History of Intellectual Culture

History of Intellectual Culture

International Yearbook of Knowledge and Society

Edited by
Charlotte A. Lerg, Johan Östling, and Jana Weiß

Current Advisory Board:
Peter Burke, University of Cambridge
Tristan Coignard, Université Bordeaux Montaigne
Heather Ellis, University of Sheffield
Tiffany N. Florvil, University of New Mexico
Adam Kola, Nicolaus Copernicus University, Toruń
Suzanne Marchand, Louisiana State University
Pierre-Héli Monot, Ludwig Maximilian University, Munich
João Ohara, Federal University of Rio de Janeiro
Herman Paul, Leiden University
Swen Steinberg, Queen's University, Kingston, and German Historical Institute, Washington, DC
Emily Steinhauer, Royal Holloway, University of London
Eugenia Roldán Vera, Center for Research and Advanced Studies (CINVESTAV), Mexico
Christa Wirth, University of Agder

History of Intellectual Culture

Volume 4
2025

Gender, Archiving, and Knowledge Production after the Holocaust. A Postwar Republic of Letters?

Edited by
Charlotte A. Lerg, Johan Östling, and Jana Weiß

Thematic section edited by
Victoria Van Orden Martínez, Christine Schmidt, and Ewa Koźmińska-Frejlak

This book has been kindly supported by the Thora Ohlsson Foundation and the Knut and Alice Wallenberg Foundation.

ISBN 978-3-11-163660-3
e-ISBN (PDF) 978-3-11-163672-6
e-ISBN (EPUB) 978-3-11-163691-7
ISSN 2747-6766
DOI https://doi.org/10.1515/9783111636726

This work is licensed under the Creative Commons Attribution-NonCommercial-NoDerivatives 4.0 International License. For details go to https://creativecommons.org/licenses/by-nc-nd/4.0/.

Creative Commons license terms for re-use do not apply to any content (such as graphs, figures, photos, excerpts, etc.) not original to the Open Access publication and further permission may be required from the rights holder. The obligation to research and clear permission lies solely with the party re-using the material.

Library of Congress Control Number: 2025941075

Bibliographic information published by the Deutsche Nationalbibliothek
The Deutsche Nationalbibliothek lists this publication in the Deutsche Nationalbibliografie; detailed bibliographic data are available on the internet at http://dnb.dnb.de.

© 2025 the author(s), editing © 2025 Charlotte A. Lerg, Johan Östling, Jana Weiß, Victoria Van Orden Martínez, Christine Schmidt, and Ewa Koźmińska-Frejlak, published by Walter de Gruyter GmbH, Berlin/Boston, Genthiner Straße 13, 10785 Berlin.
The book is published open access at www.degruyterbrill.com.

Cover image: Word Cloud generated with WordArt.com.
Typesetting: Integra Software Services Pvt. Ltd.

www.degruyterbrill.com
Questions about General Product Safety Regulation:
productsafety@degruyterbrill.com

Preface

Another year has passed, and we are grateful for our continuously growing pool of authors, peer reviewers, and readers. We are also thankful to the ones having provided financial support for this yearbook – the Thora Ohlsson Foundation and the Knut and Alice Wallenberg Foundation – as well as to our language editor, Rikard Ehnsiö.

Volume 4 features a thematic Section 2, "Gender, Archiving, and Knowledge Production after the Holocaust: A Postwar Republic of Letters?" guest-edited by Victoria Van Orden Martínez, Christine Schmidt, and Ewa Koźmińska-Frejlak. Thank you for your rich and thoughtful contributions on the production and circulation of knowledge via various forms of written communication within and among survivor historical commissions after the Second World War.

Section 1 analyzes various knowledge actors such as think tanks, insurance companies, and behavioral scientists when dealing with transnational kidnappings, commercial actors in their attempts to facilitate new digital financial markets, as well as protectionist agitators and their anti-intellectualism in the late nineteenth century.

Section 3 engages the field with two review essays on the recent works on German-American anthropologist Franz Boas and on the Europeanization of universities, respectively. The latter theme is also picked up in another contribution on new approaches in the writing of university histories, particularly the beginning of the historization of reform universities founded in the 1960s and 1970s. A theoretical think piece contemplates the link between scientific and religious thinking, using different notions of holism as an example. Last but not least, the conversation presented in this volume concerns pushing against structural injustices in the infrastructure related to knowledge and higher education by applying methodologies of "play."

This will be our last volume as a team of three as we are expanding our circle of editors for our next issue. We are delighted to announce that Isak Hammar (Lund University) and Swen Steinberg (Queen's University) will join us and are looking forward to collaborating on the many volumes to follow.

May 2025

Charlotte A. Lerg, Ludwig Maximilian University, Munich
Johan Östling, Lund Centre for the History of Knowledge (LUCK), Lund University
Jana Weiß, The University of Texas at Austin

Contents

Preface —— V

Section I: Individual Articles

Juliane Hornung
When the Practitioners Came into Play: The Emergence of a Hands-On Approach to Transnational Kidnappings in the 1970s —— 3

David Larsson Heidenblad and Axel Vikström
Creating Digital Finance for the Many: The Emergence of Online Brokerage Firms in Sweden, 1996–2000 —— 27

Fritz Kusch
Anti-Intellectualism in American Protectionism. The Protectionist Campaign against Academic Economics in the Late Nineteenth Century —— 53

Section II: Gender, Archiving, and Knowledge Production after the Holocaust

Victoria Van Orden Martínez, Christine Schmidt, and Ewa Koźmińska-Frejlak
Introduction: Gender, Archiving, and Knowledge Production after the Holocaust: A Postwar Republic of Letters? —— 93

Victoria Van Orden Martínez
Women's Work, Women's Networks: Correspondence and Knowledge Circulation Between the Polish Research Institute in Lund and Survivor Historical Commissions in the Early Postwar Period —— 105

Christine Schmidt
Gender and the Materiality of Witnessing: The Wiener Library and Postwar Holocaust Knowledge —— 129

Daniela Ozacky Stern
Letters from the Ashes: Gender, Documentation, and Holocaust Remembrance in the Work of Ruzka Korczak —— 151

Section III: Engaging the Field

Maria Simonsen
Writing the History of a Reform University: Challenges and Opportunities —— 179

Bruno Hamnell
The Numinous, the Political, and the Epistemic: Analytical Categories for Exploring the Historical Intersections of Spirituality, Ideology, and Knowledge —— 195

Valentina Mann
Review Essay: The Return of Franz Boas? —— 215

Karl Haikola and Johan Östling
Review Essay: The Europeanisation of the Universities: An Emerging Topic of Historical Research —— 237

HIC Conversation with Mariama de Brito Henn, Friedrich Cain, Evangelia (Lina) Chordaki, Stella Andrada Kasdovasili, and Katerina Stavridi
To Play is to Know: Pushing the Boundaries of Doing Academia —— 259

Contributors —— 277

Section I: **Individual Articles**

Juliane Hornung
When the Practitioners Came into Play: The Emergence of a Hands-On Approach to Transnational Kidnappings in the 1970s

Abstract: The 1970s saw the rise of a global threat: transnational kidnappings. When anti-imperialist liberation movements in Latin America and the Middle East started hijacking airplanes and kidnapping "Western" diplomats, this problem was primarily seen as a diplomatic and legal matter, and that the UN seemed to be the best place to address it. At the same time, however, a new group of non-state actors established their own way of dealing with kidnappings: practitioners. Think tanks, insurance companies, and behavioral scientists relied on various forms of applied knowledge and promoted distinctly practical solutions such as developing bargaining tactics, teaching coping strategies when in captivity, or reimbursing ransoms. Against this backdrop, this article investigates how practitioners emerged as kidnapping experts in the 1970s and how they produced, legitimated, and disseminated practical knowledge related to kidnapping. In addition, from a theoretical point of view, the article asks which larger insights into the practical dimension of knowledge may be gained from the example of transnational kidnappings.

Keywords: kidnapping, political violence, practices, think tanks, 1970s

When Jurg W. Mattman, president of a security consulting company in suburban Anaheim, California, assembled a booklet on *Executive Security & Safety* in 1982, he was on a mission.[1] In the introduction, the reader learns that the brochure was designed "to develop precautionary practices to reduce the likelihood of you or members of your family becoming targets for kidnappings and extortions," a scenario that was particularly likely "in high risk foreign areas."[2] Mattman then went on to give advice, ranging from illustrations on how to protect doors with

---

[1] This article was researched and written with the generous support of a DAAD Postdoctoral Fellowship at the Henry A. Kissinger Center for Global Affairs, Johns Hopkins University, and a Feodor Lynen Fellowship (Alexander von Humboldt Foundation) at Harvard University. I am particularly grateful to the archivists at the Hauser RAND Archives, Cara McCormick and Eric Newman, for their help.
[2] Jurg W. Mattman, *Executive Security & Safety* (Fullerton, CA: self-published, 1982), 5, 7, Karen Gardela-Treverton Papers, Box 6, Hauser RAND Archives, RAND Corporation, Santa Monica, CA.

∂ Open Access. © 2025 the author(s), published by De Gruyter. [CC BY-NC-ND] This work is licensed under the Creative Commons Attribution-NonCommercial-NoDerivatives 4.0 International License.
https://doi.org/10.1515/9783111636726-001

secured hinges to step-by-step instructions for reversing a car at a roadblock or how to behave as a hostage (e.g., "Remain calm," "Try to engage the kidnappers into light conversation," or "Immediately establish a routine for yourself – eat, sleep, read, exercise, etc.").[3] How, the readers might have wondered, did the author know all this? Why should he deserve their trust (and money)? Surely anticipating these concerns, Mattman had a simple answer: he was a former agent of the Secret Service, a hostage negotiator, "and an acknowledged expert on domestic and international terrorism."[4] In short, he was a man of practice.

Jurg W. Mattman was a small player in the global field of security policy, and for this very reason, his example vividly illustrates a broader trend characterizing the United States, as well as to some extent Europe, in the early 1980s: the belief that the threat of being kidnapped was not eliminated by legal or political countermeasures, but rather by hands-on solutions developed by practitioners. However, what Mattman's booklet presented as a matter of course was, in fact, a relatively new mode of understanding kidnappings that had emerged only about a decade earlier; that is, as a practical problem. As we know from Michel Foucault, a problem is not an objective fact. Rather, the act of problematization defines "how and why certain things (behaviour, phenomena, processes) became a *problem*" in the first place.[5] At the same time, framing a problem in a specific way determines, already at the outset, the answers that seem adequate to address it while others are ruled out.[6] Transnational kidnappings are a case in point. Since the second half of the nineteenth century, they were used as political tools. Insurgent groups captured foreign nationals for a variety of reasons: to drag other states into local conflicts, to humiliate their government on the international stage, to free imprisoned comrades, or to challenge contested borders and claim authority over a territory by seizing its inhabitants. Ransoms were often part of the motive as well. Various examples of this strategy can be found in the violent process of nation-building in Italy, Greece, and the Ottoman Balkan region between the 1860s and 1900s, in the Russian Revolution, during the Irish Revolution and subsequent civil war, in the Zionist struggle over Mandatory Palestine in the late 1940s, or in the Federal Republic of Germany and the German Democratic

---

3 Ibid., 30, 37–38, quotes: 66–67.
4 Ibid., 3.
5 Michel Foucault, *Fearless Speech*, ed. Joseph Pearson (Los Angeles: Semiotext(e), 2001), 171. See also the seminal study by Lisa Stampnitzky, *Disciplining Terror: How Experts Invented "Terrorism"* (Cambridge and New York: Cambridge University Press, 2013), 6, where she applies this approach to terrorism.
6 Foucault, *Speech*, 172.

Republic during the early years of the Cold War.[7] These kidnappings were first and foremost seen as diplomatic and legal issues, connecting discourses on state power, liability, and international relations. Hence, they had to be managed by diplomats and lawyers. This approach reached its climax when (self-proclaimed) anti-imperialist liberation movements in Latin America and the Middle East started hijacking airplanes and kidnapping "Western" diplomats in the early 1970s, while increasingly targetting foreign businessmen as the decade progressed. As a result, the General Assembly of the United Nations adopted a convention against hijacking (1970), a convention for the protection of diplomats (1973), and a convention against hostage-taking (1979).[8]

What may in hindsight seem like a success story for international cooperation was a lengthy and arduous process of negotiation between the member states, leading observers to criticize the state of the "postwar international political system" as lacking "effective order-keeping capabilities."[9] In this regard, the question of how to deal with transnational kidnappings was linked to the many challenges plaguing Europe and the United States in the 1970s, including economic and environmental crises, struggles over values and identities, military defeat and decolonization, and the rise – or rather construction – of a new threat, namely international terrorism. "By the end of the decade hijackings, kidnappings, and hostage-takings were melded together, conceptualized not simply as tactics but as identifying activities, and joined to a new and highly threatening sort of actor: the 'terrorist.'"[10] Whether it is appropriate to subsume these devel-

---

7 See, for example, Christopher A. Casey, *Nationals Abroad: Globalization, Individual Rights, and the Making of Modern International Law* (Cambridge and New York: Cambridge University Press, 2020); Russell D. Buhite, *Lives at Risk: Hostages and Victims in American Foreign Policy* (Wilmington, DE: SR Books, 1995); J. Bowyer Bell, *Terror out of Zion: Irgun Zvai Leumi, Lehi, and the Palestine Underground, 1929–1949* (New York: Avon Books, 1977); Susanne Muhle, *Auftrag: Menschenraub: Entführungen von Westberlinern und Bundesbürgern durch das Ministerium für Staatssicherheit der DDR* (Göttingen: Vandenhoek & Ruprecht, 2015).
8 Bernhard Blumenau, *The United Nations and Terrorism: Germany, Multilateralism, and Antiterrorism Efforts in the 1970s* (New York: Palgrave Macmillan, 2014).
9 David L. Milbank, *International and Transnational Terrorism: Diagnosis and Prognosis* (Washington, DC: CIA, 1976), 19. See also Stampnitzky, *Terror*, 93. For a detailed account of the negotiations, see Blumenau, *United Nations*.
10 Stampnitzky, *Terror*, 3. The fight against terrorism could provide the state with an opportunity to demonstrate strength and stability, as in the case of the Federal Republic of Germany. Here, however, state measures against "terrorists" and "sympathizers" were also viewed as excessive, thus contributing to the erosion of trust. See Karrin Hanshew, *Terror and Democracy in West Germany* (New York: Cambridge University Press, 2012); Eva Oberloskamp, "Auf dem Weg in den Überwachungsstaat? Elektronische Datenverarbeitung, Terrorismusbekämpfung und die Anfänge des bundesdeutschen Datenschutzes in den 1970er Jahren," in *Ausnahmezustände: Ent-*

opments under the catchphrase of "decline" has been disputed by historians in recent years, as has the assumption that all "Western" states shared the same experience.[11] It is nevertheless fair to say that trust in governments, states, or supranational institutions turned into a contentious issue, while the privatization of state functions materialized as a popular new solution in conservative and left-leaning circles alike.[12]

At this moment, practitioners emerged as a new group of actors who established their own interpretation of kidnappings. Even though they represented a rather diverse group encompassing criminologists, psychologists, social scientists, computer specialists, and military and law enforcement professionals, they nonetheless had one thing in common. They were not interested in abstract questions of government liability and diplomatic etiquette, nor in the noble goals of international law.[13] Relying on various forms of applied knowledge that were based on investigating the minds of kidnappers and hostages, on analyzing data, or on calculating risks, they proposed concrete actions such as developing bargaining tactics, teaching coping strategies when in captivity, or reimbursing ransoms.[14] "Knowledge," Lisa Stampnitzky states, "only becomes 'expertise' when it is made

---

grenzungen und Regulierungen in Europa während des Kalten Krieges, ed. Cornelia Rauh and Dirk Schuhmann (Göttingen: Wallstein, 2015).

11 For a critical discussion on the 1970s "decline" literature, see Sonja Levsen, "Einführung: Die 1970er Jahre in Westeuropa – un dialogue manqué," *Geschichte und Gesellschaft* 42 (2016); Frank Bösch, "Diskussionsforum Boom zwischen Krise und Globalisierung: Konsum und kultureller Wandel in der Bundesrepublik der 1970er und 1980er Jahre," *Geschichte und Gesellschaft* 42 (2016); Frank Bösch, "Zweierlei Krisendeutungen: Amerikanische und bundesdeutsche Perspektivierungen der 1970er Jahre," *Neue Politische Literatur* 58 (2013); Stéphane Porion, "Reassessing a Turbulent Decade: The Historiography of 1970s Britain in Crisis," *Études Anglaises* 69 (2016); Daniel T. Rogers, *Age of Fracture* (Cambridge, MA and London: Harvard University Press, 2011), 1–14.

12 Martin H. Geyer, "Die neue Wirklichkeit von Sicherheit und Risiken: Wie wir mit dystopischen, utopischen und technokratischen Diagnosen von Sicherheit zu leben gelernt haben," in *Die neue Wirklichkeit: Semantische Neuvermessungen und Politik seit den 1970er-Jahren*, ed. Ariane Leendertz and Wencke Meteling (Frankfurt and New York: Campus, 2016), 284–285; Ariane Leendertz, *Der erschöpfte Staat: Eine andere Geschichte des Neoliberalismus* (Hamburg: Hamburger Edition, 2022); Dietmar Süß, "Idee und Praxis der Privatisierung: Eine Einführung," in *Privatisierung: Idee und Praxis seit den 1970er Jahren*, ed. Dietmar Süß and Norbert Frei (Göttingen: Wallstein, 2012); Detlef Siegfried, "Die Entpolitisierung des Privaten: Subjektkonstruktionen im alternativen Milieu," in *Privatisierung: Idee und Praxis seit den 1970er Jahren*, ed. Dietmar Süß and Norbert Frei (Göttingen: Wallstein, 2012), 137–138.

13 Stampnitzky, *Terror*, 93.

14 To be sure, one could write the history of international lawmaking from a practical perspective as well. International law professionals were simply not viewed as practitioners in the 1970s.

applicable to a particular set of problems."[15] By defining kidnapping as a problem, the practitioners worked on their public perception as experts while linking their expertise to experience in a quite literal – or practical – sense. Against this backdrop, the goal of this article is twofold. It investigates how practitioners established themselves as kidnapping experts in the 1970s and how they produced, legitimated, and disseminated practical kidnapping knowledge. In addition, from a theoretical point of view, the article asks which greater insights into the practical dimension of knowledge can be gained from the example of transnational kidnappings.

In essence, practices "are patterned actions that are embedded in particular organized contexts and, as such, are articulated into specific types of action and are socially developed through learning and training."[16] Philosophers, sociologists, and historians such as Theodore R. Schatzki, Andreas Reckwitz, Thomas Mergel, and Sven Reichardt have argued that practice is neither the opposite of knowledge nor the opposite of language or the discursive.[17] As Emanuel Adler and Vincent Pouliot eloquently wrote: "knowledge is not only located 'behind' practice, in the form of intentions, beliefs, reasons, goals, etc. Knowledge is also 'bound up' in the very execution of the practice. For the seasoned practitioner, knowledge does not precede practice but is 'enclosed' in its execution."[18] In the context of transnational kidnappings, the related practices and knowledge intersected at material, performative, and media levels. The practitioners produced the kidnapping knowledge not just by thinking long and hard, but by physically using objects and interacting with victims, perpetrators, and political stakeholders.[19] Moreover, for the new knowledge to be accepted and applied by others, the

---

15 Lisa Stampnitzky, "Rethinking the 'Crisis of Expertise': A Relational Approach," *Theory and Society* 52 (2023): 1098, accessed February 7, 2025, doi.org/10.1007/s11186-023-09510-x. See also Achim Landwehr, "Wissen machen ist Macht: Kommissionen im frühzeitlichen Venedig," *Traverse: Zeitschrift für Geschichte* 8 (2001): 43.
16 Emanuel Adler and Vincent Pouliot, "International Practices: Introduction and Framework," in *International Practices*, ed. Emanuel Adler and Vincent Pouliot (Cambridge and New York: Cambridge University Press, 2011), 6.
17 Theodore R. Schatzki, *The Site of the Social: A Philosophical Account of the Constitution of Social Life and Change* (University Park, PA: Penn State Press, 2002), 77–80; Andreas Reckwitz, "Grundelemente einer Theorie sozialer Praktiken," in *Unscharfe Grenzen: Perspektiven der Kultursoziologie*, ed. Andreas Reckwitz, 2nd. ed. (Bielefeld: Transcript, 2010), 129–130; Thomas Mergel and Sven Reichardt, "Praxeologie in der Geschichtswissenschaft: eine Zwischenbetrachtung," in *Entbehrung und Erfüllung: Praktiken von Arbeit, Körper und Konsum in der Geschichte moderner Gesellschaften. Für Thomas Welskopp 1961–2021*, ed. Gleb J. Albert, Daniel Siemens, and Frank Wolff (Bonn: Dietz, 2021), 85.
18 Adler and Pouliot, "International Practices," 15.
19 On the materiality and performativity of practices, see Reckwitz, "Grundelemente," 113–114.

practices had to be performed in a competent way in front of an audience and disseminated through different media outlets.[20] Pictures played a particularly important role in rendering this knowledge accessible as well as in creating a notion of reliability.

Three groups of practitioners were particularly successful in cultivating their own image of being experts: think tanks, insurance companies, and behavioral scientists such as psychologists and criminologists. While often using similar methods and collaborating at international conferences, they also competed for influence and had to establish strategies that came to represent their specific fields. However, whether or not political stakeholders heeded their advice depended on national cultures of governance and perceptions of security. The US government, for instance, relied heavily on think tanks, while the insurance giant Lloyd's of London was especially powerful in influencing the government in Whitehall. The West German government, on the other hand, stayed committed to finding a solution within the UN and tied the nation's newfound international standing to the success of the conventions.[21] Focusing on the practitioners, this article revolves around three distinct practices, each of which was associated with one group of actors – computing by think tanks, profiling by behavioral scientists, and calculating by insurance companies. These practices are still prevalent today and need to be historicized.

1 Computing

Think tanks have proliferated in the United States since the late 1940s and have become an integral part of the current political landscape.[22] Independent corporations contracted by the government turned to the field of foreign relations, defense, and national security in order to develop policy advice for political stakeholders such as the Air Force, the Defense Department, and the State Department.[23] One of the most influential organizations was the RAND Corporation, RAND being an acro-

---

20 On "competent performances," see Adler and Pouliot, "Practices," 8.
21 Blumenau, *United Nations*, 4, 9.
22 In Germany, on the other hand, think tanks tended to emphasize scholarliness over pragmatic approaches. To this day, they lack the direct political influence of their US counterparts. See Josef Bramel, "The Think Tank and the Tank," in *Think Tanks, Foreign Policy and Geo-Politics: Pathways to Influence*, ed. Donald E. Abelson, Stephen Brooks, and Xin Hua (London and New York: Routledge, 2017).
23 Donald E. Abelson, "Think Tanks American Style," in *Think Tanks, Foreign Policy and Geo-Politics: Pathways to Influence*, ed. Donald E. Abelson, Stephen Brooks, and Xin Hua (London and

nym for "research and development."[24] In 1949, RAND comprised departments in physics, economics, and social sciences.[25] In the following years, a rather diverse staff of engineers, mathematicians, economists, political scientists, and social psychologists worked on Cold War military deterrence as well as counterinsurgency-related issues during the Vietnam War.[26] RAND's specialty became the so-called method of "system analysis," the practice of "modeling a situation mathematically, be it a sudden crisis of international diplomacy or the accidental detonation of a nuclear weapon, and then simulating the possible courses of action and their effects."[27] The organization was thus a vital contributor when it came to advancing the use of computers and databases.[28] When, in the early 1970s, the focus of the social science department shifted to transnational kidnappings and other "terrorist" acts, this empirical and computer-based approach proved decisive.

Brian Michael Jenkins was the associate head of the Social Science Department at RAND, while also being the initiator and director of the research program on international terrorism. He perfectly embodied the think tank version of the practitioner, even though one might argue that he did not embark on the most practical path in the early 1960s as he studied history at UCLA, in Mexico, and in Guatemala. In 1966, he served with the US Army Special Forces, first in the Dominican Republic and then in Vietnam. Thus when Jenkins joined RAND in 1972, he possessed practical experiences with political violence and so-called guerilla tactics, in addition to some first-hand geographical knowledge of Latin America.[29] The goal of Jenkins and his colleagues at RAND was to explore the dynamics of kidnappings and the actions of kidnappers, hostages, and government officials. To this end, they chose to work with case studies receiving funding from the State Department and the Defense Advanced Research Projects Agency, an agency of

---

New York: Routledge, 2017), 88. Other think tanks focused on domestic topics such as poverty or unemployment.
24 RAND launched as a research department within the Air Force in 1946 and became an independent corporation in 1948. See Thomas Medvetz, *Think Tanks in America* (Chicago and London: University of Chicago Press, 2012), 70.
25 Janet Farrell Brodie, "Learning Secrecy in the Early Cold War: The RAND Corporation Secrecy," *Diplomatic History* 35 (2011), 648.
26 Ibid., 648; Abelson, "Think Tanks," 88.
27 Medvetz, *Think Tanks*, 71.
28 Farrell Brodie, "Secrecy," 647.
29 Brian Michael Jenkins' CV, Biographical Materials, Brian Michael Jenkins Papers, Box 1, Folder 1, Hauser RAND Archives, RAND Corporation, Santa Monica, CA.

the Defense Department, between 1974 and 1976.[30] The knowledge related to the case studies obviously had to be generated, and the first step was to select the cases to be deemed relevant: 77 transnational cases between 1968 and 1975 were chosen, including kidnappings, barricade situations, and hijackings; yet the corpus did not include any local-on-local crimes.[31] The mundane practice of counting was not all that self-evident after all but already an act of classification.[32] The RAND staff had the chance to speak with members of the State Department who were in charge of the kidnapping cases involving Americans abroad, and Jenkins also put together a manual for his colleagues for interviewing former hostages.[33]

To manage all this information, a database was designed that enabled RAND to create a kidnapping chronology and relate different variables to one another, such as types of terrorist acts, national deterrence policies, and the success of past national counter-terrorism strategies.[34] In this way, the combined case studies would collectively reveal larger patterns. RAND's unique selling point was to offer "hidden" knowledge not visible to the naked eye by simply looking at the individual cases. This knowledge only revealed itself as statistical results after having been distilled by a computer and database software and translated into guidelines by the experts.[35] Indeed, the materiality of these tools considerably shaped the nature and form of the resulting knowledge. The relational database model established in 1970 made it possible to organize data into tables consisting

---

[30] Brian Michael Jenkins, David Ronfeldt, and Ralph Strauch, *Dealing with Political Kidnapping*, RAND Corporation, R-1857, 1976, iii, accessed March 15: https://www.proquest.com/government-official-publications/dealing-with-political-kidnapping/docview/1679045496/se-2.
[31] Ibid., 2.
[32] Aryn Martin and Michael Lynch, "Counting Things and People: The Practices and Politics of Counting," *Social Problems* 56 (2009): 244. See also Stampnitzky, *Terror*, 99–101.
[33] Jenkins et al., *Dealing with Political Kidnapping*, 3; "Interview Techniques," Hostage Affairs Notebook, Brian Michael Jenkins Papers, Box 2, Folder 1, Hauser RAND Archives, RAND Corporation, Santa Monica, CA.
[34] On databases and terrorism research in the 1970s with a particular focus on RAND, see Stampnitzky, *Terror*, 99–106.
[35] Margit Szöllösi-Janze, "Der Wissenschaftler als Experte: Kooperationsverhältnisse von Staat, Militär, Wirtschaft und Wissenschaft, 1914–1933," in *Geschichte der Kaiser-Wilhelm-Gesellschaft im Nationalsozialismus: Bestandsaufnahme und Perspektiven der Forschung*, vol. 1, ed. Doris Kaufmann (Göttingen: Wallstein, 2000), 49–50, in which the author stresses that the ability to mediate between different groups constitutes a key feature of being an expert. During the 1970s and 1980s, the RAND database was one of the most elaborate tools of this kind and highly praised by other terrorism researchers. See Alex P. Schmid, *Political Terrorism: A Research Guide to Concepts, Theories, Data Bases, and Literature* (Amsterdam and New Brunswick: North-Holland Publishing Company and Transaction Books, 1983), 253–255.

of rows and columns that could be related to each other.³⁶ Storing and accessing data was a distinct practice, as was creating the data for the database in the first place. For "[d]ata in itself does not really mean anything – just a cluster of numbers, words, or images out of context with no relation to the other facts."³⁷ Designing interview questions, then, did not aim so much at learning about personal experiences but at producing matchable data sets. In the early days of kidnapping and terrorism research, computing also had another function: "Techniques of quantification served to communicate the magnitude of the problem and also to establish the scientific legitimacy of its analysis."³⁸

RAND followed a greater trend that started in the 1960s and essentially came to define the 1970s: the computerization of state apparatuses such as administrations and especially police and law enforcement agencies. The latter increasingly relied on electronic data processing tools in the fight against organized crime and, as the decade progressed, "terrorism."³⁹ However, RAND's use of computers differed in two key respects. Law enforcement databases such as the British Police National Computer or the West German PIOS/Terrorismus served the purpose of digitizing large amounts of information, quickly making it available from multiple locations, and connecting scattered data on individuals, crimes, vehicles, weapons, etc. The number of possible perpetrators could then be narrowed down, leading to investigations becoming both more extensive and more efficient at the same time.⁴⁰ Jenkins and his colleagues, in contrast, did not primarily seek to manage information. They wanted to test the assumptions of US government officials regarding "terrorism" – one being Secretary of State Henry Kissinger's firm belief that a strict no-concessions policy would be the best deterrence against future kidnappings.⁴¹ Moreover, police officers did not have to program databases or even understand how they worked. They applied practical knowledge whereas

---

36 Kristi L. Berg, Tom Seymour, and Richa Goel, "History of Databases," *International Journal of Management & Information Systems* 17 (2013): 30.
37 Ibid., 29.
38 Stampnitzky, *Terror*, 106.
39 Jon Agar, *The Government Machine: A Revolutionary History of the Computer* (Cambridge, MA and London: MIT Press, 2003); James W. Cortada, *The Digital Hand, Volume 3: How Computers Changed the Work of American Public Sector Industries* (Oxford and New York: Oxford University Press, 2008); Hannes Mangold, *Fahndung nach dem Raster: Informationsverarbeitung bei der bundesdeutschen Kriminalpolizei 1965–1984* (Zurich: Chronos, 2017).
40 Mangold, *Fahndung*, 152–154; Peter Neyroud, "Police National Computer," in *Dictonary of Policing*, ed. Tim Newburn and Peter Neyroud (Abingdon and New York: Routledge, 2008), 208; Cortada, *Hand*, 106–108.
41 Carolin Goerzig, *Talking to Terrorists: Concessions and the Renunciation of Violence* (London and New York: Routledge, 2010), 2–4.

the RAND staff created it. For Jenkins, being able to master a computer thus became vital for fashioning himself publicly as an expert or, put differently, performing his practical expertise. A photograph printed by *The Oregonian* in 1982 shows him casually sitting on a desk next to a computer, where the caption, "Terrorist Tracker – Brian Jenkins, Rand Corporation's resident expert on terrorism, uses knowledge rather than cloak-and-dagger tactics," clearly linked Jenkins' expertise to the practical dimension of his work (Figure 1).[42]

Figure 1: Photograph of Brian Michael Jenkins (1982), Biographical Materials, Brian Michael Jenkins Papers, Box 1, Folder 1, Hauser RAND Archives, RAND Corporation, Santa Monica, CA.

The result of RAND's government-commissioned research on kidnapping was a classified report on *Dealing with Political Kidnapping* (1976). The database analysis disclosed no direct correlation that the "policy of not yielding to kidnappers' demands was working as a deterrent," and Jenkins advised adopting a more flexible approach instead.[43] He outlined different scenarios and practical suggestions on how the US government could respond to each of these by providing communication and negotiation strategies.[44] Since the report was only cleared for publi-

---

42 News Clipping from The Oregonian, Biographical Materials, Brian Michael Jenkins Papers, Box 1, Folder 1, Hauser RAND Archives, RAND Corporation, Santa Monica, CA.
43 Jenkins et al., *Dealing with Political Kidnapping*, 78.
44 Ibid., 11–27.

cation in the 1990s, Jenkins broke it down into several short papers without the secret information.[45] Titles such as "An Urban Strategy for Guerillas and Governments" (1972), "Hostage Survival: Some Preliminary Observations" (1976), and "Talking to Terrorists" (1982) also promised a hands-on approach. These articles and Jenkins himself were quite popular with journalists who had developed a keen interest in "terrorism" too.[46]

Why was it so important to be recognized as an expert not only by political stakeholders but also by the mass media and a wider public? On the one hand, the American think tank scene changed in the 1970s. New "advocacy think tanks" such as the Heritage Foundation and the Cato Institute specialized in aggressively marketing their ideas directly in order to "influence policy-makers, the public, and the media," thus pressuring the older post-war institutes into adopting similar media-oriented strategies to legitimate their expertise beyond state agencies.[47] On the other hand, as government funding could not be taken for granted, RAND and others had to pitch new research projects to remain relevant. Being an expert was not a state that, once achieved, would last forever. Rather, the expert status constantly had to be renewed and defended against others, in this case against other practitioners. This meant walking a fine line between stressing the accomplishments of completed projects while simultaneously indicating that the available knowledge was still incomplete. When Jenkins proposed a new project to the State Department in 1977, he started by emphasizing, "We fully agree that almost everything that can be said about policy has by now been said, at least once. The useful area of further work pertains to the actual handling of hostage incidents."[48] Hence the follow-up project should be a "lessons learned" of the previous case studies, everything that a government official "faced with a hostage situation, would want to know."[49] However, the State Department was slow to respond and Jenkins knew why. Among the staff at the State Department and CIA were psychiatrists and psychologists who questioned the value of case studies. In an internal memo to his RAND colleagues, Jenkins explained: "They jealously guard their position of access, control, and, hence, power which is based primarily on their special knowledge of human behavior. Consequently, they are resistant to the idea of case studies because such studies imply that [. . .] one – any-

---

45 Jenkins et al., *Dealing with Political Kidnapping*.
46 Interviews and Correspondence, Publicity and Media Relations, Brian Michael Jenkins Papers, Box 1, Folders 2–4, Hauser RAND Archives, RAND Corporation, Santa Monica, CA.
47 Abelson, "Think Tanks," 89.
48 Letter from Brian Michael Jenkins to Douglas Heck, June 1, 1977, Brian Michael Jenkins Papers, Box 1, Folder 8, Hauser RAND Archives, RAND Corporation, Santa Monica, CA.
49 Ibid.

one – can learn."[50] The RAND researchers and Jenkins in particular exchanged ideas with psychologists on a regular basis. Nevertheless, it becomes clear that different groups of practitioners competed for recognition, not only in terms of resources but over the (il)legitimacy of knowledge.

2 Profiling

RAND's data showed that in most hostage-takings, all or at least many of the kidnappers' demands were met while the kidnappers themselves were able to go into hiding without being punished. The RAND staff thus problematized kidnapping as a rational act, meaning that the motivations of the kidnappers were of no particular interest to them.[51] Psychologists and criminologists, on the other hand, turned to the minds and personalities of the kidnappers. Book titles such as *The Terrorist Mind*, *The Skyjacker: His Flights of Fantasy*, or *Crusaders, Criminals, Crazies* saw "*the* terrorist as a peculiar personality with clearly identifiable character traits."[52] Practically speaking, this necessitated interviewing imprisoned kidnappers to create psychological "profiles."[53] By profession, psychologists and criminologists tended to be interested in "abnormal" or "deviant" behavior, and to them, "insights from psychology and psychiatry [represented] adequate keys to understanding."[54] Profiling, then, could have a remarkably practical dimension, as psychologist Wolfgang Salewski spelled out somewhat dramatically: it enabled

---

[50] Letter from Brian Michael Jenkins to M. Landi, D. Rice, G. Shubert, R. Solomon, G. Tanham, November 7, 1978, Box 1, Folder 8, Hauser RAND Archives, RAND Corporation, Santa Monica, CA.
[51] Brian Michael Jenkins, Janera Johnson, and David Ronfeldt, *Numbered Lives: Some Statistical Observations From 77 International Hostage Episodes*, RAND Corporation, P-5905, 1977, 20–25, accessed February 13, 2025: https://www.rand.org/pubs/papers/P5905.html.
[52] Gerald McKnight, *The Terrorist Mind* (Indianapolis: Bobbs-Merrill Company, 1974); David G. Hubbard, *The Skyjacker: His Flights of Fantasy* (New York: Macmillan, 1971); Frederick M. Hacker, *Crusaders, Criminals, Crazies: Terror and Terrorism in Our Time* (New York: W. W. Norton Company, 1976). The quote comes from Schmid, *Political Terrorism*, 191, emphasis in original.
[53] Ronald D. Crelinsten, "The Study of Hostage-Taking: A System Approach," in *Final Report on Management Seminar Hostage-Taking: Problems of Prevention and Control*, ed. Ronald D. Crelinsten and Danielle Laberge-Altmejd (Montreal: self-published, 1976), 34, 36.
[54] Schmid, *Political Terrorism*, 194. Some psychologists and criminologists used statistical methods and like Crelinsten, "Study," called for big data collections. Others simply put together what to social scientists seemed like anecdotal collections. See, for instance, sociologist Doris Wilkinson's harsh review of McKnigh's *Terrorist Mind* in *Journal of Political and Military Sociology* 7 (1979): 314–315.

psychologists and criminologists "to 'overpower' the hostage-takers, 'psychologically.'"[55] For classifications and typologies offered concrete guidelines for bargaining strategies, such as advised in the FBI booklet *A Practical Overview of Hostage Negotiations*:

> When negotiating with a manic-depressive, understanding and support should be provided, along with continual reassurance that he has self-worth. Do not try to tell him that "things aren't that bad. [. . .] When negotiating with the antisocial personality, it is important to remember that he is self-centered and will attempt to make things easier for himself. Be careful about using tricks. He is sharp and expects you to try to trick him.[56]

Bargaining, moreover, was an inherently practical activity that could not "be learned in an academic environment and transferred to the field. On the job apprenticeship, training, retraining is a necessity."[57]

It would be impossible to characterize the vibrant international and interdisciplinary field of psychology, criminology, and related professions of law enforcement and psychiatry in the 1970s. However, there are a few key figures who were quoted frequently and who regularly attended important conferences such as the "Management Training Seminar Hostage-Taking: Problems of Prevention and Control" (1976) or the conference on "Dimensions of Victimization in the Context of Terroristic Acts" (1977). These included Denis Szabo, director of the International Center for Comparative Criminology in Montreal; Frank Ochberg, director of Service Programs at the National Institute of Mental Health in Rockville, Maryland; Ronald D. Crelinsten, also from the Comparative Criminology Center; Jared Tinklenberg from the Department of Psychiatry at Stanford University; Thomas Strentz, founding member of the FBI Behavioral Science Unit established in 1974; and Wolfgang Salewski, a German psychologist, director of the Institute for Conflict Research and Crisis Consulting and free-lance hostage negotiator for the Federal Foreign Office (as well as Jenkins, of course). During the conferences and based on the subsequent reports, the participants constituted a "community of practice" by sharing knowledge and by performing expertise as a group.[58] But

---

55 Wolfgang Salewski, "Panelist's Report," in *Final Report on Management Seminar Hostage-Taking: Problems of Prevention and Control*, ed. Ronald D. Crelinsten and Danielle Laberge-Altmejd (Montreal: self-published, 1976), 121.
56 G. Wayne Fueselier, "A Practical Overview of Hostage Negotiations (Part 1)," *FBI Law Enforcement Bulletin*, June 1981, 4.
57 Quote: Frank Ochberg, "Panelist's Report," in *Final Report on Management Seminar Hostage-Taking: Problems of Prevention and Control*, ed. Ronald D. Crelinsten and Danielle Laberge-Altmejd (Montreal: self-published, 1976), 119. See also Salewski, "Panelist's Report," 122–123.
58 Adler and Pouliot, "International Practices," 17. They even referred jokingly to themselves as the "terrorism mafia." See Stampnitzky, *Terror*, 42.

they also "communicated expert knowledge to other audiences [...] to establish the importance of the terrorism research project itself."[59] Indeed, they relied on public recognition beyond their specialist circles and appeared in US Congressional or Senate hearings (Jenkins), advised international organizations such as the UN or the Council of Europe (Szabo), or consulted tactical police units in kidnapping situations (Salewski).

For behavioral scientists, it was only a small step from profiling kidnappers to profiling hostages. As Crelinsten explained: "From the psychological perspective, it would be interesting to develop a victim profile, to gain insights into who would be a 'good' hostage and who would crack under the strain."[60] The dominant conceptual framework for understanding hostages in the 1970s was "identification" (with the kidnapper), a notion inspired by Sigmund Freud's "'mimetic identification' through which the boundary between self and other is breached."[61] In this way, hostages took on an active role and became an important factor for the outcome of the negotiation as well. The 1977 conference on "Victimization" reflected this novel interest in hostage behavior and grappled with a new pathological condition called "Stockholm syndrome": "the positive bond between hostage and captor, and feelings of distrust or hostility on the part of the victim toward the authorities."[62] The eponymous event that inspired this term has been surrounded by myths from the very beginning. During a failed bank robbery and ensuing hostage situation in a Stockholm bank in 1973, the two robbers took one male and three female employees hostage. The women allegedly displayed exceptionally hostile behavior when contacted by the police and seemed to believe that the kidnappers were there to protect them. Even after they were freed, all captives retained their positive attitude toward their captors. Mass media immediately jumped on the story of the siege, spreading false rumors of unfolding sexual

---

[59] Stampnitzky, *Terror*, 42.
[60] Crelinsten, "Study," 36.
[61] Celia Jameson, "The 'Short Step' from Love to Hypnosis: A Reconsideration of the Stockholm Syndrome," *Journal for Cultural Research* 14 (2010): 340.
[62] Frank Ochberg, "The Victim of Terrorism: Psychiatric Considerations," in *Final Report on Dimensions of Victimization in the Context of Terroristic Acts*, ed. Ronald D. Crelinsten (Montreal: self-published, 1977), 21. A positive attitude toward hostage-takers can be observed in many kidnapping memoires from the nineteenth and early twentieth century, when the emotional bond between kidnapper and captive was not yet seen as problematic or pathological. See Juliane Hornung, "Before Stockholm: Emotions and Victimhood in Mediterranean Kidnapping Narratives, 1866–1921," *The Historical Journal* 67 (2024).

relationships between the women and the kidnappers that were uncritically reiterated by some psychologists and criminologists, among them Ochberg.[63]

Psychologists and criminologists in the 1970s generally did not draw an explicit connection between gender and the susceptibility to bond with a hostage-taker, but the assumption that women were more vulnerable pervades a remarkably high number of publications. Tinklenberg, for instance, believed that the tendency to bond with kidnappers was "more commonly found in hysterical personalities" – hysteria, of course, being a typical female malady or at least trait since the late nineteenth century.[64] Unsurprisingly, female hostages such as the notorious Patty Hearst (who also was supposedly in love with one of her kidnappers and left her fiancé for him) typically served to illustrate this point.[65] The gender aspect also lent itself perfectly to visualizing psychological kidnapping knowledge, as demonstrated in an article by Strentz for the *FBI Law Enforcement Bulletin*, in which scenes from the Stockholm bank robbery and a hijacking are displayed (Figure 2).

Figure 2: Illustrations from Thomas Strentz's article "Law Enforcement Policy and Ego Defenses of the Hostage," *FBI Law Enforcement Bulletin* 48 (1979): 3, 9.

---

63 Ochberg, "Victim," 27. On the invention of Stockholm syndrome, see also Jameson, "Short Step."
64 Jared Tinklenberg, Peggy Murphy, and Patricia Murphy, "Adaptive Behavior of Victims of Terrorism," in *Final Report on Dimensions of Victimization in the Context of Terroristic Acts*, ed. Ronald D. Crelinsten (Montreal: self-published, 1977), 99.
65 Ibid.; Crelinsten, "Study," 8, 15, 36.

The women in both images are highly sexualized. The female bank employee screams in a manner that can only be described as hysterical while her long hair flows sensually around her, her breasts clearly visible under her blouse. The female airplane passenger clings fearfully to her male seatmate, baring her long legs while almost seductively glancing at the reader. The article demonstrates that the new knowledge had to be presented in a captivating and almost entertaining way. But the pictures are more than mere illustrations. They are tied in with the text, its gesture of expertise rubbing off on the images and testifying to their scientific value.

Examples of male kidnapping victims, in turn, were used to reveal how to resist kidnappers. Geoffrey Jackson, the British ambassador to Uruguay, and Claude Fly, an American agronomist, were both captured separately by the Tupamaros in the early 1970s. Strentz highlighted the practical side of their achievements when he wrote, almost in admiration, that Jackson "remained in thought and actions the ambassador, the Queen's representative, and so impressed his captors with his dignity that they were forced to change regularly his guards and isolate him for fear he might convince them that his cause was just and theirs foolish."[66] Equally impressive in Strentz's eyes was Fly who compiled "a 50-page 'Christian checklist,' in which he was able to create his own world and insulate himself against the hostile pressures around him."[67] In other words, these men did not identify with the "terrorists" as they remained faithful and loyal to their Western states and Christian beliefs. Women, conversely, were seen as unstable and emotional, thus posing a threat to the state and society. The 1970s were shaped by a fear of communist mind control and "brainwashing."[68] But it was also a time when prevalent notions of white masculinity were being questioned by the peace movement, the civil rights movement in the US, and leftist student protesters. On top of this, the women's movement and the so-called sexual revolution "unsettled every facet of social life and social debate."[69] At the same time, sexualized women were omnipresent in American media in the 1970s.[70] Stockholm syndrome as a psychological problematization of hostage behavior reflected and reinforced the fear of female agency, which was seemingly aimed at institu-

---

[66] Thomas Strentz, "Law Enforcement Policy and Ego Defenses of the Hostage," *FBI Law Enforcement Bulletin* 48 (1979): 9. See also Crelinsten, "Study," 36.
[67] Strentz, "Law Enforcement," 9.
[68] Timothy Melley, "Brain Warfare: The Covert Sphere, Terrorism, and the Legacy of the Cold War," *Grey Room* 45 (2022): esp. 24.
[69] Rogers, *Age*, 146.
[70] See, for example, Elana Levine, *Wallowing in Sex: The New Sexual Culture of the 1970s American Television* (Durham, NC and London: Duke University Press, 2007).

tions such as the nuclear family, marriage, and the state, as well as the new commodification of female sexuality.

3 Calculating

While psychologists and criminologists were busy studying which personality types would be at risk of identifying with their kidnappers, insurance companies also began evaluating kidnappings in terms of risk, albeit in a more fundamental way. As pointed out by Luis Lobo-Guerrero, the risk of being kidnapped is first and foremost "an interpretation that results from problematizing kidnapping in terms of risk."[71] Whereas "danger" is unavoidable, risks are taken consciously, avoided altogether, or minimized by preventive and precautionary measures.[72] They can also be calculated, which means broken down into probabilities so that they become predictable.[73] In the 1970s, kidnap and ransom (K&R) insurance emerged as "a sophisticated form of embracing kidnap risk."[74] By identifying and assessing kidnap risks, insurance companies constructed problematic spaces, such as Latin America, and situations, including travel, as well as a group of potential victims that could be targeted as clients.[75] Yet, this was not only about controlling the clients' risk of being kidnapped but also about minimizing the insurers' risk of financial loss. For "[e]liminating the most risky from an insurance pool reduces the average cost of insuring the members of the pool, allowing the insurer to offer a lower price and, possibly, obtain a greater profit."[76]

K&R insurance is based on a monthly premium paid by the insured party – a private individual or a company. In the event of a kidnapping, the ransom must be raised by the insured and will then be reimbursed by the insurance company. The existence of the insurance policy must be kept secret at all times, as its disclo-

---

[71] Luis Lobo-Guerrero, "Biopolitics of Specialized Risk: An Analysis of Kidnap and Ransom Insurance," *Security Dialogue* 38 (2007): 320.
[72] Julia Moses and Eve Rosenhaft, "Introduction: Moving Targets – Risk, Security, and the Social in Twentieth-Century Europe," *Social Science History* 39 (2015): 26.
[73] Lobo-Guerrero, "Biopolitics," 321.
[74] Ibid., 320. In the US, modern K&R insurance was offered as early as 1932 after the fatal kidnapping of the child of Charles Lindbergh, but it would not be until the 1970s that specialized providers emerged on the scene.
[75] Ibid., 323.
[76] Tom Baker, "Containing the Promise of Insurance: Adverse Selection and Risk Classification," in *Risk and Morality*, ed. Richard Ericson and Aaron Doyle (Toronto: University of Toronto Press, 2003), 263.

sure would constitute a breach of contract.[77] K&R insurance, however, is a complex tool that goes far beyond financial protection and involves a whole group of experts. Although not a conventional insurance company, one of the largest players in this field is Lloyd's of London, a marketplace where various approved syndicates specializing in different kinds of insurance operate. In the 1970s and 1980s, Lloyd's handled 70 percent of K&R policies worldwide, whereas the syndicate that accounted for most of the K&R insurance policies within Lloyd's was Cassidy Davis.[78] Cassidy Davis, in turn, collaborated with Control Risks, a consulting firm established in 1975 and funded by Lloyd's to conduct what was called "risk management": identifying, evaluating, and controlling risks.[79] Before a syndicate would talk to a potential client, let alone negotiate conditions, it had to collect knowledge regarding the levels of risk that the client represented. This is where Control Risks entered the stage. They identified the potential risks that the client was exposed to by carrying out an inspection of company and private spaces as well as an investigation of travel patterns, daily habits, and personal relations. These risks were then evaluated in terms of their probability, frequency, and severity. Purchasing a K&R insurance policy was one way of controlling the financial risk of a kidnapping.[80] But the work of Control Risks did not end there. Cassidy Davis insisted on their clients taking preventive measures, which were implemented by Control Risks consultants such as vetting staff, installing CCTV surveillance systems, developing contingency plans, or simulating kidnappings for training purposes.[81] Finally, in the event of a kidnapping, the Control Risks staff negotiated the release and made sure that the ransom would not be too high.[82] In the insurance world, Control Risks consultants clearly played a major role in creating kidnapping knowledge, defining the associated risk, and dealing with it as well. Who, then, were they? Former director of Control Risks, Richard Clutterbuck, proudly explained that they were "recruited almost entirely from people with experience in public services, notably the police, the armed forces

---

77 Anja Shortland, "Governing Kidnap for Ransom: Lloyd's as a 'Private Regime'," *Governance* 30 (2017): 286.
78 Richard Clutterbuck, *Kidnap, Hijack and Extortion: The Response* (Basingstoke and London: Macmillan, 1987), 100.
79 Ibid., 71; Julian Radcliffe, "The Insurance Companies' Response to Terrorism," in *Political Terrorism and Business: The Threat and Response*, ed. Yonah Alexander and Robert A. Kilmarx (New York: Praeger Publishers, 1979), 155; Gordon C. A. Dickinson, *Introduction to Insurance* (London: Chartered Insurance Institute, 1981), 6A.1.
80 On the process of taking out an insurance policy with Lloyd's in the 1970s, see Dickinson, *Introduction*, 5B, 5E.
81 Clutterbuck, *Kidnap*, 73–85.
82 Ibid., 128–129.

and the security and intelligence services" – that is to say, practitioners.[83] This means that K&R insurance was not limited to reactive and reparative measures after an event had occurred. Cassidy Davis and Control Risks critically shaped how kidnappings were problematized and how they should be handled on a global scale.[84]

Yet, the expertise and power accumulated by Lloyd's with regard to kidnappings did not go unchallenged. Throughout the 1970s and 1980s, West German governments, for one, thought of K&R insurance as deeply immoral and prohibited them by law until 1989.[85] K&R insurance, it was feared, would provide an incentive for kidnappers, finance terrorism, and hinder law enforcement from pursuing kidnappers. Other ECC members such as Italy, Belgium, France, and Denmark were equally opposed to K&R insurance and tried to convince the UK to ban it altogether. The Callaghan and Thatcher governments, on the other hand, were keen to protect the British economy. After all, Lloyd's earned 50 million pounds per year from K&R shares alone in the late 1970s.[86] Moreover, a government official remarked in defense of insurance companies that they "provide experts experienced in negotiating with kidnappers."[87] These experts, one should add, also relieved the state from its liability to rescue its citizens, in transnational cases as well as in domestic ones. Indeed, as concluded by Richard Aldrich and Lewis Herrington: "Control Risks were fulfilling a difficult global security role that the British government preferred to leave to proxies."[88] Just like think tanks, insurance companies too "claimed a role in the governance space" in the 1970s and thus contributed to the dissolution of what Charles S. Maier has termed the "project state."[89] To play down their key roles and discredit the allegations against K&R insurance, Cassidy Davis and Control Risks had to disclose some of their records to the Home Office. Accordingly, they compiled their data into diagrams, which are commonly believed to constitute reliable, scientific knowledge (Figure 3).

---

[83] Ibid., 126. Clutterbuck was the director of Control Risks between 1977 and 1981.
[84] Nicolai Hannig makes this important point regarding insurance companies in general in his article "Die Suche nach Prävention: Naturgefahren im 19. und 20. Jahrhundert," *Historische Zeitschrift* 300 (2015): 49.
[85] "Lösegeldversicherung," *BaFin Journal*, September 2017: 4.
[86] Minutes of ECC's Discussion on Kidnap and Ransom Insurance, November 11, 1977, FCO 76/1753, The National Archives, Kew. See also Richard J. Aldrich and Lewis Herrington, "Secrets, Hostages, and Ransoms: British Kidnap Policy in Historical Perspective," *Review of International Studies* 44 (2018): 754.
[87] Confidential memo on "Kidnap Ransom Insurance" by K. Gosh, October 24, 1977, FCO 76/1753, The National Archives.
[88] Aldrich and Herrington, "Secrets," 757.
[89] Charles S. Maier, *The Project-State and Its Rivals: A New History of the Twentieth and Twenty-First Centuries* (Cambridge, MA: Harvard University Press), 240.

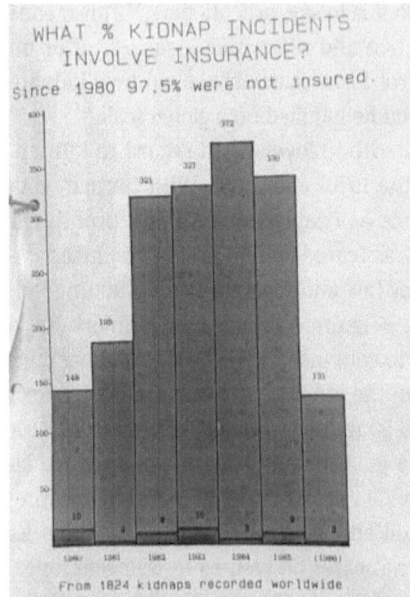 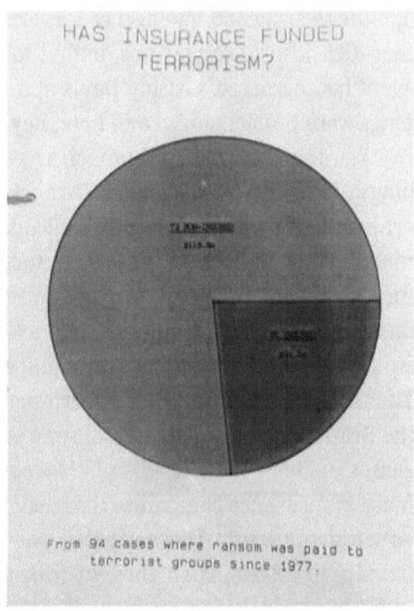

Figure 3: Presentation to the Home Secretary by Control Risks Group Limited and Cassidy Davis Limited on Kidnap and Ransom Insurance, October 13, 1986, HO 325/757, The National Archives.

In doing so, they showcased their special expertise – calculating – but in an easily comprehensible form. Rather than simply visualizing objective figures, these pictures generated evidence in a highly suggestive way. A bar chart, for example, typically implies comparability and quantifiable developments. In this case, kidnappings of people without K&R insurance spiked while remaining low for those with insurance. A pie chart, in turn, could invoke notions of proportionality and marginality, here highlighting the small share of insured hostages who had paid ransom to terrorist groups as opposed to the large segment of uninsured victims. Without being able to determine whether these numbers were correct or misleading, one point becomes very clear: Cassidy Davis and Control Risks portrayed kidnappings as individual problems that could be managed on an individual basis, not as a political problem with global implications.[90]

---

[90] The Home Office maintained a somewhat vague position on the issue of K&R insurance. It was not until 2000 that ransom payments within the UK – essentially to the IRA – were banned, while Control Risks was allowed to continue its global business endeavors. See Aldrich and Herrington, "Secrets," 757.

4 Conclusion

Analyzing the practical responses to transnational kidnappings in the 1970s may seem irritating or even cynical. Fortunately, there are extensive data collections (also from RAND, obviously) showing that most hostages survived.[91] The practitioners certainly condemned violence, but for them, it was not as ideologically or normatively charged as it was for the UN. Think tanks, behavioral scientists, and insurance companies were less concerned with high-minded goals or grand strategies to abolish kidnappings altogether. Instead, they promoted "small" but realizable solutions. The gap that emerged in the 1970s between international law and the practical handling of kidnappings proved to be long-lasting. In 1986, Brian Michael Jenkins was invited to a small gathering organized by the UN to discuss a pressing issue: "The United Nations and the Maintenance of International Peace and Security."[92] "At a time when the utility of the United Nations activities in all domains is being vigorously questioned," the invitation letter stated, "the main purpose of the meeting will be to formulate policy proposals addressed to the question of how Member States can more effectively co-operate to promote international peace and security." Jenkins' participation was desired based on his "past experience" and that he was "an innovative thinker and practitioner." Nevertheless, it took the UN – its Office on Drugs and Crime, to be precise – another twenty years before they developed their very own hands-on approach to kidnapping and published a *Manual of Best Practices to Counter Kidnapping*, which was "based on good practice identified by experienced practitioners."[93]

The knowledge produced by think tanks, behavioral scientists, and insurance companies to tackle transnational kidnappings in the 1970s was, on the one hand, quite similar. It was constituted by practitioners and legitimized as practically applicable. On the other hand, the three groups had to present their own unique offers to convince sponsors, clients, and the mass media. So, what can we learn about the practical dimension of knowledge by following these practitioners? There are three larger points to be made: First, their examples demonstrate that knowledge has a material, a media, and a performative quality. As Philipp Sarasin

---

[91] Jenkins et al., *Dealing with Political Kidnapping*, 166; Alex P. Schmid, "Prevention of Kidnappings and Hostage-Takings by Terrorists," in *Handbook of Terrorism Prevention and Preparedness*, ed. by Alex P. Schmid (The Hague: ICCT, 2021), 738, 744.
[92] Letter from UN Under-Secretary to Brian Michael Jenkins, June 4, 1986, Brian Michael Jenkins Papers, Box 1, Folder 3, Hauser RAND Archives, RAND Corporation, Santa Monica, CA. See ibid. for the following quotes.
[93] UNODC Launches Manual of Best Practices to Counter Kidnapping, April 26, 2006, accessed February 7, 2025, https://unis.unvienna.org/unis/en/pressrels/2006/uniscp530.html.

has argued, there is no knowledge without media to visualize, store, and carry it from one place to another.[94] There is also, one must add, no knowledge without objects to produce it and bodies to perform it. A practical perspective thus highlights that knowledge is more than intangible concepts "circulating" around.[95]

Second, the focus on practices helps bridge the gap between structure and actors.[96] On the one hand, practices must be performed by someone in order to come into existence.[97] In the context of transnational kidnappings, we can identify prominent figures such as Brian Michael Jenkins, Frank Ochberg, and Richard Clutterbuck. There were also a few women at RAND and among the behavioral scientists, but being a practitioner in the field of political violence was clearly coded as male in the 1970s.[98] From a structural perspective, on the other hand, practices can be understood "as structured and acted out by communities of practice, and by the diffusion of background knowledge across agents in these communities, which similarly disposes them to act in coordination."[99] The think tank or insurance world, as well as the conferences, generated communities of practical knowledge whose members learned how to present their expertise in a competent and recognizable way, which at the same time gave them a sense of self and belonging. However, a form of knowledge so fundamentally rooted in personal experience can never be completely reduced to collective structures but is first and foremost perceived as an individual quality – not least because of the mass media.

Third, emphasizing practices and the value of experience in order to become an expert also meant that the potential and actual kidnapping victims were expected to become practitioners themselves, essentially to help themselves. It was their responsibility – and not the state's – to follow psychological advice in hostage situations, to avoid kidnappings by complying with insurance company guidelines, or to purchase K&R insurance. "This tendency towards 'autonomy' and 'self-help'" was a common feature of the 1970s, not only among neoliberals

---

94 Philipp Sarasin, "Was ist Wissensgeschichte?" *Internationales Archiv für Sozialgeschichte der deutschen Literatur* 36 (2011): 168.
95 For a critical approach regarding the concept of circulation, see Stefanie Gänger, "Circulation: Reflections on Circularity, Entity, and Liquidity in the Language of Global History," *Journal of Global History* 12 (2017).
96 On knowledge and actors, see Johan Östling et al., eds, *Knowledge Actors: Revisiting Agency in the History of Knowledge* (Lund: Nordic Academic Press, 2023).
97 Adler and Pouliot, "International Practices," 15.
98 Karen Gardela-Treverton was one of RAND's leading terrorism experts who developed the terrorism database. Peggy Murphy and Patricia L. Murphy were scientists at Stanford University where they worked with Jared Tinklenberg.
99 Adler and Pouliot, "International Practices," 15.

but also within alternative communities.[100] Moreover, after having lived through a hostage situation, survivors could also claim expertise in this topic. Men like Geoffrey Jackson and Claude Fly fashioned themselves into kidnapping experts by publishing their memoirs.[101] These books, in turn, were frequently quoted by Strentz, Crelinsten, and Clutterbuck, who uncritically repeated their heroic narratives.[102] In this way, the (professional) practitioners – involuntarily – created new experts. Practices, it becomes clear, are not always intentional. They can be unpredictable and dynamic, as can knowledge.[103] A practical perspective thus rebuts the highly contested divide between "real" scientific knowledge and its simplified popular versions and replaces it with a more complex and ambivalent picture.[104]

Juliane Hornung is an associate professor at the History Department at the University of Cologne (*akadem. Rätin a.Z.*). She specializes in media history and the history of political violence in the nineteenth and twentieth centuries from a global perspective. Her current book project explores transnational kidnappings as political practices and how they were linked to political rule, international relations, and notions of trust, worth, and morality (ca. 1860–1980).

---

100 Duco Hellema, *The Global 1970s: Radicalism, Reform, and Crisis* (Abingdon and New York: Routledge, 2019), 145. For a broader perspective on modern DIY culture, see Reinhild Kreis, *Selbermachen: Eine andere Geschichte des Konsumzeitalters* (Frankfurt a. M. and New York: Campus, 2020).
101 Geoffrey Jackson, *Surviving the Long Night: An Autobiographical Account of a Political Kidnapping* (New York: Vanguard, 1973); Claude Fly, *No Hope but God* (New York: Hawthorn, 1973).
102 Strentz, "Law Enforcement," 9; Crelinsten, "Study," 36; Clutterbuck, *Kidnap*, 91–92. The point here is not to denounce Jackson and Fly as their memoires certainly served as a means to regain their agency after having been severely violated and victimized.
103 Reckwitz, "Grundelemente," 120–122.
104 Terry Shinn and Richard Whitley, "Knowledge Producers and Knowledge Acquirers," in *Expository Science: Forms and Functions of Popularisation*, ed. Terry Shinn and Richard Whitley (Dordrecht: D.Reidel, 1985); Petra Boden and Dorit Müller, "Popularität – Wissen – Medien," in *Populäres Wissen im medialen Wandel seit 1850*, ed. Petra Boden and Dorit Müller (Berlin: Kadmos, 2009).

David Larsson Heidenblad and Axel Vikström
Creating Digital Finance for the Many: The Emergence of Online Brokerage Firms in Sweden, 1996–2000

Abstract: This article analyses how a newly established set of actors – online brokerage firms (OBFs) – sought to popularise stock trading among the Swedish populace in the late 1990s. During this period, internet usage took off and stock markets surged rapidly up until the dotcom bubble burst in 2000. Sweden was at the forefront of both these international developments, and we analyse the intimate connections between digital and financial practices emerging during these years. By exploring three thematic areas – the democratisation of stock trading, the subjectification of the everyman online investor, and training on how to navigate the online trading landscape – we analyse how the communicative strategies adopted by OBFs interplayed with business journalists and the established mass media to create a new market. Our study underscores the importance for historians of knowledge to analyse the workings of self-interested commercial actors and their attempts to make, facilitate, and expand new markets by means of the circulation of knowledge.

Keywords: digital finance, online brokerage firms, popular capitalism, internet, financialisation of everyday life

Historians of knowledge have a special interest in "societal breakthroughs of knowledge"; that is, historical processes in which certain forms of knowledge and related practices enter the everyday life and consciousness of the many.[1] To be sure, such breakthroughs are rarely, if ever, all-encompassing. Societies are large and multifaceted entities. Yet, charting and analysing how various bodies of knowledge take on a new level of social significance have in recent years proved to be a productive trajectory. Studies of different time periods, settings, and phenomena have clearly shown that societal breakthroughs of knowledge do not just happen randomly or follow automatically upon scientific discoveries or technological advances. Rather, they are made and shaped by constellations of actors, or-

---

[1] James A. Secord, "Knowledge in Transit," *Isis* 95, no. 4 (2004); Johan Östling and David Larsson Heidenblad, *The History of Knowledge* (Cambridge: Cambridge University Press, 2023).

ganisations, and institutions that make knowledge circulate in wider and more profound ways.[2]

Programmatically, historians of knowledge are interested in all forms of knowledge actors, learned as well as lay individuals. It has repeatedly been argued that the study of societal circulation of knowledge requires broadening the number and kinds of historical actors being analysed. In practice, however, certain types of knowledge actors – scholars, scientists, public intellectuals, officials, and politicians – tend to take centre stage in empirical studies.[3] This means that commercial actors and motives are typically overshadowed by epistemic and political concerns. We argue that this creates a problematic blind spot for historical studies set in market-oriented societies, which is why we aim to demonstrate the usefulness of studying a societal breakthrough of knowledge through the lens of a business and market logic.

But what is the role of knowledge in commercial contexts? Should the communicative strategies of self-interested actors be analysed as knowledge, information, or propaganda (or something else)? Historians of knowledge adopt an agnostic view on the knowledge claims they analyse to rather focus on the social processes that lead to people viewing certain claims as factual, meaningful, and useful in their everyday lives. By analysing the claims as knowledge, it is possible to make comparisons to other domains, such as politics, education, science, and religion – fields in which historical actors also have a self-interest in that their claims circulate as trustworthy knowledge.[4] Economic historians and sociologists have grappled with the issues of large-scale financial systems where the flows of goods, communications, and information are instrumental. These studies show that financial capitalism is dependent on particular forms of information – such as stock prices, annual reports, economic forecasts, financial advice, etc. – being accepted as knowledge by a broad range of actors and institutions, not least po-

---

2 Erik Bodensten, "A Societal History of Potato Knowledge in Sweden c. 1650–1800", *Scandinavian Journal of History* 46, no. 1 (2021); David Larsson Heidenblad, *The Environmental Turn in Postwar Sweden: A New History of Knowledge* (Manchester: Manchester University Press, 2021); James A. Secord, "Inventing the Scientific Revolution", *Isis* 114, no. 1 (2023).
3 Philipp Sarasin, "Was ist Wissensgeschichte?" *Internationales Archiv für Sozialgeschichte in der deutschen Literatur* 36, no. 1 (2011); Simone Lässig, "The History of Knowledge and the Expansion of the Historical Research Agenda", *Bulletin of the German Historical Institute* 59 (2016); Philipp Sarasin, "More Than Just Another Specialty: On the Prospects for the History of Knowledge", *Journal for the History of Knowledge* 1, no. 1 (2020); Johan Östling, David Larsson Heidenblad, and Anna Nilsson Hammar, eds., *Knowledge Actors: Revisiting Agency in the History of Knowledge* (Lund: Nordic Academic Press, 2023).
4 Östling et al., *Knowledge Actors*.

werful ones.⁵ Hence, studies of the communicative strategies of commercial actors elucidate not only how the circulation of knowledge creates specific financial markets but also how the workings of these markets cement particular practices and claims as common knowledge.

Our empirical study is centred on how a newly established set of actors – online brokerage firms (OBFs) – sought to popularise stock trading among the Swedish populace in the late 1990s. During this period, internet usage took off and stock markets surged rapidly until the dotcom bubble burst in 2000. Sweden was at the forefront of both these international developments, and we analyse the intimate connections forming during these years between digital and financial practices. We view OBFs as a cluster of commercial knowledge actors and analyse how they sought to create a new mass market of digital finance.

To borrow a phrase from Marieke de Goede, the late 1990s represented a critical "moment of openness" where new technologies and social practices emerged but were not yet naturalised or fixed.⁶ In our case, this is true when it comes to both internet usage and online stock trading. After NetTrade, the first Swedish OBF, was launched in 1996, it was quickly joined by others wanting to seize on the opportunities offered by the popularisation of the internet. At the turn of the century, 13 different actors were operating, which meant that Sweden at this time had more OBFs per capita than any other country.⁷ While the traditional banks eventually started to offer online trading to their customers, the specialised OBFs were the most active propagators of this phenomenon, where their communicative efforts sought to forge new and deeper connections between people and financial markets.

Our study thus focuses on the OBFs, most notably Nordnet, Avanza, TeleTrade, and E-Trade as well as, to a lesser extent, hq.se, NetTrade, and Aktiespar. Our source material consists of advertisement campaigns, information brochures, and other types of material produced by these firms, in addition to media coverage of these companies and the wider phenomenon of stock trading in daily, ta-

---

5 Alex Preda, "The Rise of the Popular Investor: Financial Knowledge and Investing in England and France, 1840–1880", *The Sociological Quarterly* 42, no. 2 (2001); Marieke De Goede, *Virtue, Fortune, Faith: A Genealogy of Finance* (Minneapolis: University of Minnesota Press, 2005); Steven Marks, *The Information Nexus: Global Capitalism from the Renaissance to the Present* (Cambridge: Cambridge University Press, 2016).
6 De Goede, *Virtue*.
7 "Sverige har flest internetmäklare", *Dagens IT*, 28 April 1999. In 1999, it was also estimated that Sweden, with its 80,000 active online traders, had the busiest online traders in Europe. See "Snabba affärer på nätet", *Expressen*, 17 June 1999. The downturn of the stock market following the burst of the dotcom bubble in 2000 accelerated the consolidation process that was already in motion. Within a few years' time, only three independent OBFs remained on the scene.

bloid, business, and investor media. The mass media is of particular importance not only due to the fact that they served as a space for the OBFs to market their products but also because they covered a vast array of issues associated with the new OBFs. This meant that the journalists themselves served as knowledge actors during the emergence of online trading. By exploring three thematic areas – the democratisation of stock trading, the subjectification of the everyman online investor, and training on how to navigate the online trading landscape – we analyse how the communicative strategies adopted by the OBFs interplayed with business journalists and the established mass media to create a new market.

Financialisation of Everyday Life and the History of Popular Capitalism

The attempt of the OBFs to turn ordinary Swedes into stock investors was by no means an isolated phenomenon. The late 1990s was an era of "market populism" where politicians and pundits all over the West sang the praises of the market's ability to solve problems, create prosperity, and enhance democracy.[8] This was part of a larger historical process that current scholars conceptualise as the "financialisation of everyday life". This term refers to the way in which financial markets and practices in the last decades have become ever-more important for an increasing number of people. It also entails a mental shift where people start to think and talk about their everyday actions and lives through market logics, such as "investing" in relationships. This concept was coined in the early 2000s in the direct aftermath of the period we study, as a way for social scientists to make sense of their immediate present and the changes they were witnessing.[9]

The concept has attracted attention from historians having raised the issue of chronology. While the standard narrative up to that point had focused on the "neoliberal shift" or "market turn" around 1980, the politics of Margaret Thatcher and Ronald Reagan, deregulations of capital markets, globalisation, and the rise of a mass investment culture – historians emphasised that a longer history exis-

---

[8] Thomas Frank, *One Market Under God: Extreme Capitalism, Market Populism, and the End of Economic Democracy* (New York: Doubleday, 2000); Brooke Harrington, *Pop Finance: Investment Clubs and the New Investor Populism* (Princeton: Princeton University Press, 2008).

[9] Randy Martin, *Financialization of Daily Life* (Philadelphia: Temple University Press, 2002); Rob Aitken, *Performing Capita: Toward a Cultural Economy of Popular and Global Finance* (Basingstoke: Palgrave Macmillan, 2007); Paul Langley, *The Everyday Life of Global Finance: Saving and Borrowing in Anglo-America* (Oxford: Oxford University Press, 2008).

ted that had to be taken into account. Popular engagement with financial markets – and attempts to create more intimate connections – stretch back to at least the so-called "railway mania" of the mid-nineteenth century.[10]

The history of popular capitalism has in recent years been an expansive field, especially in an Anglo-American context. This geographic focus is hardly surprising, as the United States and the United Kingdom have for a long time been the world's most financially oriented economies, playing a leading role in the transformations of the post-war industrial economy to a knowledge- and service-based one.[11] However, sustained ambitions to increase the number of shareholders stretch back to the 1920s, when this notion was put forth as a possible solution to recurring conflicts in the labour market and as a way to safeguard traditional ideals of a proprietary democracy in an age of large corporations. In America, this ideology was called "New Proprietorship" while it was called "Property Owning Democracy" in Western Europe.

Key to its popularisation was the successful "financial mobilisation" of the First World War, where warfare was financed by special war bonds sold to the public through patriotic campaigns. Hence, income-generating securities came to be seen as a public good and the pursuit of acquiring and owning them as something socially desirable. However, the stock crash of 1929 and the Great Depression of the 1930s eroded public trust in the stock market, and it would take many decades for a new mass investment culture to emerge.[12]

In Swedish historiography, there has been a rise in scholarly interest regarding this topic in the last few years. This is informed by a now widespread insight that the Swedish economy is highly financialised and that Sweden has developed a particularly strong culture of investing in stock, including civil society organisations

---

[10] Alex Preda, "Rise of the Popular Investor"; Marieke De Goede, *Virtue, Fortune, and Faith: A Genealogy of Finance* (Minneapolis: University of Minnesota Press, 2005); Alex Preda, "The Investor as a Cultural Figure in Global Capitalism", in *The Sociology of Financial Markets*, ed. Karin Knorr-Cetina and Alex Preda (Oxford: Oxford University Press, 2005). Orsi Husz, *Bankminded: Banks as Intimate Agents of Everyday Life in Welfare State Sweden* (Basingstoke: Palgrave Macmillan 2025).
[11] Janice Traflet, *A Nation of Small Shareholders: Marketing Wall Street after World War II* (Baltimore: Johns Hopkins University Press, 2013); Kieran Heinemann, *Playing the Market: Retail Investment and Speculation in Twentieth-Century Britain* (Oxford: Oxford University Press, 2021); Amy Edwards, *Are We Rich Yet? The Rise of Mass Investment Culture in Contemporary Britain* (Oakland: University of California Press, 2022).
[12] Julia Ott, *When Wall Street Met Main Street: The Quest for an Investors' Democracy* (Cambridge: Harvard University Press, 2011); Matthew Francis, "'A Crusade to Enfranchise the Many': Thatcherism and the 'Property-Owning Democracy'", *Twentieth Century British History* 23, no. 2 (2012); Janette Rutterford and Dimitris P. Sotiropoulos, "The Rise of the Small Investor in the United States and United Kingdom, 1895–1970", *Enterprise & Society*, 18, no. 3 (2017).

such as the Swedish Shareholders' Association (est. 1966) and the Swedish Young Shareholders' Association (est. 1990). Studies have shown that attempts to popularise investing in stock can be traced back to the 1950s, which then intensified in the second half of the 1970s when state-subsidised savings schemes in mutual funds were introduced and a Stock Promotion Foundation was founded.[13]

It has also been demonstrated that the Swedish "market turn" around 1980 was remarkably rapid and sharp. During the 1980s, the number of registered shareholders rose from 900,000 to about 2,5 million (or from 8% to 26% of the total population) and the Stockholm Stock Exchange advanced about 500% (adjusted for inflation). This expansion phase ended in the early 1990s when Sweden experienced a severe banking and financial crisis, which dampened public interest in stocks and mutual funds.[14]

Hence, the period we study – the late 1990s – constituted a second wave in the popularisation of investing in stock in Sweden. In 1997, the percentage of Swedes investing in stock had bounced back up to 28%, and even though ownership in relation to the total stock value remained concentrated among the wealthiest (mainly older people living in the metropolitan areas), the surging market values in the IT sector attracted broader segments of the population to join the race.[15] This tendency was acknowledged by contemporary scholars, who analysed media discourses and conducted ethnographic studies of stock investment clubs and conferences.[16] A great deal of scholarly attention has also been directed towards

---

[13] David Larsson Heidenblad and Charlotte Nilsson, "Ungdomslivets finansialisering: Skapandet av en aktiekultur för och av unga i Sverige, 1985–1994", *Historisk tidskrift* 142, no. 4 (2022); Orsi Husz and David Larsson Heidenblad, "The Making of Everyman's Capitalism in Sweden: Micro-Infrastructures, Unlearning, and Moral Boundary Work", *Enterprise & Society* 24, no. 2 (2023); Orsi Husz, "The Birth of the Finance Consumer: Feminists, Bankers and the Re-Gendering of Finance in Mid-Twentieth-Century Sweden", *Contemporary European History* (2023). Orsi Husz, David Larsson Heidenblad, and Elin Åström Rudberg, "Wage Earners, Taxpayers or Everyman Capitalists? The Making of a Mutual Fund Culture in Sweden", in *Nordic Neoliberalisms: Perspectives on Economic, Social and Cultural Change in the Nordics after 1970*, ed. Jenny Andersson and Chris Howell (London: Routledge, 2025).
[14] Alexis Stenfors, "The Swedish Financial System", *FESSUD studies* 13 (2014); Mats Larsson, "Stockholms fondbörs 1863–2013 - en översikt" in *Stockholmsbörsen på en förändrad finansmarknad*, ed. Mats Larsson (Stockholm 2016), 32–39; Tom Petersson, "Det privata aktieägandet i Sverige", in *Stockholmsbörsen på en förändrad finansmarknad*, ed. Mats Larsson (Stockholm 2016).
[15] Petersson, "Det privata aktieägandet", 305–307. In 1997, the richest centile of Swedes controlled 62% of the total stock value while the richest decile controlled 96%.
[16] Mats Lindqvist, *Is i magen: Om ekonomins kolonisering av vardagen* (Stockholm: Natur och Kultur, 2001); Fredrik Nilsson, *Aktiesparandets förlovade land: Människors möte med aktiemarknaden* (Eslöv: Symposium, 2003).

the major pension reform enacted in 2000 (after a decision in 1994) and the privatisation of the state-owned phone company Telia that same year.[17] Hence, state initiatives have been at the centre stage, while recent studies have added novel insights regarding the workings of civil society.[18]

However, the commercial actors of the era have not yet been studied in depth. The same is true for the digital aspects of the process. Between 1995 and 2000, the percentage of Swedes with internet access rose from 2% to 51%, a trend that parallelled the emergence of new digital financial services aimed at broad segments of the population.[19] Scholars, including historians of knowledge, have recently emphasised that financialisation and digitalisation should be seen as interlinked; however, empirical studies have focused on the 2010s and 2020s.[20] Hence, we now turn to the late 1990s as a special "moment of openness" for digital finance.

Democratising Stock Trading and Financial Knowledge

For over 100 years, capitalists and socialists have quarrelled over the control of production. At the same time, people have taken matters into their own hands. Today, 3/5 of Swedes own stocks. Talk about a popular movement. Trading stocks on the internet is also well on its way to becoming one. No wonder. It's something of a revolution. In the past, the broker decided who was at the front of the line to the Stock Exchange. The greater the capital, the further ahead. Today, everyone can become their own stockbroker via the internet. And in

---

[17] Urban Lundberg, *Juvelen i kronan: Socialdemokraterna och den allmänna pensionen* (Stockholm: Hjalmarsson & Högberg, 2003); Urban Lundberg, ed., *Mellan folkbildning och fondrådgivning: Nya perspektiv på pensionssystemet* (Stockholm: Institutet för framtidsstudier, 2007); Claes Ohlsson, *Folkets fonder? En textvetenskaplig studie av det svenska fondsparandets domesticering* (Gothenburg: University of Gothenburg, 2007); Dick Forslund, *Hit med pengarna! Sparandets genealogi och den finansiella övertalningens konst* (Stockholm: Carlsson, 2008).
[18] Charlotte Nilsson, "Turning students into Stock Market Investors: The Role of Civil Society and Public Schools in Swedish Financialization, c. 1985–2010", *Enterprise & Society* (2024), 1–31.
[19] Olle Fildahl, "Svenskarna och Internet 2011", *Internetstiftelsen* (2011); "Internet och finansiella tjänster", *Finansinspektionen* (2000:3).
[20] Nick Taylor and William Davies, "The Financialization of Anti-Capitalism? The Case of the 'Financial Independence Retire Early' Community", *Journal of Cultural Economy* 14, no. 6 (2021); David Larsson Heidenblad and Charlotte Nilsson, "Personal Finance Bloggers as Knowledge Authorities: Performing, Embodying, and Circulating Knowledge Online", in *Knowledge Actors: Revisiting Agency in the History of Knowledge*, ed. Johan Östling, David Larsson Heidenblad, and Anna Nilsson Hammar (Lund: Nordic Academic Press, 2023).

Figure 1: Advertisement with Karl Marx, Avanza, advertisement, Aftonbladet, 1 May 2000.

the Stock Exchange's data system, everyone is treated equally regardless of the size of their wallet. So, in a way, Karl Marx's ideas have now become a reality. Not least for Avanza's customers.[21]

This excerpt is taken from an ad campaign launched by Avanza on 1 May 2000 (i.e., the International Workers' Day). The text was accompanied by a portrait of Karl Marx and a fictious quote reading "Stocks over the Internet? Correct me if I'm wrong, but that is exactly what 'Das Kapital' is all about" (see Figure 1). That same day, during the annual May Day demonstration, an Avanza employee marched among the protestors dressed up as Marx carrying a sign with the catchword "The capital stock to the people". Variants on the Marx ad featuring other socialist icons such as Fidel Castro ("That's what I call a revolution"),[22] Vladimir Lenin ("Another way to take control over the means of production"),[23] and Nikita Khrushchev ("Commission? Another word for exploitation")[24] were also published.

Avanza's campaign illustrates a key strand of the marketing efforts carried out by the OBFs: the representation of online trading as a way of democratising economic practices and knowledge previously only available to a small economic elite. Using working-class ideologues to advance pro-market sentiments was not a new phenomenon in Sweden: in the early 1970s, leaflets and brochures from the Swedish Employers' Confederation (SAF) used quotations from both Karl Marx and Mao Zedong in an effort to "balance the radical youths' hope for a better alternative future with the hopes of the industry for a future open to innovation and investment".[25] The specific framing of investing in stock as a "popular movement" had also been used in Sweden since the early 1980s, but it gained renewed traction in the late 1990s.[26] This was part of a larger commercial project to create a mass market for digital finance.

In the summer of 1999, the American online brokerage giant E-Trade launched a subsidiary in Sweden. Its communication strategy centred around the catchphrase "democratic capitalism", describing its mission as "our idea is to give you as much information that you can make the decisions yourself. This is called

---

21 Avanza, advertisement, *Aftonbladet*, 1 May 2000.
22 Avanza, advertisement, *Aftonbladet*, 18 May 2000.
23 Avanza, advertisement, *Expressen*, 18 May 2000.
24 Avanza, information brochure (n.d.).
25 Kristoffer Ekberg, "Capitalist fictions: Environmentalism and the Swedish industry's effort to educate for optimism and uncertainty, 1968–1988", in *Environmental Regulation and the History of Capitalism: The Role of Business from Stockholm 1972 to the Climate Crisis*, ed. Sandra Bott, Sabine Pitteloud, and Janick Schaufelbuehl (New York: Routledge, 2025), 180–198.
26 Nilsson, *Aktiesparandets förlovade land*, 137.

democratic capitalism".[27] The same phrase was also used in a TV commercial that ran in the autumn of 2000. The commercial began with a well-dressed man entering a room. He sits down on a sofa, opens the newspaper, and asks his butler for a drink. The butler responds "Yes, please" and is then shown typing away on his laptop. While the well-dressed man grudgingly gets up to make the drink, a voice-over narrator says "Everyone can now buy stocks and mutual funds online. We call it democratic capitalism".[28]

This catchphrase also appeared in interviews with representatives from the company. The CEO of E-Trade was quoted as saying that "democratic capitalism" means that customers can now quickly sell their shares if a company is exposed for using child labour "in Poland or somewhere in Asia".[29] In an article about a stock trading school for women launched by E-Trade together with the Swedish Young Shareholders' Association, the project manager used the same catchphrase, arguing that the arrival of the internet means that "everybody is able to sell and buy without first having to go to their bank or call their broker".[30]

In these examples, we see that the term democratic capitalism was used with different connotations: sometimes, it involved helping the public act swiftly in accordance with their values. Most frequently, however, it simply concerned making hitherto unavailable financial information and practices available and affordable. Indeed, a recurring trope in the strategic communication of these companies was that the internet had levelled the playing field between ordinary Swedes and professional traders. Two brochures from Nordnet were both headlined "Trade stocks on the same terms as the professional traders",[31] while a brochure from hq.se announced that its users would receive "the same information as the professional player".[32]

A similar theme ran through the media coverage, captured in phrases such as "being connected in real-time used to be a quite expensive affair, reserved for stock market professionals"[33] and "anyone with a PC and a modem have access to have the same view as the professional broker".[34] As such, the emergence of online trading was not only hailed as a democratisation of the stock market – it also served as an entry point for encouraging ordinary Swedes to manage their finances in a more "professional" way.

---

27 E-Trade, information brochure (n.d.).
28 E-Trade, TV commercial (n.d.).
29 Harry Amster, "USA-jätte startar aktietjänst i Sverige", *Svenska Dagbladet*, 3 June 1999.
30 "Kan du köpa en cd på nätet, kan du köpa en aktie", Aftonbladet, 18 November 1999.
31 Nordnet, information brochures (n.d.).
32 hq.se, information brochure (n.d.)
33 Rolf Eriksson, "Billigare börskurs i hemmet", *Dagens Nyheter*, 23 January 2000.
34 "Monopolistens ansikte", *Dagens Industri*, 29 October 1999.

An E-Trade brochure included a passage informing the reader that a mere 30 minutes on their website would give him or her enough knowledge for not having to "sit at the bank with your cap in your hand listening to so-called mutual fund advice".[35] This phrasing was indicative of how the OBFs positioned themselves against the financial establishment. Avanza marked its launch in 1998 with an ad campaign satirising the high commission fees charged by the established brokerage firms.[36] The campaign opened with a print advert headlined "Stop Avanza!" signed by a fake interest group called "Friends of the commission", who declared that Avanza's fixed price model threatened the livelihood of the "poor people" employed by the other firms.[37] Avanza also took their campaign to the streets by having people dressed up as old-fashioned stockbrokers "protesting" against the company outside the Stockholm Stock Exchange.[38]

While the media coverage did not focus on positioning specific companies, the press often stressed that stock trading used to be an elitist endeavour. One feature stated that "thanks to the computer, everyone has access to the exclusive stock market information that was previously hidden away in the dark oak-panelled rooms of the bank palaces",[39] while another heralded that you no longer had to "wear a white shirt and a tie, have a phone in each ear, and shout 'Buy! Sell!'"[40] In this way, the newspapers reinforced the persistent claim of the OBFs that online trading represented a break with an exclusionary past. In this context, it should be noted that even though more Swedish households enjoyed access to the internet compared to other countries in the late 1990s,[41] significant differences remained in terms of wealth, education level, age, and gender.[42] As such, the anti-establishment rhetoric used in the context of online trading did not necessarily match the actual experiences of large segments of the population.

The media also served as a space for the OBFs to advance their interests under the banner of democratisation. This line of campaigning was aimed at the Stockholm Stock Exchange (OM) and focused on lowering the fees charged by OM for distributing real-time information on stock prices. The issue first entered the agenda in 1998, when several firm representatives argued that the current pricing

---

35 E-Trade, information brochure (n.d.).
36 For an early discussion on the difference between "commissionaires" and "brokers", as well as the historical origins of different forms of stock trading, see Max Weber, "Stock and Community Exchanges [Die Börse (1894)]", *Theory & Society* 29 (2000).
37 Avanza, advertisement, *Svenska Dagbladet*, 28 January 1998.
38 Björn Larsson Ask, "Otidsenliga herrar raggar kunder", *Svenska Dagbladet*, 14 February 1998.
39 Leif Aspelin, "Aktiehandel via nätet ökar explosionsartat", *Svenska Dagbladet*, 10 October 1999.
40 Daniel Bergsten, "Så lätt blir du börshaj på nätet", *Aftonbladet*, 24 January 1999.
41 "Sverige etta på näthandel med aktier", *Dagens Industri*, 10 August 1999.
42 Olle Findahl, "Svenskarna och Internet År 2000", *World Internet Institute*.

model gave the professional actors a great advantage over small investors.[43] The debate intensified in 1999 when OM announced that it would not only lower its fees but also scrap the maximum amount limit that the brokerage firms had to pay to deliver the rates to their customers. The CEO of Aktiespar threatened to sue OM, arguing that "It is a question of democracy. It should be a right for us to disseminate information to our customers".[44]

In August 1999, the CEOs of four OBFs published a joint debate article where they argued that OM "discriminates" against the small investors as "larger investors should not have an information advantage".[45] A similar rhetoric would later be used in other debates concerning OM, such as its opening hours (the OBFs argued that longer open hours in the evening would benefit ordinary Swedes working full-time) and their handling of technical problems (instances where trading was allowed to continue even when OM was technically unable to distribute stock prices to the OBFs were seen as symbolic of its loyalty towards the big actors).[46]

For the OBFs, democratisation thus meant more than just supplying trading tools at an affordable price, as it also entailed the dissemination of financial knowledge – ranging from real-time stock prices to reliable information on how stock trading works. But while there is no denying that the internet served to make stock trading more available, the meaning of democratisation circulated by the online brokerage firms through their marketing campaigns also carried a specific ideology, one which, following Thomas Frank, may be labelled "market populism". The essence of market populism is that the market is seen as "*more* democratic than any of the formal institutions of democracy" – it is an "anti-elitist machine" with "no place for snobs, for hierarchies, for elitism".[47] While anti-elitist and pro-democracy rhetoric may have figured in the financial advice literature for centuries,[48] Frank views it as pivotal for understanding how American businessmen in the 1990s started to mobilise the language of social class to present the market as a site of social revolutions.

By playing on traditional socialist critiques of the stock exchange as a "conspirator's club",[49] the Swedish OBFs used socialist icons, practices, and tropes in a commercial attempt to create a mass market for their services. In doing so, they

---

43 Johan Hallsenius, "Minutkrig på börsen", *Dagens Industri*, 27 November 1998.
44 Christian Carrwik, "Nya avgifter drabbar småspararna på börsen", *Expressen*, 20 August 1999.
45 Erik Saers, Per Nordlander, Jonas Sundvall, and Magnus Lindahl, "'Småsparare utestängs'", *Dagens Nyheter*, 20 August 1999.
46 Anders Lundborg, "Kaos i aktiehandeln", *Dagens Industri*, 1 February 2000; Peter Pettersson, "Börsen ska vara till för alla", *Dagens IT*, 1 February 2000.
47 Frank, *One Market Under God*, 29–31.
48 Paul Crosthwaite et al., *Invested: How Three Centuries of Stock Market Advice Reshaped Our Money, Markets & Minds* (Chicago: Chicago University Press), 2.
49 Max Weber, "Stock and Community Exchanges", 305.

aligned themselves with the market populist tendencies at the time by advancing a new form of popular capitalism, centred on deregulating the market and reconfiguring class relations. For while the cheap distribution of financial knowledge and services could be marketed as a form of socialism, financialisation scholar Randy Martin rightly points out that it also represents "an allegory of deregulation", as the removal of intermediaries "leaves the market in its purest form, a collectivity of decision makers acting directly on maximum available information".[50] In terms of class relations, Mats Lindqvist argues that while the distinction between "large capitalists" and "small investors" that gained prominence in the 1990s might have retained an element of struggle, the goal of this struggle was limited to supplying the latter with enough financial knowledge to enable them to compete in the marketplace.[51] In this way, OBFs, journalists, and stock commentators were engaged in framing online trading as an anti-establishment movement and community, while simultaneously advancing a market populist ideology stressing the need for individuals to become well-informed competitors in the stock market game.[52] Unlike a socialist interpretation of democratisation, where political organisation and collective action are instrumental, the framing of democracy by the OBFs focused on conferring greater market participation and access to broader segments of retail consumers.[53]

The Subjectification of the Everyman Online Trader

The OBFs shook up the financial industry by implementing a business model that differed from that of their predecessors. Established banks and brokerage firms, with their high commission fees, were able to operate with a relatively small customer base. The discount online firms, on the other hand, needed a large customer base to achieve a high total volume of trades. As we recall, one of the selling points highlighted by the OBFs was that their services enabled ordinary Swedes to trade on the same terms as professionals. Consequently, the OBFs needed to

---

50 Martin, *Financialization of Daily Life*, 81.
51 Lindqvist, *Is i magen*, 84.
52 Crosthwaite et al., *Invested*, 257. On the association between stock trading and social movements, see Nilsson, *Aktiesparandets förlovade land*.
53 See also Gordon Kuo Siong Tan, "Democratizing Finance with Robinhood: Financial Infrastructure, Interface Design and Platform Capitalism", *Environment & Planning* 53(8), 2001, 1865.

cultivate a market in which a broader segment of the population acted and identified themselves as traders.

However, while the OBFs sought to appeal to a broader base, we should clarify that their ad campaigns between 1996 and 1999 mainly ran in the business-oriented newspapers *Svenska Dagbladet* and *Dagens Industri* and specific investor magazines such as *Privata Affärer* and *Aktiespararen*. The two national tabloids, *Aftonbladet* and *Expressen*, were basically void of ads until we enter 2000. This suggests that the OBFs in their early years focused on creating a market of customers who were either accustomed to trading or came from predominantly middle- or upper-class backgrounds, but that this focus gradually expanded as we approach the turn of the century.

A key first step for taking up online trading was a basic knowledge of the phenomenon. Whereas the first online firms got off to a slow start, 10,000 Swedes were using their services by the summer of 1997, which was enough for *Dagens Industri* to label it "a success".[54] In the following years, Swedish media routinely emphasised the rising popularity of online trading. Numerical accounts of the number of people engaged in trading were often accompanied by different takes on the word "explosive"; for example, phrasings such as "online trading is exploding" or "online trading is increasing at an explosive rate". Similar metaphors used to capture the magnitude of this phenomenon include "avalanche-like", "rushes towards the top", "grows so fast that it cracks", or "advances at double-quick pace". It was also recurringly said that online trading had become more popular in Sweden than in other countries, captured in phrases such as "the Swedish people love the internet – and they are definitely the best in the world when it comes to trading with stocks online".[55] This brought the phenomenon closer to home, further lowering the bar for acting and identifying as an online investor. As such, the media coverage contributed to creating and widening the new market, thereby boosting the demand for the services provided by the OBFs.

But what kind of everyday investors did the OBFs encourage their prospective customers to become? As the business models relied on making people trade without the help of a broker, these companies were actively communicating the need for individuals to take personal responsibility for their finances. To capture

---

54 Anders Billing, "Snabbköp på börsen", *Dagens Industri*, 14 August 1997.
55 Magnus Hellberg, "Svenskarna bäst på aktiehandel via nätet", *Expressen*, 24 July 2000.

this, the OBFs often resorted to different takes on the phrase "becoming your own broker".[56] In a 1997 AD campaign, Nordnet used photographs of fingers to symbolise just how easy it was "to be your own broker"[57] and that "the broker of the future is you".[58] Avanza, Aktiedirekt, and hq.se also used this phrase in their ads.[59] TeleTrade announced that its service "enables you to act entirely on your own terms",[60] while E-Trade promised to provide enough information so that "you can make the decisions by yourself".[61]

The cultivation of a subject who invested independently was closely tied to an emphasis on control. TeleTrade used the image of a model racing track accompanied by the headline "try stock trading from the driver's seat", followed by the sentence "with TeleTrade, you find yourself in the eye of the market storm with the controller in your hand".[62] E-Trade exclaimed that it enabled you to "take control over all your investments!"[63] while Nordnet boasted that "you have complete control over the market situation".[64] A variation of this message was to underline just how user-friendly the various trading programmes were. In other words, acting like "the professionals" was made easy thanks to the accessible design of the OBF services.

Another characteristic of the envisioned online investor was a person eager and ready to act swiftly. In a 1999 campaign, Nordnet illustrated this notion by using a quote from the movie *Jurassic Park*: "A butterfly can flap its wings in Peking, and in Central Park, you get rain instead of sunshine."[65] This served as a metaphor for how everyone was now tied to the global economy. Avanza asserted that "you will have time to react before the rest of the market wakes up" while guaranteeing that its customers would have access to "a lot of exciting information before it reaches the rest of the market".[66]

This ties into the notion of flexibility. Aktiespar tried to attract customers by stating that "whenever and wherever you want, you can place your orders on-

---

56 A phrase that can be traced back to title of Thomas Mortimer's *Every Man His Own Broker*, a classic guide to stock trading dating back to 1761.
57 Nordnet, advertisement, *Dagens Industri*, 31 May 1997.
58 Nordnet, information brochure (n.d.).
59 Aktiespar, advertisement, *Aktiespararen*, December 1997; Avanza, advertisement, *Aftonbladet*, 1 May 2000; hq.se, information brochure (n.d.).
60 TeleTrade, information brochure (n.d.).
61 E-Trade, information brochure (n.d.).
62 TeleTrade, advertisement, *Dagens Industri*, 5 May 1998.
63 E-Trade, information sheet (n.d.).
64 Nordnet, information brochure (n.d.).
65 Nordnet, information brochure (n.d.).
66 Avanza, information brochure (n.d.).

line".[67] Nordnet used a similar phrasing, while also stating that "the trading floor is the one you stand on at home".[68] As such, flexibility was mainly presented as a means for making trading more comfortable. But against the backdrop of having to be ready to act swiftly, it also indicated the necessity of always being present.[69] In this sense, the investor mindset was not restricted to particular times of the day, it was rather a feature of the many facets of everyday life. To quote another one of Nordnet's brochures: "At lunchtime or in the middle of the night. NordNet Aktie is open around the clock. During a break at work or in the comfort of your home. Simply, where it suits you the best".[70]

Finally, online investors were encouraged to identify and act upon their personal needs and desires. Avanza's 1999 AD campaign included an image of a factory mass-producing cars accompanied by the headline "traditional stockbrokers and their fantastic tailor-made solutions" (see Figure 2). The ad made a reference to Henry Ford, saying that it is curious that his spirit – "the same solution for all customers" – still hovers over many brokers. Avanza's counteroffer was what it called "personalisation", which meant that "you can tailor the website so that you get exactly the information that you, specifically, are interested in".[71] Nordnet also used the term "tailor" in several of their brochures.[72] This connoted that while online investors were part of a growing collective, they should still personally configure their trading according to their own needs.

The media coverage in 1999 and 2000 started to include portraits of ordinary Swedes engaged in online trading. Examples include Lars-Gunnar, "a normal small investor" who is just "one click away from the jackpot",[73] and Ingrid, who has become "a stock trading professional thanks to the internet".[74] The coverage included interviews with representatives from particular target groups, such as women or young adults, as well as famous athletes and TV celebrities.[75] These

---

67 Aktiespar, advertisement, *Aktiespararen*, December 1997.
68 Nordnet, advertisement, *Dagens Industri*, 31 May 1997.
69 Paul Langley, "The Making of Investor Subjects in Anglo-American Pensions", *Environment and Planning D: Society & Space* 24 (2006): 928.
70 Nordnet, information brochure (n.d.).
71 Avanza, advertisement, *Svenska Dagbladet*, 18 November 1999.
72 Nordnet, information brochures (n.d.).
73 Lars Söderberg, "Lars-Gunnar – ett klick från klippet", *Aftonbladet*, 12 June 1999.
74 "Ingrid – aktieproffs tack vare internet", *Aftonbladet*, 13 September 1999.
75 In the run-up to the Sydney Olympics in 2000, Avanza sponsored taekwondo athlete Marcus Thorén, who was given ample media space to talk about his interest in online trading ("There are many similarities between online trading and martial arts . . . you need to act smartly and not be too offensive". Magnus Hellberg, "Svenskarna bäst på aktiehandel via nätet", *Expressen*, 24 July 2000.

Figure 2: Advertisement with car production, Avanza, advertisement, Svenska Dagbladet, 18 November 1999.

portraits reinforced many of the character traits described above and thereby managed to provide the public with a more intimate encounter with the online investor. While there were also instances in which ordinary people were used to highlight the dangers of online trading, such as becoming addicted,[76] the portraits mostly tried to show that anyone can become an online trader.

This "ordinary people" trope was also used by the OBFs themselves. Nordnet's ad campaign in 2000 showed people in everyday settings, such as eating breakfast, vacuuming, or knitting.[77] The accompanying text started by stating: "Stock prices are talked about in the ATM queue, brokerage fees are discussed at the hairdresser, and stock trades are being boasted about at parties. Hundreds of thousands of people have already made the leap from the bank and are now investing in stocks on their own." This way of communicating reinforced the idea that the internet had democratised stock trading and enabled audiences to identify with being an online investor.

Another way of providing the audience with an intimate experience was for reporters to personally try out day trading. Sometimes, the reporters gave a summarised account of their experience, other times they included minute-by-minute accounts of everything that occurred during the day. Headlines such as "A one-day profit on stocks: SEK 73"[78] and "I failed as a day trader"[79] showcase that the articles were not centred on celebrating the phenomenon. Rather, the focus was on describing what it felt like to be day trading, such as when you have to act swiftly ("I need to free up capital!"[80]), when you are unable to take a break ("Hungry! Don't dare to leave. What if Ericsson plummets."[81]), and when you hang on to your stocks for too long ("I was simply petrified"[82]). At this point in time, the private day trader was a new and intriguing figure, and the potential hazards associated with the phenomenon arguably turned it into an enticing topic. While they did not directly encourage the readers to follow in their footsteps, these accounts gave the reader the opportunity to emotionally engage with day trading.

Based on these findings, we see how the OBFs actively sought to construct a particular investment-oriented subject fit for their commercial model. This sub-

---

[76] Kerstin Thornström, "'Jag är en aktiemissbrukare'. John spekulerade bort en kvarts miljon kronor", *Expressen*, 19 August 1999.
[77] Nordnet, advertisements, *Dagens Industri*, 17, 22, and 24 March 2000.
[78] Jon Hansson, "En dags aktievinst: 73 kronor", *Aftonbladet*, 12 February 2000.
[79] Elisabeth Montgomery, "Jag var en misslyckad dejtrejder", *Expressen*, 20 September 2000.
[80] Jonas Florén, "Daytrader för en dag", *Dagens Industri*, 8 January 2000.
[81] Hansson, "En dags aktievinst".
[82] Montgomery, "Jag var en misslyckad dejtrejder".

ject, whose characteristics were reinforced and reenacted in the media, was called upon to use the services offered by the OBFs in order to take responsibility for their personal finances. The emphasis on low fees, speed, and control, which echoes how the American OBFs communicated in their early ads,[83] was hardly surprising considering that these were the parameters where the OBFs could set themselves apart from the established banks and brokerage firms. However, there was very little focus on the notion of risk-taking, which, as argued by Brad Barber and Terrance Odean in an American context, means that beginner traders were perhaps given an "illusion of control" that led them to overestimate the importance of speed compared to other factors.[84]

While the media occasionally did bring up problems associated with online trading, the underlying message was seemingly that risk was not to be avoided but instead embraced using the tools offered by the OBFs.[85] The investment-oriented subject advanced by the OBFs thus exemplifies the new forms of independent subjectivities emerging as part of the wider transfer of risk from the state to the individual that was at the heart of the welfare cutbacks in the 1990s.[86]

Financial and Digital Knowledge for Navigating the Online Trading Landscape

When the OBFs entered the market, their most lucrative selling point was their low commission fees. However, as more firms emerged on the scene, the OBFs had to find new ways of ousting their competitors. In June 1999, *Expressen* reported that: "In the beginning, the online brokers competed to offer the lowest prices to attract customers. The trend has now shifted and the brokers' main competitive advantage is instead to offer as much information as possible".[87] Rather than being a cheap alternative, the ability to supply the best and quickest financial knowledge became increasingly important.

---

[83] Brad M. Barber and Terrance Odean, "The Internet and the Investor", *The Journal of Economic Perspectives* 15, no. 1: 41–54.
[84] Ibid., 47–48. One study also found that traders who in the 1990s switched from telephone orders to direct transactions saw their investment success rate go down, partly due to overconfidence (see Crosthwaite et al., *Invested*, 256).
[85] On the shift from "spreading risk" to "embracing risk", see Tom Baker and Jonathan Simon, eds., *Embracing Risk: The Changing Culture of Insurance and Responsibility* (Chicago: University of Chicago Press, 2002).
[86] Edwards, *Are We Rich Yet*; Martin, *Financialization*.
[87] Ulf Pettersson, "Snabba affärer på nätet", *Expressen*, 17 June 1999.

One important strand of this communication simply focused on informing customers on how to operate the online services. "The computer landscape is the same as in a normal programme. You have windows that you can open, close, and move", as stated in one of Nordnet's early brochures.[88] Customers were informed that they "can tailor their own screen image and save it so that you are always familiar with it". Screenshots were regularly used to illustrate exactly what everything looked like, and arrows were occasionally used to point out exactly where to find the different functions. This type of communication was mostly reserved for the brochures, but TeleTrade also used this design in their print ads. The OBFs emphasised that the programmes were easy and fun to use, thereby lowering the bar for ordinary people to engage in online trading. This was visualised in another TeleTrade ad that showed a man sitting by his computer while his dog muttered "Three different trading solutions? And he can't even choose the right socks".[89]

The OBFs increasingly engaged in offering their customers financial analyses and information. In 2000, Avanza boasted that its services included "everything you need to know about a stock", such as "stock price, order book, news, analyses, press releases, trading statistics, and stock data, all collected on one website".[90] The same year, hq.se introduced a virtual "real-time analyst" named Hera Qraft, a reference to the popular action character Lara Croft. In the ad campaign, she declared: "As your virtual advisor, I provide you with tips, updated statistics, current analyses, and fresh stock-driving news – 24 hours a day", as well as "the key to success in the stock market is to always have access to relevant information".[91] Here, we see how hq.se tried to counteract the stress of always having to act swiftly by ensuring its customers that it is always working for them. Or to paraphrase Hera Qraft: "You are not made to work around the clock. I am".[92]

The race for the best information gave a boost to independent analyst firms, such as Redeye, which was commissioned by several of the OBFs.[93] In March 2000, *Dagens Industri* reported that several OBFs had started recruiting business journalists in order to offer better analyses.[94] That same year, Avanza, Nordnet, and E-Trade all launched their own online TV channels.[95] Avanza and TeleTrade also had

---

88 Nordnet, information brochure (n.d.).
89 TeleTrade, advertisement, *Svenska Dagbladet*, 23 May 2000.
90 Avanza, information brochure (n.d.).
91 hq.se, advertisement, *Dagens Nyheter*, 13 February 2000.
92 Ibid.
93 Peter Benson, "Aktieanalys ska sälja nätmäklarna", *Dagens Industri*, 18 May 2000.
94 Björn-Anders Olson, "Journalister nätmäklarnas nya giv", *Dagens Industri*, 18 March 2000.
95 Jonas Leijonhufvud, "Nätmäklare lanserar finans-TV på Internet", *Svenska Dagbladet*, 20 January 2000; Hans Bolander, "'Aktiehandel på nätet är framtidens melodi'", *Expressen*, 4 May 2000; Joakim Båge, "Avanza startar digital börs-tv", *Dagens Industri*, 5 October 2000.

their own chat forums in which users could discuss their thoughts regarding particular companies or stock trading in general.[96] Avanza even launched its own bookshop selling financial literature.[97]

The OBFs also engaged in external collaborations aimed at increasing people's interest in stock trading. In this regard, E-Trade played the most active role. In 1999, it started to supply the website of the leading daily *Dagens Nyheter* with real-time stock prices from the American Stock Exchange.[98] The following year, the tabloid *Aftonbladet* launched a new finance website in collaboration with E-Trade.[99] Together with the Swedish Young Shareholders' Association, E-Trade organised events and ran a stock trading school for women.[100] It also collaborated with the commercial TV channel *TV4* and *Dagens Industri* to produce the show *Börsmatchen* [The stock market match], which was labelled as an educational programme for people who were new to the stock market.[101] In the show, four teams started out with SEK 100,000 to then try to own the most valuable stocks by the end of the series. As a way of illustrating the role of chance, the fourth team was made up of a dog that picked stocks randomly (the dog ultimately finished in second place).[102]

While the contestants only invested fictional money, the show was accompanied by an online competition where people could invest SEK 5,000 in real money and compete against each other. Besides a large prize sum for the overall winner, the participant whose portfolio had grown the most each week was awarded a trip to New York. In this way, the show encouraged viewers to try out the stock market (thus attracting them to E-Trade's services).

While the OBFs were engaged in creating a mass market of digital finance, the media took it upon themselves to help the readers navigate this environment. Several "how to" articles and "stock trading schools" appeared during the sample

---

96 Hans Bolander, "Högre krav på ryktestorget", *Expressen*, 20 April 2000; Lars Andreas Karlberg, "Tele Trade vill sälja största börschatten", *Dagens IT*, 18 October 2000.
97 "Avanza öppnar internetbokhandel", *Dagens Industri*, 23 June 1999.
98 *Dagens Nyheter*, 23 August 1999.
99 Kerstin Nilsson, "Häng med till vår nya börssajt", *Aftonbladet*, 30 May 2000.
100 Frida Johansson, "Unga aktiesparare vill locka fler kvinnor placera på börsen", *Dagens Industri*, 6 September 2000.
101 Börsmatchen, *TV4*, 2000.
102 As such, the dog served the pedagogical purpose of echoing economist Burton Malkiel's famous argument that the unpredictability of short-term changes in stock prices means that in terms of short-term gains, "a blindfolded monkey throwing darts at the stock listing could select a portfolio that would do just as well as one selected by experts" (Burton Malkiel, *A Random Walk Down Wall Street: Including a Life-cycle Guide to Personal Investing* (New York: W.W. Norton, 1973).

period. In the early years, there was a strong emphasis on how much one could save by switching from a traditional broker to an OBF, but from 1998 and onwards, these guides started to take more factors into account. The more extensive ones included separate fact boxes or tables comparing the exact services offered by different banks and OBFs, while others had a more general entry point seeking to underline what one should think about when choosing which service to use. Headlines included "Here are the best stockbrokers",[103] "Find the best broker online",[104] and "The best advice for a good stock deal online".[105] In 1999, *Privata Affärer* took this one step further by using a panel of experts to crown the "Stockbroker of the year".[106]

Similar to the OBFs emphasising personalisation discussed in the previous section, these articles encouraged readers to choose brokers based on their personal preferences. One of the guides in *Dagens Industri* urged the reader to "listen at what others have to say, but also make your own judgements and choose the online broker that fits your investment profile the best".[107] *Expressen* used a similar turn of phrase, stating that "To decide what you should choose, you first need to analyse your business needs".[108] In this way, the outlets positioned themselves as providing a knowledge base for the reader. At the end of the day, however, everyone was responsible for picking the right option for them. The guide in *Dagens Industri* continued by suggesting that investors should from time to time revaluate whether their current OBF was still the best fit for them. Not only because another OBF might have improved its services, but also because "your trading behaviour might have changed over time".[109] By encouraging the public to undertake these kinds of reviews, the press reinforced the idea of the online investor as an active subject who needed to keep up with a changing world.[110]

While the media were seemingly more thrilled by than critical of the arrival of online trading, they also took it upon themselves to report on the potential hazards. During the sampled period, we find articles covering topics such as trading addiction,[111] stock manipulation,[112] misleading rumours in online forums,[113] and

---

103 Erland Huledal, "Här är bästa nätmäklarna", *Aftonbladet*, 1 April 2000.
104 Weje Sandén, "Hitta bästa mäklaren på nätet", *Dagens Industri*, 30 October 2000.
105 "Bästa råden för en bra aktieaffär på nätet", *Privata Affärer*, September 1998.
106 "Var handlar du aktier bäst?" *Privata Affärer*, October 1999.
107 Sandén, "Hitta bästa mäklaren".
108 Johan Wallqvist, "Dyrare depåer – men allt billigare på nätet", *Expressen*, 23 September 1999.
109 Sandén, "Hitta bästa mäklaren".
110 Cf. Langley, "The Making of Investor Subjects", 928.
111 Thornström, "'Jag är en aktiemissbrukare".
112 Lars Ahnland, "Krav på samarbete och strängare lagar", *Svenska Dagbladet*, 19 August 2000.
113 Bolander, "Högre krav".

the fear of security breaches.[114] However, most of the negative press on the OBFs focused on technical malfunctions during busy trading hours.[115] In fact, these problems turned into a news angle in itself, manifested in articles purely focused on how different OBFs had managed hectic events.[116] The more critical coverage could in that sense mainly be seen as another form of consumer guidance.

To summarise, we see that the topic of knowledge played a key role during the emergence of OBFs in Sweden. The companies raced against each other to provide their customers with the cheapest services and the best and fastest information. Thanks to the internet, the OBFs could establish themselves as knowledge actors that curated platforms with chat forums, newsletters, and online TV. The media, on their behalf, provided consumer guidance by supplying knowledge that would help the public make informed choices. Arguably, emphasising both the joy and necessity of personalising and exploring one's own financial needs played an important role in establishing a market for digital finance. The OBFs and the media supplied this knowledge, but it was up to the individual to choose and act correctly. Or, to paraphrase one of E-Trade's ads: "We give you the cake, quite simply. You pick the cherries".

Concluding Remarks

In January 2000, the information officer of the Stockholm Stock Exchange declared in an interview that "more and more people invest in stocks" and that "more and more people are online". In his view, these two trends went hand in hand. He confidently declared that: "We are living in the midst of a stock revolution".[117] As we have seen, this notion circulated widely in Swedish media in the late 1990s, and the marketing campaigns of OBFs were instrumental in advancing it. Even though they competed with one another, they also jointly fostered an image of an exploding stock market with an ever-increasing number of ordinary Swedes participating. The digital financial practices were framed as everyday activities that stood in contrast to an exclusive and elitist past. "Democratic capitalism" was the catchphrase they adhered to.

---

114 Charlotte Widmark, "Nätmäklare på frammarsch", *Dagens Industri*, 6 July 2000.
115 Björn Suneson, "Näthandeln sker på kundens risk", *Svenska Dagbladet*, 28 January 1998; Sara Hammarkrantz, "Internethandeln bra för konkurrensen", *Privata Affärer*, September 1999; Kerstin Thornström, "IT-hysterin på väg att knäcka nätmäklarna", *Expressen*, 25 November 1999.
116 Liv Fries, "Nätmäklarna klarade trycket" *Dagens Industri*, 22 July 2000.
117 Rolf Eriksson, "Billigare börskurs i hemmet", *Dagens Nyheter*, 23 January 2000.

Our study demonstrates that this very notion of a breakthrough was constructed by commercial actors and mobilised the market populist rhetoric that flourished in the 1990s. The business model of the OBFs was to cater to a mass market where large trading volumes enabled them to become profitable at scale. That meant that circulating financial knowledge, information, and practices was a necessary precondition for their operation. The media coverage of the topic actively contributed to the establishment of this market – for instance, by reinforcing the "explosion" of online trading, by sharing personal experiences of online trading, and by acting as a form of consumer guidance for the public. Together, the OBFs and the media targeted and enabled a new kind of everyday online investor who was encouraged to play an active role and take personal responsibility for their personal finances with the help of the new and better financial knowledge supplied by the OBFs and the media. This shift in risk from the state to the individual was symptomatic of the welfare cutbacks characterising the 1990s, which enabled private companies to in their marketing allude to a growing scepticism towards the welfare state.[118]

To historians of knowledge, our study underscores the importance of analysing commercial actors and their attempts to make, facilitate, and expand new markets. The circulation of knowledge in society and people's lives is at the core of such endeavours. Hence, we should keep in mind that societal breakthroughs of knowledge do not just follow epistemic and political logics but also market logics. However, our findings also call for caution when studying various kinds of breakthroughs, as the historical actors in our study used this very notion to serve their own commercial ends. To create digital finance for the many, they sought to establish that they were living in the midst of a "stock revolution", despite the fact that investing in stock – notwithstanding significant growth in new segments of the Swedish populace in the 1990s – remained a distant venture for many of the households affected the most by the welfare cutbacks following the wider neoliberal market turn. Hence, as historians of knowledge interested in societal breakthroughs, we should keep in mind that the marketing campaigns of the past did not in themselves constitute a breakthrough, even though they were instrumental in the attempts of these commercial actors to achieve one.[119]

---

[118] Oskar Engdahl, "'En aktiemarknad för alla': Integritet och marknadsomsorg i (själv)regleringen av den svenska värdepappersmarknaden", *Sociologisk forskning* 49, no. 4 (2012), 270–271.

[119] We want to thank the two anonymous reviewers and editor Jana Weiß for constructive comments on earlier versions of the manuscript. The research for this article was funded by Handelsbankens forskningsstiftelser, Riksbankens Jubileumsfond (Grant M19-0231), and Ridderstads stiftelse.

David Larsson Heidenblad is an associate professor of history and deputy director of the Lund Centre for the History of Knowledge (LUCK). His research is centered on the history of investing in stock and the emergence of the knowledge society. Recent publications include "The Making of Everyman's Capitalism in Sweden" in *Enterprise & Society* (2023, with Orsi Husz) and *The History of Knowledge* (Cambridge, 2023, with Johan Östling).

Axel Vikström is a postdoctoral researcher at the Department of History, Lund University. His research is centered on the mediation of economic practices and the role of discourse and language in naturalising inequalities in terms of wealth and power. He recently published his thesis *The Mediated Representation of the Super-Rich: Secrecy, Wealth Taxation and the Tensions of Neoliberal Capitalism* (Örebro University).

Fritz Kusch
Anti-Intellectualism in American Protectionism. The Protectionist Campaign against Academic Economics in the Late Nineteenth Century

Abstract: This article examines the role of anti-intellectualism in American protectionist agitation in the late nineteenth century. It analyzes anti-intellectualism as a historical phenomenon, thus extending the empirical basis of Richard Hofstadter's classic work on anti-intellectualism and its political impact throughout American history. The article traces how protectionist agitators in this period used firmly established rhetorical tropes regarding the overly theoretical nature of free trade arguments, their supposedly foreign origins, or the alleged impracticability of free trade as an actual policy to counter the limited status of protectionist ideas among academic economists. As free trade or tariff reform positions remained dominant in the rapidly expanding academic discipline of political economy, anti-intellectualism not only constituted a reaction of protectionists to this peripheral status of their own philosophy in the academic realm but also served as a political strategy to sustain protectionists' political hegemony.

Keywords: Protectionism, Free Trade, Anti-Intellectualism, Historicism, Anglophobia

Note: I wish to thank Elke Seefried, Daniel Brewing, and the other conveners of the "2. Aachener Nachwuchs-Workshop 'Wissensgeschichte'" for inviting me to present and discuss an earlier version of this article at an inspiring and productive workshop in Aachen in 2023. In addition, I extend my gratitude to Axel Schäfer for kindly sharing some of his insights on the German roots of the American Progressive movement with me. This article is a product of the research conducted in the Collaborative Research Center 1342 "Global Dynamics of Social Policy" at the University of Bremen. The center is funded by the Deutsche Forschungsgemeinschaft (DFG, German Research Foundation) – project number 374666841-SFB 1342.

Open Access. © 2025 the author(s), published by De Gruyter. This work is licensed under the Creative Commons Attribution-NonCommercial-NoDerivatives 4.0 International License.
https://doi.org/10.1515/9783111636726-003

Introduction

In 1891, the *Protectionist*, an indicatively named monthly magazine issued by the Boston-based Home Market Club (HMC), published a "Country Grocery Discussion" (Figure 1).[1] Assuming the viewpoint and the language of a common man, the poem defended the "purtection" doctrine against an intellectual and elitist other arguing for free trade. By translating the opposition of protectionism and free trade into juxtapositions of commoner and elitist, practical application and theoretical knowledge, or common sense and academic education, the poem mirrored an important characteristic of late nineteenth-century American protectionism: its blatant anti-intellectualism. Frequently, protectionist politicians and agitators objected to the alleged hegemony of free trade in American university syllabi and lamented the disdain exhibited by professional economists with regard to protectionist ideas and policies. In this way, the elitist free trade professor came to constitute a commonly invoked bogeymen in protectionist agitation throughout the Gilded Age and Progressive Era.

In order to examine this specific aspect of protectionist ideology, this article aims to highlight key arguments and tropes frequently used to express protectionist anti-intellectualism. Thus, rather than providing a comprehensive or chronological account of this historical phenomenon, the article, by means of example, analyzes the use of anti-intellectualism as a discursive strategy adopted by American protectionist agitators. The analysis is limited to the 1880s and 1890s when the protectionist anti-intellectualist discourse was most firmly established and intersected with a major debate in the field of academic economics on the future orientation of the discipline against the backdrop of the rapid industrialization and modernization of the United States and the discipline's increasing professionalization and expansion.

It is important to note that anti-intellectualism was not in itself a necessary component of protectionist ideology, which mainly revolved around ideas on tariffs, trade, wages, the nation, and its defense. Instead, anti-intellectualism was a sentiment to which protectionist ideas could be attached and through which these ideas could be expressed. This meant that protectionist anti-intellectualism served a twofold purpose. On the one hand, it was a reaction to the peripheral status of protectionist ideas among academic economists. On the other hand, the use of anti-intellectualist stereotypes also represented an attempt to exploit a popular resentment of elite educational institutions and their representatives with the aim of popularizing protectionist ideas among ordinary Americans. Given this

---

[1] Socrates Smith: "A Country Grocery Discussion," *The Protectionist* 3, no. 1 (1891): 1.

A COUNTRY GROCERY DISCUSSION.

BY SOCRATES SMITH.

His head wuz full er theories; he talked 'em by the job;
His speech w'en shelled was one part corn an' ninety-nine parts cob.
It sounded purty; some the boys they said 'twas jest immense;
"The sound's all right," sez I to them, "but where in time's the sense?"

He called purtection "robbery," like all the Cobden school,
He said free trade wuz righteousness, the modern golden rule.
"Is't right ter rob your wife and kids," sez I ter him, "is't right
For foriners to git our work while we must starve or fight?"

"It's sound economy," sez he, "to let the cheapest sell."
Sez I, "My friend, that barb'rous rule would drag us down to hell.
Ter purtect yer home and famberly may be a deadly sin —
But them's jest the kind er sinners thet St. Peter passes in."

"Free trade 'ud save fer you," sez he, "on food, an' cloe's an' rent."
Sez I, "Meat's dear 't a cent a pound 'f ye haven't got no cent.
Free trade it robs yer wallet an' steals yer meat an' corn,
An' offers ye big bargain sales, w'en all yer money's gone."

I ast him, "Wouldn't a pauper find it purty middlin' hard
To be a dude with trouserin's at thirteen cents a yard?
We'd wear di'mon' studs fer buttons if they sol' 'em fer a nickle,
But if we had no money we'd be in the same ol' pickle."

"Free trade will usher in," sez he, "the gran' mellenial age
Foretol' by seers an' prophets ez the worl's gret heritage."
"Oh, w'en the big mellenium comes 'twill be all right," sez I,
"W'en our rivers flow 'ith honey an' our shade trees bloom 'ith pie;

W'en the angels drop down manna from the bendin' firmerment,
An' we hol' our han's an' take it an' don't have to pay a cent;
W'en food drops in our open jaws w'ile loafin' in the shade,
W'y then 'twill be a bully time to interduce free trade."

Figure 1: Socrates Smith: "A Country Grocery Discussion," *The Protectionist* 3, no. 1 (1891): 1.

attempt at popularization, the analysis focuses on political agitators as the main emissaries for bringing protectionist ideology to the American public.

First, the article outlines the political and academic standing of protectionist ideas in the United States in the late nineteenth century while also introducing popularist protectionist agitators as an important group within that movement. Then, the article discusses how academic economists of varying theoretical backgrounds treated the tariff question in their work before turning to protectionist anti-intellectualism as a protectionist counterstrategy. Delving into specific anti-intellectualist tropes, the article discusses the narrative juxtaposition of free trade as a theoretical concept and protectionism as a practical policy, the merging of anti-intellectualism and Anglophobia, and the hopes and fears projected by protectionists onto the American (college) youth as important characteristics of late nineteenth-century protectionist anti-intellectualism. Finally, the article also explores the ways in which protectionist agitators sought to establish their own positions within academic economics.

In terms of historiography, any discussion of anti-intellectualism in the United States must begin with Richard Hofstadter's 1963 book *Anti-Intellectualism in American Life*.[2] Seeking to explain the widespread anti-intellectualism of postwar American conservatism and the McCarthyist zealotry against left-leaning intellectuals, Hofstadter sought to uncover the roots of this anti-intellectualism, which he described as a cyclically recurring phenomenon throughout American history. In Hofstadter's understanding, anti-intellectualism is not a uniform ideology but rather a loose web of cultural attitudes and dispositions. The "common strain" connecting these is "a resentment and suspicion of the life of the mind and of those who are considered to represent it; and a disposition constantly to minimize the value of that life."[3] Intellect, according to Hofstadter, may be distinguished from intelligence as it is not concerned with a specific aim or its possible applicability but rather pursues intellectual exercises for their own sake, driven by a sincere thirst for knowledge and truth.[4]

With regard to the late nineteenth century, Hofstadter interprets the rise of anti-intellectualist tropes in the American political arena after the Civil War as an attempt by the Republican mainstream to repudiate the progressive reform efforts of a group of liberals, "genteel reformers" in his terminology. These reformers grew out of the Liberal Republican movement and defected as so-called Mugwumps to Grover Cleveland's Democrats in the 1880s. They were mostly from the

---

2 Richard Hofstadter, *Anti-Intellectualism in American Life* (New York: Random House, 1963).
3 Ibid., 7.
4 Ibid., 24–25.

Northeast, university-educated, and promoted a proto-progressive reform agenda centered around civil service reform. According to Hofstadter, conservatives attacking these intellectual elites was where anti-intellectualism most clearly crystallized in American politics during Reconstruction and the Gilded Age.[5] However, in his discussion on Gilded Age anti-intellectualism and the Republican dismissal of the Mugwump reform agenda, Hofstadter mostly omits the lively tariff discussions of the era and overlooks the strong impact of free trade and tariff reform ideas on the reform movement. In fact, no other issue, apart from civil service reform, provoked the break between mainstream Republicans and their liberal counterparts like the latters' deviation from protectionist orthodoxy and their call for tariff reform.[6] Protectionist anti-intellectualism was thus also a crucial component of this larger Republican anti-intellectualist backlash against these reform proposals.

Hence, this article is both an extension as well as a rectification of Hofstadter's treatment of Gilded Age anti-intellectualism. Probably due to the book's ambivalent character, scholars have interpreted *Anti-Intellectualism* quite differently. As a "scholarly polemic," *Anti-Intellectualism* oscillates between contemporary political commentary, a historically grounded philosophical essay, a formal history of a cultural phenomenon, and a personal book.[7] While political commentators welcomed the book as a suitable political diagnosis when it was published, its merits as a historical analysis have been called into question. Most scholarly treatments of the book have focused on Hofstadter's conceptualization of anti-

---

5 Ibid., 172–188.
6 Hofstadter mentions tariff reform only in passing, noting that David A. Wells lost his position as a federal revenue agent due to his free trade convictions (ibid., 173). The strong tariff reform sentiment among the majority of Liberal Republicans is in hindsight somewhat obfuscated by the fact that the party chose Horace Greeley, a convinced protectionist and as such an exception among his peers, as their presidential candidate in 1872. On the influence of free trade ideas within the Liberal Republican movement, see, for example, Marc-William Palen, *The "Conspiracy" of Free Trade: The Anglo-American Struggle over Empire and Economic Globalization, 1846–1896* (Cambridge: Cambridge University Press, 2016), 67–100, 110–115; Joanne R. Reitano, *The Tariff Question in the Gilded Age: The Great Debate of 1888* (University Park, PA: Penn State University Press, 1994), 59–61; David M. Tucker, *Mugwumps: Public Moralists of the Gilded Age* (Columbia, MO: University of Missouri Press, 1998), 26–37. Generally on the Liberal Republican Movement, see Andrew L. Slap, *The Doom of Reconstruction: The Liberal Republicans in the Civil War Era* (New York: Fordham University Press, 2006).
7 Daniel Rigney, "Three Kinds of Anti-Intellectualism: Rethinking Hofstadter," *Sociological Inquiry* 61, no. 4 (1991): 434–451, 435; Andreas Hübner and Nils Steffensen, "Von Leerstellen und Desideraten: Perspektiven über Anti-intellectualism in American Life hinaus," in *Antiintellektualismus: Ein unwahrscheinlicher Klassiker*, ed. Andreas Hübner and Nils Steffensen (Kiel: Universitätsverlag Kiel, 2024), 161–166, 164–65.

intellectualism but neglected the historical foundation underpinning his claims.[8] Lately, Hofstadter's work has found renewed attention in the wake of Trumpism and the blatant anti-intellectualism exhibited by this political movement.[9] Rather than contributing to the conceptual debate on anti-intellectualism, this article seeks to study late nineteenth-century American protectionist anti-intellectualism as a historical phenomenon. By examining it as a specific historical occurrence of the broader political phenomenon of anti-intellectualism in the United States, this article aims to underpin the empirical basis of Hofstadter's analysis. In this sense, it is also an answer to Andreas Hübner and Nils Steffensen's recent call to test the limits of the applicability of Hofstadter's ideas on anti-intellectualism in historical scholarship by providing a broader empirical basis for Hofstadter's ideas.[10]

The Tariff Question and Protectionist Pressure Groups in the Late Nineteenth Century

Stretching from Alexander Hamilton's famous *Report on Manufactures* and Henry Clay's vision of the "American System" to the pronounced protectionism that remained a consistent tenet of Republican party platforms throughout the nineteenth century, protectionism had a long tradition of being a potent political force in the United States. Intellectually, American protectionism traced its roots back to the writings of figures such as Alexander Hamilton or Matthew Carey and was carried on by a subsequent generation of protectionist thinkers. Henry C. Carey, the son of Matthew Carey, was probably the most influential thinker of the so-called American School.[11] It is important to note that throughout the

---

[8] See, for example, Tim Lacy, "Against and Beyond Hofstadter: Revising the Study of Anti-intellectualism," in *American Labyrinth: Intellectual History for Complicated Times*, ed. Andrew Hartman and Raymond J. Haberski (Ithaca, NY: Cornell University Press, 2018), 253–270, 261–265; Rigney, "Three Kinds of Anti-Intellectualism."

[9] Andreas Hübner and Nils Steffensen, "Anti-intellectualism in American Life: Fragen an einen unwahrscheinlichen Klassiker," in *Antiintellektualismus: Ein unwahrscheinlicher Klassiker*, ed. Andreas Hübner and Nils Steffensen (Kiel: Universitätsverlag Kiel, 2024), 7–16, 10; Walter G. Moss, "The Crassness and Anti-Intellectualism of President Donald Trump," *History News Network*, March 18, 2018.

[10] Hübner and Steffensen, "Anti-intellectualism in American Life," 10–12.

[11] On Henry C. Carey and his influence, see, for example, Eric Helleiner, *The Neomercantilists: A Global Intellectual History* (Ithaca, NY: Cornell University Press, 2021), 137–164. German economist Friedrich List, who had lived in Pennsylvania between 1825 and 1833, exported the ideas of the American School abroad and introduced them to economists in continental Europe: William

nineteenth century – despite this long-standing tradition of American protectionism and the at times staggeringly high American tariff rates – protectionist thought held little currency among economics professors and mostly flourished outside and at the margins of the academic realm. Protectionism was debated and developed in private discussion circles, essayistic newspaper pieces, books, and pamphlets. But for the most part, it did not enter the classrooms of American colleges and universities. The exclusion of protectionist thinkers from American universities and their reliance on private circles also meant that the arguments of these thinkers were always heavily entangled with powerful material interests in protectionist tariff policies. Wealthy industrialists from protected industries provided the financial backing for protectionist organizations and protectionist thinkers. Tellingly, Henry C. Carey never taught at a college or university but was nurtured by Philadelphia industrialists as their "guru of high-tariff economics."[12]

Still, Henry C. Carey and other protectionist thinkers were highly influential when it came to the actual tariff and trade policy of the United States. In fact, Carey himself repeatedly met with President Lincoln during the Civil War to advise him on tariff and trade matters.[13] Republicans generally remained faithful to the doctrines of the American School and pursued a heavily protectionist tariff policy from the Civil War far into the twentieth century. Nevertheless, tariff policy remained a highly controversial and divisive field. Especially in the 1880s and 1890s, bitter confrontations between protectionists (usually Republicans) and advocates of free trade or tariff reform (usually Democrats) regularly took center stage in American national politics.[14] By the late nineteenth century, the Republi-

---

J. Barber, "Political Economy and the Academic Setting before 1900: An Introduction," in *Breaking the Academic Mould: Economists and American Higher Learning in the Nineteenth Century*, ed. William J. Barber (Middletown, CT: Wesleyan University Press, 1988), 3–14, 8–9.

12 Steven A. Sass, "An Uneasy Relationship: The Business Community and Academic Economists at the University of Pennsylvania," in *Breaking the Academic Mould: Economists and American Higher Learning in the Nineteenth Century*, ed. William J. Barber (Middletown, CT: Wesleyan University Press, 1988), 225–240, 225.

13 C. D. Johnson, *The Wealth of a Nation: A History of Trade Politics in America* (New York & Oxford: Oxford University Press, 2018), 90; Douglas A. Irwin, *Clashing Over Commerce: A History of US Trade Policy* (Chicago: University of Chicago Press, 2017), 214.

14 The terminology commonly used throughout the tariff discussions in the late nineteenth century can be misleading: Demanding "protection" or a "protective tariff" typically meant support for the existing high tariff regime, often without actually specifying different tariff rates and their desired level. "Free trade" usually did not mean abolishing all duties but rather reducing them to a level that still generated the necessary revenue to finance the federal budget, thus essentially a "tariff for revenue only" – another term frequently employed by opponents of tariff protectionism. "Tariff reform" was a broad and seldomly defined term, but in the American concan Party had thus turned the ideas of Carey and others into reality by establishing a strongly protectionist tariff regime. Despite its relative political dominance, however, protectionism continued to draw only a marginal group of adherents among American economists. This peculiar disparity triggered the aggressive anti-intellectualism of late nineteenth-century protectionism.

When it comes to tracing the anti-intellectualist discourse of late nineteenth-century American protectionism, protectionist advocacy groups and their agitation material represent a promising point of departure. Backed by industrialists from protected heavy and manufacturing industries, organizations such as the American Iron and Steel Association (AISA) and the Industrial League (IL) in Philadelphia, the HMC in Boston, mainly representing the New England textile industries, or the American Protective Tariff League (APTL) in New York, representing a variety of manufacturers, formed a spectrum of private interest groups, all dedicated to popularizing ultra-protectionist ideology. These organizations sustained press outlets, published books, and distributed pamphlets by the millions to convince ordinary Americans of the benefits of tariff protectionism.[15] The discourse of protectionist anti-intellectualism crystallized most clearly in the newspapers and pamphlets, which these organizations circulated. These pressure groups were closely associated with the Republican Party and, as they simultaneously shaped and reflected the political positions of many American protectionists, they formed crucial networking forums for the protectionist cause during the Gilded Age and Progressive Era. In turn, the traditional exclusion of protectionism from academic circles reinforced the status of groups such as the APTL or the AISA and their respective outlets as important junctures for developing and circulating protectionist ideas. The strategies employed and the ideas circulated by these organizations may therefore be regarded as characteristic of the general development

---

text, it typically referred to a demand for some form of downward tariff revision and was thus rather associated with free trade than with protectionism. As Andreas Etges convincingly argues, a meaningful distinction between the various positions articulated in nineteenth-century American tariff discussions should not be derived from the level of tariff rates demanded but rather from the underlying philosophy regarding the political function of tariffs: Protectionists viewed them as a tool to shield the American economy from foreign competitors and to foster economic development, whereas free traders and tariff reformers viewed tariffs as a necessary instrument for generating the revenues needed to fund the limited activities of the national government: Andreas Etges, *Wirtschaftsnationalismus: USA und Deutschland im Vergleich (1815–1914)* (Frankfurt a. M.: Campus, 1999), 308–309. See also Reitano, *The Tariff Question in the Gilded Age*, 56–61.

15 Previous scholarship has for the most part overlooked the crucial role played by these organizations in shaping and maintaining the protectionist coalition, both politically and ideologically. The most extensive treatments are Etges, *Wirtschaftsnationalismus*, 322–324; Reitano, *The Tariff Question in the Gilded Age*, 115–117.

of protectionist thinking in this period. Given their financial backing, these organizations represented the popularist mouthpieces of elite industrial interests. Yet they frequently proclaimed that protectionism was a policy of and for ordinary Americans. This ambivalence of the protectionist cause, disguising an elite interest as a popular demand, turned anti-intellectualism into a viable strategy and a common element of protectionist agitation in this period.[16]

The protectionist anti-intellectualism of the late nineteenth century, as presented in the press outlets of these groups, was strongly underpinned by the belief held by many protectionists that American colleges were firmly in the grip of free traders. This conviction was expressed so frequently that it may be regarded as a proper truism of protectionist agitation.[17] A correspondent writing to the AISA in 1882 sought to explain "Why Our Colleges Teach Free Trade" and proclaimed that "it is unquestionably true that Free Trade is taught in a large majority of American colleges."[18] In 1897, the *American Economist*, the APTL's weekly newspaper, reported a typical anecdote:

> At one of our great universities, Free-Trade is so assiduously and consistently taught by the instructor who was hired to teach political economy that a student only a few weeks ago, asked in all good faith, "What argument is there for Protection?" and was told by the instructor, "There is no argument for Protection."

---

[16] The strategic aspect of protectionist anti-intellectualism was also mirrored in the attempts of elite industrialists to court laborers to the cause of protectionism by emphasizing the supposed wage benefits offered by protectionism to American industrial workers: Fritz Kusch, "Capital and Labor United? Workers, Wages, and the Tariff in Late Nineteenth-Century Protectionist Agitation," *Journal of the Gilded Age and Progressive Era* 24, no. 2 (2025), 157–180.

[17] In 1890, the APTL even conducted a survey to verify this claim. Based on the responses from roughly 1,400 seniors in 45 schools, including all major American universities, the poll presented an overview of the instruction in political economy. According to the poll, roughly 18% of seniors stated that the instruction at their institution leaned toward "Protection" as opposed to "Tariff Reform" (27%) and "Free-Trade" (36%). 19% reported that the instruction they had received was "Impartial." The survey also contained a list of individual universities and the names of the professors responsible for instructing political economy. Universities such as Columbia, Cornell, Dartmouth, Harvard, Princeton, Wesleyan, Williams College, and Yale emerged as bastions of free trade and tariff reform. Fewer colleges appeared as protectionist strongholds: Oberlin, Swarthmore, but especially the University of Pennsylvania. Describing their own conviction on tariff matters, 34% of seniors leaned toward "Protection," 47% toward "Tariff Reform," and 19% toward "Free-Trade," thus leaving the protectionists in the minority: *American Economist*, "Tariff Teaching: The Kind of Political Economy Taught American Collegians," May 23, 1890; *American Economist*, "Education and Economics," August 1, 1890.

[18] *Bulletin of the American Iron and Steel Association*, "Why Our Colleges Teach Free Trade," April 26, 1882.

The *American Economist* combined this anecdote with a call for action:

> It has been too long accepted as settled that Free-Trade must of necessity be taught in our colleges. It is not mere partisanship, which demands something different, but simple justice. [. . .] It is high time that Protectionists should take this matter up; and it is high time that students should not be compelled to submit to such arrogance and ignorance.[19]

The protectionist counteraction against the perceived dominance of free trade first and foremost consisted of sharp and unyielding anti-intellectualist attacks aimed at a general denigration of academic economics, its teachers, and its tenets. But before analyzing the specifics of this protectionist anti-intellectualism in greater detail, we need to take a brief look at the state of the emerging discipline of political economy within American higher education institutions and especially how American economists viewed the tariff question in order to properly contextualize the claim of protectionist agitators that free traders dominated the classrooms of American universities.

The Rise of Historicism and the Tariff Question in American Political Economy

Economics, or political economy as it was called at the time, was not established as an independent discipline until the 1870s. In the traditional American denominational college system, political economy, like all social sciences, had been a subdiscipline of moral philosophy. Most instructors were not specifically trained as economists, and their lectures were mostly intended to familiarize students with the classics of laissez-faire economics. As Daniel Rodgers put it, American colleges had "a structural commitment to the simplified and the out of date."[20] The industrialization and modernization process, which dramatically altered the American economy and American life in general in the second half of the nineteenth century, also posed new and complex economic problems and ultimately changed the structure and function of American higher education institutions. Most significantly, political economy now quickly developed into one of the lead-

---

[19] *American Economist*, "Arrogance and Ignorance," March 26, 1897.
[20] Daniel T. Rodgers, *Atlantic Crossings: Social Politics in a Progressive Age* (Cambridge, MA: Harvard University Press, 2009), 81; A. W. Coats, "The Educational Revolution and the Professionalization of American Economics," in *Breaking the Academic Mould: Economists and American Higher Learning in the Nineteenth Century*, ed. William J. Barber (Middletown, CT: Wesleyan University Press, 1988), 340–375, 349.

ing disciplines in the rapidly expanding and professionalizing colleges and universities of the country: Still in 1880, there were only three chairs exclusively dedicated to political economy in the whole country. By 1890 this number had risen to 25 and to 51 by 1900. At the turn of the century, three-quarters of all colleges and universities in the United States taught political economy and most required all students to take at least one introductory class. The number of PhD degrees awarded in political economy also rose significantly.[21]

But the discipline was not just rapidly expanding, it was also in methodological turmoil as a younger generation of scholars began to contest the established hegemony of laissez-faire. This type of economics traditionally taught by the majority of American economists consisted of a range of economic theories revolving around the self-interest of private individuals as the main driver of economic behavior, private property rights, limited government, and a positive affirmation of the forces of market capitalism. These ideas, developed by Adam Smith, Thomas Malthus, David Ricardo, and other, mostly British thinkers, formed the intellectual and philosophical underpinning of classical nineteenth-century liberalism.[22] Following the Ricardian tradition, free trade represented one of the basic tenets of laissez-faire and was thus firmly inscribed in the syllabi of American universities.

Beginning in the 1880s, a generation of younger economists, most of them trained in Germany, challenged the orthodoxy of laissez-faire economics with the arsenal of German historicism: inductive reasoning, empiricism, and historical relativism.[23] German thinkers such as Gustav Schmoller, Johannes Conrad, Karl Knies, or Wilhelm Roscher had offered a radical critique of laissez-faire to their

---

21 Judith L. Goldstein, *Ideas, Interests, and American Trade Policy* (Ithaca, NY: Cornell University Press, 1993), 85; Coats, "The Educational Revolution and the Professionalization of American Economics," 340–346; Hans-Joerg Tiede, *University Reform: The Founding of the American Association of University Professors* (Baltimore: Johns Hopkins University Press, 2015), 9; Barber, "Political Economy and the Academic Setting before 1900," 10–13.
22 Rodgers, *Atlantic Crossings*, 77–80.
23 The *Wanderjahre* of young American academics in Germany were crucial in transmitting ideas from continental political economy to the United States in the 1870s and 1880s. Germany was the preferred country of study for young Americans throughout the nineteenth century: Between 1820 and 1920, roughly 9,000 American students were enrolled at German universities, more than in any other European country. This trend was especially strong in the field of economics and would later have an enormous impact: Of the 116 leading economists in the United States and Canada, counted by Yale's Henry Farnham in 1906, 59 had studied in Germany: ibid., 86; Coats, "The Educational Revolution and the Professionalization of American Economics," 350–351; Jurgen Herbst, *The German Historical School in American Scholarship: A Study in the Transfer of Culture* (Ithaca, NY: Cornell University Press, 1965), 1.

American students. In their view, the principles of laissez-faire were not universal or natural laws but contingent human ideas, developed in and adjusted to specific historical circumstances. German historicists thus opted for historical relativism and demanded the denaturalization and historicization of market capitalism.[24] Methodologically, historicists favored an inductive approach and the empirical study of economic history to amass a broader knowledge of the changing economic realities in specific locations and specific times. They rejected deductively derived "laws" as speculative and ahistorical. Generalizations were, in their mind, always limited and required a broad empirical basis.

The main protagonists of German historicism, who gathered in the Verein für Socialpolitik, founded in 1873, also linked their economic ideas to a progressive political reform agenda centered around the rehabilitation of the state as a positive intervening force in economic and social matters. This political agenda earned them the epithet *Kathedersozialisten* – socialists of the lectern. The reappreciation of the state by German historicists was also adopted by many of their American students. With regard to trade policy, German historicists rejected the doctrinal status assigned to free trade by laissez-faire economics, instead opting for a pragmatic tariff and trade policy aimed at economic development and national prosperity. Many German historicists, most prominently Schmoller, also supported protectionist tariff policies – at least to a certain extent – as they viewed high tariffs as beneficial to the economic development of the newly founded German nation state.[25]

When some of the students of these German historicists began to occupy chairs in political economy in the United States in the 1880s, a contested reform debate emerged. This debate was more than a *Methodenstreit*, a battle for methodological supremacy between classical theorists and empirical historicists. It also concerned the future orientation of the expanding discipline as well as its position in American universities and contemporary political debates. Part of the attractiveness of the newly imported ideas was that they offered new perspectives on and potential solutions to the problems of the industrial age, such as in-

---

[24] Axel R. Schäfer, "German Historicism, Progressive Social Thought, and the Interventionist State in the United States Since the 1880s," in *Markets in Historical Contexts: Ideas and Politics in the Modern World*, ed. Mark Bevir and Frank Trentmann (Cambridge: Cambridge University Press, 2004), 145–169, 147–152.

[25] Alessandro Roncaglia, *The Wealth of Ideas: A History of Economic Thought* (Cambridge: Cambridge University Press, 2005), 303–306; Harald Winkel, "Gustav von Schmoller (1838–1917)," in *Klassiker des ökonomischen Denkens: Zweiter Band. Von Karl Marx bis John Maynard Keynes*, ed. Joachim Starbatty (Munich: C.H. Beck, 1989), 97–118, esp. 107–114; Herbst, *The German Historical School in American Scholarship*, 132–137.

dustrial concentrations, capital-labor conflicts, or urban impoverishment – problems that classical laissez-faire simply did not address.[26] The American Economic Association (AEA), founded under the auspices of Richard T. Ely in 1885, became the "rallying point for the critics of laissez-faire" among American economists.[27] The AEA was modelled on the Verein für Socialpolitik and combined a harsh critique of laissez-faire with a publicly advocated progressive political agenda that envisioned a reform path toward the institutionalization of a general welfare state in the United States.[28] But, as it quickly turned out, the AEA's original program not only alienated conservative advocates of laissez-faire but also many progressives and historicists who either did not share Ely's political agenda, were apprehensive of being branded as *Kathedersozialisten* if they participated, or did not approve of the divisive tone in the AEA's founding documents. In the late 1880s, the AEA toned down its outspokenness and included a broader spectrum of opinions, both in terms of policy and methodology.[29]

The controversies surrounding the AEA illustrate that despite the impression that the strident tone and viciousness of the debate might have given observers, the plurality of opinions, methods, and approaches among American economists went beyond a simplified dichotomy of older laissez-faire conservatives and younger historicist progressives. Many advocates of laissez-faire favored empirical historical research and did not subscribe to the absolutist aim of uncovering quasi-natural, transtemporal laws of economics. On the other side, the study in Germany did not lead to a single, unified approach among younger economists. Some, like Harvard's Frank Taussig were deeply devoted to research in economic history but did not dismiss the classics altogether or did not derive the same progressive policy conclusions from their historical investigations like Ely did.[30]

This was especially evident in the field of tariff and trade policy. Previous scholarship has mostly overlooked that for all the ideas and approaches that reform-minded American historicists had imported from Germany, many of them did not subscribe to the reappraisal of protectionist policies advocated by histori-

---

26 Barber, "Political Economy and the Academic Setting before 1900," 13–14.
27 Rodgers, *Atlantic Crossings*, 102.
28 Schäfer, "German Historicism, Progressive Social Thought, and the Interventionist State in the United States Since the 1880s," 145–146; Coats, "The Educational Revolution and the Professionalization of American Economics," 355–358.
29 Rodgers, *Atlantic Crossings*, 89, 103–106; Tiede, *University Reform*, 32–37.
30 Coats, "The Educational Revolution and the Professionalization of American Economics," 360–361.

cists such as Schmoller.³¹ Ely, for example, was an adamant critic of laissez-faire and strongly in favor of state intervention in the economy. In the case of trade policy, however, he advocated free trade even if he attempted to avoid partisan discussions on the issue and advised against devoting too much attention to it.³² Francis Amasa Walker at the Massachusetts Institute of Technology, the founding president of the AEA, took a similar position.³³ Tariffs also played only a minor role in the work of Henry Carter Adams at the University of Michigan, the first vice president of the AEA in 1885, but he too was critical of protectionism.³⁴ Similarly, Edwin R. A. Seligman at Columbia, the AEA's treasurer, advocated a progressive income tax and opposed excessive tariffs.³⁵ Edmund Janes James from the University of Pennsylvania, a traditional stronghold of American protectionism, served as the AEA's second vice president. Supervised by Johannes Conrad in Halle, James had written a PhD thesis on the American tariff debate. In his thesis, he was generally sympathetic to protectionism as a developmental philosophy but critical of the excesses of the contemporary American tariff regime.³⁶ The position of John Bates Clark at Smith College, the third vice president, was similar to that of James.³⁷

---

31 For a recent example of the frequently repeated conflagration of German historicism and protectionism in the literature, see Marc-William Palen, *Pax Economica: Left-Wing Visions of a Free Trade World* (Princeton, NJ: Princeton University Press, 2024), 22–23.

32 Richard T. Ely, *Problems of To-Day: A Discussion of Protective Tariffs, Taxation, and Monopolies* (New York: Thomas Y. Crowell, 1888), 6–86; Reitano, *The Tariff Question in the Gilded Age*, 36; Benjamin G. Rader, *The Academic Mind and Reform: The Influence of Richard T. Ely in American Life* (Lexington, KY: University of Kentucky Press, 1966), 132.

33 Francis A. Walker, *Political Economy* (New York: Henry Holt, 1884), 388–402.

34 Henry C. Adams, *The Science of Finance: An Investigation of Public Expenditures and Public Revenues* (New York: Henry Holt, 1912), 414–420.

35 Edwin R. A. Seligman, *Principles of Economics: With Special Reference to American Conditions* (Cambridge: Cambridge University Press, 1905), 505–516. See also Franek Rozwadowski, "From Recitation Room to Research Seminar: Political Economy at Columbia University," in *Breaking the Academic Mould: Economists and American Higher Learning in the Nineteenth Century*, ed. William J. Barber (Middletown, CT: Wesleyan University Press, 1988), 169–202, 194–196.

36 Edmund J. James, *Studien ueber den amerikanischen Zolltarif: Seine Entwickelung und seinen Einfluss auf die Volkswirtschaft* (Jena: Herrmann Dufft, 1877).

37 While he made a moral argument for the right of governments to protect their national economies against foreign competition, Clark was critical of unchecked partisan protectionism, which he regarded as a political favor to industrialists. He would later advocate a tariff commission to adequately set tariff rates only high enough to eliminate differences in terms of cost of production: John B. Clark, *Philosophy of Wealth: Economic Principles Newly Formulated* (Boston: Ginn, 1886), 149–173; John B. Clark, *Essentials of Economic Theory: As Applied to Modern Problems of Industry and Public Policy* (New York: Macmillan, 1918), 552–560. See also Rozwadowski, "From Recitation Room to Research Seminar," 199–201.

If anything, most American historicists were rather critical of protectionist policies. Mostly, however, they did not intervene in the political tariff debates of the era, and the AEA never ended up officially endorsing any tariff law.[38] There are two reasons for this development. First, many German-trained American economists exhibited a relative disinterest in the tariff question and sidelined the issue as they focused their attention on the new and urgent problems of industrial society. Their focus was not on tariffs and trade but on money, land, rent, labor, and social reform. Influential scholars such as Ely, Adams, or Seligman might have been critical of tariff protectionism, but it was not a major part of their research and, typically, they did not publicly state their opinion on the matter. The same applied to economists such as Arthur T. Hadley and Henry W. Farnam at Yale, or Jeremiah Jenks at Cornell. All of them had studied in Germany – Farnam even with Schmoller in Strasbourg. All of them were critical of tariff protectionism, but their research was focused on issues that they viewed as more pressing.[39] Consequently, American economists hardly produced any new analyses of the tariff question in this period, the works of Frank Taussig and Simon Nelson Patten being notable exceptions.[40] Taussig authored an influential, often republished, and frequently expanded *Tariff History of the United States*, which came to be a standard work for decades but exhibited a marked preference for free trade that Taussig also voiced in other publications.[41] Patten, on the other hand, was an avid protectionist. Yet, his style of protectionism differed markedly

---

38 Things looked fundamentally different in the German case. While tariff policy was a controversial issue among German historicists, a majority favored some form of protectionist policy. In a narrow vote, the Verein für Socialpolitik followed Schmoller and opted to support Bismarck's protectionist turn in 1879. The AEA, in comparison, never came close to this level of openly advocating protectionist policies. Steven L. McClellan, "German Economists and the Intersection of Science and Politics: A History of the Verein für Sozialpolitik, 1872–1972" (PhD diss., University of Toronto, 2022), 23–24, 55–57.
39 Arthur T. Hadley, *Economics: An Account of the Relations Between Private Property and Public Welfare* (London & New York: Putnam, 1899), 421–446; Henry Villard and Henry W. Farnam, "German Tariff Policy: Past and Present," *Yale Review* 1, no. 1 (1892): 10–34, 20–34; Irving Fisher, "Henry Walcott Farnam," *American Economic Review* 24, no. 1 (1934): 175–177, 175; Jeremiah W. Jenks, *The Trust Problem* (New York: McClure, Phillips & Co., 1901), 44–55. See also William J. Barber, "The Fortunes of Political Economy in an Environment of Academic Conservatism: Yale University," in *Breaking the Academic Mould: Economists and American Higher Learning in the Nineteenth Century*, ed. William J. Barber (Middletown, CT: Wesleyan University Press, 1988), 132–168, 154–163.
40 Goldstein, *Ideas, Interests, and American Trade Policy*, 90; Coats, "The Educational Revolution and the Professionalization of American Economics," 367–368.
41 Frank W. Taussig, *The Tariff History of the United States*, 7th ed. (New York: Putnam, 1923). See also Frank W. Taussig, *Free Trade, the Tariff and Reciprocity* (New York: Macmillan, 1920);

from the Careyite variety. He advocated tariff protectionism not as a transient developmental strategy but as a tool of government administration and social planning, which he believed to be crucial in the transition from an economy of scarcity to the economy of abundance that he envisioned.[42]

Taussig's historically grounded critique of American protectionism points to the second reason for the fact that many American historicists did not emulate the protectionism of some of their teachers: the conditionality of any historicist reasoning. Even if Schmoller and other German historicists in the Verein für Socialpolitik were supportive of protective tariffs, they did not seek to replace laissez-faire's universal dogma of free trade with a countervailing protectionist dogma. Their protectionism was not universal and absolute but contingent, relative, and dependent on the economic circumstances of late nineteenth-century Germany.[43] Schmoller, for example, declared: "In my view, protective tariffs and free trade are not questions of principle but subordinate means of government therapy or economic therapy."[44] Hence, it is hardly surprising that Schmoller and other historicists pragmatically endorsing Germany's protectionist turn did not translate into an endorsement of American protectionism by their American students. Their mostly critical view of American protectionism was, in turn, the result of their assessment of the economic circumstances of Gilded Age America. This relativist and pragmatic perspective on the tariff issue also made it difficult for Careyite protectionists, who watched the heated debates between traditionalists and historicists from the sidelines of the academic discourse, to align their unconditional and doctrinal support of protectionist tariff policies with the historicist critique of laissez-faire.

Robert A. Cord, "Frank W. Taussig (1859–1940)," in *The Palgrave Companion to Harvard Economics*, ed. Robert A. Cord (Cham: Palgrave Macmillan, 2024), 113–142, esp. 117–122.

42 Simon N. Patten, *The Economic Basis of Protection* (Philadelphia: J. B. Lippincott, 1890); Reitano, *The Tariff Question in the Gilded Age*, 54–56; Sass, "An Uneasy Relationship," 233–34; Daniel M. Fox, *The Discovery of Abundance: Simon N. Patten and the Transformation of Social Theory* (Ithaca, NY: Cornell University Press, 1967), 55–57.

43 Schmoller himself had been a free trader at the onset of his career but had little difficulty in justifying his later reorientation as it depended on the rapidly changing economic circumstances of a unifying Germany in a globalizing economy: Jens Herold, *Der junge Gustav Schmoller: Sozialwissenschaft und Liberalkonservatismus im 19. Jahrhundert* (Göttingen: Vandenhoeck & Ruprecht, 2019), 67–71, 263–269.

44 "Schutz- und Freihandel sind für mich gar keine prinzipiellen Fragen, sondern untergeordnete Mittel der staatlichen oder volkswirtschaftlichen Therapie oder Diätetik" [author's translation]. Gustav Schmoller, "Correferat über die Zolltarifvorlage" in *Verhandlungen der sechsten Generalversammlung des Vereins für Socialpolitik über die Zolltarifvorlagen am 21. und 22. April 1879 in Frankfurt a. M.: Auf Grund der stenographischen Niederschrift hrsg. vom Ständigen Ausschuß. (Schriften des Vereins für Socialpolitik XVI)*, ed. Verein f. Socialpolitik (Berlin: Duncker & Humblot, 2022), 19–29.

Support for protectionist policies was even scarcer beyond the historicist camp. Conservative traditionalists such as J. Laurence Laughlin at Harvard opposed protectionism in their defense of laissez-faire.[45] Other scholars were ardent free traders. Charles Graham Sumner at Yale, who merged laissez-faire economics with social Darwinism, was perhaps the most influential contemporary advocate of free trade among American economists and frequently lectured at free trade clubs and societies.[46] Arthur Latham Perry, a moral philosopher at Williams College, was another influential voice. His *Political Economy*, in which he fiercely defended the principle of free trade, remained the most commonly used political economy textbook of the time.[47]

Thus, general sympathies and support for free trade and tariff reform among the majority of economists clearly outweighed the few protectionist dissenters among late nineteenth-century American economists. Beyond the University of Pennsylvania, some scholars, such as Charles Franklin Dunbar at Harvard, upheld protectionist positions, and some colleges featured protectionist ideas in their teaching.[48] However, these minor pockets of protectionist influence faced a majority of economists – historicists, progressives, and laissez-faire advocates alike – who either favored free trade, tariff reform, or some form of downward tariff revision.[49] Whereas American protectionists clearly overstated the ideological uniformity and dogmatism of this free trade hegemony in American colleges, their self-diagnosis as a marginalized minority within the field of American economics was thus not all that inaccurate.

Before turning to anti-intellectualism as the discursive strategy, which American protectionists used to counter the hegemonic position of free trade, this over-

---

[45] J. L. Laughlin, *The Elements of Political Economy: With Some Applications to Questions of the Day* (New York: D. Appleton, 1887), 289–302.
[46] See, for example, William G. Sumner, *Protectionism: The -Ism Which Teaches That Waste Makes Wealth* (New York: Henry Holt, 1887). See also Reitano, *The Tariff Question in the Gilded Age*, 57; Barber, "The Fortunes of Political Economy in an Environment of Academic Conservatism," 145–151.
[47] Arthur L. Perry, *Political Economy*, 20th ed. (New York: Charles Scriber's Sons, 1888), 461–533. See also Arthur L. Perry, *Protectionism Obviously Opposed to the Plan and Purpose of God and the Welfare and Happiness of Mankind* (Boston: New England Free Trade League, 1901); Reitano, *The Tariff Question in the Gilded Age*, 57.
[48] E. H. Hall, "Charles Franklin Dunbar (1830–1900)," in *The Palgrave Companion to Harvard Economics*, ed. Robert A. Cord (Cham: Palgrave Macmillan, 2024), 101–112, 105–108; Byrd L. Jones, "A Quest for National Leadership: Institutionalization of Economics at Harvard," in *Breaking the Academic Mould: Economists and American Higher Learning in the Nineteenth Century*, ed. William J. Barber (Middletown, CT: Wesleyan University Press, 1988), 95–131, 104–108.
[49] Goldstein, *Ideas, Interests, and American Trade Policy*, 88.

view of late nineteenth-century American economics and the position of American economists on the tariff question needs to be supplemented to include Henry George, whose 1886 book *Protection or Free Trade* was perhaps the most-read treatise on the issue.[50] As he was both an ardent free trader and a passionate critic of academic economics with anti-intellectualist leanings, George also represents an interesting case in strong contrast with the protectionist type of late nineteenth-century anti-intellectualism.[51] An autodidactic and highly idiosyncratic economist, George was best known for his advocacy of a single tax on land value and his outspoken support for the labor movement. Even though he had briefly been considered to serve as a professor of political economy at the University of California in 1877,[52] George remained outside the academic realm, engaged in a long-term feud with the established discipline of political economy, and displayed a considerable degree of anti-intellectualism.[53] Throughout his public career, George constantly railed against the condescension with which most professors treated his populist advocacy of a single tax.[54] George also criticized the anti-labor bias of the established class of political economists, insisting that "it is in the nature of things that professors of political economy should either belong to or consciously or unconsciously be influenced by the very class who profit by the wrong, and who oppose, therefore, all means for its remedy."[55]

This critique of established economists was also a prominent feature of George's *Protection or Free Trade*. On the one hand, George endorsed free traders' critique that protectionist doctrine was illogical and self-contradictory, maintaining that "Protectionism viewed in itself is absurd."[56] In his view, the peculiar cir-

---

[50] It was even read in full into the Congressional Record in 1892: Christopher W. England, *Land and Liberty: Henry George and the Crafting of Modern Liberalism* (Baltimore: Johns Hopkins University Press, 2023), 79.
[51] George even joined the Cobden Club in 1881: Palen, *Pax Economica*, 64.
[52] Charles A. Barker, *Henry George* (New York: Oxford University Press, 1955), 240–243.
[53] As an example of Gilded Age anti-intellectualism, Hofstadter even retells an anecdote about George allegedly advising his own son not to attend college but to pursue a career in journalism to remain in touch with the "practical world": Hofstadter, *Anti-Intellectualism in American Life*, 237.
[54] In 1890, for example, the American Social Science Association at its meeting in Saratoga discussed George's idea of a single tax. During the meeting, George engaged in a heated debate with Edwin R. A. Seligman over his critique of American professors of political economy: American Social Science Association, *The Single Tax Discussion: Held at Saratoga Sept. 5, 1890*, transcribed by F. B. Sanborn (Concord, MA: American Social Science Association, 1890), 84–89. See also England, *Land and Liberty*, 84–86.
[55] American Social Science Association, *The Single Tax Discussion*, 84.
[56] Henry George, *Protection or Free Trade* (New York: Robert Schalkenbach Foundation, 1886), 250.

cumstances of the American context – scarcity of capital and labor coupled with an abundance of available land – meant that free trade, not protectionism, was the most beneficial trade policy for American workers. Also, the Georgist idea of a single tax made tariffs superfluous as a source of government revenue.[57] On the other hand, George also scolded the established free trade advocates as "men who derive their ideas from the emasculated and incoherent political economy taught in our colleges"[58] and criticized the narrowness of their arguments. In his view, too many free traders contented themselves with pointing out the logical fallacies of the protectionist argument but failed to address the reasons for its continued appeal to working-class Americans, which George saw in the promise of work and good wages that tariff protectionism seemed to offer. To George, the tariff debate was thus inherently tied to the labor question: "the Ohio of the tariff question flows into the Mississippi of the great social question."[59] As long as both sides of the argument failed to address this underlying connection, their endorsement or rejection of either free trade or protectionism – regardless of their logical soundness – was meaningless to him:

> It need not surprise us that both parties to the controversy, as it has hitherto been conducted, should stop here for it would be as rational to expect any thorough treatment of the social question for the well-to-do class represented in the English Cobden Club or the American Iron and Steel Association, or from their apologists in professorial chairs, as it would be to look for any thorough treatment of the subject of personal liberty in the controversies of the slave-holding Whigs and slave-holding Democrats of forty years ago, or in the sermons of the preachers whose salaries were paid by them.[60]

George thus refocused the American tariff debate on the social question and, in turn, tied his advocacy of free trade to his pervasive endorsement of a single tax: "[T]o make either the abolition of protection or any other reform beneficial to the working-class we must abolish the inequality of legal rights to land, and restore to all their natural and equal rights in the common heritage."[61]

Henry George and his anti-intellectual, pro-labor advocacy of free trade may serve as a reminder that anti-intellectualism was not monopolized by protectionists during the Gilded Age and Progressive Era. Georgists and Careyite protectionists were the polar ends of the political spectrum with regard to tariff and trade

---

[57] Palen, *Pax Economica*, 72–75; Thomas L. Martin, "Protection or Free Trade: An Analysis of the Ideas of Henry George on International Commerce and Wages," *American Journal of Economics and Sociology* 48, no. 4 (1989): 489–501; Barker, *Henry George*, 448–451.
[58] George, *Protection or Free Trade*, 315.
[59] Ibid., 229.
[60] Ibid.
[61] Ibid., 278.

policy, but their respective outsider status in academic economics turned anti-intellectualism into a viable strategy for both groups. Indeed, the protectionist anti-intellectualism of the era may also be interpreted as an attempt to exploit the anti-intellectualist potential, which George's appeal among working-class Americans clearly showcased, for the protectionist cause.

The "Cult of Experience": Theory and Practicality in Protectionist Anti-Intellectualism

Figure 2: *American Economist*, "Practice Always Beats Theory," May 16, 1902.

To counter the perceived hegemony of free trade among American economists, protectionist agitators continued to engage in aggressive anti-intellectualist polemics. Borrowing talking points from the historicist critique of laissez-faire, they presented protectionism as the outgrowth of experience and astute observation of actual economic developments whereas free trade was presented as a mere theory, an abstract calculation not applicable to the real world (Figure 2). Protectionists thus attacked the proponents of free trade not based on inconsistencies in their arguments but, perhaps more substantially, based on their approach in itself. Free trade might be soundly reasoned and follow a perfect internal logic, but as it was divorced from economic reality, protectionists warned, it was unsafe when applied as actual government policy. In short, protectionists alleged that free traders produced little more than "theories based on assumptions."[62]

For example, in 1882 the AISA explained that free trade

> is so simple. It requires no severe study, no knowledge of history, no deep and profound thought, in order to trace out the causes of events daily happening before one's eyes. With its single maxim of government "Hands off" it solves all problems of statesmanship and promises the immediate advent of the millennium. No wonder that our professors teach Free Trade.[63]

Similarly, Cyrus Hamlin, a theologian who was especially active in the protectionist campaign against free trade professors, argued in 1893 that free trade was "based upon abstract principles" and that "facts have nothing to do with it. You might as well bring facts to disprove the multiplication table." In Hamlin's view, free trade was "a very easy and delightful system to teach. It requires no knowledge of the world of commerce and the arts, or of the industries and designs of other nations. [. . .] It is clear abstract truth; but the economy of Protection demands statesmanship and a great knowledge of human affairs."[64]

Complaints about the overly theoretical nature of free trade were frequently tied to the stereotype of the unworldly college professor who had lost touch with real-world phenomena with his head "in a Cloud of Theory" (Figure 3).[65] In 1882, William "Pig-Iron" Kelley, a staunchly protectionist congressman from Pennsylvania, promoted experience as a practical teacher of protectionist doctrine when attacking American professors' support for free trade:

> But does this measure of uniformity of opinion attend their students, who, having secured diplomas, go forth to engage in practical business? No! Experience controverts the theories they accepted in the class-room. They find themselves involved in the management of affairs, and compelled to deal with results which demonstrate the absurdity of the assumptions from which their professors' "absolute truths" were deduced. The doctor, the clergyman, the *littérateur*, freed from this rough contact with the course and vicissitudes of trade, may cherish the views with which he quits college; but his classmates who engage in any department of productive industry soon come to regard the doctrines of our Sumners and

---

62 Robert P. Porter, "The College Professor: His Political Responsibility Explained by Hon. Robert P. Porter," *American Economist*, April 13, 1894.
63 *Bulletin of the American Iron and Steel Association*, "Why Our Colleges Teach Free Trade," April 26, 1882.
64 Cyrus Hamlin, "Why is Free-Trade so Largely Taught in Our Colleges?" *American Economist*, June 9, 1893.
65 *American Economist*, "His Head In A Cloud Of Theory," February 17, 1905.

Figure 3: *American Economist,* "His Head In A Cloud Of Theory," February 17, 1905.

> Perrys as beautiful and seductive theories, which must be classed with the airy nothings bodied forth by poets.[66]

In alignment with their appreciation of experience, protectionists regularly claimed that many students who had left college as convinced free traders were quickly converted to protectionism as a result of their experience in the business world: "[W]e find college graduates shedding their notions on political economy as soon as they come in contact with the world of action."[67] As the *Protectionist*

---

[66] William D. Kelley, *A Science Based on Assumptions* (Philadelphia: American Iron and Steel Association, 1882), 2.
[67] *Bulletin of the American Iron and Steel Association,* "Why Our Colleges Teach Free Trade," April 26, 1882.

summarized in 1900, "It is often said of college men that the free trader of twenty-one is sure to be a protectionist at forty."[68]

The contrast between free trade as theoretical knowledge acquired through intellectual endeavors and protectionism as practical knowledge based on experience was closely tied to the conviction of protectionist industrialists that arrogant economists neglected and denigrated their views as practitioners. In 1890, for example, the *American Economist* proclaimed that "It has long been a peculiarity of Free-Traders to think their scholastic ways wiser and surer than the work of legislators and business men; that their theories were sounder than experience." Van Buren Denslow, editor of the *American Economist*, claimed that

> political economy has fallen into odium, because men not acquainted practically with either Statesmanship, politics or industry have sought to build up on *a priori* reasoning or by means of such experience as is accessible to a man not in public life a speculative and metaphysical body of theories concerning the effect of legislation upon business, as they appear to men who have never been engaged in either legislation or business.[69]

The juxtaposition of theoretical and practical knowledge in protectionist anti-intellectualism also reflected a broader characteristic of American culture during the Gilded Age: its strong appreciation of practicality. This "unreflective instrumentalism," the tendency to judge the merit of any idea exclusively based on its immediate applicability and thus, by extension, on its potential to generate commercial profit, originated among the industrial tycoons of the era. As these captains of industry seemed to embody a new culture, created by and best adapted to the emerging industrial society of late nineteenth-century America, their worldview wielded great influence over Gilded Age culture. Apart from their appreciation of practicality and applicability, the fact that most business leaders had little or no formal education and styled themselves as self-made men contributed to their common disdain for intellectual life.[70] Hofstadter argues that this class had "brought to anti-intellectualist movements more strength than any other force in society."[71] The cultural dominance of the business community manifested itself in "a persistent hostility to formal education and a countervailing cult of experience."[72] This anti-intellectualist "cult of experience" was heavily intertwined with a dislike for Mugwumps and other college-educated reformers.

---

68 "The Tariff Not a Dead Issue," *The Protectionist* 12, no. 134 (1900): 62–64, 64.
69 *American Economist*, "Education and Economics," August 1, 1890.
70 Lacy, "Against and Beyond Hofstadter," 255–256; Rigney, "Three Kinds of Anti-Intellectualism," 444–447.
71 Hofstadter, *Anti-Intellectualism in American Life*, 237.
72 Ibid., 257–260 (quotation on p. 257).

Hence, Hofstadter argues, the general upsurge of anti-intellectualism during the Gilded Age was linked to the cultural dominance of the business community. As the same class, business leaders from protected heavy and manufacturing industries, also formulated and propagated the main tenets of contemporary protectionist doctrine, it is no surprise that the same anti-intellectualist tropes and the "cult of experience" also surfaced in contemporary protectionist agitation. Yet, as indicated above, Hofstadter overlooked the industrialists' hostility to free trade theory as a key strain of the Gilded Age's conservative backlash against the progressive reform proposals originating in academic circles.

The strong emphasis on experience and practical knowledge also mirrored a major shift in the general argument presented by protectionists to justify maintaining a high tariff regime. Traditionally, American protectionists had relied on the infant industry argument and had promoted protectionism as a developmental strategy. When, however, the rapid modernization and industrialization of the American economy had nurtured many American industries to reach a high degree of competitiveness in the late nineteenth century, this strategy was no longer viable. Orthodox protectionists developed a new line of argument that revolved around the lived experience of industrial growth under tariff protectionism. The meteoric rise of the United States to industrial supremacy under a continuously ultra-protectionist tariff regime was interpreted as practical proof of a permanent causal relationship between protectionism and prosperity. Protectionism, they argued, was an economic panacea that needed to be maintained as it would continue yielding further prosperity in the future.[73] Protectionism was no longer imagined and promoted as a transient tool of economic development but as a necessary and permanent precondition for the creation and maintenance of economic prosperity.

As a result of this change in argument, the temporal orientation of American protectionists also changed. As a developmental strategy, protectionism had been oriented toward the future and the prosperity that protectionism had yet to produce. Now, the protectionist argument increasingly centered around the prosperity that protectionism had allegedly already produced and attempted to justify the continued application of protectionist tariffs by projecting previous experiences into an expected future. In this sense, the protectionist argument critically hinged on a supposed knowledge of experience: Americans had in their own lives witnessed the nation's rise to prosperity and industrial modernity under tariff protectionism. As the AISA wrote in 1886, "Experience is cruel to the theories borrowed by college professors from British teachers. It has taught the people of this

---

[73] Etges, *Wirtschaftsnationalismus*, 324–28.

country that they have never grown so rapidly in wealth or industry, and never been so prosperous, as under the Protective system."[74] Any deviation from this path, especially if based on flimsy theoretical reasoning, was branded as a dangerous experiment with potentially disastrous results. Accordingly, the argument concerning the proven value and positive effects of tariff protectionism went hand in hand with a heavy load of fearmongering about the risky and experimental nature of free trade.

The link between protectionism, practicality, and experience, coupled with the denigration of free trade as theoretical and abstract, also echoed the contemporary *Methodenstreit* among economists. Occasionally, the rise of historicism was also directly addressed by protectionists seeking to link it to their own ideas. For example, when discussing the results of a survey among college students of political economy in 1890, the APTL claimed that

> in nearly every instance where the college correspondents disclosed their personal opinions, and especially when this was done by the abler and by the younger of them, they disclaimed English orthodoxy and hastened to enroll themselves under the historical school so vigorously expanded in Germany. The best collegiate thought of the country no longer regards Protection as a narrow, unscientific thing, but as legitimate and a question of practical politics.[75]

Robert P. Porter, a leading figure in the APTL, also alluded to historicism in 1894: "I say boldly that the cold facts and figures of industrial progress in the United States would have long sent the political economy of the old British school kiting to Jupiter and Mars if it had not already been ground to dust by the more enlightened and broad-minded European economists of the present time."[76]

The fact that most historicists among the younger generation of American economists were, at best, ambivalent regarding the merits of protectionism typically did not feature in protectionists' evocation of historicism as an antidote to free trade economics. Accordingly, references to specific economists were scarce, and, typically, the alleged disdain of younger economists for free trade policies was asserted rather than demonstrated. The fact that protectionist agitators were relatively apprehensive of directly embracing historicism as an academic vindication of protectionist convictions demonstrates that they knew that many historicists did favor tariff reductions and that even the tacit sympathy held by some regarding the general notion of protective tariffs did not align with their own un-

---

[74] *Bulletin of the American Iron and Steel Association*, "Tariff Here and in Great Britain," August 18, 1886.
[75] *American Economist*, "Education and Economics," August 1, 1890.
[76] Porter, "The College Professor."

conditional support of the existing ultra-protectionist tariff regime. In other words, protectionists welcomed historicism as it promised to unsettle the established hegemony of laissez-faire, but it was far from the type of political economy that they envisioned as the ideal.

John Bull in American Classrooms: Anglophobia in Protectionist Anti-Intellectualism

Anglophobia was a ubiquitous feature of American culture throughout the Gilded Age and, characteristically, also of American protectionism in this period. According to Stephen Tuffnell, it served "as the leitmotif for a variety of forms of economic nationalism."[77] Consequently, Anglophobic stereotypes also heavily permeated the anti-intellectualism of late nineteenth-century American protectionism. Many protectionist agitators used "English" as a synonym for "laissez-faire," lamented the dominance of "English" free trade in American classrooms, and feared that an American deviation from protectionist orthodoxy might benefit Great Britain. Moreover, they alleged that a British-led conspiracy existed, poisoning the minds of young Americans with dangerous free trade theories. In a general sense, the marriage of Anglophobia and anti-intellectualism in late nineteenth-century American protectionist agitation can be understood as the result of the same popularist impulse to attach a political idea – protectionism – to given popular resentments – a disdain for academics and intellectual life or widespread hostility toward Great Britain – in order to garner public support for this very idea.

Protectionist agitators frequently referred to the British descent of the leading theorists of laissez-faire in order to frame free trade as a British concept that, in turn, was denigrated as unsuitable for the American context. In this way, both free trade and protectionism were in the protectionist imagination nationalized as essentially "British" or "American" doctrines. This nationalization of knowledge not only constructed a supposedly national origin for certain ideas but also tied the question of their validity to this supposed national origin: British free trade,

---

[77] Stephen Tuffnell, "'Uncle Sam is to be Sacrificed': Anglophobia in Late Nineteenth-Century Politics and Culture," *American Nineteenth Century History* 12, no. 1 (2011): 77–99, 87. See also Marc-William Palen, "Foreign Relations in the Gilded Age: A British Free-Trade Conspiracy?" *Diplomatic History* 37, no. 2 (2013): 217–247; Reitano, *The Tariff Question in the Gilded Age*, 98–101. This Anglophobic tradition in American protectionism also had far-reaching roots going back to the early republic. See, for example, Sam W. Haynes, *Unfinished Revolution: The Early American Republic in a British World* (Charlottesville, VA: University of Virginia Press, 2010), 136–141.

the argument went, might be beneficial to Great Britain and its specific contexts but certainly not to the United States. Here, protectionists proclaimed, American ideas on trade and tariff policy, which had been developed by Americans to specifically fit the American context, namely the Careyite American School of political economy, should reign supreme. By merging American nationalism, traditional American Anglophobia, protectionism, and anti-intellectualism, protectionist agitators thus created a powerful and frequently wielded rhetorical weapon.

For example, in an 1885 pamphlet, entitled "English Free Trade Taught in American Colleges" (Figure 4), Cyrus Hamlin wrote:

> In all our universities and colleges, we have been content to learn of our dear old mother, England. We have stretched up our heads and opened our mouths and she has graciously fed us. Adam Smith, and Ricardo, and Malthus, and Fawcett, and Mill, and Jevons, and Sedgwick, and Senior Mc Leod, have given us our text-books of economics. Our universities, if they have done anything have only re-echoed this foreign teaching.[78]

In an earlier instance, Cyrus Elder, the general secretary of the IL, had appeared before the commission appointed by President Arthur in 1882 to prepare a general revision of the tariff. In his statement, Elder strongly rejected "what is now known and recognized as English political economy." He read from a letter sent to the AISA by a student of Arthur Latham Perry:

> Our American Colleges [. . .] prefer to study John Stuart Mill or Professor Perry in preference to Henry C. Carey or any other writer of the American school; and it is my experience under Professor Perry that Henry C. Carey's name has never been mentioned in the classroom except to be cursed.[79]

Hamlin complained that "the college has ceased to be American and has become decidedly English." He asserted that American schools were "of English Birth" and that American professors were promoting "a purely British policy." Dramatically, he warned that in American universities, "the tendency is to put Free-Trade in the lead, and to make John Stuart Mill a higher authority than Henry C. Carey."[80] Writing from Ohio in 1894, a correspondent with the *American Economist* complained, "We are tired of studying Political Economy from John Bull text books."[81]

---

[78] Cyrus Hamlin, *English Free Trade Taught in American Colleges and Universities* (Milwaukee, WI: Northwestern Tariff Bureau, 1885).
[79] *Report of the Tariff Commission: Appointed Under Act of Congress Approved May 15, 1882*, Volume II (Washington, D.C.: Government Printing Office, 1882), 2355–2356.
[80] Hamlin, "Why is Free-Trade so Largely Taught in Our Colleges?"
[81] G. L. Chilcota, "They Should All Use Them," *American Economist*, March 2, 1894.

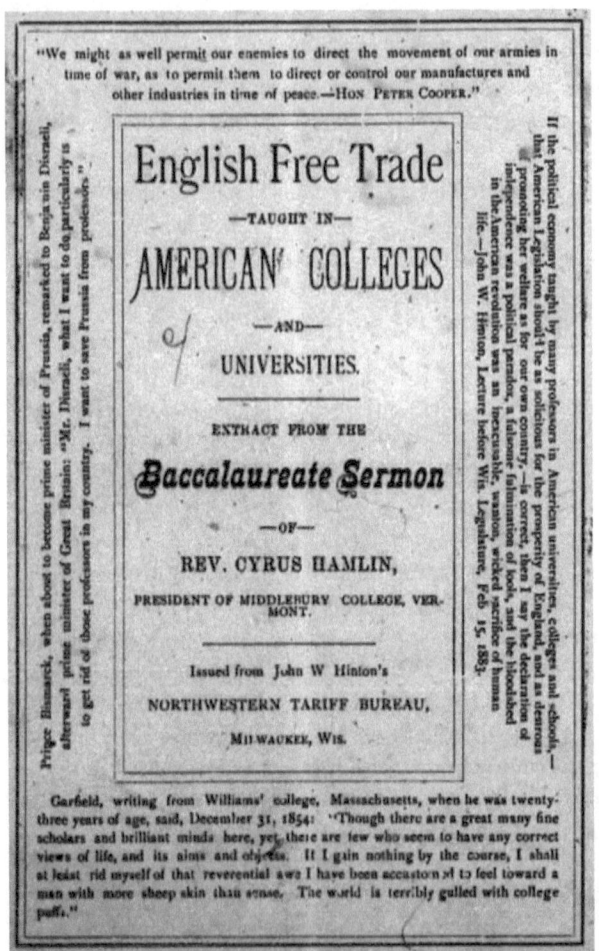

Figure 4: Cyrus Hamlin, *English Free Trade Taught in American Colleges and Universities* (Milwaukee: Northwestern Tariff Bureau, 1885), Coverpage.

In the protectionist mind, moreover, the dominance of British thinkers in American universities was not just a problem of imbalance but an acute danger to American interests. Teaching British theories, protectionists warned, also served the political and economic interests of Great Britain. In their view, supporting American protectionism was thus not just a question of intellectual conviction but also of patriotism. In 1882, the AISA asserted

> that the Free Traders are deliberately and studiously poisoning the very fountains of knowledge on the subject of industrial and commercial economy; in other words, that the colleges

of America are being used by the Free Trade missionaries as a means of undermining the "American system" of Protection, for the benefit of the British manufacturers and the New York importers.[82]

The conviction that British free trade theory inherently contradicted American interests lent a sense of urgency to the warnings constantly voiced by protectionists. This notion was enhanced even more through the frequently expressed fear of an encompassing conspiracy. The dominance of free trade in American colleges was, many protectionists argued, not incidental. Rather, they portrayed it as the result of deliberate efforts by British and American free traders acting in a broad and powerful conspiracy. Hamlin, for example, was sure of the power behind American free trade professors: "The great Cobden Club composed of the elite of England with regard to status, learning, and wealth, has poured out its publications and its gold, in order to promulgate its blessed doctrines of Free-Trade, and to denounce its opposite as belonging to the dark ages."[83] In 1885, he claimed that American professors

> cover with British fog the real field of our national life, do almost irreparable injury by encouraging foreign hopes and plans. The Cobden Club, which has at its command more wealth, talent, and influence, than any organization of its kind ever formed, and whose declared and sole purpose is, giving up the great nations of Europe to subdue the United States to the British system, takes courage from all its coadjutors in our colleges and universities.[84]

That same year, the AISA warned of the Cobden Club's alleged reach: "[T]hey have agents all over this country; [. . .] I now tell you that they are very busy, that they are in your towns, and even in your colleges, your institutions of learning. [. . .] They are in Harvard College, they are in Yale College, they are in Williams College, and I do not know in how many other institutions of learning, distributing their medals."[85]

These kinds of shrill, almost paranoid warnings of a British conspiracy constituted a defining feature of late nineteenth-century American protectionism. Whereas the Cobden Club, a British free trade organization founded in 1866, was, in fact, quite active in the United States and could count prominent American free traders among its members, the alleged conspiracy was mostly a myth. There was little secrecy in the Club's activities: Like other advocacy groups, it published pamphlets and organized speakers. Lists of its members were publicly available.

---

82 *Bulletin of the American Iron and Steel Association*, "Free Trade in Colleges," March 29, 1882.
83 Hamlin, "Why is Free-Trade so Largely Taught in Our Colleges?"
84 Hamlin, *English Free Trade Taught in American Colleges and Universities*, 4.
85 Thomas H. Dudley, "Something about the Cobden Club," *Bulletin of the American Iron and Steel Association*, January 7, 1885.

Still, the idea of the alleged conspiracy triggered a strong counter-reaction by American protectionists, who imagined themselves fighting a heroic defensive battle against a mighty, foreign foe.[86] Regardless of whether or not their conspiracy allegations actually conformed to reality, the mere belief among American protectionists that the Cobden Club and other British free traders were conspiring against the United States served as a powerful driver of protectionist agitation and frequently merged with protectionist anti-intellectualism.

American Youth in the Protectionist Imagination

The American youth and particularly college students occupied a special, somewhat ambiguous position in the anti-intellectualist discourse of American protectionists. On the one hand, protectionists exhibited a great fear that the negative influence of free trade indoctrination would endanger the continuation of American protectionism. On the other hand, protectionists also recognized a chance to break the objectionable hegemony of free trade by winning over the minds and hearts of young Americans for protectionism.

The obsession with colleges and universities among American protectionists was grounded in their conviction that there was no more harmful place for free traders to spread their ideas. John Hinton, a protectionist activist from Milwaukee, emphasized this point in 1899:

> No reform clubs in this country; no efforts of partisan oratory; not even the vast expenditures of foreign free traders [. . .] nor yet the Cobden Club's money and literature, expended in this country, all combined, have done so much harm to the welfare of the United States as has been wrought by the teachings of free trade in the colleges and universities [. . .] to the youth of the country.[87]

According to this line of thought, what turned the allegedly ubiquitous teaching of free trade in American colleges from a nuisance into an imminent threat was the feared impact on the future leaders of the country. The position of aspiring young American academics on the tariff issue was, as the APTL pointed out in 1890, crucial because

---

[86] Palen, *The "Conspiracy" of Free Trade*, 59–67; Palen, "Foreign Relations in the Gilded Age," 246–247.
[87] John W. Hinton, "Free Trade Prophecies and Professors," *The Protectionist* 11, no. 122 (1899): 65–68, 65.

They become ministers, lawyers, doctors, teachers, engineers, journalists, manufacturers and merchants and rapidly reach positions of commanding influence. It is a matter of much moment in the industrial and legislative history of the country how these young men are trained in political economy, what views they will advocate in turn and how they can best be made serviceable in maintaining a national policy.[88]

John Hinton argued similarly when polemizing against free trade instruction at American universities in 1895:

But when a preacher, college or university president, a professor or school teacher, one trained, taught, and paid to instill sound principles into the minds of young Americans, to inspire love of country, desire for the promotion of the general welfare of his own country and people; when such a one teaches that our youth should be as ardent for the promotion of the welfare of another country, sometimes more so than for his own; that man, be he who he may, is guilty of high treason. He, I say, is unfit to teach American youth; he is un-Americanizing them; he is destroying the *amor patriae* of our youth, our rising generation; those upon whom depend the perpetuity of American liberty and free government.[89]

In a populist fashion, protectionists frequently stressed the connection of college students with ordinary Americans or "the people" and juxtaposed them with the remoteness ascribed to elitist university professors: "Many of the professors have no real sympathy with the people [. . .] We have colleges with a large number of Free-Trade professors and a small following of Free-Trade students. The latter come from the people, the professors are separate from the people and cannot understand them."[90] In 1890, Hamlin quoted a "mechanic who has risen by his industry, enterprise, and capacity to great wealth and influence," saying, "I send my son to college, and in the class-room he hears his father as a protectionist set down as an idiot, a robber, a lobbyist, and a thief. Can I respect an institution that allows such things?"[91]

However, American college students were not just the object of scaremongering regarding allegedly being indoctrinated with harmful free trade ideology. Protectionists also invested great hopes in the coming generation of American economists to strengthen the protectionist tariff regime. This ambiguity of the American youth in the protectionist imagination was closely tied to yet another, perhaps somewhat paradoxical strand of protectionist anti-intellectualism. De-

---

88 *American Economist*, "Education and Economics," August 1, 1890.
89 John W. Hinton, *Free Trade Professors and Free Trade Preachers in the Campaign of 1894* (Milwaukee, WI: Northwestern Tariff Bureau, 1895), 6–7.
90 Hamlin, "Why is Free-Trade so Largely Taught in Our Colleges?"
91 Joseph Wharton, *Is a College Education Advantageous to a Business Man? Address Delivered Before the Wharton School Association, University of Pennsylvania, February 20, 1890* (Philadelphia, 1890), 14.

spite all their sweeping, shrill, and polemic denigrations of academic economics, protectionist agitators did not dismiss the sphere of intellectual arguments altogether. Rather, they combined their radical critique of free trade economics with attempts to establish their own positions within academic discourse – often by means of attempting to influence the teaching of political economy and thus the coming generation of American economists.

Like perhaps no other aspect of late nineteenth-century protectionist agitation, this attempt to establish protectionist positions within academic discourse reveals the instrumental character of the anti-intellectualist fervor exhibited by many protectionists. Their tirades against free trade professors and universities often took the form of a general denigration of intellectuals, academic institutions, and their ways of producing knowledge. In essence, however, what bugged American protectionists was not academic life per se but the relatively meager status of their own ideas within that world. Professors who defended protectionist positions and universities that included protectionist ideas in their curricula were commonly excluded from protectionist scolding. As Hofstadter observes, this ambivalence is actually a characteristic feature of most historic forms of anti-intellectualism. As the carriers of anti-intellectualism often consist of groups from the margins of intellectual life, who obsessively focus on a specific idea or ideology, "anti-intellectualism is not the creation of people who are categorically hostile to ideas."[92]

In the late 1880s and early 1890s, the APTL offered prizes to protectionist essays written by college students, which were supposed to demonstrate the persistence of protectionist thought among American college youth. Furthermore, the competition was intended to counter a similar initiative by the Cobden Club. The prizes amounted to $250, $100, and $50 for the three best essays, in addition to 15 silver medals awarded to participants. The APTL widely advertised its competition in college newspapers and also ensured the annual publication of the winning essays.[93]

---

92 Hofstadter, *Anti-Intellectualism in American Life*, 21.
93 For the advertisement, see, for example, *Yale Daily News*, "Prizes for Tariff Essays," November 6, 1889; Edward H. Ammidown and Henry M. Hoyt, "American Protective Tariff League – Prize Essay Proposal for 1890," *The Concordiensis*, December 1, 1889. For the published essays, see Crawford D. Hening, *The Advantages of a Protective Tariff to the Labor and Industries of the United States* (New York: American Protective Tariff League, 1890); C. D. Todd, *Home Production Indispensable to a Supply, at Low Prices, of the Manufactured Commodities Required for the People of the United States, and Adequate Home Production of these Commodities Impossible Without a Protective Tariff* (New York: American Protective Tariff League, 1888); Homer B. Dibell, *What Are Raw Materials? Would Free Raw Materials be Advantageous to the Labor and Industries of the United States* (New York: American Protective Tariff League, 1889); John Ford, *The American Pol-*

In the late 1880s, the APTL was also instrumental in sponsoring and promoting Van Buren Denslow's decidedly protectionist textbook *Principles of the Economic Philosophy of Society, Government, and Industry*.[94] Denslow, a journalist and former law professor, was an ardent protectionist and, for a while, the editor of the *American Economist*.[95] The APTL boasted that his book was

> destined to mark a new departure in the study of Economic Science in this country. For the first time in many years this science is treated from an exclusively American point of view, free from that servile adherence to antecedent foreign theories or schools which have characterized, with few exceptions, the more conspicuous American economic writings. Professor Denslow adopts broadly and fully the new historic methods of economic science.[96]

The fact that the APTL chose to sponsor and promote Denslow's textbook is part of the long extra-academic tradition of American protectionism. Still, the APTL clearly envisioned that Denslow's book should be read by students of political economy. The League was not shy about the book's purpose: "Mr. Denslow's book is the best of its class ever published, and should be the text book of political economy in all American academies and colleges."[97] However, albeit meticulously compiled and extensive, Denslow's textbook was a heavily partisan and at times polemic account that was not just created outside of the academic realm but also failed to live up to the standards of the rapidly professionalizing discipline. It was not received well among academic economists.

Joseph Wharton, the enormously wealthy cofounder of the Bethlehem Steel Corporation, was perhaps the most influential figure in the protectionist attempt to shape college curricula. Wharton, an avid disciple and acquaintance of Henry C. Carey, was an untiring lobbyist, activist, and financier of the protectionist cause.[98] As financial donors, Wharton and other Pennsylvania industrialists also wielded a strong influence on the instruction of political economy at the University of Pennsylvania. It was mainly due to their influence that Robert E. Thompson, a trained

---

icy of Protection Applied to American Shipping Engaged in International Commerce (New York: American Protective Tariff League, 1890).
94 Van Buren Denslow, *Principles of the Economic Philosophy of Society, Government and Industry* (New York: Cassell & Company, 1888), esp. 555–630.
95 "Van Buren Denslow: Lawyer, Journalist, and Political Economist," *The Protectionist* 11, no. 128 (1899): 441–464; Reitano, *The Tariff Question in the Gilded Age*, 53–54.
96 *Tariff League Bulletin*, "Principles of the Economic Philosophy of Society, Government and Industry," June 22, 1888.
97 *Tariff League Bulletin*, "Denslow's Political Economy," October 12, 1888.
98 He was a founding member of the IL in 1868 and became the driving force behind its tariff agitation and lobbying. He also became the AISA vice president for tariff matters in 1875 and the organization's president in 1904.

theologian, a strict adherent to Careyite doctrines, and a close associate of Wharton, became the university's principal instructor of political economy. In 1875, Wharton and the IL financed the printing and distribution of Thompson's protectionist textbook *Social Science and National Economy*, which the IL sent to colleges across the country to foster the teaching of protectionist doctrine.[99]

Wharton's greatest contribution came in 1881 when he donated $100,000 to the University of Pennsylvania to create the Wharton School of Business and Finance. Here, Wharton planned to train a new class of university-educated businessmen, ideally prepared for the demands of the modern business world. The curriculum was focused on practical skills directly applicable to economic life, but it also included lectures on the social sciences and political economy.[100] The latter prominently featured a decidedly protectionist perspective that Wharton had made into a precondition for his financial support. According to Wharton's demands, the school was obligated to teach

> The necessity for each nation to care for its own, and to maintain by all suitable means its industrial and financial independence; no apologetic or merely defensive style of instruction must be tolerated upon this point, but the right and duty of national self-protection must be firmly asserted and demonstrated.[101]

Wharton hired some of the most renowned academic economists with protectionist leanings to establish his "scholarly home for protection."[102] In 1883, Edward Janes James was appointed as the school's dean, and in 1888, the semi-professional theologian Thompson was moved to the history department and replaced as the chair of political economy by Simon Nelson Patten. It was primarily Patten and his original defense of protectionist policies that ended up securing the Wharton School's reputation as a protectionist stronghold within academia.[103]

For all these relative successes of the Wharton School project, it is indicative that economists such as Patten and James came to be the figureheads in the process of successfully establishing the Wharton School as a respected part of the dis-

---

[99] Sass, "An Uneasy Relationship," 225–229; Steven A. Sass, *The Pragmatic Imagination: A History of the Wharton School, 1881–1981* (Philadelphia: University of Pennsylvania Press, 1982), 34–35, 149–151, 184, 191.
[100] Sass, *The Pragmatic Imagination*, 35–39.
[101] Joseph Wharton, Deeds and Indentures of the Wharton School, June 22, 1881, Joseph Wharton Family Papers, Ser. 8. Wharton School (established 1881) papers, 1881–1849 [sic], Deeds and indentures, 1881–1902, Box 52, Swarthmore College, Friends Historical Library, Philadelphia.
[102] Reitano, *The Tariff Question in the Gilded Age*, 52.
[103] James and Patten also upheld their connection to their common German *alma mater* and in the 1880s and 1890s regularly sent Wharton students to study with their former professor Johannes Conrad in Halle: Rodgers, *Atlantic Crossings*, 85; Sass, "An Uneasy Relationship," 229–232.

cipline of political economy in the United States. While they were sympathetic to protective tariffs in principle, Patten and James never exhibited the kind of unconditional support for a continued ultra-protectionist tariff regime that characterized protectionist writers outside or at the margins of the academic realm, such as Van Buren Denslow. The fact that even such an ardent protectionist as Wharton realized that there was little chance of establishing his school as a serious academic institution if it taught the ultra-protectionism advanced by groups like his own IL speaks to the difficulties this style of radical protectionism continued to face in the rapidly developing and professionalizing discipline.

Conclusion

The protectionist anti-intellectualism of the late nineteenth century grew out of the uneasiness experienced by protectionist industrialists with regard to the limited currency their own convictions held among academic economists, whose public influence simultaneously grew rapidly at this time. The disparity between the established protectionist hegemony in the political arena and the reverse situation in the emerging discipline of political economy led protectionists to worry about the continuation of their preferred ultra-protectionist tariff regime. Against the backdrop of the advent of German historicism in the 1880s, they hoped that the time had come to push back against the dominance of free trade in the academic world. Yet, while their anti-intellectualist attacks on British thinkers in American universities or on the theoretical and detached sophism of laissez-faire contained echoes of the contemporary *Methodenstreit* in American economics, the lack of support from American historicists regarding the given protectionist tariff regime meant that the few attempts to establish their own ultra-protectionist positions within academic discourse ultimately remained unsuccessful.

Anti-intellectualism remained a crucial feature of American protectionism as the rift between the continued application of protectionist tariff policies and the simultaneous hostility toward these policies among American economists only grew wider in the following decades. The confrontation between the dominance of protectionism in the political arena and the strong preference among most academics for tariff reform reached a pinnacle when over 1,000 economists from all over the nation, among them the most prominent names in the field, in May 1930 published a resolution urging Congress and President Hoover not to pass the later infamous ultra-protectionist Smoot-Hawley Tariff.[104] However, anti-intellectualism

---

[104] "Economists against Smoot Hawley," *Econ Journal Watch* 4, no. 3 (2007): 345–358.

was still a powerful weapon in the rhetorical arsenal of American protectionists. When the economists' resolution was read in the Senate, Senator Samuel Shortridge of California spouted, "I am not overawed and I am not at all disturbed by the proclamation of the college professors who never earned a dollar by the sweat of their brow by honest labor – theorists, dreamers – I am not overawed or disturbed by their pronunciamentos." Fellow Republican Henry Hatfield, Senator of West Virginia, agreed: "Cloistered in colleges as they are, hidden behind a mass of statistics, these men have no opportunity to view the practical side of life in matters pertaining to our industrial welfare as a nation."[105] The protectionist anti-intellectualism, which had developed in the late nineteenth century, thus still wielded political influence as an important component of American protectionist discourse in the early 1930s. The long-term trajectory of protectionist anti-intellectualism in the United States, especially during the following era of trade liberalization that accompanied the New Deal and dominated American trade policy in the postwar period, thus still offers a potential for further research but is beyond the scope of this article.

In a general sense, the case of late nineteenth-century protectionist anti-intellectualism should direct the attention of historians to the complicated relationship between dominant economic ideas and their application as government policies. Newer global histories of economic nationalism have highlighted shifts in the hegemony of certain economic ideas within the intellectual sphere in order to explain the changing tides of national tariff and trade policies.[106] Yet, exactly how this translation occurred, the ways in which these economic ideas were (or were not) converted into national trade policies to a large degree remain understudied. In this regard, the use of anti-intellectualist tropes in American protectionist agitation can serve as a reminder for historians of knowledge and intellectual culture not to assume a mechanical relationship in which ideas popular or even universally supported in the academic realm automatically inform government policies. Rather, we need to pay close attention to external factors, structural conditions of knowledge circulation, and actors attempting to influence the complex relationship between the academic and political spheres. Robert Shiller has recently emphasized the importance of narrativity in economic policymaking. In his view, economic thinking and decision-making are primarily characterized by narrative explanations of economic phenomena and rarely take the form of a

---

[105] Quoted from Douglas A. Irwin, *Peddling Protectionism: Smoot-Hawley and the Great Depression* (Princeton, NJ: Princeton University Press, 2017), 85–86.
[106] See, for example, Marvin Suesse, *The Nationalist Dilemma: A Global History of Economic Nationalism, 1776–Present* (Cambridge: Cambridge University Press, 2023); Helleiner, *The Neomercantilists*.

rational process of weighing possible benefits and risks against each other.[107] In this process, actors such as the protectionist agitators, who sparked the anti-intellectualist protectionist discourse, could be enormously influential as they intentionally shaped the generally accepted narrative explanation of economic phenomena such as tariffs and their effects, popularized their own doctrines, and prevented the implementation of opposing ideas.

Fritz Kusch is a PhD candidate at the University of Bremen, Germany, and a research associate at the Collaborative Research Center 1342 "Global Dynamics of Social Policy." His research interests include the political and social history of tariffs and trade in the United States and German-American history. He is currently working on a PhD project on the history of protectionist advocacy groups in the United States and their impact on American trade policy in the late nineteenth and early twentieth centuries.

---

107 Robert J. Shiller, *Narrative Economics: How Stories Go Viral and Drive Major Economic Events* (Princeton, NJ: Princeton University Press, 2020).

Section II: **Gender, Archiving, and Knowledge Production after the Holocaust**

Victoria Van Orden Martínez, Christine Schmidt, and Ewa Koźmińska-Frejlak

Introduction: Gender, Archiving, and Knowledge Production after the Holocaust: A Postwar Republic of Letters?

Abstract: Behind the production and circulation of knowledge about Nazi atrocities during the Second World War and the Holocaust is a history of documentation and archives-building carried out by victims of these atrocities. Although more women than men were involved in these efforts, women typically held subordinate roles to men and have largely been invisible in the historiography of these endeavors. This thematic section addresses this lacuna by focusing on the circulation of knowledge via correspondence within and among survivor historical commissions after the Second World War with an emphasis on the interplay of gender and other differences. Just as with the Republic of Letters during the Age of Enlightenment, the mass destruction and upheaval caused by the Second World War and the Holocaust enabled narrow cracks to form in social and organizational hierarchies through which some women managed to gain access, something that correspondence provides glimpses of through intersections between gender, class, and migration.

Keywords: archives, gender, the Holocaust, postwar period, survivors

Behind the production and circulation of knowledge about Nazi atrocities during the Second World War and the Holocaust is a history — or rather histories — of documentation and archives-building conducted by the victims of these atrocities. Even while crimes against Jews and other victim groups were being perpetrated, efforts to "collect and record" evidence of Nazi crimes against humanity sprang from and contributed to an intellectual culture that placed the perspectives of victims and witnesses at the center of historicizing catastrophe.[1] Jewish victims and survivors drew on and developed what historian Laura Jockusch has described as

---

[1] Laura Jockusch, *Collect and Record! Jewish Holocaust Documentation in Early Postwar Europe* (New York: Oxford University Press, 2012; Mark Lee Smith, *The Yiddish Historians and the Struggle for a Jewish History of the Holocaust* (Detroit: Wayne State University Press, 2019).

"a distinct 'historiography of trauma'" known as *khurbn forshung* (destruction research). Originally formulated and used at the beginning of the twentieth century, this approach to documenting history included gathering eyewitness and victim testimonies.[2] The objectives set by *khurbn forshung* were in line with the postulate advocated by historian Simon Dubnow, who called on Jews to write the history of their own people based on all kinds of sources: official documents as well as personal records, sources produced by social elites and ordinary people. This research was also shaped by Jewish ethnography, which emerged from Dubnow's ideas and as a result of projects dedicated to the study of Jewish folklore developed and carried out even before the First World War. In all these efforts, great importance was placed on the participation of volunteers — *zamlers* (collectors) — who gathered data similarly to professional researchers or prominent figures in Jewish culture and politics at the time. Another influence was the method of social memoir, which had been developed in Poland during the interwar period to document the personal stories of the public, particularly as they related to social and political issues.[3] In addition to placing the experiences of common people at the center of documenting history, *khurbn forshung* and social memoir enabled women to have both a hand and a voice in historiography. From the beginning, *khurbn forshung* involved women working as *zamlers* as well as providing testimony.[4] Social memoir, likewise, enabled women's voices to enter into the historical record through various forms of autobiographical writing.[5]

Both during and after the Second World War and the Holocaust, these methods continued to be used and developed to document Nazi atrocities. In 1938 and 1939, Polish-Jewish historian Emanuel Ringelblum began gathering witness testimonies from Polish Jews who had been expelled from Germany and were living in the Zbąszyń refugee camp in Poland.[6] Soon after, Ringelblum was imprisoned in the Warsaw Ghetto, where in Autumn 1940 he organized a secret archive called *Oyneg Shabes* to document and preserve the experiences of Jews during the German occupation (1939–1942) and the murder of Jewish people. Numerous staff and volunteers contributed to this effort by gathering eyewitness testimonies of Jewish persecution within and outside the ghetto, collecting diaries, and distribut-

---

2 Jockusch, *Collect and Record!*, 19–20.
3 For example, Katherine Lebow, "Autobiography as Complaint: Polish Social Memoir Between the World Wars," *Laboratorium: Russian Review of Social Research* 6, no. 3 (2014): 13–25.
4 Jockusch, *Collect and Record!*, 32–33.
5 Lebow, "Autobiography as Complaint."
6 Joseph Kermish, "Introduction to Polish-Jewish Relations During the Second World War," in *The Nazi Holocaust - Part 5: Public Opinion and relations to the Jews in Nazi Europe*, ed. Michael R. Marrus (Berlin and New York: K. G. Saur, 1989), 266–298, 269–270.

ing questionnaires about life in the ghetto and other war experiences.⁷ Similar initiatives were conducted in other Jewish ghettos as well, including in Riga, Latvia, where Simon Dubnow encouraged the Jews imprisoned in the ghetto to record their experiences.⁸ At the same time, non-Jewish underground resistance groups and governments-in-exile engaged in efforts to document and disseminate knowledge about what was happening to their citizens.⁹ One of these was the Polish underground resistance group, the Home Army (AK), which gathered details of Nazi atrocities against Poles in Nazi-occupied Poland and the mass murder of Jews in the gas chambers of Auschwitz and other death camps.¹⁰ Even though many of the individuals who participated in these efforts – especially those who were Jewish – were murdered in ghettos and extermination and concentration camps, the efforts themselves lived on with the survivors, who reorganized under new circumstances after the war to serve justice and history.

While many of the wartime and postwar documentation initiatives were or began as grassroots efforts, many more were or developed into institutional or professional endeavors. Regardless, their organizational structures tended to mirror the social and gender hierarchies of the period. At the same time, because women's participation in these efforts had already been established, they were not barred by tradition. The result was that although more women than men were involved in efforts to document the Nazi atrocities, they typically held subordinate roles to men and have thus largely been invisible in the historiography of these endeavors. In recent years, scholars have started to correct this with works on women who held leading positions in survivor documentation initiatives, such as Nella Rost, Miriam Novitch, Rachel Auerbach, and Eva Reichmann.

---

7 For instance, Samuel Kassow, *Who will Write our History: Emanuel Ringelblum and the Oyneg Shabes Archive* (Bloomington, IN: Indiana University Press, 2007); "Introduction" in *The Ringelblum Archive. Underground Archive of the Warsaw Ghetto*. Volume Three, *Oyneg Shabes. People and Works*, ed. Aleksandra Bańkowska and Tadeusz Epsztein (Warsaw: Jewish Historical Institute, 2020).

8 See, for instance, Jockusch, *Collect and Record!*, 33–34; Annette Wieviorka, "The Witness in History," *Poetics Today: International Journal for Theory and Analysis of Literature and Communication* 27, no. 2 (2006): 385–398; Łukasz Krzyżanowski, *Ghost Citizens: Jewish Return to a Postwar City*, trans. Madeline G. Levine (Cambridge & London: Harvard University Press, 2020); Szymon Datner, *Zagłada Białegostoku i Białostocczyzny. Notatki dokumentalne* [The Holocaust of Białystok and Bialystok Region. Dokumentary notes] (Warsaw: Jewish Historical Institute, 2023); Aleksandra Bańkowska and Weronika Romanik, *Podziemne Archiwum Getta Białostockiego. Archiwum Mersika-Tenenbauma* [The Underground Archive of the Białystok Ghetto. The Mersik-Tenenbaum Archive] ("Zagłada Żydów. Studia i materiały" 2013).

9 Jockusch, *Collect and Record!*, 43–45.

10 Michael Fleming, "The Polish Government-in-Exile: The United Nations War Crimes Commission and the Holocaust," *Holocaust and Genocide Studies* 36 (2022): 19–34.

For example, historian and journalist Rachel Auerbach's work of collecting under the German occupation as part of the secret *Oyneg Shabes* group in the Warsaw Ghetto has to some extent been treated within the context of histories written about this group by Samuel Kassow, while more of her work has recently been translated from Yiddish.[11] Sharon Geva has shed important light on the documentation work of Miriam Novitch, a French Holocaust survivor and member of the French Resistance and one of the founders of the world's first museum dedicated to the Holocaust – the Ghetto Fighters' House in Israel. In her earliest work on Novitch, Geva lamented, "The dissonance of the gap between her achievements in documenting the history of the Holocaust and her marginal position [in historiography] is disturbing, perhaps even outrageous."[12] Likewise, Christine Schmidt has increased awareness of Dr. Eva Reichmann (including in this thematic section), a German Jew and scholar in her own right who fled to London in 1939 and in 1945 joined what is now The Wiener Holocaust Library in London as director of research. In the 1950s, she led an effort to gather what ultimately amounted to more than 1,200 eyewitness accounts from Jewish victims and witnesses.[13] Even less has been written about the efforts undertaken outside the countries most affected by the Second World War and the Holocaust, such as Sweden, where no fewer than three survivor-led documentation efforts were undertaken in the early years after the Holocaust. One of these, the Jewish Historical Commission in

---

[11] Kassow, *Who will Write our History*; Rokhl Auerbach, *Warsaw Testament* (Amherst, MA: White Goat Press, 2024). See also Boaz Cohen, "Rachel Auerbach, Yad Vashem, and Israeli Holocaust Memory," trans. Erica Nadelhaft, in *Polin: Studies in Polish Jewry*, vol 20: *Making Holocaust Memory*, eds. Natalia Aleksiun et al., (Liverpool: Liverpool University Press, 2007), 197–221; Karolina Szymaniak, "On the Ice Floe: Rachel Auerbach – the Life of a Yiddishist Intellectual in Early Twentieth Century Poland," in *Catastrophe and Utopia: Jewish Intellectuals in Central and Eastern Europe in the 1930s and 1940s*, ed. Joachim von Puttkamer and Ferenc Laczó (Berlin: Walter de Gruyter GmbH, 2017), 304–351.

[12] Sharon Geva, "'To collect the tears of the Jewish people': The Story of Miriam Novitch," *Holocaust Studies* 21, no. 1–2 (2015): 73–92, 75. See also Sharon Geva, "Documenters, Researchers and Commemorators: The Life Stories and Work of Miriam Novitch and Rachel Auerbach in Comparative Perspective," *MORESHET Journal for the Study of the Holocaust and Antisemitism* 16 (2019): 56–91.

[13] See "Gender and the Materiality of Witnessing: The Wiener Library and Postwar Holocaust Knowledge" in this volume; Christine Schmidt, "'We Are All Witnesses': Eva Reichmann and the Wiener Library's Eyewitness Accounts Collection," in *Agency and the Holocaust: Essays in Honor of Debórah Dwork*, ed. Thomas Kühne and Mary Jane Rein (Cham: Springer International Publishing, 2020), 123–140; Christine Schmidt, "'Historical Meaning Beyond the Personal': Survivor Agency and Mediation in the Wiener Library's Early Testimonies Collection," *EHRI Document Blog*, 17 April 2019, accessed March 5, 2025, https://blog.ehri-project.eu/2019/04/17/historical-meaning-beyond-the-personal

Stockholm, was led by Polish Holocaust survivor Dr. Nella Rost, who had previously been involved with the Central Jewish Historical Commission in Poland. Although Rost is mentioned in several works, the most extensive treatment of her is a 2021 anthology chapter by Swedish historian Johannes Heuman.[14] As important as these contributions are, it is alarming that not a single monograph has been published about these women and their work — either collectively or individually.

The growing research on women and their involvement in documentation and archives-building related to the Nazi atrocities during and after the Second World War and the Holocaust has come with an increased overall focus on grassroots documentation efforts and the archival collections they generated during and after the Nazi period, particularly concerning Jewish collecting efforts.[15] However, the women who conducted the work behind the scenes are rarely named. For instance, Ewa Koźmińska-Frejlak has studied the work of Klara Mirska, one of the most active interviewers at the Central Jewish Historical Commission in Poland (CJHC). The collections of the Jewish Historical Institute (JHI) contain approximately 250 transcripts of testimonies recorded by her between 1945 and 1949 during her employment at the CJHC and later, after the CJHC was transformed into the JHI, at the JHI's Łódź branch. The comparison made by Koźmińska-Frejlak between the handwritten testimonies recorded by Mirska and their edited versions submitted to the CJHC demonstrates that Mirska's contribution to

---

[14] Johannes Heuman, "In Search of Documentation: Nella Rost and the Jewish Historical Commission," in *Early Holocaust Memory in Sweden: Archives, Testimonies and Reflections*, ed. Johannes Heuman and Pontus Rudberg (Basingstoke & New York: Palgrave MacMillan, 2021), 33–65. See also Laura Jockusch, "Historiography in Transit: Survivor Historians and the Writing of Holocaust History in the Late 1940s," *Leo Baeck Institute Year Book*, 2013, 75–94, 85; Izabela Dahl, "Witnessing the Holocaust: Jewish Experiences and the Collection of the Polish Source Institute in Lund," in *Early Holocaust Memory in Sweden: Archives, Testimonies and Reflections*, ed. Johannes Heuman and Pontus Rudberg (Basingstoke & New York: Palgrave Macmillan, 2021), 67–91, 78. The other two were the Polish Research Institute (PIZ) in Lund (see Victoria Van Orden Martínez's chapter in this volume) and the documentation efforts carried out by Germaine Tillion, a non-Jewish ethnologist and member of the French Resistance who survived imprisonment in Ravensbrück and came to Sweden as a repatriate in the spring of 1945. She would collect accounts from other former prisoners of Ravensbrück while in a Swedish sanatorium. See Emma Kuby, *Political Survivors: The Resistance, the Cold War, and the Fight against Concentration Camps after 1945* (Ithaca, NY and London: Cornell University Press, 2019), 26.

[15] For instance, Jason Lustig, *A Time to Gather: Archives and the Control of Jewish Culture* (New York: Oxford University Press, 2022); Dora Osborne, *What Remains: The Post-Holocaust Archive in German Memory Culture* (Rochester, NY: Camden House, 2020); Dan Stone, *Fate Unknown: Tracing the Missing after World War II and the Holocaust* (London: Oxford University Press, 2023).

documenting the Holocaust went far beyond simply transcribing the stories she heard. By structuring the testimonies and giving coherence to the narratives, Mirska effectively co-created the final accounts. A similar process applied to other interviewers as well. However, researchers referring to the testimonies they collected tend to omit their names entirely. Despite their significant contributions, there has thus far not been any scholarly analysis focusing on the work of any of these women.[16]

Moreover, few studies have framed the documentation efforts in terms of gender and its intersections with class, nationality, ethnicity, sexuality, and other contexts in terms of shaping knowledge production and dissemination in the early postwar period. It is perhaps indicative that upon issuing the call for abstracts for this thematic section of the *History of Intellectual Culture*, we only received a few proposals in response, even with an extension. While several factors may contribute to this, we believe it suggests that questions regarding the relationship between gender and knowledge production and archives-building are still in their nascency and are yet to fully capture the imagination of researchers capable of providing the research and amplification necessary. The chapters in this thematic section thus depart from most previous research by orienting our focus to the gendered aspects of collecting and documentation work in ways that focus on women's contributions within male-dominated spaces and institutions as they developed in the postwar period.

Likewise, little attention has been paid thus far to the behind-the-scenes work that was conducted by the largely female workforce of interviewers, typists, archivists, etc. Unlike the women in higher positions, there is often very limited source material on these women and their specific contributions to the documentation efforts. Even when ample source material does exist, however, historians and others have largely overlooked it. Victoria Van Orden Martínez has written about two women — one on each end of this spectrum — who were involved in the Polish Research Institute (PIZ) in Lund, Sweden, an initiative that involved both Jewish and non-Jewish Polish survivors gathering testimonies and evidence from other Polish survivors in Sweden as refugees in the early years of the postwar period.[17] On one end of the spectrum, there is very limited source material about Polish Holocaust survivor Luba Melchior, who was the only Jewish em-

---

[16] Ewa Koźmińska-Frejlak, "Właściwym autorem tej książki jest . . . [A true author of this book is . . .]," in Lejb Zylberberg, *Żyd z Klimontowa opowiada* . . . [A Jew from Klimontow tells . . .] (Warsaw: Jewish Historical Institute, 2022): 9–30.

[17] See "Women's Work, Women's Networks: Correspondence and Knowledge Circulation Between the Polish Research Institute in Lund and Survivor Historical Commissions in the Early Postwar Period" in this volume. See also Victoria Van Orden Martínez, "Afterlives: Jewish and

ployee of PIZ. On the other hand, there is relatively extensive source material on Ludwika Broel-Plater, who began working with PIZ soon after arriving in Sweden in 1945 and who continued to work for the institute until she died in 1972.[18] Despite the presence and availability of sources on Broel-Plater, she has fared no better in historiography than Melchior, demonstrating that, as historian Gerda Lerner wrote in 1969, the neglect of women in history is not always about a lack of empirical material.[19] This is evidenced by a more recent surge in scholarship highlighting the continued neglect of women's archives, women in archives, and women archivists as key actors in the production and circulation of knowledge.[20] As emphasized by Michelle Caswell, the archives profession and associated discipline, although readily referenced by historians, is often engaged as a "handmaiden" to history and viewed as a "feminine service industry" rather than as culturally constructed based on decades of theoretical debate.[21] As demonstrated by this small but growing body of work, fragments can be as useful as archives when it comes to reconstructing the past, leaving no excuse for historians to con-

---

Non-Jewish Polish Survivors of Nazi Persecution in Sweden Documenting Nazi Atrocities, 1945–1946" (PhD diss., Linköping University, 2023).
18 Victoria Van Orden Martínez, "Documenting the Documenter: Piecing together the history of Polish Holocaust survivor-historian Luba Melchior," *EHRI Document Blog*, 12 December 2022, accessed 6 February 2025, https://blog.ehri-project.eu/2022/12/12/luba-melchior/; Victoria Van Orden Martínez, "An Eternally Grateful Refugee? Silences in Swedish Public Discourse and the (De)Historicization of Polish-Swedish Activist Ludwika Broel-Plater," in *Forced Migrants in Nordic Histories*, ed. Johanna Leinonen et al. (Helsinki: Helsinki University Press, 2025), 203–223.
19 Gerda Lerner, "New Approaches to the Study of Women in American History," *Journal of Social History* 3, no. 1 (1969): 53–62, 59.
20 For instance, Nupur Chaudhuri, Sherry J. Katz, and Mary Elizabeth Perry, eds., *Contesting Archives: Finding Women in the Sources* (Urbana, IL: University of Illinois Press, 2010); Patricia Owens, *Erased: A History of International Thought Without Men* (Princeton, NJ: Princeton University Press, 2025); Elizabeth Shepherd, "Hidden voices in the archives: Pioneering women archivists in early 20th-century England," in *Engaging with Records and Archives: Histories and Theories*, ed. Fiorella Foscarini, Heather MacNeil, Mak Bonnie, and Oliver Gillian (Cambridge: Cambridge University Press, 2018), 83–103. See also, for instance, Malin Thor Tureby, "'No, I never thought that we were different': Vulnerability, Descriptive Discourses and Agency in the Archive," in *From Dust to Dawn: Archival Studies After the Archival Turn*, ed. Ann Öhrberg, Tim Berndtsson, Otto Fischer, and Annie Mattsson (Uppsala: Uppsala University, 2021), 333–358; Lisa Leff, *The Archive Thief: The Man who Salvaged French Jewish History in the Wake of the Holocaust* (New York: Oxford University Press, 2015); and Elisabeth Gallas, *A Mortuary of Books: The Rescue of Jewish Culture after the Holocaust* (New York: New York University Press, 2019).
21 Michelle Caswell, "'The Archive' is not an Archives: Acknowledging the Intellectual Contributions of Archival Studies," *Reconstruction* 16, no. 1 (2016): loc 23, accessed March 10, 2025, https://escholarship.org/uc/item/7bn4v1fk.

tinue overlooking women in various historical contexts. Although the work conducted by women involved in postwar documentation and archives-building of the Nazi atrocities primarily took place behind the scenes, the editors and contributors of this thematic section have all recognized that the personal and official correspondence of these women represents invaluable source material that – just like the women – has largely been overlooked. By drawing on this material for insight into how women contributed to knowledge production and archives-building, we contribute to and uncover what historian Antoinette Burton has described as "the fugitive work of gender and the equally fleeting presence of women as subjects across a vast landscape of the past."[22]

This thematic section focuses on the circulation of knowledge via letters and other forms of written communication within and among survivor historical commissions after the Second World War with an emphasis on the interplay of gender and other differences.[23] This material serves as a window through which the behind-the-scenes labor and construction of the archival collections in focus can be viewed, which makes it productive for exploring the intersection between gender, class, and migration relative to knowledge production. As was the case with the Republic of Letters during the Age of Enlightenment, the Second World War, the Holocaust, and the resulting mass destruction and political and social upheaval enabled narrow cracks to form in social and organizational hierarchies through which some women managed to gain access. In both cases, this access was partially possible because it entailed work that kept women relatively invisible in the "private" sphere of correspondence and intimate personal engagements, which in the more contemporary context included personal interviews, administrative tasks, etc.[24] Even though women's involvement in the traditionally male-dominated work of historical documentation was accompanied by deeply embedded gender barriers that affected them in their own time and historiographically, the chapters in this thematic section demonstrate that the product of the postwar documentation efforts – namely, the archives they helped to create – is certainly not the beginning of the story of how knowledge of the Second World

---

[22] Antoinette Burton, "'Small Stories' and the Promises of New Narratives," Foreword in *Contesting Archives: Finding Women in the Sources*, ed. Nupur Chaudhuri, Sherry J. Katz, and Mary Elizabeth Perry (Urbana, IL: University of Illinois Press, 2010), vii.

[23] We are inspired by works such as Johan Östling, Erling Sandmo, David Larsson Heidenblad, Anna Nilsson Hammar, and Kari H. Nordberg, eds., *Circulation of Knowledge: Explorations in the History of Knowledge* (Lund: Nordic Academic Press, 2018); Susanne Korbel and Philipp Strobl, eds., *Cultural Translation and Knowledge Transfer on Alternative Routes of Escape from Nazi Terror: Mediations through Migrations* (London: Routledge, Taylor & Francis Group, 2022).

[24] For instance, Susan Dalton, *Engendering the Republic of Letters: Reconnecting Public and Private Spheres in Eighteenth-Century Europe* (Montreal: McGill-Queen's University Press, 2004).

War and the Holocaust was produced and circulated in the aftermath. As acknowledged by historian Carolyn Steedman, "nothing starts in the Archive."[25]

With these considerations in mind, the authors have been particularly interested in exploring aspects of the "unseen labor" – various forms of work, often "administrative" in nature and thus primarily carried out by women – behind these documentation efforts that remain underexplored and marginalized in studies on the production, circulation, and history of knowledge, as well as of intellectual culture. Individually and together, these contributions provide insight into two key questions. First, how did gender and other differences affect the circulation of knowledge through written communications about war crimes investigations and postwar trials, the publication and dissemination of scholarly and popular literature, archiving, the collection of oral histories and testimonies, and other outputs? By nature of the geographies of the Second World War and the Holocaust, the German and Polish contexts are at the forefront of the analyses. However, none of the documentation efforts examined took place in these geographies but were instead carried out in England, Sweden, and Mandatory Palestine (later Israel). As a result, the contributions reinforce the transnational aspect of the circulation of knowledge in this context, which was embedded in migrant knowledge.[26] This leads us to the second key question considered in this thematic section: How was knowledge about these activities amassed and circulated in national and transnational contexts?

The first two contributions address initiatives carried out by Jewish and non-Jewish Polish survivors of Nazi persecution in three distinct geographical settings. Victoria Van Orden Martínez's chapter seeks to understand the role of women's informal networks, activated through correspondence, in the circulation of knowledge during the early postwar period – both about the Nazi atrocities and the efforts themselves (methods, materials, etc.) – between the Polish Research Institute in Lund, Sweden (PIZ) and other similar initiatives, especially those conducted by survivors of Nazi persecution. In addition to gender, religion and other differences represent important analytical tools used in this study to understand if and how communications were carried out across these categories. Martínez's

---

25 Carolyn Steedman, *Dust: The Archive and Cultural History* (New Brunswick, NJ: Rutgers University Press, 2002), 45.
26 Andrea Westermann and Onur Erdur, eds., "Histories of Migrant Knowledge: Transatlantic and Global Perspectives," *Bulletin of the German Historical Institute*, Supplement 15 (2020), accessed February 20, 2025, https://www.ghi-dc.org/publication/histories-of-migrant-knowledge-transatlantic-and-global-perspectives; Simone Lässig and Swen Steinberg, "Knowledge on the Move: New Approaches toward a History of Migrant Knowledge," *Geschichte und Gesellschaft* 43, no. 3 (2017); Simone Lässig, "The History of Knowledge and the Expansion of the Historical Research Agenda," *Bulletin of the GHI Washington* 59 (Fall 2016).

findings shed important light on the limits to women's agency created by gendered social and institutional hierarchies in the early postwar period, including "benevolent sexism," and the impact of this gendered gatekeeping on the circulation of knowledge between similar initiatives.

Moving from institutions to the actions of individuals within them, Daniela Ozacky Stern's chapter examines the significant role of Ruzka Korchak (1921–1988), a Polish-born survivor of the Vilna Ghetto and a partisan fighter, in shaping early Holocaust memory and documentation in postwar Israel. Korchak arrived in Mandatory Palestine (later Israel) in December 1944 and immediately began sharing her experiences through public speeches and writing. Her 1946 book, *Flames in the Ashes*, was one of the earliest survivor accounts published in Hebrew. Ozacky Stern's chapter explores Korchak's multifaceted contributions to Holocaust remembrance, including her subsequent efforts to collect and preserve documents from the Holocaust as well as her founding role in the Moreshet Holocaust Archive. Based on Korchak's personal letters and interviews, the study sheds light on her complex position as a central figure in early Holocaust commemoration and as a woman often overshadowed by male counterparts in the public's memory. By analyzing Korchak's life and work, Ozacky Stern's contribution highlights the crucial role of women in preserving and sharing Holocaust experiences while also examining the gendered nature of public memory efforts in postwar Israel.

Christine Schmidt's chapter also focuses on the role of an individual woman in a survivor historical commission. In the mid-1950s, the Wiener Library in London launched a project led by German-Jewish refugee scholar Eva Reichmann (1897–1998) to collect eyewitness accounts by survivors of Nazi persecution. Reichmann organized the project to "fill gaps" that she believed existed in the knowledge having been amassed by the institution's existing activities and collection, shaped at their foundation by the undercover activist efforts of its predecessor organization, the Jewish Central Information Office, during the Nazi period. Schmidt's chapter examines the impact and intersection of gender on the forms that the Library's postwar transnational collecting activities took, particularly the material contexts of and challenges to its implementation (networking, administrating, appraising, describing, cataloging, indexing, and other acts of archiving – all forms of "unseen labor" in this context often carried out by women). Schmidt's analysis of the Wiener Library's rich corpus of more than 1,200 eyewitness accounts and related correspondence brings to light the lesser-known contributions of women who circulated within the orbit of the Library and who created and disseminated Holocaust knowledge after the war.

Together, the contributions in this thematic section point to some of the ways investigating previously overlooked knowledge actors through a gendered lens contributes to understanding knowledge production and circulation in specific contexts. In this case, the studies do not merely confirm that women played important roles in the production and circulation of knowledge about the Nazi atrocities. Each study specifically explores how gender combined with other influential factors, such as culture, class, intellectual background, and forced migration not only contributed to *what* women did within these initiatives but also *how*. Moreover, although each of the contributions highlights the specific ways in which women contributed to documentation and archives-building about the Second World War and the Holocaust, they also point to how gender norms, roles, and expectations shaped and even limited the knowledge production and circulation related to these cataclysms. The chapters thus serve as a prompt for further analysis to explore transnational connectivity in early Holocaust documentation efforts and the transfer and transformation of knowledge across different borders. However, in so doing, they also center the frequently marginalized voices and labor within that analysis.

We hope that even though only a few scholars expressed an interest in contributing to this volume, the contributions that are published here serve as important case studies and raise additional queries for analysis. Moreover, we hope that this thematic section encourages further interdisciplinary analyses of the history of ideas and knowledge production, taking on board explorations of the intersections between gender, class, and culture in the analysis of knowledge circulation and transformation. We are also keen to spur further dialogue and scholarship on the relationship between knowledge produced by and through archives-building and the material conditions for these as well as the establishment of different fields of study (e.g., Jewish studies and Holocaust studies) and beyond the geographies addressed in the chapters that follow. How are these factors related to the establishment of the "canon" in Jewish and Holocaust studies, the fairly recent wider recognition of women's issues and women historians in Holocaust studies, and major debates (*Historikerstreit*) within the field, largely articulated by men? These are all queries beyond this special section, but we aim to provoke further debate and analysis.

Victoria Van Orden Martínez is a researcher at the Department of History at Lund University in Sweden. Her current research focuses on how survivors of Nazi persecution who became migrants and refugees after the war were involved in various sociohistorical processes, with a focus on gender and other differences. Victoria is currently working on a project about women survivors of Nazi persecution who were medical professionals during and after the Second World War aiming to gain insight into how their wartime experiences impacted their lives and careers in medicine and science.

Christine Schmidt is deputy director and head of research at The Wiener Holocaust Library. Her research has focused on the history of postwar tracing and documentation efforts, the concentration camp system in Nazi Germany, comparative studies of collaboration and resistance in France and

Hungary, and the collection of survivor accounts recorded by The Wiener Library. Schmidt is co-editing *Holocaust Letters: Methodology, Cases, and Reflections* (London: Bloomsbury, 2026) and *Older Jews and the Holocaust: Persecution, Displacement, and Survival*, eds. Christine Schmidt, Elizabeth Anthony and Joanna Sliwa (Detroit: Wayne State University Press in association with the US Holocaust Memorial Museum, 2026).

Ewa Koźmińska-Frejlak is an associate professor at the Jewish Historical Institute (JHI) in Warsaw. Her research focuses on Jewish life during the Holocaust and its aftermath, Polish-Jewish relations during these periods, and the early Jewish historiography of the Holocaust. She is currently working on a book on the social history of the Central Jewish Historical Commission in Poland as well as on a book on the interviewers who collected testimonies from Holocaust survivors immediately after the war.

Victoria Van Orden Martínez

Women's Work, Women's Networks: Correspondence and Knowledge Circulation Between the Polish Research Institute in Lund and Survivor Historical Commissions in the Early Postwar Period

Abstract: Research on early postwar documentation efforts related to the Second World War and the Holocaust conducted by survivors of Nazi persecution has expanded over the past two decades. Yet, research on how knowledge circulated between these efforts – especially across various "borders" – is still nascent. This chapter seeks to gain a better understanding of the role of women's informal networks during the early postwar period, activated through correspondence, in the circulation of knowledge – with regard to both the Nazi atrocities and the efforts themselves (methods, materials, etc.) – between the Polish Research Institute in Lund, Sweden (PIZ) and other similar initiatives, especially the ones conducted by survivors of Nazi persecution. In addition to gender, religion and other differences are also important analytical tools used in this study to understand if and how communications were carried out across these categories. The findings provide new insights into the roles of women in early efforts to document the Nazi atrocities, the interplay of gender dynamics in the organizational structure and hierarchy of one of these efforts, and their impact on the circulation of knowledge between similar initiatives.

Keywords: survivors of Nazi persecution, survivor historical commissions, Polish Research Institute in Lund (Sweden), correspondence

Introduction

In late 1949, Germaine Tillion, a former member of the French resistance who had been imprisoned in the Ravensbrück concentration camp, wrote an urgent letter to Ludwika Broel-Plater, a former member of the Polish resistance who had also been imprisoned in Ravensbrück. Tillion was a witness at the French Military Tribunal trial of SS officer Fritz Suhren, commandant of Ravensbrück from September 1942. She was also involved in efforts to document the experiences of individuals persecuted by the Nazis. Broel-Plater, a stateless resident of Sweden, was responsible for

∂ Open Access. © 2025 the author(s), published by De Gruyter. This work is licensed under the Creative Commons Attribution-NonCommercial-NoDerivatives 4.0 International License.
https://doi.org/10.1515/9783111636726-005

the objects and documentation gathered from former prisoners of Nazi concentration camps by the Polish Research Institute (Polski Instytut Źródłowy) in Lund, Sweden (hereafter PIZ). Among this material was a certified copy of the "Mittwerda List" of 480 prisoners who supposedly had been sent to the fictional "Mittwerda rest camp" but who were, in fact, executed in the gas chamber. This list was signed by Suhren and dated April 6, 1945.[1]

"The Mittwerda list is of great importance because it is an irrefutable document proving SUHREN's responsibility for the extermination of the camp," Tillion wrote to Broel-Plater in French. However, she explained, the French Examining Magistrate feared that if the document was requested through "the hierarchical channel" it would arrive too late for the trial, so asked Tillion to use her personal connections to obtain it in a timelier fashion. Tillion had originally written to former PIZ employee Helena Dziedzicka, whom she had known in the camp, before ultimately writing to Broel-Plater. Tillion closed the letter by writing that she had fond memories of Broel-Plater in Ravensbrück.[2] Broel-Plater fulfilled Tillion's request in time for the list to be used as evidence in Suhren's trial, which ended with a guilty verdict.[3]

This letter, held in the PIZ archive, is an example of knowledge pertaining to the Nazi atrocities being shared between similar initiatives in the early postwar period by means of informal networks crossing geographical, linguistic, national, and other borders. These networks, as the letter demonstrates, were often based on shared wartime experiences in, for example, concentration camps and resistance groups. Because men and women were separated as prisoners in camps and other settings, these networks frequently developed along gender lines, with some scholars arguing that women developed more extensive and enduring networks than men.[4] Following liberation and the dispersal of survivors, the networks could be maintained and activated through correspondence. For example, other letters and documents in the PIZ archive reveal that the formation of PIZ as a survivor historical commission in the early postwar period as well as many of the internal operations of the institute – including gathering witness testimonies –

---

[1] The Polish Research Institute in Lund (PIZ) archive (Lund University Library, Sweden), volume 30: 5. "Mittwerda."
[2] Zygmunt Łakocińskis arkiv (ZL) (Lund University Library, Sweden), volume 41, letter from Germaine Tillion to Ludwika Broel-Plater, in French, datelined Paris, December 31, 1949. Capitalizations in original. Translated from French by me. All translations are my own unless otherwise noted.
[3] Tillion writes about Mittwerda and mentions Dziedzicka and Broel-Plater in Germaine Tillion, *Ravensbrück*, trans. Gerald Satterwhite (New York: Anchor Books, 1975), 147–152.
[4] For instance, Judith Tydor Baumel-Schwartz, "Women's Agency and Survival Strategies during the Holocaust," *Women's Studies International Forum* 22, no. 3 (1999): 329–347, 338.

were supported by and/or conducted through former concentration camp prisoners' networks of support and resistance, particularly those of women. These internal operations at PIZ were focused on gathering knowledge about the German occupation of Poland and the experiences of Poles in ghettos, concentration and labor camps, in hiding, and so forth. This was done through face-to-face interviews as well as by means of correspondence, which was often carried out through informal networks. In addition, important knowledge was circulated "from below" through these networks that informed the ways in which the institute members conducted their work, such as by adapting collection methods and deviating from the established methodology.[5]

The letter regarding the Mittwerda List constitutes tantalizing potential evidence that women's informal networks also served as an important conduit for disseminating this knowledge and sharing knowledge about how these efforts were being carried out through correspondence with other organizations and initiatives concerned with documenting the Nazi atrocities. Throughout much of history, women's participation in public debates, politics, business, philosophy, and other arenas was restricted by social norms. Correspondence conducted in the "feminine" domestic sphere was one of the few ways women could participate in these arenas, which were otherwise reserved for men in the "masculine" public sphere. Through letters, women were also able to build and maintain informal networks of support and resistance. Correspondence is thus a fruitful source of material right up to the modern period, especially when seeking to understand the role of women in historical events and the interplay between gender and other differences in various contexts, such as transnational and diaspora knowledge networks.[6]

While research on early postwar documentation efforts, especially those conducted by survivors of Nazi persecution, has expanded over the past two decades, research on how knowledge was circulated between these efforts – especially across various "borders" – is still nascent.[7] Understandably, most research has fo-

---

[5] Victoria Van Orden Martínez, "Afterlives: Jewish and Non-Jewish Polish Survivors of Nazi Persecution in Sweden Documenting Nazi Atrocities, 1945–1946" (PhD diss., Linköping University, 2023).

[6] Relevant studies address both historical and contemporary actors. See, for instance, Susan Dalton, *Engendering the Republic of Letters: Reconnecting Public and Private Spheres in Eighteenth-Century Europe* (Montreal: McGill-Queen's University Press, 2004); Sami Mahroum, ed., "Transnational Knowledge Through Diaspora Networks," *International Journal on Multicultural Societies* 8, no. 1 (2006), accessed February 26, 2025, https://unesdoc.unesco.org/ark:/48223/pf0000149086.locale=en

[7] This is in line with the previous lack of studies on migrant knowledge. See, for instance, Simone Lässig, "The History of Knowledge and the Expansion of the Historical Research Agenda,"

cused on knowledge *about* the atrocities and how this knowledge was collected rather than on how both forms of knowledge were circulated between documentation commissions and other initiatives concerned with the Nazi atrocities. Similarly, research on gender and religious dynamics within and across these efforts is still in its infancy. In her foundational book on Jewish documentation efforts in early postwar Europe, historian Laura Jockusch observes that the high level of involvement of women in these efforts "undermined established gender roles." At the same time, only a few women held leading roles, as most of them worked as collectors, interviewers, archivists, and secretaries.[8] Scholars are just now beginning to investigate the "behind-the-scenes" work carried out by these women.[9]

Bulletin of the GHI Washington 59 (2016), 29–58, accessed February 26, 2025, https://www.ghi-dc.org/publication/bulletin-59-fall-2016; Simone Lässig and Swen Steinberg, "Knowledge on the Move: New Approaches toward a History of Migrant Knowledge," *Geschichte und Gesellschaft* 43, no. 3 (2017): 313–346. Previous research exploring the topic of correspondence across these types of boundaries includes Ari Joskowicz, *Rain of Ash: Roma, Jews, and the Holocaust* (Princeton, NJ: Princeton University Press, 2023); Nicolas Berg, *The Holocaust and the West German Historians*, trans. and ed. Joel Golb (Madison, WI: University of Wisconsin Press, 2015). An exception here is historian Laura Jockusch's foundational book *Collect and Record! Jewish Holocaust Documentation in Early Postwar Europe* (Oxford: Oxford University Press, 2012).

8 Jockusch, *Collect and Record*, 186. Some women did play lead roles. See, for instance, Boaz Cohen, "Rachel Auerbach, Yad Vashem, and Israeli Holocaust Memory," in *Polin: Studies in Polish Jewry*, ed. Gabriel N. Finder, Natalia Aleksiun, and Antony Polonsky, Volume 20 of *Making Holocaust Memory* (Liverpool: Liverpool University Press, 2007), 197–221; Sharon Geva, "'To collect the tears of the Jewish people': The story of Miriam Novitch," *Holocaust Studies* 21, no. 1–2 (2015): 73–92, accessed February 26, 2025, https://doi.org/10.1080/17504902.2015.1062276; Christine Schmidt, "'We Are All Witnesses': Eva Reichmann and the Wiener Library's Eyewitness Accounts Collection," in *Agency and the Holocaust: Essays in Honor of Debórah Dwork*, ed. Thomas Kühne and Mary Jane Rein (Cham: Springer International Publishing, 2020), 123–140; Johannes Heuman, "In Search of Documentation: Nella Rost and the Jewish Historical Commission," in *Early Holocaust Memory in Sweden: Archives, Testimonies and Reflections*, ed. Johannes Heuman and Pontus Rudberg (Basingstoke & New York: Palgrave MacMillan, 2021), 33–65.

9 For instance, Leora Bilsky, "Rachel Auerbach and the Eichmann Trial: A New Conception of Victims' Testimonies," *The Journal of Holocaust Research* 36, no. 4 (2022): 327–345; Sharon Geva, "Documenters, Researchers and Commemorators: The Life Stories and Work of Miriam Novitch and Rachel Auerbach in Comparative Perspective," *MORESHET Journal for the Study of the Holocaust and Antisemitism* 16 (2019): 56–91; Christine Schmidt, "'Historical Meaning Beyond the Personal': Survivor Agency and Mediation in the Wiener Library's Early Testimonies Collection," *EHRI Document Blog*, April 17, 2019, accessed February 6, 2025, https://blog.ehri-project.eu/2019/04/17/historical-meaning-beyond-the-personal/; Ewa Koźmińska-Frejlak, "Właściwym autorem tej książki jest . . .," in *Żyd z Klimontowa opowiada . . .* (Wydanie Krytyczne Prac Centralnej Żydowskiej Komisji Historycznej, ed. Lejb Zylberberg and Żydowski Instytut Historyczny Im Emanuela Ringelbluma (Warsaw: Żydowski Instytut Historyczny im. Emanuela Ringelbluma, 2021), 9–30; Victoria Van Orden Martínez and Christine Schmidt, "Survivor-Interviewers as Companions of

Likewise, they are increasingly turning to the personal correspondence by victims of Nazi persecution to gain insight into the Second World War, the Holocaust, and the early postwar period.[10] This study brings together these complementary threads of research to gain a better understanding of the role of women's informal networks during the early postwar period, activated through correspondence, in the circulation of knowledge – both regarding the Nazi atrocities and these efforts themselves (methods, materials, etc.) – between PIZ and other similar initiatives, especially the ones conducted by survivors of Nazi persecution. In addition to gender, religion and other differences – such as nationality and language – are also important analytical tools that are used in this study to understand if and how communications occurred across these categories. By examining the PIZ correspondence in relation to organizational structures and hierarchies as well as the role of gender and other differences within these, this chapter offers new and important insight not only into postwar efforts to document the Second World War and the Holocaust but also into how power dynamics associated with the gender and religion of those involved in these efforts helped or hindered the circulation of knowledge between similar initiatives.[11]

Misery: A Comparative View from Post-War England and Sweden," in *Survivors' Toil*, ed. Éva Kovacs and Natalia Aleksiun (Toronto: University of Toronto Press, forthcoming 2026); Victoria Van Orden Martínez, "Documenting the Documenter: Piecing together the history of Polish Holocaust survivor-historian Luba Melchior," *EHRI Document* Blog, December 12, 2022, accessed February 6, 2025, https://blog.ehri-project.eu/2022/12/12/luba-melchior/

10 In addition to the contributions in this thematic section, see also, for instance, Ewa Koźmińska-Frejlak, "List należy do życia . . . Listy prywatne jako źródło badań nad Zagładą" [A Letter is Part of Life . . . Personal Letters as Source Materials for the Study of the Holocaust], *Kwartalnik Historii Żydów/Jewish History Quarterly* 250, no. 2 (2014): 321–340; Christine Schmidt and Dan Stone, "What was Known? Holocaust-Era Letters, Archives, and Knowledge," in *Holocaust Letters*, ed. Christine Schmidt and Sandra Lipner (London: The Wiener Holocaust Library, 2023), 10–11; Daniela Ozacky Stern, "Out of Africa: Letters of Jewish detainees in the British internment camps, 1944–1948," *Journal of Modern Jewish Studies* 23, no. 2 (2023): 444–469, accessed October 31, 2024, https://doi.org/10.1080/14725886.2023.2292800; Clara Dijkstra, Charlie Knight, Sandra Lipner, and Christine Schmidt, eds., *Holocaust Letters: Methodologies, Cases and Reflections* (London: Bloomsbury, forthcoming 2026).

11 In addition to the works already cited, this body of research includes Pieter Lagrou, "Historiographie de guerre et historiographie du temps présent: cadres institutionnels en Europe occidentale, 1945–2000," in *Bulletin du Comité international d'histoire de la deuxième guerre mondiale* 30–31 (1999–2000): 191–215; Pieter Lagrou, "L'histoire du temps présent en Europe depuis 1945, ou comment se constitue et se développe un nouveau champ disciplinaire," *La Revue pour l'histoire du CNRS* 9 (2003): 4–15.

Documenting the Second World War and the Holocaust

PIZ was a historical commission collecting material on the German occupation of Poland and atrocities committed against Poles starting in late 1939. In the spring and summer of 1945, some 30,000 Jewish and non-Jewish survivors of Nazi persecution were brought to Sweden for medical care and recovery, including around 13,000 Poles. Some of these Polish "repatriates," as they were termed by the Swedish government, became involved with PIZ in a new effort to collect evidence and written testimonies from other Polish survivors regarding the Nazi atrocities. In 1945 and 1946, nine Polish repatriates – seven women and two men who were all former prisoners of Nazi concentration camps – were employed by the Swedish Labor Market Commission to conduct this work in a formal capacity. They were led by PIZ co-founder Dr. Zygmunt Łakociński, a Polish art historian who came to Sweden in 1934 and worked at Lund University.[12] Today, the PIZ collection assembled by these individuals consists of an impressive array of material artifacts from the concentration camps, art and poetry about life during and after the Second World War and the Holocaust, and hundreds of witness testimonies.[13]

PIZ was one of many documentation efforts established during and after the Second World War and the Holocaust by individuals directly affected by the Nazi atrocities. What is now known as The Wiener Holocaust Library in London originated in 1933 when Dr. Alfred Wiener, a German Jew fleeing Nazi persecution, established the Jewish Central Information Office in Amsterdam to collect material about the Nazis and their actions against Jews.[14] Following the invasion of Poland by Soviet and Nazi forces in 1939, the Polish government-in-exile began gathering material and evidence related to the Nazi occupation of Poland with the assistance of the Polish underground resistance movement.[15] Starting in 1940, clandestine archives were created in several Polish ghettos, most notably the

---

[12] On Łakociński, see, for instance, Izabela A. Dahl, "Witnessing the Holocaust: Jewish Experiences and the Collection of the Polish Source Institute in Lund," in *Early Holocaust Memory in Sweden: Archives, Testimonies and Reflections*, ed. Johannes Heuman and Pontus Rudberg (Basingstoke & New York: Palgrave Macmillan, 2021), 67–91.
[13] Lund University Library, "Witnessing Genocide," accessed October 31, 2024, https://www.ub.lu.se/hitta/digitala-samlingar/witnessing-genocide
[14] Ben Barkow, *Alfred Wiener and the Making of the Holocaust Library* (London and Portland, OR: Vallentine Mitchell, 1997).
[15] For instance, Michael Fleming, "Geographies of obligation and the dissemination of news of the Holocaust," *Holocaust Studies* 23, no. 1–2 (2017): 59–75, accessed February 26, 2025, https://doi.org/10.1080/17504902.2016.1209834

Oyneg Shabes (Oneg Shabbat) archive in the Warsaw Ghetto, which was founded by Polish-Jewish historian Emmanuel Ringelblum to "capture the experiences of Polish Jews under German occupation."[16] In France, the *Centre de Documentation Juive Contemporaine* (Contemporary Jewish Documentation Center, CDJC) was established in 1943, "to collect evidence on the persecution of the Jews in order to bear witness and demand justice after the war."[17] As these examples demonstrate, many of the documentation efforts initiated during the war were grassroots initiatives undertaken by Jewish organizations and individuals. Laura Jockusch in her comprehensive account of Holocaust documentation efforts notes that "German persecution and extermination policies elicited widespread and multifaceted individual and collective Jewish documentation efforts across Europe."[18] In contrast, the wartime efforts by both the Polish government-in-exile and PIZ were concerned with documenting the Nazi occupation of Poland and the persecution of Polish citizens in general, which they understood as *including* Polish Jews.[19] However, PIZ operated independently of the Polish government-in-exile during the war and was, like the Jewish documentation commissions, a grassroots effort.

The end of the war led to a flood of new initiatives to document the Nazi atrocities led by both Jewish and non-Jewish survivors, as well as non-survivors, living in Europe. Just as during the war, many of these were or began as grassroots efforts, while others were founded with the support of existing institutions. Some of the most well-known survivor historical commissions include the Central Jewish Historical Commission, founded following the liberation of Lublin, Poland in August 1944,[20] and the Central Historical Commission in Munich founded in November 1945, which – although founded in Germany – was established by two Jewish survivors, one originating from Poland and one from Lithuania.[21] In 1946, Polish-Jewish survivor Dr. Nella Rost, who had previously worked with the Central Jewish Historical Commission in Poland, established a historical commission in Sweden as part of the Swedish section of the World Jewish Congress.[22]

---

16 For instance, Samuel D. Kassow, *Who will write our history? Emanuel Ringelblum, the Warsaw Ghetto, and the Oyneg Shabes Archive* (Bloomington, IN: Indiana University Press, 2018).
17 "The history of the CDJC," Mémorial de la Shoah, accessed February 6, 2025, https://www.memorialdelashoah.org/en/archives-and-documentation/the-documentation-center/the-history-of-the-cdjc.html
18 Jockusch, *Collect and Record*, 33.
19 Fleming, "Geographies of obligation."
20 Jockusch, *Collect and Record*, 89; Natalia Aleksiun, "The Central Jewish Historical Commission in Poland 1944–1947," in *Polin: Studies in Polish Jewry* 20, ed. Natalia Aleksiun et al. (Liverpool: Liverpool University Press, 2008), 74–97.
21 Jockusch, *Collect and Record*, 128.
22 Heuman, "In Search of Documentation."

Within the realm of postwar survivor historical commissions, PIZ was unusual in the sense that its focus on Germany's crimes against Poland and all Poles meant that it was concerned with documenting both Jewish and non-Jewish suffering, rather than just one or the other. Accordingly, the volunteers and employees of PIZ included both Jewish and non-Jewish Poles – something that apparently rarely occurred among survivor historical commissions in the postwar period.[23] These unusual dynamics meant that suffering under the German occupation and in ghettos and concentration camps was mediated across religious boundaries in the internal work of the institute, albeit to a limited extent due to the involvement of fewer Jews than non-Jews.[24] These dynamics mean that the religion of those involved with PIZ represents an important analytical category for this analysis. A key consideration when examining the correspondence is thus to what extent religious boundaries were crossed – and, hence, knowledge circulated – via external correspondence between, for instance, PIZ and the many Jewish survivor historical commissions.

Similarly, because more female than male repatriates were employees of PIZ, gender is also an important factor to consider in terms of institutional dynamics, not least because I have argued in previous research that much of the day-to-day internal operations were conducted through women's existing and reconstructed networks of resistance and support – the kind of informal networks that facilitated the use of the Mittwerda List at Suhren's trial.[25] Hence, another key consideration when examining the correspondence concerns the role of gender in how external correspondence was conducted and the impact of this on the circulation of knowledge.

---

[23] For instance, Lagrou, "Historiographie de guerre," Lagrou, "L'histoire du temps." Another example of a survivor historical commission established by non-Jewish survivors is Die Vergessenen (The Forgotten). It was founded by Gentile concentration camp survivors Karl Jochheim-Armin and Georg Tauber, who gathered the testimonies of Roma survivors. See, for example, Ari Joskowicz, "Separate Suffering, Shared Archives: Jewish and Romani Histories of Nazi Persecution," *History and Memory: Studies in Representation of the Past* 28, no. 1 (2016): 110–40, accessed February 26, 2025, https://doi.org/10.2979/histmemo.28.1.110

[24] Victoria Van Orden Martínez, "Witnessing against a divide? An analysis of early Holocaust testimonies constructed in interviews between Jewish and non-Jewish Poles," *Holocaust Studies* 28, no. 4 (2021): 483–505, accessed October 31, 2024, https://doi.org/10.1080/17504902.2021.1981627

[25] Martínez, "Afterlives."

Material and Method

Historians engaged in research on and through correspondence are increasingly using technology to facilitate the digital mapping of letters and the production of useful metadata.[26] Unfortunately, although parts of the PIZ archive have been digitized, this material does not include the correspondence. Nothing in the related personal archive of the institute's founder, Zygmunt Łakociński, has been digitized. However, the inventory lists of both archives are comprehensive and well-organized, thus lending themselves to an analog analysis that is sufficient for the kind of understanding needed to ground this study. In this chapter, I utilize these lists not only as guides to the primary sources in the archives but also as primary sources in their own right. The correspondence analyzed in this chapter is located in two archives held in the Special Collections of the Lund University Library in Lund, Sweden: The Polish Research Institute in Lund archive (here referred to as the PIZ archive) and Zygmunt Łakociński's archive (here referred to as the ZL archive).

The postwar collection and documentation work undertaken by PIZ was the most intense in the first three years after the war. At the end of 1946, Swedish government funding for the initiative ended and little additional funding was subsequently obtained. In 1947 and 1948, most of the repatriates who had been involved with PIZ left Sweden and/or found paid work elsewhere. After that, Ludwika Broel-Plater and Łakociński continued the work of PIZ in a limited manner until Broel-Plater's death in 1972 prompted Łakociński to terminate the work of the institute. The focus of this analysis is primarily on the early correspondence, which was sent and received during the first five years after the war. The details of the contents of this correspondence are beyond the scope of this article but were generally bureaucratic in nature (requests for funding and other kinds of support, sharing methods and materials, etc.).

Many Polish repatriates were involved with PIZ in various ways, particularly during the period analyzed here. As a result, the PIZ and ZL archives contain voluminous correspondence between Łakociński and Polish repatriates in Sweden,

---

26 See, for instance, Javier Ureña-Carrion et al., "Communication now and then: Analyzing the Republic of Letters as a communication network," *Applied Network Sci*ence 7, no. 26 (2022): 1–16, accessed October 31, 2024, https://doi.org/10.1007/s41109-022-00463-1; Dan Edelstein et al., "Historical Research in a Digital Age: Reflections from the Mapping the Republic of Letters Project," *The American Historical Review* 122, no. 2 (2017): 400–424, accessed October 31, 2024, https://doi.org/10.1093/ahr/122.2.400; Institute for War, Holocaust and Genocide Studies (NIOD), *First-Hand Accounts of War: War letters (1935–1950) from NIOD digitized*, accessed October 31, 2024, https://www.niod.nl/en/projects/first-hand-accounts-war

as well as personal correspondence between Łakociński and private individuals in Sweden. I have examined this larger body of correspondence in previous research, which has offered me useful knowledge for this analysis while providing context and depth to the findings. However, since this chapter is concerned with how PIZ communicated with other organizations, institutes, and historical commissions, this correspondence falls outside of the scope of the present analysis. Instead, this analysis primarily focuses on what I consider external communications – correspondence sent and received by Łakociński, as founder and head of the institute, and the nine Polish repatriates employed by the Swedish Labor Market Commission to work for PIZ in 1945 and 1946 – Ludwika Broel-Plater, Krystyna Karier, Luba Melchior, Helena Dziedzicka, Bożysław Kurowski, Józef Nowaczyk, Halina Strzelecka, Helena Miklaszewska, and Irena Jaworowicz (see Figure 1).

Figure 1: Group photo taken by Maria Helena Kurowska, 1946 (public domain image). According to the caption associated with the image: Back row (left to right) Bożysław Kurowski, Ludwika Broel-Plater, Carola von Gegerfelt (Zygmunt Łakociński's wife), Józef Nowaczyk, unidentified in original caption but almost certainly Krystyna Karier, Zygmunt Łakociński. Front row (left to right): Helena Dziedzicka, Luba Melchior, Halina Strzelecka. Image courtesy Wikimedia Commons.

As in all organizations, each PIZ employee was assigned specific responsibilities based in part on their experience and skills during the period the institute was funded by the Swedish government. This work was carried out in addition to the overall interviewing and collection activities that all employees to some extent participated in. Krystyna Karier, who had studied mathematics, was responsible for accounting, oversaw general correspondence, and served as secretary in charge of meetings and conferences. Luba Melchior, who had a business degree, was responsible for the Jewish and literary departments of PIZ as well as for archiving and organizing the institute's documents. Ludwika Broel-Plater, a qualified teacher and linguist, was responsible for creating a list of vocabulary used in the concentration camps and for documenting the history of PIZ. Helena Dziedzicka, who had studied languages, was responsible for translations and correspondence in English and French. Bożysław Kurowski, a lawyer, was responsible for legal issues. Józef Nowaczyk, a diplomat with a background in economics, was responsible for a geographical dictionary of the concentration camps and related locations. Halina Strzelecka, who had a master's degree in literature, was responsible for maintaining the PIZ files. Helena Miklaszewska, a historian, was responsible for maintaining a list of deceased former prisoners, while Irena Jaworowicz, a librarian, was responsible for typing all PIZ documents.[27] By nature of their responsibilities, some of these individuals were more engaged in correspondence than others. Accordingly, this chapter focuses on those who were active correspondents.

Gender and feminist studies scholar Maria Tamboukou views archives "as an assemblage of documents, institutional practices, power/knowledge relations as well as space/time/matter rhythms."[28] The word assemblage denotes that these are not merely qualities of the archives and the material within them but rather a *process* that involves researchers. Encountering and engaging with an archive in various ways, at different times, through distinct lenses, and by asking diverse questions, researchers not only analyze the documents of life within it, but they also become part of the life of the archive, creating new assemblages in the process. Each encounter with an archive is a new beginning, the start of a new assemblage with the potential for unexpected outcomes that the researcher must be open to. Tamboukou argues that:

> Although we always go to the archive with some questions in mind, we should also let its documents surprise us, allow them to interrogate our a-priori judgements, understandings and prejudices and let them redirect our analytical paths and routes of interpretation.[29]

Methodologically, this means adopting an open and flexible approach to research that is informed by the rhythms of the archive and the individual researcher's

---

[27] PIZ 44.5g, p. 5.
[28] Maria Tamboukou, "Archival Rhythms: Narrativity in the Archive," in *The Archive Project: Archival Research in the Social Sciences*, ed. Niamh Moore, Andrea Salter, Liz Stanley, and Maria Tamboukou (London and New York: Routledge, 2017), 93.
[29] Maria Tamboukou, "Reassembling Documents of Life in the Archive," *European Journal of Life Writing* 6 (2017): 1–19, 4, accessed October 31, 2024. https://doi.org/10.5463/ejlw.6.215

engagement with the material within it. Tamboukou also stresses the importance of embracing the multi-modality of archival research by considering archival material in different formats. Through my past encounters with the PIZ and ZL archives, I have developed a sense of some of the rhythms – for instance, the assemblages of institutional practices and power/knowledge relations – of the lives of and in archives. "Mapping" these rhythms has served both as a method for analyzing this material and been a result of my research and continues to be so in this analysis. In this chapter, I continue this mapping of the PIZ and ZL archives by asking them different research questions to gain a better understanding of how knowledge of the Nazi atrocities was circulated during the early postwar period between PIZ and other organizations, including other survivor historical commissions.

The analysis is divided into two main parts. The first part identifies rhythms in the correspondence that begin to reveal institutional practices and hierarchies that had a bearing on which knowledge was circulated in the context of PIZ and how. It considers the correspondence both from a bird's eye view and through close readings of select correspondence to gain an understanding of how the material breaks down into various categories linked to recipient and sender, such as gender, religion, nationality, and language. These findings are extrapolated in the second part of the analysis, which adopts an actor-centered approach to elucidate how knowledge was communicated at PIZ and by whom, thereby enabling me to address the specific research questions.[30]

Mapping the PIZ and ZL Archives

The PIZ and ZL archives are thoroughly cataloged in extensive archive lists.[31] This means that these lists are already maps that can be used to navigate their respective archives. But just like road maps, archival maps are traversed differently by various users. Through specific research questions, researchers do not merely follow an existing map, they also contribute to the mapping of the archives.[32] Since my research questions involve gaining an understanding of gender and other differences in the context of institutional, social, and knowledge hierarchies, it is

---

30 Lässig, "The History of Knowledge," 43–44.
31 "[Archival description for] Zygmunt Łakocińskis arkiv," (Lund, Sweden: Lund University Library), accessed October 31, 2024, http://urn.kb.se/resolve?urn=urn:nbn:se:alvin:portal:record-64405; "Archival description: The Polish Research Institute in Lund (Polski Instytut Zrodlowy [sic] w Lund, PIZ)" (Lund, Sweden: Lund University Library), accessed October 31, 2024, https://www.ub.lu.se/sites/ub.lu.se/files/2020-11/PIZ_archival_description.pdf
32 Tamboukou, "Archival Rhythms."

through these categories that I map the PIZ and ZL archives in this part of the analysis.

In the PIZ archive, most of the correspondence is organized into clear categories across five volumes, 46 to 50, and dispersed in three others, 43 to 45.[33] For example, the overarching category for volumes 46 to 47 reads "Letters and documents exchanged between PIZ and authorities, institutions and organizations." The sub-categories include, for example, volume 46 "Letters and documents: Sweden," under which several additional sub-categories can be found, such as volume 46:8 "Letters/documents to/from World Jewish Congress: Historical Commission, Stockholm 1946" and volume 46:11 "Letters/documents to/from Rada Uchodzstwa Polishiego w Szqwcji [sic] (Polish Council for Refugees in Sweden), Stockholm, 1945–1973."[34] More general correspondence is found in volumes 48 to 50 "Correspondence between PIZ and private individuals." This analysis does not use these latter volumes extensively, instead focusing on examining the correspondence in volumes 43 to 47, as this involves exchanges between the repatriates associated with PIZ and/or Łakociński and external actors and organizations. The correspondence in the ZL archive naturally includes a large amount of Łakociński's personal correspondence, as well as correspondence submitted to the editorial team of the Polish-language publication *Polak*, which was founded by Łakociński.[35] This material, however, is outside the present scope. From the ZL archive, this analysis only considers Ludwika Broel-Plater's early postwar correspondence.[36]

On the PIZ side of the correspondence, all individuals were Polish. Accordingly, many letters written in Polish passed between PIZ and Polish individuals and organizations. Correspondence with Polish governmental and other organizations in Sweden, such as the Interim Treasury Committee for Polish Questions in Stockholm, the Polish Aid Committee in Sweden (Polski Komitet Pomocy w Szwecji), and the Polish Council for Refugees in Sweden (Rada Uchodźstwa Polskiego w Szwecji), was primarily handled by Łakociński in his capacity as head of PIZ.[37] He was also the primary correspondent with Polish organizations and indi-

---

33 PIZ archival description, 32–80.
34 Ibid, 38–39, 45, 47. Should read: *Rada Uchodźstwa Polskiego w Szwecji*.
35 Ibid, 71–80.
36 This material – Broel-Plater's personal archive – is contained in five volumes (41–45) in the Łakociński archive. In addition to her material, one of the volumes (41) also includes material related to her death, including tributes written by Zygmunt Łakociński. See Victoria Van Orden Martínez, "An Eternally Grateful Refugee? Silences in Swedish Public Discourse and the (De)Historicization of Polish-Swedish Activist Ludwika Broel-Plater," in *Forced Migrants in Nordic Histories* ed. Johanna Leinonen et al. (Helsinki: Helsinki University Press, 2025), 203–223.
37 For instance, PIZ 46:9, 46:10, 46:11, 46:12.

viduals in Poland and around the world.[38] However, there are exceptions to this pattern. For example, Bożysław Kurowski and Krystyna Karier – responsible for legal matters and general correspondence, respectively – corresponded with Polish organizations in countries such as Germany and Belgium, and they both wrote letters to the Polish Red Cross.[39] Karier also corresponded with the Institute of National Remembrance (Instytut Pamięci Narodowej, IPN) in Warsaw, as did Łakociński.[40] Broel-Plater, who was responsible for camp vocabulary and the history of PIZ, and Karier also engaged in limited communications with Polish publications and organizations in Sweden, Britain, and Uruguay.[41] The bulk of the PIZ associates' written communication in Polish with Polish individuals and organizations is of a less formal nature compared to that of Łakociński; that is, in correspondence between Łakociński, other Polish repatriates in Sweden, and Poles in the diaspora.[42] An exception to this is Melchior's official correspondence – in her role as head of the Jewish section of PIZ – with fellow Pole Nella Rost, who was the head of the Jewish Historical Commission in Stockholm.[43]

Of course, PIZ engaged in extensive correspondence with organizations and individuals of various nationalities and in different languages. Łakociński was responsible for correspondence with Swedish individuals and organizations, both as the head of PIZ and as the only person who could correspond in Swedish.[44] Correspondence between Łakociński and the Norwegian Association of Political Prisoners in Oslo was carried out in Swedish on his part and Norwegian on theirs, mainly focusing on the two organizations' activities and collection procedures.[45] He corresponded in English with individuals and organizations in the United States, such as the Hoover Institute and Library at Stanford University (where the PIZ testimonies were sent for safekeeping between 1949 and 1972), and in Swedish, English, and German with the Dutch Legation in Stockholm regarding Dutch citizens interned in Ravensbrück.[46] In addition to Łakociński, PIZ employees Broel-Plater, Karier, and Helena Dziedzicka (who was responsible for correspondence in English and French) also communicated to a relatively limited extent across national and language barriers. Karier and Dziedzicka both corresponded

---

38 For instance, PIZ 47:6, 47:7, 47:8, 47:9, 47:10, 47:12.
39 For instance, PIZ 47:11b, 47:11d, 47:5.
40 PIZ 47:4.
41 For instance, PIZ 46:13b, 47:12a, 47:11 b.
42 PIZ 44:3, 48–50; ZL 41.
43 PIZ 46:8.
44 PIZ 46:1 to 46:6.
45 PIZ 47:2.
46 PIZ 47:14, 46:7.

in English with Major A.K. Mant at the War Crimes Investigation Unit in Germany regarding the Hamburg Ravensbrück Trial.[47] Broel-Plater also corresponded in French, as seen in her communications with Germaine Tillion.

Except for Luba Melchior, all repatriates employed as part of PIZ were Catholic, while Łakociński was a Protestant. Melchior was placed in charge of "Jewish matters" for PIZ, which meant that the correspondence involving Jewish organizations should have been handled by her. However, Łakociński was also involved with this correspondence. Together with Melchior, he signed or co-signed several letters to Nella Rost at the Jewish Historical Commission in Stockholm.[48] He also sent a letter, without Melchior's involvement, to the Jewish Historical Commission in Munich, although no response is to be found in the archives.[49] Finally, he corresponded with Dr. Jacob Robinson at the Institute of Jewish Affairs (IJA) in New York (again, without Melchior's involvement) to request financial support for the "Jewish Section" of PIZ headed by Melchior.[50] Beyond this communication, there is no other external correspondence between Łakociński or the non-Jewish PIZ employees, on the one hand, and Jewish individuals or organizations, on the other. Moreover, Melchior's extant correspondence with Jewish organizations is limited to the Jewish Historical Commission in Stockholm. In short, the primary actors corresponding with PIZ were non-Jewish individuals and organizations. It has already been shown that Łakociński corresponded with many Polish organizations in Sweden, Poland, and elsewhere. Ludwika Broel-Plater's personal correspondence also contains letters between herself and Polish organizations and individuals. Some of these pertain to religious or spiritual matters that she was concerned with as a Catholic.[51]

As revealed thus far in the analysis, only four of the seven women – Luba Melchior, Krystyna Karier, Ludwika Broel-Plater, and Helena Dziedzicka – and two of the three men – Zygmunt Łakociński and Bożysław Kurowski – were engaged in external correspondence to any notable degree. Of these, Kurowski has the least amount of extant correspondence in the archives, followed by Dziedzicka. On the other hand, as we have already seen, Łakociński – in his role as head of PIZ and as the only person with roots in Sweden – was the most prolific correspondent, as the sender and receiver of most of the letters to and from Polish and Swedish organizations. Given the conditions at the time, the individuals he corresponded with were primarily men in positions comparable to his own,

---

47 PIZ 47:1.
48 PIZ 46:8.
49 Ibid.
50 PIZ 47:13.
51 ZL 41.

such as academics, heads of institutes, etc. In the few cases where a woman was his equal, he usually shared the responsibility for correspondence with the female repatriates at PIZ. As we have seen, this was true in the case of Nella Rost, whom he continued to correspond with even though it dealt with "Jewish matters," which were technically the responsibility of Melchior. Similarly, he did not fully delegate correspondence with Major Mant to Karier and Dziedzicka but continued to engage in active correspondence. Likewise, he and Karier shared responsibility for corresponding with Polish historian Wanda Kiedrzyńska at the Institute of National Remembrance (IPN) in Warsaw.

By mapping the correspondence, patterns have emerged related to the institutional dynamics and hierarchies within PIZ. Even though more women than men were involved in the PIZ correspondence, Łakociński held the dominant position in terms of volume. He was also heavily involved with the women's correspondence, at least between 1945 and 1947, when most of the correspondence analyzed was written. Although Karier, Melchior, and Dziedzicka had all been made responsible for some type of correspondence – general correspondence, correspondence with Jewish organizations, and correspondence in English and French, respectively – the archives reveal that these responsibilities were, in fact, shared with Łakociński.

In late 1946, PIZ lost the funding from the Swedish Labor Market Commission that enabled it to employ the repatriates. Although some of the repatriates continued to work without remuneration for various lengths of time, most of them eventually left Sweden and/or PIZ behind. By 1949, Ludwika Broel-Plater was the only remaining repatriate involved with PIZ. Łakociński also became less involved with PIZ, in part because his work took him away from Lund. The result was that Broel-Plater was primarily responsible for carrying on the work of PIZ – albeit in a limited way and without compensation – until her death in 1972.[52] Her correspondence from the late 1940s and early 1950s reflects this shift for PIZ with regard to responsibility as it occurred.[53] However, the archives demonstrate that Łakociński through his continued correspondence with Polish organizations around the world never fully relinquished his position as head of PIZ.[54]

---

52 Martínez, "An Eternally Grateful Refugee?"
53 ZL 41.
54 For instance, PIZ 47:4 (1949–1969), 47:9, 47:10c, 47:11f, 47:12.

Knowledge Actors and Institutional Hierarchies

The findings of the archival mapping provide important insight into how the formal institutional hierarchy of PIZ, which officially divided the responsibility for external correspondence between Łakociński and five of the nine PIZ workgroup employees, did not necessarily bear out in practice. This, however, did not entail departing from hierarchical networks. Rather, rigid hierarchies were the norm in the official, external correspondence of PIZ. Historian Lorraine Daston argues that epistemological hierarchies are often intertwined with social hierarchies (and, I would add, institutional hierarchies) that "rank knowers and the epistemic virtues they are expected to display."[55] Within institutional hierarchies, individuals play certain "roles" as defined by the organization, both through specific responsibilities and through knowledge cultures embedded in a particular context.[56] The result is that individuals act as specific types of knowledge actors – individuals involved in the production and circulation of knowledge – depending on the dynamics of the situation in which they find themselves.[57]

The first part of the analysis reveals that Łakociński was heavily involved in PIZ correspondence with external individuals and entities, including when such correspondence was supposed to be the domain of the repatriates working for PIZ. He acted as a knowledge gatekeeper – a knowledge actor who controls the circulation of knowledge in a particular context.[58] In this case, Łakociński shaped the institutional hierarchy through which knowledge was circulated, affecting what, how, and to whom knowledge was exchanged through formal PIZ correspondence. This is especially evident in the case of Luba Melchior. Although she was ostensibly responsible for Jewish matters – including correspondence with

---

55 Lorraine Daston, "Comment," in *Debating New Approaches to History*, ed. Marek Tamm and Peter Burke (London: Bloomsbury Academic, 2020), 176.
56 Martin Mulsow, "History of Knowledge," in *Debating New Approaches*, ed. Marek Tamm and Peter Burke (London: Bloomsbury Academic, 2020), 162–163.
57 Johan Östling et al., "Introduction: Revisiting agency in the history of knowledge," in *Knowledge Actors: Revisiting Agency in the History of Knowledge*, ed. Johan Östling et al. (Lund, Sweden: Nordic Academic Press, 2023), 12. See also, for instance, Marian Füssel, *Wissen: Konzepte, Praktiken, Prozesse, Historische Einführungen* (Frankfurt: Campus, 2021); Philipp Sarasin, "Was ist Wissensgeschichte?" *Internationales Archiv für Sozialgeschichte der deutschen Literatur* 36, no. 1 (2011): 159–172, accessed February 26, 2025, https://www.zgw.ethz.ch/fileadmin/ZGW/PDF/sarasin_wissensgeschichte_2011.pdf; Stephanie Zloch, "Migrationswissen: Das Beispiel der Bundesrepublik Deutschland aus zeithistorischer Sicht," in *Aus Politik und Zeitgeschichte* 71, no. 3–4 (2021), accessed February 26, 2025, https://www.bpb.de/shop/zeitschriften/apuz/wissen-2021/325611/migrationswissen/
58 Simone Lässig, "The History of Knowledge," 44.

other Jewish organizations – Łakociński participated in the correspondence with Nella Rost at the Stockholm Jewish Historical Commission and wrote directly (and without Melchior's involvement) to other Jewish organizations and individuals. In previous research, I have argued that Łakociński was interested in the efforts of the Jewish historical commissions and wanted to have more contact with them to compare methodologies and share material.[59] This is the reason why he initiated contact with Nella Rost and sent the letter to the Central Historical Commission in Munich in June 1946.[60] He was also, as already shown, interested in developing and expanding the "Jewish section" of PIZ, and this is why he appealed directly to Jacob Robinson at the IJA in New York for potential funding.

While knowledge gatekeepers can be individuals seeking power over the circulation of knowledge for negative reasons, they can also be benevolent figures. Łakociński almost certainly belonged to the latter category of knowledge gatekeepers. There is no indication that his direct involvement in the bulk of external correspondence was anything other than well-intended, as he appears to have respected all institute employees, regardless of gender or religion. Yet, good intentions are not incompatible with maintaining power and authority, as demonstrated by the concept of benevolent sexism. Benevolent sexism differs from hostile sexism in the sense that it "does not require that individual men consciously intend to control or dominate women. Gender inequality becomes routinized through the widespread diffusion and acceptance of sexist ideology."[61] In workplaces, benevolent sexism "subtly [filters] women into low status, low power positions."[62] As in most institutional structures at the time, few women held top positions in the organizations that PIZ communicated with. Thus, official correspondence between organizations often took place between men in positions of authority, who acted as figureheads and decision-makers even though women did much of the behind-the-scenes work.[63]

The findings of this analysis demonstrate that the institutional hierarchy at PIZ reflects the gendered social and institutional structures of the period because

---

[59] Martínez, "Afterlives," 144–147.

[60] PIZ 46:8, letter to the Central Historical Commission in Munich, in Polish, signed by Łakociński, and dated June 10, 1946.

[61] For instance, Rachel A. Connor, Peter Glick P, and Susan T. Fiske, "Ambivalent Sexism in the Twenty-First Century," in *The Cambridge Handbook of the Psychology of Prejudice*, ed. Chris G. Sibley and Fiona Kate Barlow, Cambridge Handbooks in Psychology (Cambridge: Cambridge University Press, 2016), 295–320, 299.

[62] Kristen Jones et al., "Negative consequence of benevolent sexism on efficacy and performance," *Gender in Management: An International Journal* 29 (2014): 171–189, 172, accessed February 26, 2025, https://doi.org/10.1108/GM-07-2013-0086

[63] See, for instance, Jockusch, *Collect and Record*, 186. See also Cohen, "Rachel Auerbach," 220.

this is how Łakociński arranged and administered it. Although Melchior, Karier, and Dziedzicka had all been assigned "responsibility" for some aspect of correspondence, they were essentially secretaries for Łakociński and PIZ with little power to take direct initiative on behalf of the institute. This helps explain why the informal networks, especially of the female PIZ employees, having been utilized with such positive results in the internal communications – such as the establishment of the postwar collection and documentation efforts and the gathering of witness testimonies – were not utilized to the same extent in the external correspondence. The example of the Mittwerda List is obviously a notable exception. However, that was an *incoming* request made and received at a time when Broel-Plater, rather than Łakociński, was primarily responsible for the operations of PIZ. By that time, he had at least partly relinquished his role as knowledge gatekeeper, which he then shared with Broel-Plater. Moreover, Tillion in her letter indicates that the French Examining Magistrate *asked her* to use her personal connections to obtain the list, supporting the idea that these types of initiatives came from above in this context.

Łakociński's gatekeeping may have prevented better communication and knowledge circulation with and among Jewish survivor historical commissions and other Jewish institutions and individuals. Apart from Nella Rost, whom Melchior met with in person and shared PIZ testimonies, Łakociński's personal outreach to Jewish organizations was unsuccessful.[64] For instance, he received no response from the Jewish Historical Commission in Munich. He did receive a response from Robinson at the IJA but no assistance. The only other contact with a Jewish organization was facilitated by Luba Melchior's link to the Council of Jewish Associations of Belgium in Brussels (Conseil des Associations Juives de Belgique), which was affiliated with the World Jewish Congress. Melchior took a temporary leave of absence from PIZ to work with this organization, which resulted

---

64 As shown by historian Johannes Heuman, after Nella Rost's departure in 1951, the Stockholm commission ceased to exist and its archive was dispersed, parts of it presumed lost or destroyed. In her continued capacity with the World Jewish Congress, Rost took some of the commissions' documents with her when she left Sweden. See Heuman, "In Search of Documentation." Among these were several testimonies that originated with PIZ, including at least five that Luba Melchior had been responsible for. These were among the ones that Nella Rost sent to Joseph Wulf in the 1970s, which is why they are now part of the Joseph Wulf papers at the Central Archives for Research on the History of the Jews in Germany (Zentralarchiv zur Erforschung der Geschichte der Juden in Deutschland).

in one testimony in the PIZ collection given by a Polish survivor living in Belgium.⁶⁵ The result was that, in contrast to the religious crossover that occurred in the internal efforts to collect witness testimonies, there was very limited circulation of knowledge between PIZ and the large number of Jewish survivor historical commissions. Moreover, the minimal communication with other Jewish organizations came to very little. The reason may at least in part be found in the sense of distrust found in some Jewish efforts with regard to non-Jewish actors, whom, Jockusch writes, they feared "might have an interest in denying the historical truth, distorting the facts, or barring Jewish historians from access to the evidence."⁶⁶ Had Łakociński fully handed "responsibility" for Jewish matters to Melchior, it is possible that trust could have been established between PIZ and similar Jewish initiatives and organizations, leading to the circulation of knowledge between them.

While the repatriates employed by PIZ took a backseat to Łakociński in terms of corresponding with other organizations, this does not mean that they were not also knowledge actors in the circulation of knowledge through PIZ's external correspondence. To begin with, whether they corresponded with various individuals on their own or as co-signers with Łakociński, they were involved in the transnational circulation of knowledge concerning the Nazi atrocities and how this knowledge was being collected and used in various contexts. I suggest that they were what might be called behind-the-scenes knowledge actors, and that they were recognized as such by Łakociński. We can look at this in at least two ways. First, Łakociński acknowledged to his male correspondents how essential the women repatriates working for PIZ were to the Institute and its operations.⁶⁷ In his correspondence with Jacob Robinson at the IJA, for example, Łakociński in his appeals for funding repeatedly mentions Melchior and the importance of her work with PIZ.⁶⁸ Second, there is evidence that the limited amount of correspondence that occurred between the female repatriates of PIZ and other institutions benefited knowledge circulation in the longer term. One example is the five PIZ

---

65 PIZ Record of Witness Testimony 492, datelined Brussels, September 4, 1946, attributable to Luba Melchior, accessed October 31, 2024, http://urn.kb.se/resolve?urn=urn:nbn:se:alvin:portal:record-103889. For more, see Martínez, "Documenting the Documenter."
66 Jockusch, *Collect and Record*, 131.
67 One example of this pertains to a woman not mentioned in this study, Helena Salska, whom Łakociński told a Swedish correspondent was "the soul of the whole company." See PIZ 46:4, Letter from Łakociński to Sven Dahl, in Swedish, dated September 1, 1945.
68 PIZ 47:13, Letter from Zygmunt Łakociński to Dr. Robinson of the World Jewish Congress Historical Commission, in Polish, dated November 12, 1946, p. 1; PIZ 47:13, Letter from Zygmunt Łakociński to Dr. Robinson of the World Jewish Congress Historical Commission, in Polish, dated November 12, 1946, p. 2.

testimonies gathered that are now in the Joseph Wulf papers at the Central Archives for Research on the History of the Jews in Germany (Zentralarchiv zur Erforschung der Geschichte der Juden in Deutschland). Melchior shared these with Nella Rost, who later shared them with Wulf.[69] Ultimately, however, as important as the repatriates' knowledge may have been and as much as it may have influenced PIZ, its operations, and even Łakociński's correspondence, the circulation of this knowledge among other institutes and historical commissions was left largely in the hands of Łakociński in the first years following the Second World War and the Holocaust.

This analysis demonstrates that PIZ adhered to standard social and institutional norms in its external communications. That said, women were in other ways actively involved with postwar collection and documentation initiatives, among them many survivors, such as Rachel Auerbach, Miriam Novitch, and Eva Reichmann.[70] Moreover, during Germaine Tillion's time as a repatriate in Sweden immediately after the war, she conducted her own initiative to collect "detailed depositions" from other former prisoners of Ravensbrück.[71] Yet, at least in the PIZ archive, there is no evidence of any correspondence between these women and anyone at PIZ, with the exception of the 1949 correspondence between Germaine Tillion and Broel-Plater. Acknowledging the possibility that not all correspondence remained in the PIZ and ZL archives, this suggests that the networks of the PIZ workgroup – male and female alike – were primarily Polish, as the correspondence in the PIZ archive actually points to. It is possible that the narrow, national focus of PIZ was at least part of the reason why women's networks were not deployed in external correspondence, which had been the case internally. As Polish women, few if any of the members of these networks had any institutional power or authority, particularly since most of them were refugees themselves.

Conclusion: Unexpected Results

This chapter has sought to gain a better understanding of the role of women's informal networks, activated through correspondence during the early postwar

---

[69] See, for instance, Zentralarchiv zur Erforschung der Geschichte der Juden in Deutschland, Heidelberg, Nachlaß Joseph Wulf, B2-1, Serie C, 390, 393, 394, 498.
[70] See, for instance, Cohen, "Rachel Auerbach"; Geva, "Documenters, Researchers and Commemorators"; Schmidt "'We Are All Witnesses."
[71] Emma Kuby, *Political Survivors: The Resistance, the Cold War, and the Fight against Concentration Camps after 1945* (Ithaca, NY and London: Cornell University Press, 2019), 26.

period, in the circulation of knowledge – both about the Nazi atrocities and the efforts themselves (methods, materials, etc.) – between PIZ and other similar initiatives, especially those conducted by survivors of Nazi persecution. Analyzing the PIZ correspondence while considering the interplay of gender, religion, and other differences, the chapter also looks at to what extent external communications were conducted across these categories. The findings indicate that unlike the internal PIZ operations, the external operations were not to any notable extent carried out across religious (e.g., Jewish and non-Jewish) or even cultural boundaries. Likewise, while the women repatriates associated with PIZ utilized networks of resistance and support in the establishment and internal operations of PIZ as a survivor historical commission, these networks were only used to a limited degree in external correspondence. Rather, external correspondence at PIZ was conducted through a hierarchical institutional structure in which the role of women was to support the role of Łakociński as head of the institute. The example presented at the beginning of this chapter, in which hierarchical networks were intentionally bypassed in order to expedite knowledge circulation – was the exception, at least where PIZ was concerned. The kind of cultural and identity boundary crossings I observed with regard to the gathering of testimonies and the internal work of PIZ are not to any significant degree repeated in the external correspondence. This lack of crossover contributed to inhibiting knowledge circulation between, for example, Jewish and non-Jewish initiatives.

The results of this analysis are unexpected. My previous findings on the important role of networks of resistance and support in the internal operations of PIZ, and thus also regarding the circulation of knowledge about the Nazi atrocities in the postwar period, were partly what encouraged me to ask the questions considered in this chapter. To me, the correspondence between Tillion and Broel-Plater seemed like an early indicator that non-hierarchical networks might also have played an important role in how various forms of knowledge circulated between other institutions dealing with similar issues in the early years following the Second World War and the Holocaust. It was thus essential for this analysis that I keep in mind that each encounter with an archive is a new beginning – a chance to ask new questions that requires an openness to the rhythms of the archive, not least to discontinuities, ruptures, and breaks.[72] As suggested by Tamboukou, "the events that erupt in the process of doing archival research often radically change our practices, our prior knowledges, as well as the objects of our inquiry."[73] The methodological mapping of the PIZ correspondence with other in-

---

72 Tamboukou, "Archival Rhythms."
73 Ibid., 84.

stitutions did indeed reveal unexpected results, not least that women's informal networks of support and resistance were rarely deployed in the correspondence between PIZ and other organizations.

These findings provide better insight into the complex institutional dynamics at PIZ and the ways in which knowledge of the Nazi atrocities and the documentation of these was circulated between PIZ and similar initiatives, including other survivor historical commissions. They also provide important insight into the limits of the women's informal networks in the organizational structure of PIZ. Moreover, the findings create a clearer picture of how the national nature of the PIZ initiative to some extent inhibited the circulation of knowledge across national and religious lines. Ultimately, at least as far as PIZ was concerned, exchanges such as that between Ludwika Broel-Plater and Germaine Tillion, which helped convict Fritz Suhren, were the exception rather than the norm. Further studies of the PIZ correspondence are clearly needed to gain a more complete picture of the institutional dynamics and the role of women and others who worked behind the scenes with the essential day-to-day work of the institute. Similar studies of the institutional dynamics in other documentation efforts and a closer analysis of communications between these initiatives would also broaden the fields of Holocaust Aftermath studies, migrant knowledge, and gender history, as well as the intersections between these.

Victoria Van Orden Martínez is a researcher at the Department of History at Lund University in Sweden. Her current research focuses on how survivors of Nazi persecution who became migrants and refugees after the war were involved in various sociohistorical processes, with a focus on gender and other differences. Victoria is currently working on a project concerning female survivors of Nazi persecution who were medical professionals during and after the Second World War. The aim of this project is to gain insight into how their wartime experiences impacted their lives and careers in medicine and science.

Christine Schmidt
Gender and the Materiality of Witnessing: The Wiener Library and Postwar Holocaust Knowledge

Abstract: In the mid-1950s, the Wiener Library launched a project led by German-Jewish refugee scholar Eva Reichmann to collect eyewitness accounts by survivors of Nazi persecution. This chapter examines the impact and intersection of gender on the Library's postwar collecting activities, in particular with regard to the material contexts and challenges related to their implementation (networking, administrating, appraising, describing, cataloging, indexing, and other acts of archiving – all forms of "unseen labor" in this context often carried out by women). Based on extensive correspondence in the Library's institutional archive, analyzed through cultural and social historical frameworks, it is possible to map influences that shaped the creation and dissemination of the eyewitness reports collection. The role of gender in this intellectual transfer and knowledge production remains under-explored, and the more than 1,200 accounts and related correspondence, which document building this collection, provide a rich corpus to better understand the lesser-known contributions of German-Jewish women who were part of the orbit of the Library and who created and disseminated Holocaust knowledge after the war.

Keywords: Holocaust, correspondence, archives, gender, eyewitness accounts, German-Jewish history

Introduction

Nearly a decade after other post-Second World War historical documentation efforts embarked on their work of recording survivor accounts, the Wiener Library (now The Wiener Holocaust Library) in London in the mid-1950s launched an ambitious project to collect written eyewitness accounts from survivors of Nazi persecution and the Holocaust. This effort was based on the foundational work of the Library, which had extended the work of its predecessor organization, the Jewish Central Information Office (JCIO). The JCIO, led by German-Jewish scholar Dr. Alfred Wiener, resisted the Nazis and their sympathizers after being exiled from Berlin to Amsterdam, where it was established in 1933. It conducted information campaigns and other covert acts of collecting and disseminating information and was the first organization to document the Nazi persecution of the Jews.[1] Wiener and his colleagues carried on their activities after moving to London in 1939, just before the outbreak of the war, and their foundational work formed the basis of its activities going forward. By continuing to gather published works and documentation, the institution acted as an information service. It provided evidence to Allied governments during and after the war, including supporting war crimes trials, while also developing and promoting new research on the rise of the Nazis and the Holocaust.[2]

Building on its prior work, the Library's initiative to gather persecutee accounts after the war was led by the Library's first director of research, German-Jewish refugee and scholar Dr. Eva Reichmann. Supported by grants from the Conference on Jewish Material Claims against Germany (Claims Conference), the project began in London, from where Reichmann managed a small team of paid staff members and volunteers, including many women.[3] Interviewers were located throughout Europe and were paid to trace, contact, and persuade potential interviewees to participate. The process of constructing the Eyewitness Accounts (EWA) collection continued until the mid-1960s and proceeded in a concentric and centrifugal manner: the organizers began close to London using their network of professional and social contacts within middle-class, intellectual German-Jewish circles, to gradually go out further and further as the network of interviewers and interviewees widened and diversified. For example, it ended up including Romani survivors, those in "mixed" marriages, and other groups of witnesses.[4] The resulting collection placed in the Library's repository consists of more than 1,200 "reports" (including letters, poems, songs, and other types of written materials predominantly recorded in or translated from German and other languages).[5] The

---

[1] Ben Barkow, *Alfred Wiener and the Making of the Holocaust Library* (Elstree: Vallentine Mitchell, 1997); Michael Berkowitz, "Introduction," *The Fatherland and the Jews*, by Alfred Wiener (London: Granta Books, 2021), 3–43.
[2] Barkow, *Alfred Wiener*, 104–125.
[3] The JCIO had collected anonymous eyewitness accounts in the days and weeks following the November Pogrom in 1938. Christine Schmidt, "'We are all Witnesses': Eva Reichmann and the Wiener Library's Eyewitness Accounts Collection," in *Agency and the Holocaust – Essays in Honor of Debórah Dwork*, ed. Mary Jane Rein and Thomas Kühne (London: Palgrave Macmillan, 2020), 123–140.
[4] On the collection of Romani eyewitness accounts, see Ari Joskowitz, *Rain of Ash: Roma, Jews, and the Holocaust* (Princeton, NJ: Princeton University Press, 2023), 154–156.
[5] A considerable amount of the EWA collection has been translated into English and published on the digital resource *Testifying to the Truth*, https://testifyingtothetruth.co.uk (accessed October 29, 2024) and https://whlcollections.org (last accessed 7 July 2025).

project illustrates the reach and impact of transnational networks that German-speaking Jews sought to reconstitute after the Holocaust, and the methodology employed by the project organizers and staff exemplifies the efforts by German-Jewish refugees to shape Holocaust research and memory in the postwar period.[6]

Moreover, the EWA collection highlights the important yet under-researched role of German-speaking Jewish women in early postwar documentation efforts. Examining the activities of the project director and interviewers in terms of crafting and mediating the accounts demonstrates how cultural, professional, and other kinds of knowledge were transferred, such as shared personal experiences of forced migration and life in exile. This chapter argues that the EWA collection is a site of knowledge production shaped by former refugee women working for a diasporic German-Jewish institution displaced to Britain. This, in turn, makes it useful for assessing the impact of gender and culture on archives-building and producing knowledge after the Holocaust.[7] Andrea Westermann has noted that "[i]mmigrants, refugees, 'illegal aliens,' and other subaltern subjects inhabited and often actively interrogated the contradictory categories and conflicting goals confronting them. Consequently, researchers are coming to understand migrant responses as knowledge in its own right, even though it does not manifest itself in the learned books of émigré scholarship."[8] Furthermore, according to Westermann and Onur Erdur, there are three interconnected epistemological strands of migrant knowledge: knowledge about migrations, scientific knowledge carried from its original locale by means of migration, and knowledge that migrants carry before, during, or after being displaced.[9] The displacement of "Wiener's Library" (as the JCIO came to be called) to Amsterdam and then to London may be

---

[6] Christine Schmidt and Ben Barkow, "Early Holocaust Research, 'Testimony', and the Wiener Library," in *Crimes Uncovered: The First Generation of Holocaust Researchers*, ed. Hans-Christian Jasch and Stephan Lehnstaedt (Berlin: Metropol, 2019), 302–327; Schmidt, "'We Are All Witnesses'," 123–140; Christine Schmidt, "Refugees, Survivors, Archives: The Wiener Library in 1960s Britain," in *Holocaust Consciousness in Britain in the 1960s*, ed. Dan Stone and Johannes-Dieter Steinert (London: Bloomsbury, 2026).

[7] For a useful discussion on the limits and possibilities of archives as sites of knowledge production and a review of relevant literature, see Malin Thor Tureby, "To Hear with the Collection: The Contextualisation and Recontextualisation of Archived Interviews," *Oral History* 4, no. 2 (2013): 63–74.

[8] Andrea Westermann, "Migrant Knowledge: An Entangled Object of Research" (March 14, 2019), online at: https://migrantknowledge.org/2019/03/14/migrant-knowledge/#fnref-2.

[9] Andrea Westermann and Onur Erdur, "Migrant Knowledge: Studying the Epistemic Dynamics that Govern the Thinking in and around Migration, Exile, and Displacement," *Histories of Migrant Knowledge: Transatlantic and Global Perspectives, Bulletin of the German Historical Institute*, Supplement 15 (2020): 5–16. Further useful frameworks for understanding the relationship between migration and knowledge production can be found in Simone Lässig and Swen Stein-

considered migrant responses to the Nazi onslaught. And the EWA project launched by Reichmann as part of the Library's postwar activities reveals all three epistemological strands of migrant knowledge – migrant response, a reflection of carried scientific knowledge (particularly with regard to the disciplinary framing of the project through Reichmann's academic background), and evidence of the knowledge carried by migrants before and after being displaced.

The concept of "migrant knowledge" leads to Peter Burke's point that knowledge is never unmediated or transmitted without ambiguity, and I will examine the multiple points of mediation of the knowledge gathered for the EWA project.[10] This chapter analyzes extensive, recently cataloged correspondence and administrative documentation held in the Library's institutional archive, which chronicles the planning and implementation of the project and serves as a useful corpus from which to assess gendered and German-Jewish cultural interventions in archives-building after the Holocaust. The voice and perspective of Eva Reichmann and other contributors to the project are gleaned from this documentation as well as from Reichmann's published works. Using these different frames of analysis makes it possible to understand multiple influences on the development and implementation of this project, the changing role of the Library, and the frequently undervalued role of Jewish women as knowledge producers in the postwar diaspora.

Hence, I will examine the impact and intersection of gender on post-Holocaust archives-building efforts in relation to the material contexts and challenges concerning the implementation of the EWA project (networking, administrating, appraising, valuing, describing and cataloging, indexing, and other acts of archiving – all forms of "unseen labor" in this context often carried out by women). Building on the work of Michelle Caswell and Jessica Lapp, who have identified the ways in which archiving has been "feminized" and dismissed as a subservient "handmaiden" to scholarship, while also uncovering and challenging gendered assumptions regarding archival work, this essay focuses on the little-known but important contributions of the German-Jewish women working for and within the orbit of the Library in the 1950s and 1960s.[11]

---

berg, "Knowledge on the Move: New Approaches toward a History of Migrant Knowledge," *Geschichte und Gesellschaft* 43, no. 3 (2017): 313–346.

10 Peter Burke, *What is the History of Knowledge?* (Cambridge: Polity, 2015), 5–6.

11 Michelle L. Caswell, "'The Archive' is not an Archives: Acknowledging the Intellectual Contributions of Archival Studies," *Reconstruction* 16, no. 1 (2016): https://escholarship.org/uc/item/7bn4v1fk (accessed October 15, 2024); Jessica M. Lapp, "'Handmaidens of History': Speculating on the Feminization of Archival Work," *Archival Science* 19 (2019): 215–234.

Eva Reichmann and the (Forced) Migration of Knowledge

Eva Reichmann played a key role in the creation of the EWA collection, thereby solidifying the Library's position as an institution that not only collected evidence, chronicled the study of antisemitism, the rise and fall of Nazism, the Holocaust, and related topics but also compiled and disseminated its own original research after the war.[12] Her biography, briefly outlined here, demonstrates that her academic expertise, her experiences of forced migration and resettlement in Britain, and her social networks underpinned the creation of the EWAs for the Library.

Prior to fleeing to Britain in 1939, Reichmann (née Jungmann) had studied economics and sociology, earning her first doctorate from Heidelberg University in 1921 with a second to follow from the London School of Economics. Just like Alfred Wiener, she had joined the Centralverein deutscher Staatsbürger jüdischen Glaubens (CV), an important organization fighting for the rightful place of German Jews in German society, the civil rights of German Jews, and against rising antisemitism.[13] Although she was sympathetic to Zionism and the intellectual challenges it entailed for German Jewry, Reichmann firmly believed in the significance of the Jewish diaspora as a legitimate and positive "Jewish path," one that she did not see in a negative light or as a sign of the decline of Judaism but as something that had value and purpose in its own right.[14] Starting in 1933, she became the editor of *Der Morgen*, the monthly periodical focusing on a range of issues of Jewish interest, especially German-Jewish life under the Nazis. The CV not only shaped her professional life but also her personal circumstances, as this is where she met Hans Reichmann, who became her husband. Reichmann also worked for the Jewish Agency in Berlin as well as the Reich Representation of German Jews (Reichsvertretung der Deutschen Juden). This organization was led

---

12 Barkow, *Alfred Wiener*, 108–111; see also *The Wiener Library Bulletin*, issued between 1946 and 1981.

13 On Reichmann's biography, see, inter alia, Eva G. Reichmann, "Trägt ihn mit Stolz, den gelben Fleck," in *Die andere Erinnerung. Gespräche mit jüdischen Wissenschaftlern im Exil*, ed. Hajo Funke (Berlin: Fischer Taschenbuch, 1989), 311–335; Kirsten Heinsohn, "Biografien jüdischer Frauen: Eva Gabriele Reichmann (1897–1998) – eine jüdische Intellektuelle des 20. Jahrhunderts," *Medaon* 15 (2021): 28, http://www.medaon.de/pdf/medaon_28_heinsohn.pdf (accessed October 29, 2024); and Hannah Villette-Dalby, "German-Jewish Female Intellectuals and the Recovery of German-Jewish Heritage in the 1940s and 1950s," *The Leo Baeck Institute Year Book* 52, no. 1 (January 2007): 111–129.

14 Eva G. Reichmann, "Diaspora als Aufgabe," in *Grösse und Verhängnis deutsch-jüdischer Existenz: Zeugnisse einer tragischen Begegnung*, ed. Eva Reichmann (Heidelberg: Verlag Lambert Schneider GmbH, 1974), 46–47.

Figure 1: Eva Reichmann at the Wiener Library, 1952. Courtesy, Wiener Holocaust Library Collections.

by Rabbi Leo Baeck and served as an umbrella organization for coordinating Jewish groups in Germany starting in 1933. Her commitment to remaining in Germany was shaken when Hans was arrested during *Kristallnacht*, after which he was sent to the Sachsenhausen concentration camp. After she arranged for his release on the condition that the couple would emigrate, they settled in London and became embedded within the refugee German-Jewish community where they continued their activist work.

In 1945, Reichmann joined the Wiener Library as its first director of research (Figure 1). Wiener, Reichmann, and other German-Jewish colleagues sought to build a research institution based on the foundations laid by the JCIO's prewar and wartime collection efforts. After the war, Reichmann often traveled with Alfred Wiener to West Germany to promote interfaith dialogue and to give lectures eschewing the concept of collective guilt despite her personal experiences, even though returning to Germany permanently after the war was out of the question.[15] She continued to publish on the history of German Jewry and the legitimacy of the German-Jewish diaspora, defending the emancipation of Jews in Germany against

---

[15] Hannah Villette-Dalby, *Central Voices from the Margins: Hannah Arendt, Eva G. Reichmann, Eleonore Sterling, Selma Stern-Taeubler and German-Jewish Traditions in the Twentieth Century* (PhD Diss, University of Southampton, 2005), 132–136.

any insinuation of its failure.[16] Although she described her relationship with Germany as "complicated," she staunchly retained her German language, identity, and commitment to German-Jewish culture during her postwar life and work in Britain, both for the Library and for other institutions. As an academic who worked outside the academy largely due to forced exile, she nevertheless contributed significant scholarship on the history of antisemitism and the German-Jewish experience.[17] As argued by Joseph Malherek, émigré scholars forced by the Nazis to become intellectual refugees were "both victims of national exclusion and agents of scholarly analysis in a time of disintegrating liberal democracy, rising fascism, and the global specter of authoritarianism."[18] The EWA collection, being rich in its diverse imprints of the intellectual and cultural markers of Reichmann and other German-Jewish refugee women, is also important for understanding, as noted by Westermann and Erdur, "how place-specific material resources shaped the migrants' professional and economic engagements."[19]

With the appointment of Reichmann as research director, several initiatives emerged that positioned the Library as a significant and active early documentation center. As shown in previous research, survivor historical commissions in the postwar period were, at the highest ranks, dominated by men, among them historians and other academics. Women, on the other hand, were more numerous than men but less likely to hold high-profile positions in the commissions while also to a lesser degree being professional historians or academics in other fields. However, the archival and administrative work they carried out was the lifeblood of the commissions and included conducting interviews, collecting material, and working as archivists and secretaries.[20] In general, women's contributions to the survivor historical commissions have been under-analyzed, especially in comparison with the contributions by men, in part because the women's work often con-

---

[16] See the collection of writings, Reichmann, *Grösse und Verhängnis deutsch-jüdischer Existenz* (Heidelberg: Verlag Lambert Schneider GmbH).
[17] In addition to the works already cited, see Eva Reichmann, *Hostages of Civilization: The Social Sources of National Socialist Anti-Semitism* (London: Gollancz, 1950).
[18] Joseph Malherek, "Displaced Knowledge and its Sponsors: How American Foundations and Aid Organizations Shaped Emigre Social Research, 1933–1945," in *Histories of Migrant Knowledge: Transatlantic and Global Perspectives* (Washington, DC: GHI Bulletin, 2020), 113.
[19] Westermann and Erdur, "Migrant Knowledge," 16.
[20] Laura Jockusch, *Collect and Record! Jewish Holocaust Documentation in Early Postwar Europe* (Oxford: Oxford University Press, 2012), 5. See also Boaz Cohen, "Rachel Auerbach, Yad Vashem, and Israeli Holocaust Memory," in *Polin: Studies in Polish Jewry*, vol. 20: *Making Holocaust Memory*, ed. Natalia Aleksiun et al. (Liverpool: Liverpool University Press, 2007), 220; Victoria Van Orden Martínez, *Afterlives: Jewish and Non-Jewish Polish Survivors of Nazi Persecution in Sweden Documenting Nazi Atrocities, 1945–1946* (PhD diss, Linköping University, 2023).

cerns behind-the-scenes efforts required to launch and maintain such projects. As convincingly argued by Michelle Caswell, this devaluation may be understood further within the framework of "the construction of archival labor as a feminine service industry and archival studies (if it is ever acknowledged as existing) as imparting merely practical skills."[21] Even in instances where women occupied high-profile positions for long periods of time – such as in the case of Reichmann or Rachel Auerbach and Miriam Novitch – the significance of their work related to survivor historical commissions has for a long time been ignored. The reason for this, argues historian Sharon Geva, is because their task of documenting, researching, and commemorating the Holocaust "reflected distinctly feminine attributes" and that "their work as documenters took place behind the scenes."[22] This phenomenon is more widely reflected in the history of archives and institutions more broadly. Elizabeth Shepherd notes, for example, the lack of attention to the role of female archivists and their professional interventions that shaped the archival field in early twentieth-century England.[23] Therefore, a closer examination of the activities of Reichmann and other women involved in the project further increases our understanding of the role of women in archival knowledge production more generally.

As Reichmann aimed to fill what she viewed as gaps in the existing record, she saw the value of the eyewitness accounts as a chronicle of what had been previously unspoken but also as evidence for future researchers.[24] Building on her academic research and activating surviving Jewish communal defense networks, she launched the EWA collection project among several other important research and communal initiatives undertaken by the Library. The EWA project reveals how Reichmann thought "archivally" – even though she was not a professional archivist – and serves as an important locus for analyzing the relationship between gender and knowledge production by building archives. Although she has been presented "mainly [as] an organizer of knowledge" with regard to the collection of eyewitness accounts, I contend that Reichmann was a *producer* of knowledge in creating this collection (among her other work), which can be as-

---

21 Caswell, "'The Archive'," https://escholarship.org/uc/item/7bn4v1fk#main.
22 Sharon Geva, "'To collect the tears of the Jewish people': The Story of Miriam Novitch," *Holocaust Studies* 21, no. 1–2 (2015): 73–92, here 80.
23 Elizabeth Shepherd, "Hidden voices in the archives: Pioneering women archivists in early 20th-century England," in *Engaging with Records and Archives: Histories and Theories* (Cambridge: Cambridge University Press, 2018), 83–103. I here wish to thank the anonymous reviewer of this chapter for introducing this helpful reference.
24 Ciaran Trace, "On or Off the Record? Notions of Value in the Archive," in *Currents in Archival Thinking*, ed. Terry Eastwood and Heather MacNeil (Santa Barbara, CA: Libraries Unlimited, 2009), 47–68.

sessed through her and other individuals' recording of the material and its "organization" (or archiving).[25] Following Caswell, I analyze the intellectual contributions of a selection of German-Jewish women work in different ways contributed to the EWA project while focusing on their work as worthy of engagement in its own right, not solely as organizers "in service" to researchers, in order to understand multiple mediations shaping knowledge production at the Library in London (Figure 2).

Gender and the Materiality of Archiving

One way of orienting this study toward the impact of gender on the production and circulation of knowledge within the diaspora is to consider the materiality of archiving; in particular, the behind-the-scenes labor that supported gathering and preserving evidence after the Holocaust.[26] The preservation of this evidence and the work performed to make it accessible to researchers situates archiving as a kind of indispensable (and definitely not neutral) work that supported the establishment of Holocaust studies as an academic discipline – including in its earliest stages in contemporary German history and the study of antisemitism and fascism, as well as a discipline with its own intellectual foundations and legacies. The EWA collection is useful for further exploring the gendered material conditions of archiving, since it was led by a German-Jewish woman scholar whose work was later subsumed by a male-dominated field focusing on debates such as the decision-making process related to the "Final Solution," the history of the SS and the concentration camps, and resistance (especially German resistance) against the Nazis. As argued by Hannah Villette-Dalby, Reichmann was "neither [a] member of the male guild of historians nor working within mainstream German historical studies."[27] Moreover, many women contributed to the EWA project as interviewers, as interviewees, and as cataloguers and indexers, and their concerns shaped many of the project's outputs – for example, its methodological approaches, the contents of the interviews, and the index, which formed a descriptive taxonomy that enabled cross-referencing and searching of the collection.

---

25 Joskowitz, *Rain of Ash*, 156.
26 This follows Verne Harris's concept of "archives" focused on the external characteristics as well as the labor related to various interventions, such as preserving and cataloging. Verne Harris, "Genres of the Trace: Memory, Archives, and Trouble," *Archives and Manuscripts* 40, no. 3 (2012): 150.
27 Villette-Dalby, *Central Voices*, 15.

As noted above, the Claims Conference supported the project financially through a grant that, for the most part, was distributed to the Library in partnership with Yad Vashem, which had been established in 1953. In essence, Reichmann and the staff of the Library planned the gathering of the eyewitness accounts, after which these accounts were duplicated and "sold" to Yad Vashem in order to fund the work in arrears. Yad Vashem held and distributed the budget for the project, which was provided by the Claims Conference.[28] The Claims Conference grant funded the Library to pay the salaries for interviewers and cataloguers to process the collection. A full exploration of the cooperation with Yad Vashem and the Claims Conference is beyond the scope of this article, but the at times fraught relationship was managed by both Wiener and Reichmann through correspondence, contract negotiations, and in-person visits to the Library, facilitated by Marc Uveeler on behalf of the Claims Conference.[29] The negotiations with Yad Vashem and the Claims Conference situated the Library within the emerging landscape of a small number of contiguous and collecting institutions established in the early postwar era that had begun to gather materials, research, and publish about the Holocaust.[30] Indeed, the creation of Yad Vashem catalyzed cooperation with international institutions, such as the Library and the Centre de Documentation Juive Contemporaine in Paris, but also a competition of sorts between the emerging official memory institution in the Jewish state and organizations located elsewhere.[31] As a Jewish diasporic institution whose postwar funding – and at times, even location – was precarious, one should not underestimate the importance of the EWA project for the continued existence and reputation of the Library.[32]

---

28 Barkow, *Alfred Wiener*, 128–129; Schmidt, "'We are all Witnesses'," 126. The Library was one of the four institutions receiving Claims Conference funding under the category "Commemoration and Documentation of the Jewish Catastrophe" along with Yad Vashem in Israel, YIVO in New York, and the Centre de Documentation Juive Contemporaine in Paris. See also Wiener Holocaust Library (hereafter, WHL) 3000/7/2: Eyewitness testimony project correspondence, and WHL 3000/9/1/291: Correspondence with the Conference on Jewish Material Claims Against Germany.
29 Schmidt, "Refugees, Survivors, Archives"; Central Archives for the History of the Jewish People (CAHJP) CC-18528: Conference on Jewish Material Claims Against Germany/Yad Vashem Wiener Library Agreement.
30 Jockusch, *Collect and Record*, and Jason Lustig, *A Time to Gather: Archives and the Control of Jewish Culture* (Oxford: Oxford University Press, 2022).
31 See David Silberklang, "More than a Memorial: The Evolution of Yad Vashem," *Yad Vashem Quarterly Magazine* (Fall 2003): 6–7. On the public and parliamentary debate, see Roni Stauber, *The Holocaust in Israeli Public Debate in the 1950s: Ideology and Memory* (Elstree: Vallentine Mitchel, 2007), 67–77, 119–132.
32 Barkow, *Alfred Wiener*, 104–134; Schmidt, "Refugees, Survivors, Archives."

Reichmann drew on the academic disciplines of sociology and history, especially contemporary history, in order to develop the methodology for the project. Like other survivor historical commissions, the Library's project followed an academic historical methodology designed to ensure that the witness testimonies remained credible and were able to withstand the scrutiny of historians. Due to the involvement of many professional scholars, including historians, the methodologies adopted by the Library and other survivor historical commissions reflect the influence of traditional historical methods at the time, which meant setting guidelines for how "impartial collectors" should obtain "objective facts" from witnesses.[33] These methodologies might also reflect a disciplinary influence and transfer from sociological survey methods, including the Chicago School, which also emphasized qualitative methods and personal life history, given the close disciplinary links between contemporary history and sociology.[34] Reichmann was committed to the process of witnessing that recognized the value of interviewers' subjectivity as fellow victims of persecution, while arguing that only contemporaries could interpret the language of the Third Reich, particularly with regard to press, books, letters, and other personal documents, meaning there was a somewhat urgent need to record the witnesses. "Everything is coloured and distorted," she wrote.

> And only contemporaries can decipher the secret language. Experiential truth, personal opinion, and even feelings could not be committed to writing, at least not if they conflicted with the party line. Thus an immense vacuum was created, which must be, at least partly, filled as soon as possible.[35]

Both publicly and privately, Reichmann saw the purpose of gathering eyewitness accounts from the persecuted as a means not only to "fill in gaps" in the historical record rendered imperfect and fragmented by Nazism in order to thereby convey the truth "as it really was" (after Ranke), but also as a kind of memorial to a communal past, similar to other documentation projects looking upon "their accumu-

---

33 See, for instance, Jockusch, *Collect and Record*, 186–187 and Victoria Van Orden Martínez and Christine Schmidt, "Survivor-Interviewers as Companions of Misery: A Comparative View from Post-war England and Sweden," in *Survivors' Toil*, ed. Éva Kovacs and Natalia Aleksiun (Toronto: University of Toronto Press, 2026).
34 This disciplinary transfer requires further analysis. See Martin Bulmer, *The Chicago School of Sociology: Institutionalization, Diversity, and the Rise of Sociological Research* (Chicago: University of Chicago Press, 1984) and Alan Sica, "Defining Disciplinary Identity: The Historiography of US Sociology," in *Sociology in America: A History*, ed. Craig Calhoun (Chicago: University of Chicago Press, 2007).
35 Eva G. Reichmann, "We all Bear Witness," *AJR Information* IX, no. 100 (November 1954): 1.

lated documents and chronicles of the past as 'memorials' or 'gravestones' for their dead."[36]

Reichmann developed an administrative framework and guidelines for interviewing, outlined in internal meetings and memos as well as external appeals describing the structure and aims of the project, in addition to the psychological dimensions of interviewing in a non-coercive manner.[37] On February 18, 1957, she signed off the summary of a meeting she had held with other Library staff, including Dr. Leo Kahn, a German-Jewish refugee and lawyer by training who headed up the Library's project to catalog its copy of the Nuremberg Trial documents and who conducted some interviews; Bertha Cohn, another German-Jewish refugee who compiled bibliographies of scholarship for the Library and who also interviewed witnesses; and Elisabeth Zadek, a German-Jewish refugee originally from Berlin, formerly active in the Jüdische Frauenbund (League of Jewish Women) and Jüdische Waisenhilfe (Jewish Orphans' Aid), who was employed by the Library to conduct interviews.[38] The meeting outlined the status of the EWA project in fifteen points. These included taking inventory of the reports and the status of the compilation of each report; establishing the extent to which the reports had been analyzed, copied, and indexed by Zadek; the assignment of serial numbers by Cohn; classifying with regard to their readiness to duplicated for Yad Vashem and monitoring the transfer progress by Zadek; and numbering the reports.[39] The memo demonstrates Reichmann's central oversight of the project, which helped her establish and monitor the progress of the duplicate reports to Yad Vashem and thereby receive funds to further the project and the Library's work.

Another important facet of the archival work underpinning the project was the creation of cross-indexed terms identified from the interviews and described by the team. These are found on each cover sheet, the only standardized aspect of the reports, which contains basic information about the author, the title given by

---

36 Jockusch, *Collect and Record*, 187.
37 Eva Reichmann, "A Memo to all friends of the Wiener Library," May 1958, WHL 3000/7/2/1: Eyewitness Testimony Project: Administration.
38 18 February 1957, meeting notes, WHL 3000/7/2/1. Kahn also later worked on collections for the Imperial War Museum. See Suzanne Bardgett, "The Depiction of the Holocaust at the Imperial War Museum since 1961," *Journal of Israeli History* 23 (2004): 146–156. On his experiences of internment, see Leo Kahn, Oral History, 1979, Imperial War Museum, https://www.iwm.org.uk/collections/item/object/80004270. By Cohn, see, for instance, "Post-War Publications on German Jewry, Compiled on Behalf of The Wiener Library, 1966," *Leo Baeck Institute Year Book* 12, no 1. (January 1967). On Zadek's work for the Library, see correspondence in WHL 3000/9/1/1604: Correspondence with Elisabeth Zadek.
39 18 February 1957, meeting notes, WHL 3000/7/2/1.

the interviewer to the account, the interviewer's name, the date of when the interview was recorded and received, and a short abstract under "form and contents." This abstract included terms that were underlined: typically locations, people, and subjects. Even when the reports were in German, French, or other languages, the cover sheet was in English, as was the term index, apart from Nazi-related German terms and proper nouns. A review of the index developed based on these terms suggests an emerging taxonomy of the geographies ("sites of Nazi crimes") and experiences of the Holocaust, but also a suggestion that gendered experiences of the Holocaust were recognized by Zadek and others who contributed to the index, including "abortions (in camps)" with at least two interviews noted in relation to this subject and cross-listed as "pregnancies, interruption of"; "artificial insemination, experiments with"; "Aryan wives, demonstration in Berlin"; "'marriages' in camps"; "maternity hospital"; "rape"; "sexual assaults (on a Jewish girl by Latvian police)"; "sexual behavior in camps"; "women"; "women in concentration camps"; and "women, resistance of." Other interesting terms took note of emotional landscapes, including "angst" and "anxiety."[40]

The Wiener Library's institutional archive is replete with pages of Reichmann's correspondence with interviewers and project staff, while her appraisal and valuation of the submitted reports within the aims of the project and for the wider collection emerges throughout this extensive correspondence. From her letters to Zadek, who moved to Switzerland and would continue to contribute to the project as a freelancer while working at the Ecole d'Humanité, we see the ongoing material struggles to sustain the project through the reimbursement procedure facilitated by Yad Vashem, including its impact on the Library's cash flow to pay interviewers.[41] Reichmann attempted to curtail Zadek's apparent eagerness to systematically conduct interviews from different Swiss locations due to the additional travel and accommodation expenses that this would incur. In August 1958, Reichmann admonished Zadek, who seemed to have written to her about several interviews she planned to undertake, implying some impatience with the (lack of) timeliness of her submissions:

> Your enthusiasm and interest are not only appreciated by me, but also by Dr Wiener. But please remember that you should not allow yourself to be swept away with them without proper supervision. In my opinion, you will not be able to support yourself in Switzerland

---

40 EWA Index, WHL Collections.
41 Reichmann to Elisabeth ("Li") Zadek, 18 June 1958, WHL 3000/9/1/1604/12. Each travel expense incurred by Zadek had to be approved before being reimbursed: "You are aware of our chronic financial difficulties in this department. Unfortunately they are particularly acute at the moment, so unfortunately we cannot avoid such a regulation [. . .]"

Figure 2: Women working in the Wiener Library, London, 1950s. Courtesy of The Wiener Holocaust Library Collections.

with this work, unless you live almost for free and can use most of the fees as pocket money. It would certainly be very tempting for the Library, and especially for the eyewitness department, to be able to maintain a Swiss branch. But we cannot do that, and I have told you that repeatedly [. . .] I would like to be pleased about your plans, but they always worry me. Please understand, dear Miss Zadek. After all, so far only two average reports, as we both agreed, have emerged from all the plans and long letters. I have already told you how sorry I am that there are not more of them and that we therefore cannot transfer the full £25 to you.[42]

Reichmann, Wiener, and Zadek continued to correspond regarding various material challenges in the project, including the difficulties of transferring funds to Zadek internationally as well as the publication of an inaccurate news article written for the *Bern Tagblatt* by one of Zadek's interviewees, Dr. Franz Glaser. According to the exchanges, Glaser had interviewed Zadek informally after she had compiled his report after their interview, but he misrepresented several details about the Library, the project, and Zadek's own personal history. Wiener wrote to Zadek to ask her to refrain from speaking to the press in Bern without consulting the Library and first obtaining its permission, after which Zadek wrote an effusive apology. To prove her sincerity to Wiener and Reichmann, she included copies of her strident note to Glaser and to the editorial team at the *Tagblatt* asking for a retrac-

---

[42] Reichmann to Zadek, 21 August 1958, WHL 3000/9/1/1604.

tion.⁴³ It is clear from subsequent exchanges with other women working at the Library, such as Ilse Wolff, who created and disseminated bibliographies of published works in this emerging field, and Ruth Rudas that Zadek was worried that she had left an enduringly bad impression on Reichmann and Wiener. The letters paint a picture of Zadek as enthusiastic and wanting to impress them through her contributions to the EWA project, while Reichmann, although warm in her responses, was wary and reinforced the material boundaries and archival frameworks she had established and which sustained the project.

Gender and Witnessing

Zadek and the Library exchanged a further lengthy correspondence, not without friction, about the content and process for archiving another report being developed in Switzerland with an interviewee named "E.S." E.S. gave a lengthy (over 40 pages) report written in the first person, describing the persecution of her and her family first in Fiume (or Rijeka), their flight, and eventually their separation.⁴⁴ E.S. was deported to Auschwitz-Birkenau where she worked in the "Kanada" commando, sorting through the belongings of deportees. After being deported to and subsequently liberated from Theresienstadt, she was reunited with some of her family, and having been contacted by Zadek, she provided an interview in 1958. Regarding the experience of interviewing and developing this report, Zadek wrote to Wiener in September of that year:

> There is such a wealth of material that I can hardly manage it. Apart from the fact that the sessions with [E.S.] were tremendously exciting for both of us – for me, in living through this fate, for her in reliving it again – I now have to find my way through this factual material 'at home'. [. . .] It concerns unusual experiences even for us, and are at a highly human level.⁴⁵

In an exchange later that year, Reichmann called the report draft "extraordinary," particularly for its discussion of "Kanada" and the harrowing description of survival, which included graphic descriptions of fraught negotiations, includ-

---

43 Wiener to Elisabeth ("Li") Zadek, 14 July 1958, WHL 3000/9/1/1604/14.
44 For a fuller discussion of this account, see Christine Schmidt, "Historical Meaning Beyond the Personal: Survivor Agency and Mediation in the Wiener Library's Early Testimonies Collection," EHRI Document Blog, April 17, 2019, https://blog.ehri-project.eu/2019/04/17/historical-meaning-beyond-the-personal/ (accessed February 28, 2023). I have used the initials for this interviewee as she requested that her report remain anonymous.
45 Li (Elisabeth) Zadek to Alfred Wiener, September 1958, WHL 3000/7/2/4/20.

ing sexual barter, between prisoners.[46] Yet, equally compelling and significant as the contents of the report itself, the internal correspondence and materiality of the report demonstrate the relational aspects of the interview as well as E.S.'s perception of her own agency as she sought to maintain a certain amount of control over the afterlife of the narrative she had compiled together with Zadek.

After receiving the report, Reichmann first wrote to E.S. in a warm and compassionate manner, demonstrating Reichmann's sense of the historical value of what had been collected as well as her empathic care for the witness. Reichmann acknowledged that the report must have been tremendously difficult for E.S. to compile:

> I am still so completely under the impression of your terrible suffering that every word that I could thank you with for this [report] seems inadequate. [. . .] You have thus demonstrated that you have faced up to a moral task, which, as I hope, carries a reward in itself: You have helped to ensure that your experiences are now kept in an archive and preserved for posterity. They have thus received historical meaning beyond the personal.[47]

Reichmann closed another letter, laden with emotion, with the following: "the most important thing to me is that you find inner and outer peace, that you will get well and stay healthy and that the future will pay off much or even everything for everything you've suffered so bravely."

Yet the story of this report was far from over. Some years later, E.S. wrote to the Library to retract portions of the account, at which time C.C. Aronsfeld, who had succeeded Wiener as director, notified her that Reichmann had since left her position as director of research for the Library. The fact that the account had been copied in multiple locations meant that withdrawing it was not a straightforward process. And in Aronsfeld's view, moreover, the report was important for the historical record and should remain in the Library's collection.

For her part, E.S. was "surprised" and "disappointed" with the Library's position, emphasizing that in addition to allowing some personal aspects of the testimony that she had wished not to be included in the record to remain, she had wanted certain information that she felt Zadek had omitted from the final submission to be included. Due to these discrepancies, she marked her report "strictly confidential" (as of now, the report has not been published in the Library's online archive, nor is it available online in Yad Vashem's archive).[48] This is the only copy held in the Library's collection, and visual clues indicate parts that have been crossed out, explained, or underlined – likely by E.S.'s own hand. Although Reich-

---

46 Reichmann to Zadek, 24 October 1958; 10 December 1958, WHL 3000//9/1/1604.
47 Eva Reichmann to E.S., 10 December 1958, WHL 3000/9/1/1370.
48 See *Testifying to the Truth*, testifyingtothetruth.co.uk (accessed October 29, 2024).

mann in her remarks referred to the account as having "historical meaning beyond the personal," the correspondence with E.S. regarding the "afterlife" of her narrative brought the discussion back primarily to the "personal." The elements she wanted removed, she felt, reflected problematic personal opinions that she had expressed during her interview. Aronsfeld favored retaining the report in the archive nevertheless, and after a somewhat terse exchange during which E.S. acquiesced, the copy remained in the collection. Its materiality – the author's markings – is a testament to the fact that the subjectivity of the survivor-witness was integral to the report's authorship, even when the witness was ambiguous regarding its inclusion.[49] While E.S. exercised some agency over her narrative, the Library project – which continued after Reichmann's departure – tried to balance the subjectivities and feelings of the witnesses with its institutional priorities.[50] Had Reichmann remained involved in the project, one can imagine that she would have responded similarly to Aronsfeld; meaning that in this instance, archival and institutional priorities were more impactful than gender. It is also possible that the report collected by Zadek was revealing, candid, and focused on gendered experiences due to the fact that the interviewer, Zadek, was a woman.[51]

In addition to the administrative and financial constraints negotiated with contributors, the correspondence reveals how culture and gender were in some cases combined to shape the contents of the accounts and the process through which they were made accessible. For example, Ottilie Schönewald, a former member of the Jüdische Frauenbund (as were Reichmann and Zadek), wrote about her experiences organizing aid at railway stations to Jews who were deported during the *Polenaktion* in October 1938.[52] Like Reichmann, she had worked in communal defense organizations prior to the war and fled Germany after her husband was arrested during *Kristallnacht*. Her account offers a vivid description of the logistical challenges involved in providing aid to deportees before they embarked on the train journey across the border in 1938. She wrote candidly:

---

[49] Correspondence between C.C. Aronsfeld and E.S., 19 March 1962, WHL 3000/9/1/1370.
[50] Noah Shenker, *Reframing Holocaust Testimony* (Bloomington, IN: Indiana University Press, 2015).
[51] Martínez and Schmidt, "Companions."
[52] See Michal Frankl, "Citizenship of No Man's Land? Jewish Refugee Relief in Zbąszyń and East-Central Europe, 1938–1939," *S.I.M.O.N.* 7, no. 2 (2020): 37–49; Alina Bothe and Gertrud Pickhan, eds., *Ausgewiesen! Berlin, 28.10.1938. Die Geschichte der "Polenaktion"* (Berlin: Metropol, 2018); and Christine Schmidt, "Finding the Archival Traces of 'Misery Trains': Early Accounts of Train Transport before the Holocaust," *Journal of Transport History* 45, no. 2 (2024): 242–263.

> Why am I so frightened merely to write about this event, why does my heart beat so hard as to take my breath away, even today, as soon as I think about it? Events that directly threatened my own fate and life occurred before then and afterwards, but this day lives in my memory like an abyss, a tear that can never close, a wound that will never heal. And yet, it all happened so calmly, so 'organised', no murder, no manslaughter, no torture, I almost wrote. But that was exactly what it was, a long-drawn-out, cold, cruel torture.[53]

The frank, emotional remarks with which she begins her account mirror the private, intimate correspondence she had with Reichmann, where we, based on Reichmann's responses (the ones by Schönewald do not survive in the Library's archive), may infer that Schönewald was initially reluctant to submit this report. Reichmann was impressed by Schönewald's account, she wrote on October 11, 1956, linking the "facts" of her report to Reichmann's ability to experience them from the immediacy of the prose in a kind of double witnessing:

> I read them through immediately – breathlessly, so to speak. The fact that you demand that I be honest to the point of impoliteness is an imposition that I am sorry to have to disappoint you in fulfilling. It is precisely honesty that forces me to tell you that the reports have inspired me directly. However, as I have not expected anything different from you, you have represented the facts so vividly that one believes to experience them.

Reichmann writes further, referring to Schönewald's reputation and status:

> You have succeeded magnificently in describing the roundup of stateless Eastern European Jews [*Ostjuden*]. I have read a lot about it, but I have not yet experienced it in the way you have made me experience it. [. . .] Should you find the time and strength to write down more of your rich memories, you will fill me with great happiness each time. There are really only a few people left who can draw on so much as you do, and who, by virtue of their personage, have witnessed and been involved in so many important events.[54]

Writing in a previous letter, Reichmann had (apparently successfully) countered Schönewald's seeming reluctance to contribute to the Library's project, reacting to what Schönewald considered a "dead monument":

> What you mean by a "dead monument", which you reject, I don't quite know [. . .] on this point I beg to differ, as they say so politely in English. Should an epoch be sunk and forgotten if the goddess of history has not granted it a longer life? Rather, shouldn't the testimony of thought, struggle and creation, which this historical era saw, be preserved? I wholeheartedly commit myself to the creation of such a memorial, when life itself has already passed into the past.[55]

---

[53] Eyewitness account by Ottilie Schönewald, WHL PIIe. No. 338, https://www.testifyingtothetruth.co.uk/viewer/fulltext/104888/en/.
[54] WHL 3000/9/1/1221/2: Correspondence with Ottilie Schönewald.
[55] WHL 3000/9/1/1221/1.

For Reichmann, the emotion and subjectivity of Schönewald's account made it *more* credible as a source rather than the other way around, and their shared cultural and gendered framework of Jewish communal defense, women's issues, and social networks led to the solicitation, composition, and incorporation of this report.

As Reichmann did not provide a standardized set of questions to be used by interviewers (or at least not one left in the archives), each interviewer shaped the interviews with their own concerns, values, priorities, and considerations. Therefore, multiple interviews conducted by a single interviewer can prove very useful for analyzing how gendered migrant knowledge impacted the interviews and archival process. Nelly Wolffheim, for example, a feminist specialist in Freudian psychoanalytic pedagogy, who at the age of sixty had fled Nazi Germany for Britain in 1939, and who was never able to reestablish herself as a pedagogue in her newly adopted country, was both an interviewee and an interviewer for the Library. Wolffheim submitted twenty-three reports that became part of the collection during the period 1957–1960. These included interviews with thirty refugees and survivors of Nazi persecution, most of whom were Jewish.[56] The experiences of married couples were usually reported together in a single account, which typically began with brief biographical details as well as the professions of the interviewees' parents – a genealogy of class and cultural attributes. Of the accounts submitted by Wolffheim, twenty-three were conducted with women, including eleven single or widowed women. The interviewed men were generally interviewed as being a part of married couples and they often remained unnamed.[57] Wolffheim shaped the reports she co-developed with interviewees around issues that were of particular importance to her, such as age, class, and gender, especially women's experiences in relation to fleeing persecution, survival, and the long-term psychological torment experienced by many victims.[58] Moreover, the interviews conducted by Wolffheim for the Library echo her experiences of displacement and loneliness, loss of profession, and desire for financial and emotional self-sufficiency at an older age. They reveal Wolffheim's intellectual back-

---

[56] Christine Schmidt, "'Head of an Old Woman': Nelly Wolffheim and the Voices of the Aged," in *Older Jews and the Holocaust: Persecution, Displacement, and Survival*, eds. Christine Schmidt, Elizabeth Anthony and Joanna Sliwa (Detroit: Wayne State University Press in association with the US Holocaust Memorial Museum, 2026).

[57] Wolffheim's submissions included three letters written by Gertrude Hammerstein in 1942 prior to her being deported to Theresienstadt, where she perished. Wolffheim received the surviving letters from the author's daughter and son-in-law and submitted them to the Library. Three letters by Gertrude Hammerstein, WHL PIIIc No. 1062; https://www.testifyingtothetruth.co.uk/viewer/metadata/105301/1/ (accessed October 31, 2024).

[58] Schmidt, "'Head of an Old Woman'."

ground in child psychology and Freudian theory, which she carried with her to Britain, as well as her focus on the upper-middle-class Jewish milieu, its genealogy, and fate. Among the short biographical details at the top of each account, Wolffheim listed the profession of the interviewee and the interviewee's parents. Finally, changes to "privileged" status were commonly addressed and commented on in her interviews.

Wolffheim was particularly concerned with women's struggles to emigrate, as well as professional, financial, and other material losses brought on by persecution and forced migration. For example, the signed narrative of Lotte Lewin, recorded in March 1960 after an interview with Wolffheim when she was sixty-eight years old, immediately opens with a remark that "[f]ollowing inflation, the salary rate at the university [of Breslau, where Lewin worked] worsened considerably," which compelled her to move into her father's textile industry.[59] Lewin was overheard by a male (Christian) employee at the company referring to Joseph Goebbels as the "spawn of filth and fire" (in the style of Faust). Her words were passed on and eventually reported to the Gestapo, after which she was imprisoned for three days. The account takes an interesting "editorial" turn in which Wolffheim describes the Jewish community of Breslau as seemingly unaware and unresponsive to the growing threat of Nazism:

> Back then in 1936 in Breslau, where there was an especially large number of Jewish people living, one generally seemed not to be sufficiently perturbed and viewed the whole matter of the Nazis more as a transitional period. The businesses carried on and so relatively few Jewish people emigrated.

This is followed by a rare direct quotation from Lewin, who apparently agreed with this assessment, in which she expressed that "One was more angry than fearful."

Wolffheim continues to interpret Lewin's activities: "Lotte Lewin distinguished herself through a misguided optimism, and following the experience described above [imprisonment], even traveled for Pentecost to see friends in Czechia, Gräfenberg, for 10 days." There, and later when she traveled to Switzerland, she was warned not to return to Germany by relatives in England, who promised to help her emigrate. The following excerpt implies that both Lewin and Wolffheim reached similar conclusions regarding the former's naiveté, clearly based on knowledge amassed in hindsight: "However, she wanted, for as long as she

---

[59] Eyewitness account by Lotte Lewin, WLA PIIc No. 1182, 1; https://www.testifyingtothetruth.co.uk/viewer/metadata/104842/1/ (accessed October 31, 2024).

had her existence, not to emigrate and be a burden to others."⁶⁰ Lewin was brought to trial once again not long after, in 1936, for her comments and sentenced to a further nine months in prison. The account describes her experiences and treatment in prison, from which she was freed in July 1937. The account ends with Lewin emigrating to England with the help of relatives.⁶¹ Here, Wolffheim's experience of forced migration as an older woman shaped the content of the interview and subsequent report, and both women reflected (together) on the difficult decisions and material limits related to emigration and flight.

On the other hand, Wolffheim conducted other interviews that Reichmann ultimately rejected for the EWA collection, something that once again demonstrated the boundaries set by her concepts for the collection as well as the material restrictions with which she operated from London. For example, correspondence from Reichmann to Wolffheim regarding a report that the latter drew up for Ms. K. Lalouve reveals that Reichmann declined this report as there was already an existing report with this interviewee conducted by another colleague, Midia Krause. Reichmann was surprised that Lalouve did not reveal this to Wolffheim.⁶² Reichmann's correspondence with Wolffheim includes many corrections of spelling mistakes, incorrect dates, and queries regarding aspects of draft reports that were unclear or historically dubious, which shows the extent of the editorial and research work behind the creation of the reports. In other words, the reports were heavily mediated co-constructions and productions between the interviewee, interviewer, and staff of the EWA team, who through this iterative approach sought to establish accounts that were factually reliable by credible witnesses. The dynamics of gender and culture as influences on how the reports were shaped are revealed through a close reading not only of the interviews themselves but also the extensive correspondence chronicling their production.

Conclusion

This chapter has examined the conceptualization and implementation of the EWA project by the Wiener Library in the 1950s as a site of knowledge production. Through several illustrative examples, I have explored the impact of gender and culture on different forms of knowledge production through the Library's post-

---

60 Lewin, 2.
61 Lewin, 5.
62 Correspondence with Nelly Wolffheim, 6 October 1958, WHL 3000/9/1/1573/17, 6 October 1958. See WHL PIII.i. (France) No. 95, or 1656/3/9/95.

war work. Gender shaped the ways in which the EWAs were constructed, mediated, and archived as documentary evidence of Nazi atrocities. Examining the materiality of the EWA production as an archival collection developed at a diasporic Jewish institution after the war necessarily centers the work of German-Jewish women in the diaspora who not only led these efforts but also conducted interviews and engaged in archival work to conceptualize and construct the collection. This reinforces the idea that archiving itself derives from its own theoretical and non-neutral traditions, produces knowledge, and should be considered an integral part of the development of Holocaust research and memory after the war.

Furthermore, analyzing the different imprints and mediations on the EWA collection – a collection developed within and for an institution born of forced migration – furthers our understanding of the contributions of Jewish women to archives-building after genocide and helps reinforce the significance of correspondence in relation to gathering and mediating knowledge about Nazi atrocities. Through correspondence held at the Library's institutional archive, it is possible to map influences that shaped the creation and dissemination of the EWA collection as a serious project of intellectual transfer as well as to better understand the under-researched contributions of German-Jewish women, who not only organized but also created and disseminated Holocaust knowledge after the war.

Christine Schmidt is deputy director and head of research at The Wiener Holocaust Library. Her research has focused on the history of postwar tracing and documentation efforts, the concentration camp system in Nazi Germany, comparative studies of collaboration and resistance in France and Hungary, and the collection of survivor accounts recorded by The Wiener Library. Schmidt is currently co-editing (with Clara Dijkstra, Charlie Knight, and Sandra Lipner) *Holocaust Letters: Methodology, Cases, and Reflections* (London: Bloomsbury, 2026) and (with Elizabeth Anthony and Joanna Sliwa) *Older Jews and the Holocaust: Persecution, Displacement, and Survival* (Wayne State University Press in association with the US Holocaust Memorial Museum, 2026).

Daniela Ozacky Stern
Letters from the Ashes: Gender, Documentation, and Holocaust Remembrance in the Work of Ruzka Korczak

Abstract: This chapter examines the significant role of Ruzka Korczak (1921–1988) in shaping early Holocaust memory and documentation in postwar Israel. A Polish-born survivor of the Vilna Ghetto and a partisan fighter, Korczak arrived in Mandatory Palestine in December 1944 and immediately began sharing her experiences through public speeches and writing. This chapter explores Korczak's contributions to Holocaust remembrance, including her later efforts to collect and preserve documents from the Holocaust as well as her role in founding the Moreshet Holocaust Archive. Based on Korczak's personal letters and interviews, this study sheds light on her complex position as a central figure in early Holocaust commemoration and as a woman often overshadowed by male counterparts in the public's memory. By analyzing Korczak's life and work, this research contributes to broader discussions on gender, memory, politics, and historical representation in Holocaust studies. It highlights the crucial role of women in preserving and sharing Holocaust experiences.

Keywords: Jewish resistance, Holocaust commemoration, Holocaust archive, Holocaust aftermath, letters

Introduction

Immediately after the Holocaust, there was a surge in efforts to document and commemorate the atrocities against Jews that unfolded across Europe during the Second World War. Survivors started to tell their stories, and their testimonies were collected by Jewish historical commissions in Europe.[1] It took some time for

---

[1] See the excellent book by Laura Jockusch, *Collect and Record! Jewish Holocaust Documentation in Early Postwar Europe* (New York: Oxford University Press, 2010).

survivors to reach the Yishuv[2] in Mandatory Palestine, still under British rule. One of the pioneers in this critical endeavor was Ruzka Korczak (1921–1988), a Polish-born Jewish woman and member of the Socialist Zionist youth movement Hashomer Hatzair.[3] She was incarcerated in the Vilna Ghetto, joined the ghetto underground, and later escaped to the forests to join the partisans. Korczak's commitment to preserving Holocaust memory began as early as September 1943, when her group left the ghetto through the sewage system while she insisted on bringing a large number of papers from the underground archive. Against all odds, these documents survived and were brought to Israel.[4] In December 1944, she reached Mandatory Palestine and immediately started to share her experiences through numerous public speeches. She also wrote down her accounts in a book published in 1946.[5] At the same time, she kept corresponding with her friends remaining in Poland and thus served as a liaison between them and the movement's leadership in Mandatory Palestine.

This chapter explores Korczak's role in producing knowledge and sharing it in the years immediately after the war and over the next years. Her experiences during the Holocaust greatly influenced her subsequent dedication to preserving its memory, commemorating its victims and heroes, and highlighting Jewish resistance in the ghettos and forests. She was one of the founders of the Moreshet Holocaust Archive in the 1960s, which became a cornerstone of Holocaust research in Israel, and she tirelessly sought to collect testimonies, documents, and artifacts as well as to educate youth and adults about the Holocaust and resistance.[6] Korczak's later scholarly and personal contributions to the *Moreshet Journal* enabled a more

---

2 The Yishuv refers to the Jewish community in Mandatory Palestine before the establishment of Israel (1882–1948), during which this community developed autonomous political institutions and social structures.
3 Hashomer Hatzair is a Socialist-Zionist youth movement founded in Galicia in 1913, which combines Jewish nationalism with socialist ideology and played a significant role in the Zionist movement.
4 These documents are now preserved in the Moreshet Archive.
5 Ruzka (Reizl) Korczak, *Flames in the Ashes* (Merhavia: Hakibbutz Haartzi, 1946). The Hebrew title is *Lehavot Baefer*.
6 For comprehensive discussions on the complex relationship between the Yishuv, the early Israeli state, and Holocaust memory, including the impact of the Eichmann trial, the role of survivor resistance fighters in kibbutzim, and the development of formal commemoration practices, see Neima Barzel, "The Concept of Bravery in the Holocaust, From Collective National Memory to Privatized National Memory," *Dapim for the Holocaust Research* 16 (2000), 86–124; Roni Stauber, *A Lesson for this Generation: Holocaust and Heroism in Israeli Public Discourse in the 1950s* (Jerusalem: Yad Ben Zvi, 2000); Boaz Cohen, "Holocaust Heroics: Ghetto Fighters and Partisans in Israeli Society and Historiography," *Journal of Political & Military Sociology* 31, no. 2 (2003): 197–213; Idith Zertal, *Israel's Holocaust and the Politics of Nationhood* (Cambridge: Cambridge University Press, 2005); Dalia Ofer, "We Israelis Remember, But How? The Memory of the Holocaust and the Israeli Experience," *Israel Studies* 18, no. 2 (2013): 70–85.

comprehensive understanding of the Holocaust and resistance. Despite her central role in Holocaust commemoration and archiving, Korczak often remained in the background, ceding the spotlight to male figures such as Abba Kovner, who had become the dominant voice in shaping the story of Vilna Ghetto and the partisans.

This chapter seeks to address this gap by examining Korczak's life and work through various sources with a particular focus on a unique collection of letters she wrote in 1945–1946 to her wartime friend Vitka Kempner (1920–2012) in addition to interviews with Korczak and her contemporaries. Analyzing her work may shed light on the complex task of memory construction in the aftermath of the Holocaust and serve as a powerful reminder of the crucial role of women in exposing the horrors of the war while it was still ongoing, as well as preserving the memory of it for future generations. My hope is that this analysis contributes to discussions on gender, memory, and historical representation in Holocaust studies.

Figure 1: Ruzka Korczak, Courtesy of the Ghetto Fighters' House Museum / Photo Archive.

Biographical Note: In the Ghetto and Forests

Ruzka Korczak (Figure 1) was born on April 28, 1921, in the small town of Bielsk, some 20 kilometers from Płock, a city in central Poland about 100 kilometers northwest of Warsaw. Her father Gedaliah was a cattle merchant, and her mother Hinda was a housewife. Ruzka was the oldest of three sisters. The family was observant and Zionist, and she was brought up in the hope that she would one day immigrate to Mandatory Palestine.⁷

She studied in a Polish school, but as a Jew, she also engaged in additional studies with the town's rabbi that included the Hebrew language, Jewish history, and the Bible. She recalled that she experienced antisemitism in her childhood, but she nevertheless developed the idea and behavior of being a proud Jewish woman. Every Saturday, she would go to the synagogue with her grandmother. As the economic situation for Jews deteriorated in the mid-1930s, the family moved to Płock in search of better opportunities and education for the children. Ruzka loved to learn things and to read books that she borrowed from the city library. To help support the household, she worked in a shop selling bread and rolls, giving her earnings to her parents. She also adopted socialist ideas of justice and equality, joined the Hashomer Hatzair movement, and soon became an instructor and member of the leadership in the city branch.⁸

Here, she found a sense of belonging to something greater and more meaningful than everyday life. Being among friends who shared her ideas would help her during the war years. Her parents argued with her regarding her affiliation with the movement and that she distanced herself from religion, so she tried to keep some religious customs for the sake of her father.⁹

She was very active socially, and one of her major public activities before the war was to organize aid for the Jews affected by the Zbąszyń deportation in October 1938 – the German expulsion of Jews with Polish citizenship to this town, where they lived under harsh conditions. When the Second World War broke out in September 1939, the Jews of Płock tried to flee the city, just as in many other occupied cities. The Korczak family discussed what to do and decided to stay. A difficult period now began for the Jews, full of decrees and prohibitions. As a natural documenter, Ruzka kept a diary during this time, which was later lost. She witnessed the abuse of the Jews in the city, which greatly affected her. Fear was in the air. Hashomer Hatzair members who stayed would occasionally meet and discuss what to do. Ruzka decided to escape eastward and saying goodbye to her parents was difficult. In November 1939, she left Płock for Warsaw, where she accidentally on the street met Tosia Altman, a friend from Hashomer Hatzair. Tosia convinced her to head further east toward Vilna, which was still free, and where many members of youth movements had already gathered. "This meeting with Tosia, which lasted maybe two minutes in the devastated Warsaw

---

7 Carmela Lachish, interview, in Yehuda Tuvin, Levi Dror, and Yosseph Rav, eds., *Ruzka Korczak-Marle: The Personality and Philosophy of the Life of a Fighter* (Tel Aviv: Moreshet, 1988), 7.
8 Tuvin, Dror, and Rav, *Ruzka*, 9.
9 Tuvin, Dror, and Rav, *Ruzka*, 9.

under German occupation, is really what determined the course of my life," she said years later.[10]

She traveled for days, eventually reaching Lviv. From there, she continued alone on a winding path until she arrived in Rivne, where her fellow Hashomer Hatzair members had gathered. Together, they crossed the lines, and she finally arrived in Lithuania. Here, she lived with her comrades in a kibbutz-like community they called Rikuz Vilna ("Vilna Assemblage"). Their main focus at the time was to procure certificates to immigrate to Mandatory Palestine.[11] In Vilna, she met Vitka Kempner, and the two became close friends until Ruzka's death forty-nine years later.

While in Vilna, she received a letter from her family informing her that they had been deported to Piotrków near Łódź. She would later receive news that her father had died of typhus. During the war years, she did not know what had become of her mother and sisters. In the first years after arriving in Israel, she met someone (she was unable to remember his name) who told her that he had stayed with her mother and two sisters in a camp. "Your mother spoke about you and hoped you would survive," he said, "I could have saved your sister, but she said she wouldn't leave her mother."[12]

Ruzka stayed in the Vilna Rikuz until it was disbanded in mid-1940 when the Soviets occupied Lithuania and banned Zionist activities. The Hashomer Hatzair members went underground. Nazi Germany invaded the Soviet Union in June 1941, which led to the remaining members deciding to leave Vilna. "For us, the refugees, it was easier than for the people of Vilna who had homes, families, and children. We, a group of young people, could take our walking sticks and leave. We decided to go east, cross the border, and join the Red Army to fight the Germans."[13]

However, they did not succeed in this and were forced to return to Vilna, which had fallen into German hands. Decrees against Jews were issued immediately, which led to widespread panic and uncertainty. From this moment on, as Ruzka testified, she ceased to view herself as an individual and began to see herself as part of a group and a movement. Perhaps this was a kind of survival mechanism, a way of compensating for her family that was far away. She felt like an equal among equals in the group, sharing with her comrades the chaotic situation arising with the beginning of the Soviet-German war and struggling together for survival.

---

10 Shmuel Hupert, interview, in Tuvin, Dror, and Rav, *Ruzka*, 15.
11 On the "kibbutz" in Vilna, see Daniela Ozacky Stern, "Collective Documentation from the Beginning of WWII: The 'Rikuz' in Vilna as a Case Study," *Jewish Culture and History* 23, no. 2 (2022): 115–136.
12 Lachish, interview, in Tuvin, Dror, and Rav, *Ruzka*, 13.
13 Hupert, interview, in Tuvin, Dror, and Rav, *Ruzka*, 16.

Two ghettos were set up in Vilna in September 1941 into which the Jews were crammed. Ruzka remembered how she stood in front of the ghetto gate and saw baby carriages and scattered packages. She and her friends arrived at a courtyard in the ghetto and entered an apartment already full of people. She lived there with Vitka Kempner and Abba Kovner as well as several others, and the three of them became a "trio." Vitka would years later say that: "We were very close friends and lived in complete partnership."[14] Indeed, they remained inseparable later when living in the forests and once again in Israel.

Soon, the Germans started deporting Jews to the murder site in the Ponary forest, where they were shot to death in pits. During one of these *Aktionen*, Ruzka hid with Vitka behind a large closet, and they comforted each other that "whatever would be, would be." Ruzka, just like others, faced death many times in the ghetto but survived.[15]

In January 1942, an underground body called the United Partisan Organization (Fareynikte Partizaner Organizatsye, FPO) was established in the Vilna Ghetto, and Ruzka joined it on behalf of Hashomer Hatzair. In the Vilna Ghetto, she was also part of the Paper Brigade, whose members had to organize the collection of Jewish books and other documents in Vilna that would otherwise be appropriated by the Nazi looting agency Einsatzstab Reichsleiter Rosenberg. These brave scholars then smuggled and hid these materials, thereby preserving them for the future.[16]

On the day that the ghetto was liquidated (September 23, 1943), she escaped the ghetto with the last group of underground members through the sewage tunnels. Chaya Shapira Lazar would years later recall that she saw Ruzka on that day just before leaving the ghetto together with Zelda Treger, a fellow underground member and a good friend of Ruzka from Hashomer Hatzair. The two women approached each other, shook hands, while Zelda said: "Hazak ve'ematz.[17] See you in Eretz Israel."[18] Together with this group, Ruzka reached the Rudniki forests, located some 40 kilometers south of Vilna, and joined a Jewish partisan unit where she served until her departure a year and a half later.[19]

---

14 Abraham Atzili, 1998 interview, in Vitka Kempner-Kovner, *Vitka: Fighter for Life* (Moreshet and Kovner family, 2013), 28.
15 Hupert, interview, in Tuvin, Dror, and Rav, *Ruzka*, 22.
16 David Fishman, *The Book Smugglers: Partisans, Poets, and the Race to Save Jewish Treasures from the Nazis* (Lebanon, NH: ForeEdge, 2017), 65, 72.
17 "Be strong and of good courage" is the Hashomer Hatzair motto.
18 Chaya Shapira-Lazar, testimony, 1997, USC Shoah Foundation Visual Archive, 30239, tape 4.
19 On her partisan experience, see M. Gefen, C. Grossman, Y. Segal, A. Kovner, and R. Korczak, eds., *The Book of the Jewish Partisans* (Merchavia: Sifriat Poalim, 1958), 106–159. Being part of the editorial board of this book represents another commemoration initiative by Korczak.

This is how she described her experience among the partisans: "Although it wasn't common for women to take an active part in partisan fighting, in the Jewish units in Rudniki, there were many young women. [. . .] They participated in operations against the Germans." She added that they viewed themselves as just as worthy and capable of participating in operations as the men. "I remember that for the first operation, I was chosen along with another one of our female comrades, and we felt that the fate of the entire female gender depended on us. If we succeed in the mission, if we fulfill the role assigned to us – we would pave the way for all the women."[20]

Ruzka served as a quartermaster in the forest: "Someone had to organize all the food and clothing matters for the unit."[21] In addition, she was involved in guarding the camp. Benjamin Levin, a fellow partisan, recalled how he stood guard with Ruzka one day and what they talked about: "My team to the patrol was Ruzka Korczak [. . .] we were always going together. [. . .] I was sitting on a tree and watching and then she climbed too and started watching. [. . .] She was one of the nicest people I have met. She was very intelligent, very straight, and very honest, and she took everything very seriously. She was a party member, a born party member [of Hashomer Hatzair]." She showed him how to use his weapon. They engaged in long discussions during their guard duty and enjoyed sitting together for six hours. "She was a very brave person. [. . .] She told me about Zionism, about Israel. [. . .] She was a terrific person."[22]

With the liberation of Vilna in mid-July 1944, Ruzka returned to the city with the partisans and the Red Army. "After the war, one had to first and foremost find oneself," she said,[23] "Just as leaving the ghetto for the forest was a crisis for many of us because everything started anew, so was the crisis at the end of the war. Suddenly, you felt as if you were free, liberated." She recounted that when the news of liberation came to the Jewish partisan camp, there was a deadly cemetery-like silence. What was the point of being liberated? At least while in the forest, they were fighters and their life had meaning. There was hope that their relatives might have survived. This hope gave them the strength and motivation to live. And then, when they entered Vilna in a military parade, they discovered a city empty of Jews while encountering antisemitic remarks from locals, such as "Look how many of them Jews are still alive."[24] In one of the streets, she met a

---

20 Hupert, interview, in Tuvin, Dror, and Rav, *Ruzka*, 40.
21 Hupert, interview, in Tuvin, Dror, and Rav, *Ruzka*, 41.
22 Benjamin Levin, testimony, 1997, USC Shoah Foundation Visual Archive, 26425, tape 6.
23 Hupert, interview, in Tuvin, Dror, and Rav, *Ruzka*, 42.
24 Lithuania saw one of the highest Jewish death rates during the Holocaust: of approximately 200,000 Jews living under Nazi occupation, only about 10,000 survived – a devastating 95% mor-

woman with a child who spoke Yiddish. This was the first time that Ruzka burst into tears after not having cried for a very long time. She stood in the street and wept loudly "because I saw and heard a Jewish child."[25] Despite this first reaction, they soon understood that the war was not over for them and the other Jewish survivors.

In an interesting report written by Ruzka Korczak after the war, she described the feelings of the survivors gathered in Vilna and the beginning of their efforts to collect and preserve information:

> Everyone is alone and solitary, and family is a rare phenomenon. It's no wonder that Jews seek the closeness of other Jews. Organized activity began among them. A Jewish Museum was created on the initiative of Abraham Sutzkever, Abba Kovner, and Shmuel Amarant. The collection of items of cultural value began. There are quite a few exhibits, first of all from the YIVO collections: documents, sculptures, and even Herzl's diary, as well as a large archive from the ghetto, in fact, all the documents of the Judenrat.[26]

Former partisans, including Ruzka, documented the role of Jews in the partisan movement and collected testimonies from individual Jews who had survived the extermination in various towns. Ruzka also noted that people who returned from the Soviet Union and met the Jewish women were surprised that some of them were partisans.[27] They discussed the possibility of transferring all this documentation to Mandatory Palestine as this was the only location where it would be possible to write down the whole truth. The museum was the only Jewish center in Vilna at the time, and it was the address used for letters and the main community organization.

This report offers a unique perspective on the immediate aftermath of the Holocaust for survivors in Vilna. It reveals the complex interplay between trauma, survival, and the urgent need to act, document, and preserve their history. Ruzka's observations highlight the survivors' remarkable resilience and foresight in establishing cultural institutions amidst the chaos of postwar Europe.

She only stayed in Vilna for a short while and went to Kovno (Kaunas) in early August 1944 to "search for people, partisans and movement members, and tell them: fellows, we don't have a reason to stay here, we are not staying in Lithuania. We would gather and search ways to go to Eretz Israel."[28] When she re-

---

tality rate. See Yitzchak Arad, *History of the Holocaust: The Soviet Union* (Jerusalem: Yad Vashem, 2004), 1011.

25 Hupert, interview, in Tuvin, Dror, and Rav, *Ruzka*, 43.
26 Ruzka Korczak, undated report, Moreshet Archive, D.1.442. For more on the Jewish Museum in postwar Vilna, see Fishman, *The Book Smugglers*, 145–155.
27 Korczak, Moreshet Archive, D.1.442.
28 Hupert, interview, in Tuvin, Dror, and Rav, *Ruzka*, 44.

turned to Vilna, Kovner gave her a new mission and sent her together with Dr. Shmuel Amarant, a partisan and former principal of the famous Tarbut gymnasium in Vilna, to check the roads in the east and establish transit points on the way toward Romania. From there, they inquired regarding the possibilities of illegally immigrating to Mandatory Palestine, which was then ruled by the British.

Amarant was disguised as a journalist with Korczak as his secretary. They arrived in Bucharest at the end of November. Here, her mission took an unexpected turn following a meeting with emissaries from her movement having just arrived from Mandatory Palestine. Unaware of the enormity of the Holocaust, they gathered around her to listen to the story of an eyewitness member of their movement. Korczak at length told them about the experiences in the ghettos and the forests and the destruction of the Jews in Europe. The information she presented was not limited to Lithuania alone. On her way to Romania, she had gathered evidence about the situation of Jewish survivors in more places and told them everything she knew.[29]

The listeners were shocked by her words and could not hold back their tears. A decision was made on the spot that instead of going back to report on the results of her mission, Korczak should travel to Mandatory Palestine to share this information, in person, with the leaders and members of Hashomer Hatzair.[30]

She initially resisted, as she wanted to stay with her friends in Europe and be a part of the newly launched Bricha (Escape) movement.[31] However, she was persuaded to go, knowing that she must spread this crucial information about the Holocaust, which no one else could do. From that moment on, telling became Ruzka Korczak's mission. She devoted her life to sharing knowledge on the Holocaust and the various ways and methods of Jewish resistance with the public. "And so, I was 'glued' as a wife to a man who had a vacant place in his passport and a certificate." She sailed on a ship from the Port of Constanta on the Black Sea to Mandatory Palestine, arriving on December 12, 1944, as one of the first survivors to do so.[32]

---

[29] Dina Porat, "With Forgiveness and Grace: The Encounter between Ruzka Korczak, the Yishuv and Its Leaders 1944–1946," *Journal of Israeli History* 16 (1995): 101–132.
[30] Porat, "With Forgiveness," 119.
[31] The Escape movement, also known as the Bricha (Hebrew for "escape" or "flight"), was a clandestine effort to help Jewish Holocaust survivors flee postwar Europe and reach Mandatory Palestine, which was then under British rule. See the testimony of Korczak on this period, Moreshet Archive, A.1587–38 (no date).
[32] Hupert, interview, in Tuvin, Dror, and Rav, *Ruzka*, 45.

In Eretz Israel (Mandatory Palestine)

Upon arrival, Korczak was for a short time interned in the British detention camp in Atlit where newcomers to the country were "classified" by the British authorities. "No one was waiting for me; no one knew I had arrived," she remembered.[33] It took two weeks for her to ask around and finally meet with the Hashomer Hatzair representative in the camp as well as other influential people. The person who finally succeeded in getting her out of the camp was Yitzhak Greenbaum,[34] who signed a paper saying that she had tuberculosis and endangered the other camp dwellers, declaring that he would take her directly to a hospital.[35] They traveled to his kibbutz, Gan Shmuel, and this was the first time in years that she had a room for herself to sleep in. "This was when I finally realized that I am indeed in Eretz Israel."[36]

Korczak joined Kibbutz Eilon on the northern border with Lebanon but still felt lonely without her friends who had stayed behind. In January 1945, merely three months after her arrival, she addressed the executive meeting of Hashomer Hatzair in Kibbutz Gan Shmuel, for the first time in detail telling them about the extermination of Jews and Jewish resistance during the war. "A petite young woman with delicate features and a modest smile at the corners of her mouth, speaking Yiddish in a quiet, subdued tone, she was among the first who introduced the story of the Holocaust and heroism to the Palestine Jewish elite."[37] She started with an explicit description of the annihilation of Jewish communities in Europe, saying that "up until now no one could have grasped its extent" and that they – who had not been there – obviously could not fully understand what had happened.[38] Through this speech and the ones that followed, Korczak established the narrative that Hashomer Hatzair was the leading movement in the resistance while downplaying the role of others.

In the first weeks of her stay in the country, she met with several leaders of the Yishuv and spoke about her experience on various occasions. A famous event

---

33 Hupert, interview, in Tuvin, Dror, and Rav, *Ruzka*, 45.
34 A member of the Jewish Agency Board who would later become the first interior minister in the Israeli government.
35 Hupert, interview, in Tuvin, Dror, and Rav, *Ruzka*, 45.
36 Korczak's speech in Gan Shmuel, January 3, 1945, Moreshet Archive, A.990; see also Tuvin, Dror, and Rav, *Ruzka*, 119.
37 Neima Barzel, "Rozka Korczak-Marla," *Shalvi/Hyman Encyclopedia of Jewish Women* (February 27, 2009), Jewish Women's Archive, https://jwa.org/encyclopedia/article/korczak-marla-rozka.
38 For the full text in Hebrew, see Tuvin, Dror, and Rav, *Ruzka*, 87–106.

was the sixth Histadrut conference in Tel Aviv on February 1, 1945.[39] They allocated just a few minutes for her speech, and she once again spoke in Yiddish since her Hebrew was not yet sufficiently good. Her words aroused great emotion. People approached the stage and surrounded her, wishing to hear more. The next speaker was David Ben-Gurion, the head of the Histadrut who would become the first prime minister of the new state of Israel three years later. He stood up and started his speech by notoriously criticizing Korczak for speaking in "a foreign and grating language." However, he was unable to continue his speech and was forced to step down due to the rage engulfing the attendees.[40] It was not the Yiddish that was grating, Ruzka said afterward, it was Ben-Gurion's words, which testified to "exemplary insensitivity and disregard for good taste." Once again, she met with misunderstandings and ignorance from people in the Yishuv concerning what had happened in Europe. At this early stage, when the Second World War was still going on and communication was disrupted, people could not grasp the magnitude of the Holocaust.

That same month, she met with a large group of women, members of Moetzet Ha'poalot, "the Female Workers Council," established in 1921 as part of the Histadrut to improve women's representation in the organization and their rights as workers. Unsurprisingly, the presentation focused on the situation and roles of the *haverot*, "female members" and their bravery during the Holocaust. "My story about them is completely objective," said Ruzka, "because the truth is strong, and there is no need to adorn it." She went on to describe the central role of women during those dark days. "I see them everywhere, in every circumstance. They are the ones who maintain the only contact between the ghetto and the outside world. They are the lionesses who travel between cities, with forged papers. [. . .] Delivering the idea of resistance, they managed the technical actions in the ghettos and later took part in the military operations as partisans."[41] The percentage of women was not high in the forests, and many of them were too old to participate in combat. Nevertheless, they took it upon themselves to carry out the important tasks of maintaining the daily life and needs of their comrades.

---

39 The Histadrut, established in 1920 as the General Organization of Workers in the Land of Israel, was one of the most powerful institutions in the Yishuv, not only operating as a trade union but also as a major employer, healthcare provider, and key force in the pre-state Jewish economy and society.

40 Ben-Gurion's opposition to Yiddish was part of a broader Zionist ideology seeking to establish Hebrew as the national language of the new Jewish state. See Rachel Rozanski, "'A Foreign and Grating Language' Indeed? The Question of Ben-Gurion's Attitude to Yiddish after the Holocaust," *Iyunim Be'tkumat Israel* 15 (2005): 463.

41 Tuvin, Dror, and Rav, *Ruzka*, 102.

She went on to mention the names of several women who were involved in the underground and the partisans, most of them perished and only a few survived. One of these was her dear friend Vitka Kempner, whose exploits Ruzka elaborated on, telling the female audience about Vitka's missions to save Jews from the Vilna Ghetto and sabotage German trains, but also how she identified the roads from the ghetto to the forest and organized their escape on the day of liquidation.[42] "But I want you to understand," she added, "this was not exceptional. I want you to envisage the image of the female members who grew and developed through these events and could not have behaved otherwise." And during all this time, their longing for Eretz Israel did not cease, "because those young women had a pioneering education, belonged to youth movements, and were connected so strongly to their People, and therefore became its most beautiful figures."[43] So, on the one hand, she strengthened the notion of women's role in the Jewish resistance while, on the other hand, she created the narrative that heroism and fighting were dominated by the socialist pioneering movements and ignored the contribution of other political sections in the Jewish resistance.

In the following year, Korczak traveled around the country, met with people from all walks of life, and talked extensively about her experiences during the war, as if possessed by the mission to share as much as she could with as many as possible (Figure 2). She also met privately with various women. One of them was Sarah (Surika) Braverman, one of the first female fighters to serve in the Palmach.[44] She was trained as a parachutist with the group sent to Europe in 1944 (however, her mission was canceled) and later founded the Women's Corps in the IDF.[45] Braverman was deeply impressed by Ruzka, and they established a warm relationship right from the beginning of their encounter. According to Braverman, the traits that characterized Korczak were honesty, simplicity, and a lack of dramatizing things: "these were the secrets of her strength."[46] Braverman instructed a course on weapons use for fifty-two female trainees in the Palmach and invited Ruzka to address them. As usual, she spoke Yiddish, and Braverman intended to translate her words when something extraordinary occurred. "We sat

---

42 Tuvin, Dror, and Rav, *Ruzka*, 103.
43 Tuvin, Dror, and Rav, *Ruzka*, 106.
44 The Palmach ("strike forces") was an elite fighting force of the Haganah established in 1941. Haganah served as the main military force of the Jewish community in pre-state Israel and formed the backbone of the early Israel Defense Forces.
45 The IDF (Israel Defense Forces) is Israel's unified military force established in 1948 when the state was founded.
46 Words of Surika Braverman from Kibbutz Shamir about Ruzka Korczak after her passing. July 25, 1988, Moreshet Archive, A.1501.

on a hill; Ruzka spoke in her wonderful deep voice, and no one moved, so I could not interrupt her. I kept noting down what I would translate for the audience and let her speak." When she started translating Ruzka's words, the participants told her that there was no need. "They understood everything. They did not understand Yiddish, but they felt her, they sensed. She conveyed to them what she wanted to tell through her gaze and voice." This first encounter with women fighters in the country was very important to Ruzka.[47]

Korczak's reports offer profound insights into her early communication with people who had not experienced the Holocaust. By framing her account as "a greeting from the past," she humanized the victims and survivors, transforming historical facts into personal messages. Her emphasis on the diverse forms of murder across different locations highlighted the complex and varied nature of the Jewish Holocaust. Her narrative also offered a valuable insight into the evolution of Jewish resistance. Her account actively countered the misconception of Jewish passivity, thus rejecting the narrative of "going as sheep to the slaughter" by emphasizing the conscious decision to resist and fight.[48] Her presentation and her book, presented at such an early stage, in a way prove the notion of early scholars of the Holocaust, such as Lucy Dawidowicz, who underestimated the survivors' testimonies as an objective historical resource. Dawidowicz argued that:

> Survivor chroniclers can seldom transmit more than their individual circumscribed experiences, however harrowing, however extraordinary. [. . .] Few survivors had an overview of the events beyond their immediate experience. [. . .] Only a few survivors might be able to achieve the necessary distance by an act of will, by the imposition of discipline over self.[49]

However, as one of the earliest formal witnesses of the Holocaust in Mandatory Palestine, Korczak represents the immediate efforts to communicate the incomprehensible to the Yishuv, thereby setting the stage for future Holocaust remembrance and education in Israel. In April 1946, another female fighter, Zivia Lubetkin, who took part in the Warsaw Ghetto Uprising, spoke at Kibbutz Yagur to the members of her movement, Hakibbutz Hameuhad, and had a similar effect on her audience and the entire Jewish society in the country. Both women set the

---

47 Braverman, Moreshet Archive.
48 The stereotype of "Jews going like sheep to the slaughter" was a misleading post-Holocaust narrative that ignored both the reality of Nazi control systems and the many forms of Jewish resistance that actually materialized. See Yael S. Feldman, "'Not as Sheep Led to Slaughter?' On Trauma, Selective Memory, and the Making of Historical Consciousness," *Jewish Social Studies: History, Culture, Society* 19, no. 3 (2013): 139–169.
49 Quoted in Jockusch, *Collect and Record!*, 196.

narrative of an exclusive connection between heroism in the ghettos and left-wing pioneering youth movements during the Holocaust.

And yet, despite the warm welcome and appreciation and the good contacts with the leaders of her movement, Korczak still felt lonely and missed her friends as she had always seen herself as part of them. It seems as if her fellow underground comrades, the former partisans and members of the movement, had become an alternate family for her, and she longed to be with them. The person she missed the most was her closest friend, Vitka Kempner, as expressed in the letters she wrote to her.

Figure 2: Ruzka Korczak speaking at a memorial rally held at Kibbutz Yad Mordechai on the tenth anniversary of the Warsaw Ghetto Uprising, April 12, 1953. Courtesy of the Ghetto Fighters' House Museum / Photo Archive.

Letters to Vitka

A unique collection of letters written by Korczak in 1945–1946 to her friend Vitka offers invaluable insights into her inner thoughts and experiences as she navigated the challenges of rebuilding her life in the Yishuv. Vitka Kempner, later Kovner, was born in 1920 in Kalisz in western Poland. After completing her high school studies, she entered the University of Warsaw and joined Hashomer Hatzair. When the Germans entered Kalisz in September 1939, she fled eastward and reached the Rikuz in Vilna, where she met Korczak, and they became soulmates. Their lives were intertwined until Ruzka died from illness in 1988.

Eight months had passed since Korczak arrived in Mandatory Palestine, and she had not heard from the friends who remained in Europe. She was worried, restless, and sad, and when a letter from Vitka finally arrived, she could not hide her feelings: "I tried to explain to myself and understand why you did not write but could not. How can one explain your silence? How is it possible to understand that the closest people to me – and you know what you mean to me, as do the others – how could you avoid writing even one word?!"[50] She could not contain her worry and disappointment. However, the main focus of the letter is the deep gap she encountered between the movement in the Yishuv and its surviving members in Europe. Surprisingly, Ruzka tried to defend the leadership's criticism of the survivors, who had established a joint organization with other youth movements after the war.[51] She begged Vitka to understand their position. "It is not true that they do not understand you [. . .] you must realize that in a reality of peace and life of labor, there is a [different] perspective of life, and there is no way we would continue in the perspective of a bunker and a forest."[52] In other words, during the few months that she had lived in the Yishuv, and after long conversations with the movement's leaders, Ruzka learned to accept their attitude of separatism and their focus on the movement's uniqueness and ideology. Despite what happened in Europe, they maintained the political rivalry in the Yishuv, did not support the need of the survivors to join forces, and could not understand the survivors' urgent wish for Jewish unity after the Holocaust.

This tragic attitude, which had also been seen in meetings between survivors and political emissaries coming to Europe after the war, caused a continued rift between the different movements and affected the joint efforts of survival and rescue during the three years between the end of the Second World War in 1945 and the establishment of the state of Israel in 1948. Despite the testimonies of Korczak and others, the Yishuv leaders did not at that time fully comprehend what had happened in the Holocaust and were not ready to change.

Moreover, it is clear from the letters that the feelings Ruzka had toward Vitka were stronger than just close friendship: "Sometimes I think about the connection

---

50 Ruzka to Vitka, letter, August 1, 1945, in Tuvin, Dror, and Rav, *Ruzka*, 127. The original letters are preserved in the Moreshet Archive, C.68–4.
51 On this unification attempt, see Dina Porat, "Eastern European Remnants Brigade – All Its Minutes, April 4–July 23, 1945," *Massuah* 28 (1999): 177–200.
52 Ruzka to Vitka, letter, August 1, 1945, in Tuvin, Dror, and Rav, *Ruzka*, 128.

between us, and I am scared of its intensity," she wrote at the end of one letter, asking "Are you certain that our paths are separated? This is the deepest and most painful blow that can happen to me."[53] These feelings recur in the following letters, even after Ruzka receives words of comfort from her friend.[54] In November, she received two letters from Vitka and was once again not satisfied. "I feel emptiness," she wrote after reading them, "I don't know what to write back." Still, however, she expresses her wish to meet and talk face to face: "If only I could stroke your curly hair, everything could have been simpler. You may have felt that our relationship is so strong and firm that we could lean on it and not suffer. [. . .] I wish I could just say a few good words to you with no ideological or smart comments. Just simple words you say to a close person."[55]

Behind these emotional words, there is a hidden serious gap. At that time, Vitka, Abba Kovner, and a group of former partisans were planning revenge actions against the Germans. This was a controversial matter and obviously secretive, which meant that they could not discuss it openly in the letters. Ruzka knew that the Hashomer Hatzair leadership in the Yishuv opposed these plans and that their members should collaborate with members of right-wing movements, whom they called "fascists," in this endeavor. Ruzka took it upon herself to negotiate between the two sides[56] and tried her best to dissuade her friend from engaging in the revenge plans. Writing in code, she appealed to her: "You should not live with death. It is impossible and unnecessary."[57] But when she met Kovner, who arrived in the country in late 1945 and took part in an eleventh-hour meeting with Meir Ya'ari, the movement's leader,[58] she decided to back her friends' efforts and tried to help them get money and poison to realize their revenge plans.[59] From then on, Ruzka would express her frustration of being away and not being able to help more. "There are moments that I feel like I am going crazy. The worst time is when I realize that I am not useful."[60] Between the lines,

---

53 Ruzka to Vitka, in Tuvin, Dror, and Rav, *Ruzka*, 128.
54 Vitka Kempner's letters were not found, but some of her comments are reflected in Korczak's responses. The letters suggest that the feelings Ruzka had toward Vitka were stronger than just close friendship. The intensity and intimacy of Ruzka's letters suggest a deep emotional connection that might have gone beyond conventional bonds.
55 Ruzka to Vitka, November 13, 1945, in Tuvin, Dror, and Rav, *Ruzka*, 132.
56 Dina Porat, *"To Me Belongeth Vengeance and Recompence": The Yishuv, the Holocaust and the Abba Kovner Group of Avengers* (Haifa: Pardes, 2019), 156.
57 Ruzka to Vitka, November 13, 1945, in Tuvin, Dror, and Rav, *Ruzka*, 133.
58 Meir Yaari (1987–1897) was one of the main leaders and ideologists of Hashomer Hatzair, Hakibbutz Haarzi, and Mapam.
59 Porat, *"To Me Belongeth,"* 157, 184.
60 Ruzka to Vitka, January 8, 1946, in Tuvin, Dror, and Rav, *Ruzka*, 135.

she confessed to Vitka about her loneliness and that she felt like a "strange element" in Kibbutz Eilon, "like a dog without a kennel." She did not socialize with the people there and did not work in the kibbutz, which was very rare at the time. Instead, she devoted her time to writing a book about her experiences during the war. She wrote to Vitka: "I wish so much to finish it soon because I urgently need to see you, so I am working like a horse."[61]

Despite her sadness, Ruzka learned to appreciate her life in the Yishuv and described it to Vitka in a letter dated November 28, 1945: "Only now I see the difference. Here, every kibbutz, every village is like the FPO [the Vilna Ghetto underground]. The struggle is for life and not for death." She finally admitted that her situation was much better than that of her friend. "Fate has been graceful for me; here, I have come to recognize the positive side of life."[62] Based on Vitka's letters, she understood that her situation had worsened after Kovner's departure, and she tried to encourage her friend by complimenting her virtues and her faith in the idea of revenge. "If I could have been with you now, I know that it would have been much easier for both of us [. . .] but you should reinforce the people [. . .] let them believe that the mission will be fulfilled [. . .] the despair and pessimism are not final. I believe things are about to change," she wrote in January 1946.[63]

It took a long time for the letters to get to their destination, sometimes as long as three months. Vitka moved from Vilna to Lublin in January 1945 and later to Italy, and she had no permanent address, so they tried to send their letters with emissaries of the movement and not by mail. The letters from 1946 mainly deal with the whereabouts of Kovner, who was arrested by the British and put in jail in Cairo and Jerusalem, and how his absence affected the revenge plans. Both women were worried about his condition. They used codes and false names – he was called Uri (his underground alias) in the letters – and their mood went up and down based on the news. "My beloved, rest assured that I'm doing everything possible [for him], please be strong and patient," Ruzka wrote in April 1946, saying that she was happy that "things are moving."[64]

In the last letter, dated May 5, 1946, written following Kovner's release, Ruzka did not hide her disappointment in what she saw as the failure of a revenge action carried out by the group in Germany.[65] She understood that for her friend, it was not just a strong jolt but "the end of it all," and she tried to comfort her. "We

---

[61] Ruzka to Vitka, October 1, 1945, in Tuvin, Dror, and Rav, *Ruzka*, 131.
[62] Ruzka to Vitka, November 28, 1945, in Tuvin, Dror, and Rav, *Ruzka*, 134–135.
[63] Ruzka to Vitka, January 8, 1946, in Tuvin, Dror, and Rav, *Ruzka*, 137.
[64] Ruzka to Vitka, April 20, 1946, in Tuvin, Dror, and Rav, *Ruzka*, 138.
[65] They poisoned bread in a German POW camp, which resulted in hundreds of sick people but no deaths. See Porat, *"To Me Belongeth,"* 231–241.

are used to failures, but they never broke us. [In the past] we managed to move on, by some incomprehensible power, and continue with our ventures till they bore fruit."[66] She suggested that Vitka put aside this one-time disappointment and look at the greater picture, mainly the success of saving people and sending them to Mandatory Palestine through the Escape movement. "It is only the first battle that we failed, not the entire war. This is still ahead of us, and we need to gather our powers," she wrote as if she were an integral part of the group. Ruzka tried to persuade Vitka that her real life was still waiting for her in Eretz Israel, that this was the place where she would find meaning. "This is why I am so looking forward to you and I wish to see all of you here. I know it will not be easy [. . .] but it has not been easy for us anywhere else." In a long paragraph, she repeats her deep faith in Vitka's strength and ability to influence others, meaning her fellow members of the revenge group, who were frustrated. "You must support them. They do not have the resources you possess. You must help bring back and spark their hope, their desire for life."[67]

She concluded by telling Vitka about her and Kovner's plan to create a group (Garin – "nucleus" in Hebrew) that would join a kibbutz so they could all stay together. She was already impatient to meet them all and contribute to their wellbeing in the country. Then, all of a sudden, at the end of the last letter, she lost her self-confidence and, out of the blue, wrote a sentence that is difficult to elucidate: "You may think all I have written is silly, but this is what I feel."[68] Was she troubled by the gap between them and the coming meeting with the friend so dear to her who might have changed? Did she fear that the difference between them was unbridgeable? The fact that we do not have Vitka's letters makes it hard to judge, but the trio of Korczak, Kempner, and Kovner would live side by side in Kibbutz Ein Hahoresh for years to come, maintaining good relationships between their families, and joining forces in projects commemorating the Holocaust.[69]

Writing *Flames in the Ashes*

A year and a half into her stay in Mandatory Palestine, after numerous presentations and talks, Korczak's book was published and immediately attracted massive attention. She wrote in Polish, sitting alone in her room in Eilon and not showing

---

66 Ruzka to Vitka, May 5, 1946, in Tuvin, Dror, and Rav, *Ruzka*, 139.
67 Ruzka to Vitka, May 5, 1946, in Tuvin, Dror, and Rav, *Ruzka*, 140.
68 Ruzka to Vitka, May 5, 1946, in Tuvin, Dror, and Rav, *Ruzka*, 140.
69 Vitka married Abba Kovner while Ruzka married Avi Marla. Both families raised their children in the kibbutz.

up to work, which was criticized in the kibbutz. Interestingly, this was not her first attempt to write, as she had kept a diary since leaving Vilna after the war. However, it was lost, "or maybe someone stole it from me," she recounted many years later.[70] She had it in her: the need to document, remember, and memorialize.

Flames in the Ashes was one of the earliest testimonial accounts of the Holocaust and resistance published in the aftermath of the war. It focused on the Vilna Ghetto, the Jewish underground, and the partisans in the forests. "It was the obligation to testify, not any literary pretense or an urge to become famous that led me to write this book," she wrote thirty years later in the introduction to its Russian version in January 1977. "This is not a biography of me and my friends but the story of an entire generation."[71]

Originally written in Polish in 1945, it was simultaneously translated into Hebrew by Benjamin Tene (Tenenbaum), a member of Kibbutz Eilon, who translated her work daily. It was edited by David Hanegbi and published in 1946. The swift translation and publication of the book underscore the urgency of the Yishuv to document and understand this tragedy.[72] Not everyone welcomed it – some fellow partisans who did not belong to her movement were annoyed by the one-sided representation of the events in the Vilna Ghetto and the book denying the role of others in the underground, such as the Bund, the Communists, and Betar.[73] A forceful critique was written by Chaim Lazar, a Betar member who belonged to the FPO underground in the ghetto and was a fellow partisan, still living in Europe at the time. He blamed Korczak for distorting the truth and published two long articles in his movement's organ *Ha'mashkif*, one by one correcting the many details in the book he viewed as errors.[74] But the dominant sentiment supported Korczak, and the book became a success.

Twenty years later, in 1965, an expanded third edition of *Flames in the Ashes* was published, edited by Mordechai Amitai and the author herself. This version added a significant second part titled "The Forest Episode," which detailed the experiences of Jewish partisans. This addition was based not only on Korczak's

---

[70] Tuvin, Dror, and Rav, *Ruzka*, 109.
[71] Quoted in Tuvin, Dror, and Rav, *Ruzka*, 153.
[72] Mendel Piekarz, *The Literature of Testimony as a Historical Source of the Holocaust and Three Hasidic Reflections to the Holocaust* (Jerusalem: Mosad Bialik, 2003), 70–71.
[73] Betar was a Revisionist Zionist youth movement founded by Ze'ev Jabotinsky in 1923 and known for its nationalist ideology and emphasis on military training.
[74] *Ha'mashkif* ("The Observer") was a daily newspaper published in Mandatory Palestine as the main publication of the Revisionist Zionist movement. Chaim Lazar, "Ashes in Flames," *Hamashkif*, February 14, 1947.

memory but on the testimonies of other former partisans. The extended edition also included appendices and corrections based on documents and testimonies that were unavailable to the author when the book was first written. This evolving nature of the book reflects the ongoing process of uncovering and understanding the full scope of the Holocaust experience.

The book's reach expanded further in 1976 with a Russian edition, making these crucial testimonies accessible to a broader audience of former Soviet partisans. In 1988, a fourth Hebrew printing was released, cementing the book's position as a foundational text in Holocaust literature. In 2011, parts of the book were translated into Lithuanian as well.[75]

For Korczak, the act of writing was an integral part of her mission to bear witness, but it was emotionally taxing for her. She often regretted taking on such a challenging task, as the act of writing and speaking would immerse her deeply in the past, thus making it difficult for her to disconnect and return to the present reality. This struggle highlights the profound psychological impact of bearing witness and the complex relationship between survivors and their memories. The process of documenting was not just about creating a historical record but also about grappling with personal trauma and the responsibility of representing the people who did not survive.

The multiple editions, translations, and expansions of *Flames in the Ashes* over several decades demonstrate its enduring significance. It not only serves as a crucial historical source but also as a testament to the evolving nature of Holocaust memory and documentation. The book's journey from its initial spontaneous writing process to its various more accurate publications mirrors the broader process of how Holocaust testimonies over time have been collected, shared, and integrated into the public consciousness and scholarly research.

Holocaust Commemoration and Building an Archive

Korczak's dedication to commemoration extended beyond her testimony and writing the book to recognizing the importance of a centralized repository for documenting the Holocaust. She actively worked together with other Hashomer Hatzair survivors to establish the Moreshet Holocaust Archive in Givat Haviva,

---

75 Evaldas Balčiūnas, "Why I Am Translating Rozka Korczak's Vilna Ghetto Memoir," December 10, 2011, in www.defendinghistory.com.

the educational and ideological center of the movement named after Haviva Reik, a parachutist during the war who was murdered in Slovakia in 1944. Founded in the 1960s, Moreshet engaged in Holocaust research, publishing books and an annual journal, and organizing conferences and educational activities. The archive has collected and preserved survivor testimonies, historical documents – including from people who were brought to Mandatory Palestine from Vilna after the war – and various artifacts. Korczak remained a vital contributor to the institute until her passing in 1988. Her tireless efforts positioned Moreshet at the forefront of Israel's Holocaust memory institutions.[76]

Korczak's commitment to understanding the Holocaust led to her actively researching various related topics, such as the experiences of children in the Nazi concentration camp Buchenwald, the life of Warsaw Ghetto fighter David Nowodworski, etc.[77] She explored both individual stories and broader historical trends. Some of her works were published in the *Moreshet Journal*, while others are collected in the memorial book, which also includes interviews and words of appreciation related to her personality and work.[78]

A Gendered Perspective to Remembering and Commemorating

Even before it became common, Korczak had the foresight to focus her commemoration efforts on the female perspective and acknowledge the immense position of her female comrades in Jewish defiance during the Holocaust. In her testimonies and interviews over the years, she made consistent efforts to bring them to light and depict their actions and bravery. Her early contribution in this field helps scholars pay attention to the important role of women in the resistance movement. In a 1982 interview, for example, she talked about an unknown female hero, Rashka Markovich, referring to her story as "intimate": "Who was Rashka Markovich, 'Rashu'? I don't know if others have written about her. [. . .] She was a Vilna native, a member of Hashomer Hatzair, a young woman, very dark, not

---

[76] For additional information on the establishment of Moreshet, see Adi Portugez's article, "The Beginning of 'Moreshet'," *Moreshet Journal* 80 (2015): 13–25.
[77] Ruzka Korczak, "Children in the Concentration Camp Buchenwald," *Moreshet Journal* 8 (1968): 42–74; Ruzka Korczak, "David Nowodworski – An Image of a Fighter," *Moreshet Journal* 35 (1983): 79–100; Ruzka Korczak, "An Image of a Fighter: Mira Melamed (Buz)," *Moreshet Journal* 42 (1986): 155–172.
[78] Tuvin, Dror, and Rav, *Ruzka*.

beautiful, but her eyes were like no other's. Full of life, full of intelligence, full of sadness. What a pair of Jewish eyes."[79]

Reading this short depiction, one can sense Korczak's rare insights as she describes her friend, who perished during the war. By paying attention to her physical appearance, one can almost sense the intimacy Korczak felt toward her. Two powerful anecdotes linked to Rashka accompanied Ruzka for many years, and she had the chance to tell them openly in an interview that was conducted as late as 1982.

The first one occurred on the last day in the ghetto when the two of them walked toward the meeting point of the group planning to escape through the sewage system. The streets were deserted when they suddenly met Rashka's mother. She crossed the street and greeted her daughter. "It's hard to describe this scene," Ruzka recalled. None of them knew what the future held for them. The mother was not aware of her daughter's plan, and the daughter could not tell her anything. "I stood a bit away to give them a chance to say goodbye. This was one of the few moments in my life where I thought: It is easier for me, because I don't have a mother anymore. I don't have to face this kind of goodbye."[80]

The other incident took place in the partisan forests. Ruzka and Rashka were lying on a bunk when, after a deep silence, her friend said: "Ruzka, you must stay alive." The unexpectedness of this statement surprised Ruzka, who asked, "Wait, what are you talking about? Why all of a sudden?" Rashka repeated her words firmly, "Yes, I mean exactly what I said. You have to stay alive to tell everyone what happened here. You will be the one to tell our story."[81] This was her last request. Not long afterward, Rashka was shot during a partisan action.[82]

Korczak possessed an extraordinary ability to, with remarkable sensitivity and meticulous detail, depict the intricate relationships between women in the ghetto and the partisans. Her writing expresses the profound interpersonal bonds forming amidst the chaos of war. This unique talent to capture the smallest details and paint vivid scenes immerses readers in a comprehensive and nuanced portrayal of her story. She also captures the complexities of female camaraderie during the war and the subtle nuances of interactions, revealing the deep-seated emotions, unspoken understandings, and unwavering support that sustained these women through unimaginable hardship. Beyond the vivid portrayal of indi-

---

79 Ruzka Korczak, interview, 1982, Yad Yaari Archive.
80 Korczak, interview, 1982.
81 Korczak, interview, 1982.
82 Yechiel Gernstein and Moshe Kahanovitz, eds., *The Lexicon of Bravery*, vol. 2 (Jerusalem: Yad Vashem, 1965), 53.

vidual relationships, Korczak managed to paint a broader picture of the collective experiences of women in the resistance.

Conclusion

Jewish historical commissions were established right after the war in various European countries, and one of these even focused specifically on commemorating the Jewish partisans.[83] One of the major efforts of these commissions involved collecting testimonies of survivors when they were still fresh in their memory as well as establishing documentation centers to create a basis for future Holocaust research. While debating the question of historical objectivity and professionalism vis-à-vis memories, which are subjective and selective, they acknowledged that "the experience of survival, commitment to the cause of documentation, and will to act in the present counted more than professional training."[84]

At the same time, private initiatives emerged initiated by survivors who felt the need to tell their stories and write them down. This was the case with Ruzka Korczak's pioneering project of writing *Flames in the Ashes* as early as 1945, following her arrival in Mandatory Palestine in December 1944. At the same time, she traveled the country and met with leaders and large audiences who gathered to hear her story, thus becoming a pioneer in contributing to understanding the Holocaust in the Yishuv in that early stage.

She was not the only one. In March 1944, Elisheva Ingster (Weiss), Fredka Oxenhandler (Mazia), and Chaika Klinger, three ghetto underground members, had arrived in Mandatory Palestine from Poland. They too appeared at the meetings of various official bodies and told their stories, which shocked people. Some of their accounts also appeared in the press but somehow did not achieve the expected impact.[85] The war was still ongoing, and it was still difficult to comprehend the scale of this tragedy. When Korczak arrived, she not only talked about the horrors of the Holocaust but also about Jewish heroism and resistance in the ghetto and the forests as well as the liberation by the Red Army. The context of liberation created a more receptive audience, as people were more prepared to hear and process the full extent of the Holocaust.[86]

---

83 Jockusch, *Collect and Record!*, 156.
84 Jockusch, *Collect and Record!*, 186.
85 Porat, "With Forgiveness and Grace," 114.
86 Porat, "With Forgiveness and Grace," 115.

Despite the earlier arrivals, the perception of Korczak as the "first witness" might also reflect the cumulative impact of testimonies. Each successive account is built upon the previous ones, with Ruzka's testimony perhaps being seen as the most comprehensive or impactful due to its timing and her ability to articulate her experiences. This phenomenon underscores the complex process of how information about the Holocaust was received, understood, and integrated into the consciousness of the Yishuv.

I would add that there was also a political reason behind her better reception. The fact that Korczak represented the movement Hashomer Hatzair, whose leaders were quick to understand the importance of her story and helped spread it, played a major role in creating the dominant narrative she presented. The pioneering youth movements and the socialist parties dominated the Yishuv institutions and used the heroism of their people in Europe in many different ways: to ease their pangs of conscience for not coming to the rescue of the Jews during the Holocaust, to create a narrative of heroism to contradict the notion of "going like sheep to the slaughter," to highlight the members of their own movements as the spearheads of Jewish resistance, to exclude political rivals such as the right-wing Betar and non-Zionist Bund from the pantheon, and to establish a one-sided Israeli narrative, which prevailed for many years.

Korczak's arrival in Mandatory Palestine, all alone, was not planned. She traveled from Vilna to Romania on a mission to find routes and border crossings to transfer survivors across Europe to the Black Sea ports and from there to their homeland. But her meeting with the Hashomer Hatzair emissaries, to whom she told her account of the Holocaust and resistance, changed her path. They convinced her, indeed forced her, to turn toward Mandatory Palestine on a new mission to spread the word.

It seems as if Korczak was the right person to deliver the voices of the survivors to the Yishuv. She was eloquent – albeit in Yiddish. She was an impressive woman, a fighter who took part in the resistance. She had a good sense of history, and she was a dedicated member of Hashomer Hatzair, praising her fellow members and showing sympathy to the movement leaders in the Yishuv, despite differences of opinion and their lack of a full understanding of the Holocaust.

This is reflected in a series of letters she sent to her soulmate Vitka Kempner (later Kovner), who stayed behind and was involved in plans of revenge against the Germans, which the leadership in the Yishuv opposed. In a letter written in August 1945, Korczak begged her friend to show "consideration" to them and their motives, since "the reality here is of productive labor which bears a lot of fruits [. . .] and the perspective must be of life and not of death. [. . .] Here we should fight for life, and all the rest is unimportant."[87] The letters also reflect how deep their friendship was, how she longed for her friend, and how important Vitka's opinion was to her. Despite the appreciation she received in the Yishuv, as well as the hundreds of people she had met and talked to, Korczak felt lonely without her wartime friends. She was welcomed as a hero but felt lonely among those who did not share her wartime experiences.

Korczak's early dedication to collecting testimonies, establishing a commemoration institute such as Moreshet in the early 1960s, and advocating for a better understanding of Jewish resistance during the Holocaust laid the groundwork for future generations of scholars and educators. By bringing Korczak's story to light, we gain a richer appreciation for the complex task of memory construction in the aftermath of the Holocaust. Furthermore, her life and work serve as a powerful reminder of the crucial role of women in the resistance and subsequently when it comes to strengthening and preserving the memory of the Holocaust.

Daniela Ozacky Stern is a scholar of Jewish resistance during the Holocaust and the Second World War. She is a lecturer in the Holocaust Studies Program at Western Galilee College, Israel. Ozacky Stern earned a PhD in Jewish History, specializing in Jewish partisans in Lithuania and Belarus during the Holocaust, and a master's degree focusing on Nazi propaganda under Joseph Goebbels. She conducted post-doctoral research at Yad Vashem on Holocaust documentation and Jewish resistance movements. She was an Archive Fellow at the Fortunoff Video Archive for Holocaust Testimonies at Yale University, where she researched survivor testimonies and resistance narratives. Her publications deal with Jewish partisans in Eastern Europe, the Vilna Ghetto, and Holocaust documentation. She is the book review editor of the *Jewish Culture and History* journal.

---

87 Tuvin, Dror, and Rav, *Ruzka*, 128

Section III: **Engaging the Field**

Maria Simonsen
Writing the History of a Reform University: Challenges and Opportunities

Abstract: The 1950s and 1960s witnessed a global expansion of modern universities aiming to reform pedagogical, research, and governance practices in higher education. Established in the mid-1970s, Aalborg University was among Denmark's last reform universities to be created at the tail end of this period. In 2024, the university celebrated its fiftieth anniversary, which was marked by a series of jubilee events and the publication of *At bygge et universitet: Aalborg Universitet 1974–2024*, an account of its historical trajectory that I co-authored with Mogens Rüdiger. The article reflects on the process of writing this book, while emphasising the unique challenges and opportunities we faced when documenting the history of Aalborg University in the absence of a centralised university archive, from piecing together dispersed sources to integrating diverse voices often overlooked in the conventional biographical narratives of more traditional universities. Situating the rapid expansion of Aalborg University within its broader social context required a broad narrative approach illustrating how the study of a modern university can enrich university historiography and the broader field of the history of institutional knowledge.

Keywords: university history, modern university, reform university, Aalborg University

1 The New Reform Universities

In the 1950s and 1960s, a wave of educational expansion swept several parts of the world. During the 1960s alone, annual enrolments of new students doubled across many Western European countries, with even greater increases in countries such as France, Norway, and Finland.[1] One significant consequence of this

---

[1] Johan Östling, *Kunskapens stora hus: Huvudlinjer i universitetets historia* (Gothenburg: Makadam, 2024), 103; Heike Jöns, "Modern School and University," in *A Companion to the History of Science*, ed. Bernard Lightman (New York: Wiley & Sons, 2016), 332; Hans Fink et al., *Universitetet og videnskab. Universitetets idéhistorie, videnskabsteori og etik* (Copenhagen: Hans Reitzels Forlag, 2003), 130.

Note: The author is grateful to Else Hansen, Mogens Rüdiger, Lise Thorup-Pedersen, Jon Wilcox, and Johan Östling for their helpful advice and comments during the preparation of this article.

ථ Open Access. © 2025 the author(s), published by De Gruyter. This work is licensed under the Creative Commons Attribution-NonCommercial-NoDerivatives 4.0 International License.
https://doi.org/10.1515/9783111636726-008

surge was the establishment of numerous new universities across Europe and the United States. Several factors contributed to this massive expansion. The large post-war birth cohorts started to enter higher education just as universities became more accessible to previously underrepresented groups. Increasingly, women and students from non-academic backgrounds gained access to higher education.[2] Furthermore, various forms of financial support for education, introduced in many countries starting in the 1960s, further bolstered this rise in enrolment.

Many of the new universities established in the 1960s and 1970s differed significantly from traditional universities. In her article "Modern School and University", Heike Jöns describes these modern schools and universities as "post-medieval institutions that were subsequently modernized at various occasions through new intellectual movements and related institutional reform".[3] However, the term 'modern' only partially captures the unique and radical nature of the universities that emerged in this period. These institutions represented a clear departure from older universities, both in terms of their approach to education and their institutional structures. In British scholarship, the new universities of this period are typically described as 'utopian',[4] while in Germany, the term *Reformuniversität* is preferred.[5] Here, I use "modern university" in a general sense (to distinguish them from traditional or older universities) and "reform university" when specifically discussing the universities established in the 1960s and 1970s that had a transformative impact on academia. These institutions not only modernised but actively *reformed* educational practices and structures in numerous ways, hence my use of this term. Perhaps the most distinctive characteristic of the reform universities was their attempts at reforming the studies and structure at these universities by abolishing faculties.

Many of the new reform universities shared several defining characteristics. They were often located on integrated campuses outside city centres, typically in medium-sized regional cities that previously, at most, had a college or a small

---

2 Julian Lamberty, *Universitetet og konkurrencestaten: Et studie af Syddansk Universitet 1990–2016* (Odense: Syddansk Universitetsforlag, 2022), 31; Maria Simonsen, "Between Tradition and Experiment: The Idea of a New University", *Nordic Journal of Educational History* 10, no. 2 (2023): 45–58.
3 Jöns, "Modern School and University", 310.
4 In Britain, the term 'utopian' is largely limited to universities established in the 1960s up to the turn of the decade. As noted by Jill Pellew and Miles Taylor, "by the early 1970s [. . .] the 'utopian' moment had passed". Jill Pellew and Miles Taylor, eds., *Utopian Universities: A Global History of the New Campuses of the 1960s* (London: Bloomsbury, 2021), 5.
5 Moritz Mälzer, *Auf der Suche nach der neuen Universität. Die Entstehung der 'Reformuniversitäten' Konstanz und Bielefeld in den 1960er Jahren* (Göttingen: Vandenhoeck & Ruprecht, 2016).

number of higher education programmes. Another common feature was their architecture, which frequently included examples of modernist-inspired construction.[6] However, they also differed significantly, particularly in terms of the societal conditions under which they were established. The favourable economic climate characterising much of the West in the 1960s – leading, among other things, to considerable investments in higher education – had shifted drastically by the 1970s, when the oil crisis and economic recession affected many countries. In Denmark, for example, this affected the university expansion, which was planned during the economic boom to then be realised under far more constrained financial conditions.

Another factor shaping these institutions was the influence of the student movement. The ideology and rhetoric that defined the political left and student activism in the mid-1960s differed markedly from those of the late 1970s. As suggested by the terms 'reform' or 'utopian', these universities were often experimental, introducing innovative curricula and pedagogical approaches while also exploring new models for organising research and engaging with local and regional communities.[7] The focus on testing and experimentation led to significant changes in the educational landscape. Arguably, no other period saw "so much experimentation in what a university should look like physically; how, what and whom it might teach; and how it should be governed".[8] These universities often took inspiration from one another. For example, new Danish universities founded in the early 1970s introduced a "base year" model, drawing on American and Swedish examples.[9] In these institutions, the base year allowed students to switch programmes without delaying their education. This flexible model was even considered by the University of Copenhagen – an institution founded in the medieval period – but was ultimately deemed too radical for its traditional framework.[10] Over time, however, elements initially regarded as experimental, such as interdisciplinary research and group work, gradually came to permeate even the oldest universities.[11]

---

6 For more on campus architecture, see Pellew and Taylor, *Utopian Universities*, 15, note 32.
7 Pellew and Taylor, *Utopian Universities*, 2–6.
8 Pellew and Taylor, *Utopian Universities*, 2.
9 Else Hansen, *En koral i tidens strøm: Roskilde Universitetscenter 1972–1997* (Roskilde: Roskilde Universitetsforlag, 1997), 53.
10 Maria Simonsen and Mogens Rüdiger, *At bygge et universitet: Aalborg Universitet 1974–2024* (Copenhagen: Nord Academic, 2024), 40.
11 Marianne Rostgaard, *Aalborg Universitet: En billedfortælling 1974–2004* (Aalborg: Aalborg University, 2004), 19, 25–26.

The extensive changes across universities also placed education policy and pedagogical reform high on the political agenda in the late 1960s and early 1970s. Public spending on higher education increased on an unprecedented scale[12] as education came to be seen as an investment just as crucial as those in production and technology.[13] This shift had a lasting impact on higher education, especially in the West. Between 1960 and 1980, the university sector is estimated to have expanded by 300 to 400 per cent.[14] The establishment of many new universities and the transformation of the educational landscape marked a clear break from earlier generations and traditions, affecting both modern and traditional institutions. During this period, particularly around 1968, tensions flared between the student movement and representatives of both old and new universities. While Scandinavian countries experienced relatively peaceful protests compared to the disruptive demonstrations in France and Germany, the generational conflicts in Tokyo and Mexico City were far more intense as several lives were lost amid the clashes.[15] In Denmark, too, the demands of the student movement turned into a catalyst for modernising university governance, teaching, and research orientation. As described by Peter C. Kjærsgaard and Jens Erik Kristensen, these demands were often made "in direct alliance with government officials and politicians".[16]

Today, the modern universities founded across the globe in the 1960s and 1970s have reached maturity, where many have celebrated multiple major anniversaries. As numerous new universities have since been established, the reform universities of this era are no longer seen as the youngest or most modern. In fact, some have even trended towards 're-traditionalisation', adopting elements of older, more traditional universities – such as ceremonial graduation events or formal installations of new professors – to reflect a more conventional institutional identity. Anniversaries and other celebrations often prompt reflection.[17] For traditional and modern universities alike, these milestones offer an opportunity to narrate and frame their histories. In the early years of many modern universities, they documented their histories in small, in-house publications. How-

---

12 Pellew and Taylor, *Utopian Universities*, 2; Fink et al., *Universitetet og videnskab*, 130.
13 Simonsen and Rüdiger, *At bygge et universitet*, 41.
14 Östling, *Kunskapens stora hus*, 107.
15 Notker Hammerstein, "Social Sciences, History and Law", in *A History of the University in Europe*, ed. Walter Rüegg (Cambridge: Cambridge University Press, 2011), 392; Östling, *Kunskapens stora hus*, 107–108; Louis Vos, "Student Movements and Political Activism", in *A History of the University in Europe*, ed. Walter Rüegg (Cambridge: Cambridge University Press, 2011), 107–108.
16 Fink et al., *Universitetet og videnskab*, 131.
17 Simonsen and Rüdiger, *At bygge et universitet*, 182; Rostgaard, *Aalborg Universitet*, 7.

ever, as they have reached their fiftieth, sixtieth, or seventieth anniversaries, more extensive anniversary volumes have emerged in recent years that offer in-depth accounts of their beginnings, development, and, in some cases, future prospects.[18] In addition to these anniversary publications, more thematic studies have also appeared, offering fresh perspectives on university history. Anthologies or monographs often explore topics such as modern universities' architecture, pedagogical practices, and relationships with the state.[19] These thematic works shed light on various aspects of the university experience, including life on campus, working conditions, and interactions with surrounding communities, often presenting a more nuanced view than the biographical focus of anniversary publications.[20] This trend has also sparked a greater reflection on university history as a field of academic inquiry, which has contributed to a notable increase in historiographical articles on the subject.[21] The growing body of recent publications underscores that the time has come to historicise modern universities and to situate them within a broader historical context.

The present study should be seen within this broader context of recent historiographical developments in university history. In the early spring of 2024, my colleague Mogens Rüdiger and I completed *At bygge et universitet: Aalborg Universitet 1974–2024* (Designing a University: Aalborg University, 1974–2024). This is an anniversary book about Aalborg University – a modern institution established in the mid-1970s as the last of Denmark's reform universities amid the post-war educational expansion of higher education.[22] Just like hundreds of other university campuses worldwide, Aalborg University was a product of the significant educational reforms of the era. Reflecting the spirit of the new university move-

---

[18] Examples of more comprehensive anniversary publications include Hansen, *En koral i tidens strøm*; Jürgen Lüthje and Dietmar Schütz, eds., *50 Jahre Universität in Oldenburg: Ein Glücksfall für Stadt und Region* (Oldenburg: Isensee, 2024); Andreas Beaugrand, ed., *50 Jahre Zukunft: FH Bielefeld 1971–2021* (Bielefeld: Transcript, 2021).
[19] See, for instance, Pellew and Taylor, *Utopian Universities*; Lamberty, *Universitetet og konkurrencestaten*; Johanna Ringarp, *Frihetsretorik och marknadslogik. En analys av den svenska högskolepolitiken 1970–2014* (Gothenburg and Stockholm: Makadam förlag, 2024).
[20] Simonsen and Rüdiger, *At bygge et universitet*.
[21] Peter Dhondt, ed., *University Jubilees and University History Writing: A Challenging Relationship* (Leiden: Brill, 2015); Peter Josephson and Thomas Karlsohn, eds., *Universitetets gränser* (Gothenburg: Freudianska föreningen, 2019); Johan Östling, "Contemporary Nordic Histories of the Universities: The Renewal of An Old Field", *Nordic Journal of Educational History* 10, no. 2 (2023): 37–44. See also Östling, *Kunskapens stora hus*, 130–131 and Sylvia Paletschek, "Stand und Perspektiven der neueren Universitätsgeschichte", *NTM Zeitschrift für Geschichte der Wissenschaften, Technik und Medizin* 19 (2011): 169–189.
[22] Lüthje and Schütz, *50 Jahre Universität in Oldenburg*; Simonsen and Rüdiger, *At bygge et universitet*.

ment, Aalborg University Centre – as it was known during its first two decades – was experimental in terms of both research models and pedagogical approaches,[23] traits that continue to define the institution to this day.[24] In the following three sections, I reflect on the process of writing the history of Aalborg University. While working on the anniversary book together with Mogens Rüdiger, I observed key differences between publications on older, more traditional universities and accounts of the younger universities founded in the 1960s and 1970s. I soon realised that narrating the history of these universities may require a distinct narrative approach. At the same time, I recognised that writing the history of a reform university presents specific challenges as well as unique opportunities to renew the institution's historical narrative. Many of the experiences, challenges, and opportunities we encountered in documenting the history of Aalborg University are shared more broadly in efforts to chronicle modern universities. Moreover, current trends in university historiography suggest potential future directions for the field. In the concluding section of this article, I argue that future studies would benefit from comparative analyses of modern and traditional universities, both nationally and transnationally, to better understand the evolution of university history. I begin by offering a brief overview of the establishment of Danish universities from the Middle Ages to the 1970s, when Aalborg University and the other reform universities were founded.

2 Writing the History of Aalborg University

Up until the latter half of the 1960s, Denmark had only two universities: the University of Copenhagen, established by King Christian I in 1479, and Aarhus University, founded in 1928. In addition, there were several specialised schools of higher education, such as Den Polytekniske Læreansalt (The Polytechnic, founded 1829), Kongelige Veterinær- og Landbohøjskole (The Royal Veterinary and Agricultural University, 1856), and Foreningen til Unge Handelsmænds Uddannelse (The Association for Young Tradesmen's Education, 1880), now known as Copenhagen Business School. The polytechnic model, based on the French École Polytechnique, had gained widespread influence across Europe in the nineteenth century. Rooted in the practical application of research, this model led to the establishment of several specialised colleges (*højskoler*) in Denmark, a trend that contin-

---

23 Simonsen, "Between Tradition and Experiment", 51.
24 Simonsen and Rüdiger, *At bygge et universitet*, 85–87.

ued into the twentieth century.[25] Following the Second World War and a period of rapid population growth, it became increasingly clear that the Danish higher education sector needed to expand. One key reason was the rising number of students from the large post-war birth cohorts; another was the growing recognition among policymakers regarding the need for academic research within the public sector.[26] However, determining where and how this expansion should take place was a complex issue that took some time to resolve. Various local and regional groups began advocating for establishing universities outside Copenhagen and Aarhus, the two largest cities in the country, which led to a significant transformation of the higher education landscape, including through greater political oversight of higher education programmes.[27] Within just fifteen years, Denmark saw a sharp increase in student enrolment, faculty numbers, and public investments in universities and higher education.[28] Between the mid-1960s and mid-1970s, three new universities were founded: Odense University in 1966, Roskilde University Centre in 1972, and, finally, Aalborg University Centre in 1974.

These new universities shared several key characteristics. They were primarily intended to alleviate pressure on the older universities in Copenhagen and Aarhus. However, they were also part of a broader transformation of universities from elite institutions to mass universities. They were expected to introduce pedagogical and research reforms, particularly based on interdisciplinary and project-based approaches.[29] The universities in Roskilde and Aalborg were established as "university centres" – a term reflecting the vision of integrating both traditional university programmes and professional education, such as the welfare officer programme, which had previously not been part of university institutions.[30] At Odense University, there was also a debate over whether the institution should be designated a university centre, but a consensus was never reached. Discussions on the matter continued for nearly a decade to conclude in 1976 when

---

25 Fink et al., *Universitetet og videnskab*, 122–124.
26 Fink et al., *Universitetet og videnskab*, 130.
27 In Denmark, the so-called Governance Act (Styrelsesloven) for universities was adopted in 1970 and revised in 1973. The Act abolished the exclusive right of professors to manage universities and granted greater influence to all teachers, students, and technical/administrative staff. However, it also reflected a broader political desire for increased governmental oversight of universities.
28 Fink et al., *Universitetet og* videnskab, 130; Simonsen, "Between Tradition and Experiment", 48, 52.
29 Simonsen and Rüdiger, *At bygge et universitet*,154–173.
30 Hansen, *En koral i tidens strøm*, 75.

the idea of Odense as a university centre was ultimately abandoned.[31] However, important differences among the new universities gradually became more apparent. Even though all three were influenced by the political left, the degree and intensity of this influence varied. Roskilde University Centre quickly became politically controversial due to the dominance of left-wing forces, especially among the students,[32] to the extent that some politicians even advocated for closing it down. In Aalborg, the left-wing students also dominated campus politics for several years, but in view of the experience in Roskilde, the university management sought to maintain tighter control over the movement.[33] Meanwhile, the regional role of the universities in Odense and Aalborg was particularly pronounced. As a regional institution, Odense University had much in common with Aalborg University. For both Odense and Aalborg, securing a university was a blessing for the surrounding region. The universities not only brought in students but also development and new opportunities.

Aalborg University celebrated its fiftieth anniversary in 2024. To mark this occasion, the university management funded the research project "Knowledge for the World: The History of Aalborg University, 1974–2024" aimed at producing, among other outputs, a substantial book on the university's first fifty years.[34] Tasked with this project, we also wanted to write a book accessible to a wider audience, including technical/administrative staff and students, and not just researchers with an interest in university history or Aalborg University specifically. When Mogens Rüdiger and I embarked on our research in early 2021, we did not venture into an entirely uncharted territory; some aspects of Aalborg University's history had already been documented. However, our project marked the first time that the university management had actively sponsored a dedicated historical study of the institution. Previous anniversaries had produced various publications – some written by enthusiastic individuals from specific departments keen to preserve the history of their generation, others offering brief overviews accompanied by photos and general accounts of the early years of the university and its founders. Additional formats, such as interview books and commemorative mag-

---

31 Tønnes Bekker-Nielsen, "Det tredje universitet. Fra de glade tressere til de flade tiere", in *En verden af viden: Syddansk Universitet, 1966–2016*, ed. Jeppe Nevers (Odense: Syddansk Universitetsforlag, 2016), 28.
32 Hansen, *En koral i tidens strøm*, 146–147.
33 The political student movement also had a significant impact on the older universities in Copenhagen and Aarhus. See, for instance, Finn Hansson, *1968 Studenteroprør og Undervisningsrevolution. En fortælling om opgøret med traditionel universitetsundervisning* (Roskilde: Roskilde Universitetsforlag, 2018).
34 In addition to Aalborg University, the project was also supported by Det Obelske Familiefond.

azines, had also contributed to summarising aspects of Aalborg University's history.[35] Yet, a common characteristic of these earlier publications was their limited scope: the majority focused on a particular institute, department, theme, or period, and none of them provided a comprehensive account linking together the different facets of the university. Given this background, one of our primary objectives was to create a more complete and integrated history of Aalborg University.

In the following, I reflect on this process and discuss some of the challenges and opportunities we encountered when writing our book. I focus on two key factors that significantly shaped our work: the availability of extensive archival materials and the role of the university's founding figures. I start with a brief overview of the historiography of Danish universities in order to place the history of Aalborg University within a broader historiographical framework. Much of the history of Danish universities has been written in the context of anniversaries or other celebrations, often by individuals within the institutions themselves. Scholarly research on the history of both modern and traditional Danish universities has been relatively limited and often leans towards biographical narratives.[36] However, the extensive publication on the University of Copenhagen by Svend Ellehøj and Leif Grane stands out, both in terms of its depth and the long period of publication.[37] Many anniversary publications recount the establishment of the university in question with a traditional emphasis on key figures – vice-chancellors, prominent professors, or others who played a significant role in shaping the institution – while often overlooking broader questions regarding university policy, conflicts, or issues such as gender.

Some notable exceptions challenge this conventional approach to Danish university historiography.[38] Else Hansen's works on Roskilde University Centre and welfare state university policy – *En koral i tidens strøm* (1997) and *Professorer, studenter og polit.er* (2017) – as well as Jens Frøslev Christensen's *Oprøret på CBS* (2016), which examines the series of missteps at Copenhagen Business School that

---

[35] For a complete overview of publications on Aalborg University, see Simonsen and Rüdiger, *At bygge et universitet*, 279–285.
[36] On the history of the University of Southern Denmark, Roskilde University, and Aalborg University, see Jeppe Nevers, ed., *En verden af viden: Syddansk Universitet, 1966–2016* (Odense: Syddansk Universitetsforlag, 2016); Hansen, *En koral i tidens strøm*; Rostgaard, *Aalborg Universitet*; Else Hansen, *Professorer, studenter og polit.er: om velfærdsstatens universitetspolitik, 1950–1975* (Copenhagen: Museum Tusculanums, 2017); Lamberty, *Universitetet og konkurrencestaten*.
[37] Svend Ellehøj and Leif Grane, eds., *Københavns Universitet 1479–1979* (Copenhagen: C.E.C Gads Forlag, 1986–2005).
[38] See also Hansen's discussion on university history in Denmark in *Professorer, studenter og polit.er*, 26–38.

ultimately led to the departure of its president in 2011,[39] represent examples of studies that courageously confront the conventions in this field by addressing the conflicts that were central in the histories of these universities.[40] Ning de Coninck-Smith's pioneering research on two female students who later became employees at Aarhus University goes even further,[41] experimenting with the genre by using an "imaginative archive [. . .] to imagine how the two women's lives unfolded" and thus compensating for gaps in the archival record.[42] These recent works undoubtedly contribute to advancing the field of Danish university historiography. Nevertheless, there is still a need for more research-based studies of individual universities, as well as comprehensive histories of Danish higher education as a whole. Institutional narratives often become insular, whereas a broader historical approach could offer a more nuanced understanding of the mission and significance of each university within its intellectual, societal, and cultural contexts. In other words, a more expansive historiographical perspective is essential for the field to evolve. This call for a broader perspective extends beyond Denmark. Most histories of Danish universities, including my own publications, are framed within a national context, overlooking factors such as the impact of Europeanisation or other significant international influences on higher education, but this limitation is also evident in much of the scholarship on university history in other countries.

3 The Status of the Archival Record

Writing university history, above all, requires access to source material. At the outset of this project, Mogens Rüdiger and I were surprised to discover that no centralised university archive exists for Aalborg University. Previous publications

---

[39] The firing of the president, Johan Roos, followed the bodged merger of one of the business programmes at the Copenhagen Business School with its management institute, which led to several graduate students not receiving their degree accreditations. However, the board of the school suggested that this was just one of the reasons for Roos' departure. Jens Frøslev Christensen, *Oprøret på CBS: Forandring, ledelse og modstand i en professionel organisation* (Frederiksberg: Samfundslitteratur, 2016).

[40] Hansen, *En koral i tidens strøm*; Hansen, *Professorer, studenter og polit.er*; Christensen, *Oprøret på CBS*.

[41] Ning de Coninck-Smith, "Gender Encounters University – University Encounters Gender: Affective Archives Aarhus University, Denmark 1928–1953", *Women's History Review* 29, no. 3 (2020), 413–428.

[42] Coninck-Smith, "Gender Encounters University", 17.

had relied on scattered sources available at the Danish National Archives, local archives in Aalborg, and the university library – without a centralised overview of the available materials.[43] Beyond preserving the basic records mandated by Danish archive legislation, there had been no concerted effort to collect secondary materials during the early years of the university. There are likely several reasons why this was neglected. One explanation may be found in the nature of a young university: its leadership and employees focused on the future rather than on the past, prioritising development over preservation. It was not until the fiftieth anniversary that the importance of archiving materials in order to document the university's history was fully recognised. The rapid expansion of Aalborg University further complicated efforts to trace the development of its departments and institutions. Few faculty members or staff had documented their experiences in personal biographies,[44] and while some employees and departments had published isolated historical insights, these accounts remained unconnected. Piecing together these disparate fragments became a major challenge. Furthermore, little attention had been paid to materials that did not neatly fit into formal collections – such as artefacts, songs, and photos from daily life or special events – materials that are typically valued in cultural history but had never been systematically collected at Aalborg University.

For a book like ours, this type of material was crucial in creating a fuller and more nuanced history of everyday university life. Even though we had access to official records, such as the rector's speeches and board meeting minutes, these mostly reflected a narrow managerial perspective. Fortunately, through a "call for material" aimed at past and present staff and students, we were able to collect more personal artefacts. Many contributors sifted through attics, basements, and old offices, uncovering invaluable materials that captured everyday university experiences – items that might otherwise have been discarded during office moves or cleanouts. In fact, we still receive archival contributions even months after the project was concluded. However, one question remains: What will happen to the collected materials now that the project has ended? This issue is yet to be resolved. While collecting the materials was an essential first step, it has also sparked discussions at various levels within the university on how to establish a permanent archival solution in the future.

---

[43] The value of official documents, such as those in the Danish National Archives, should not be underestimated. Meeting minutes and other records offer an insight into internal disagreements and the early stages of new initiatives.

[44] Peter Plenge, "Min tid på Aalborg Universitet", Aalborg University, 2003; Lars Lönnroth, *Dörrar till främmande rum – minnesfragment* (Stockholm: Atlantis, 2009).

The lack of a centralised archive in Aalborg also led us to explore alternative sources for documenting and preserving institutional memory. We found that local and regional press coverage, alongside internal publications such as university newspapers, student magazines, and websites, offered valuable insights into the university's activities and culture, thus providing new perspectives on the evolution of Aalborg University. These broader archival challenges are not unique to Aalborg University or even to newer universities in general; they are equally relevant to older institutions. Today, universities generate vast amounts of both digital and physical material, and archiving practices vary from country to country. Preserving these diverse materials is essential, as they illuminate different facets of university history and help reconstruct institutional operations in past periods. Maintaining archives is also a financial consideration, but this investment is worth making – ensuring that a university retains its institutional memory as a key component of its future vision.

The absence of a well-defined archival system at Aalborg University posed a significant challenge, but it also created unique opportunities. Without a predefined collection, we had the flexibility to include materials often overlooked in conventional university histories, thereby reducing the risk of merely reproducing the official narrative. During interviews, we aimed to gather insights from a broad spectrum of individuals – secretaries, caretakers, students, principals, and senior executives – embracing the motto: "as many voices as possible". Our goal was to build a history that truly reflected the diversity of people essential to a university's daily operations.

4 The Founding Fathers

Many of the individuals who helped establish and shape the universities of the 1960s and 1970s are still alive today, and they often feature prominently in university histories – for good reason.[45] Their testimonies provide important insights and help historians trace the development of the reform universities. Here, the term 'founding fathers' extends beyond the initial management to also include technical/administrative staff and former students, who later played a crucial role in shaping the learning environment, campus culture, student publications,

---

45 Examples include Beaugrand, *50 Jahre Zukunft*; Lüthje and Schütz, *50 Jahre Universität in Oldenburg*; Jes Adolphsen, *I satte os i jeres baner: Interviews med 19 vigtige personer i AUC's historie* (Aalborg: Aalborg Universitetsforlag, 1984); Peter Ditlev Oldenburg, *Glimt fra nordjysk universitetshistorie gennem 40 år* (Aalborg: Aalborg Universitetsforlag, 1999).

and other formative practices and institutions. At Aalborg University, the early founders, leaders, and many engaged students were predominantly men; over time, however, more women entered leadership roles both within the university administration and the student community. It took years, however, for their contributions to gain visibility in, for instance, student publications.

Many of those who helped establish Aalborg University remain linked to it. Several early lecturers are now emeritus professors, and some first-generation students later became staff members. Long-time rector Sven Caspersen, university director Peter Penge,[46] and information officer Allan Clausen were key supporters of our project and shared their extensive understanding of university management and the early years of life at Aalborg University, among other things through both official and informal interviews and by sharing material from their working life.[47] Inevitably, the history of the university in some respects also serves as an evaluation of their collective efforts. A key challenge in involving these founders, however, concerns managing the potential for conscious or unconscious attempts to influence how their contributions and legacies are portrayed. To mitigate this, we carefully cross-checked information with written documents such as university annual reports and corroborated personal accounts through multiple interviews.[48] Still, the fact that many of Aalborg University's founding employees are still alive presented invaluable opportunities for our research. We could ask direct questions about specific events in the university's history, gather diverse perspectives from students across decades, and engage the past and present management in reflecting on both strategic and practical decisions with the benefit of hindsight. What had they succeeded in? Where had they gone wrong?

Obviously, it was not possible to interview or contact all employees, students, or external partners who had been part of Aalborg University over the past fifty years. This limitation inevitably led to some disappointment, particularly among members of the university's earliest generations, who felt that their voices were not sufficiently represented. Even after half a century, emotions remained strong.

---

[46] Sven Caspersen and Peter Plenge have been key figures in developing Aalborg University. Sven Caspersen was appointed rector in 1976 and served until 2004, after which he chaired the university's first board until 2006, when he retired. Peter Plenge was employed in the Planning Secretariat, which prepared the university. In 1977, he became head of administration. After seven years as university director at the University of Copenhagen, he was appointed to the same position at AAU in 1998 until he retired in 2014.

[47] Simonsen and Rüdiger, *At bygge et universitet*.

[48] In our work on the history of Aalborg University, we conducted approximately 25 interviews and collected approximately the same number of written testimonies.

A small group of former students, some of whom later became staff members, were especially dissatisfied with the anniversary publication, feeling it did not adequately capture their experiences – particularly the significance of the base year at Aalborg University. In response, they produced their own anniversary publication where they shared personal memoirs from the university's formative years.[49] This reaction highlights the deep attachment many feel towards the institution and underscores the challenge of crafting a history that resonates with a broad and diverse community.[50]

5 The Future of University History

There are many ways to tell the story of a reform university. By adopting innovative approaches that place the institution within a broader social context and by incorporating diverse sources often absent from traditional accounts, our study demonstrates how the history of a single modern university can enrich the broader tapestry of university historiography. Despite the long history of the academy, university historiography has often been characterised by a conservative and somewhat limited approach. As Johan Östling observes, "historians of the universities have not always belonged to the avantgarde of historical research".[51] However, since 2010, the field has undergone renewal, driven by new historical lenses – such as gender, media, and information history – as well as the "radical changes in academic reality around the year 2000".[52] Moreover, the reform universities of the 1960s and 1970s have reached milestones in recent years

---

49 This publication, also financed by Aalborg University, is titled *Gåsen og guldægget* and is authored by Mogens Ove Madsen, Jan Holm Ingemann, and Steen Ørndorf (Aalborg: Aalborg Universitetsforlag, 2024). It is discussed in Lasse Højsgaard, "Aalborg Universitet", Forskerforum, 21 June 2024, https://dm.dk/forskerforum/magasinet/2024/forskerforum-nr-3-2024/i-projektarbej det-kunne-man-tage-fat-i-struben-og-faa-rystet-en-ordentlig-akademiker-ud-af-dem/; Maria Simonsen and Mogens Rüdiger, "Replik Forskerforums artikel om Aalborg Universitet: Dårlig journalistik", Forskerforum, 27 June 2024, https://dm.dk/forskerforum/debat/replik-til-forskerforums-artikel-om-aalborg-universitet-daarlig-journalistik/.
50 This kind of a challenge is not unique to Aalborg University. On the occasion of the twenty-fifth anniversary of Roskilde University Centre, three anniversary books were published – there were many thoughts on how the history of the university should be told. Hansen, *En koral i tidens strøm*; Henrik Toft Jensen, *RUC i 25 år* (Roskilde: Roskilde Universitetsforlag 1997); Henning Salling Olesen, *Utopien der slog rod. RUC – radikalitet og realisme* (Roskilde: Studenterrådet Roskilde Universitetscenter,1997).
51 Östling, "Contemporary Nordic Histories", 37.
52 Östling, "Contemporary Nordic Histories", 38.

having prompted institutional introspection regarding their trajectories. Why did we evolve the way we did? Where are we heading in the future? Anniversaries – marking fifty, sixty, or even seventy years (for the earliest reform universities) – have offered opportunities to place these institutions within a larger historical framework.

How will the study of university history evolve? Judging from current trends, it is a field marked by increasing dynamism and innovation. Recent publications on modern university history reveal a growing willingness to experiment, thus challenging a discipline once known for its conservatism. Future comparative studies of traditional and reform universities could prove enlightening, especially when it comes to the question of how traditional and modern universities have influenced each other. In the case of Aalborg University, I have observed how it, in important ways, has moved towards the organisational structures of traditional universities – for instance, in relation to interdisciplinary collaboration. Another crucial avenue for future research is the internationalisation of university operations and governance, particularly the increasing Europeanisation of higher education since the transformative years around the fall of the Berlin Wall in 1989. Understanding these broader influences will be essential when tracing the evolution of universities in the decades to come.

As one of the youngest universities in Denmark, Aalborg University may have been lulled into a sense of perpetual youth, perhaps in one way or another overlooking the importance of systematic documentation – until its fiftieth anniversary prompted a moment of reflection. In addition, the work in connection with the anniversary has also demonstrated the significance of history in terms of creating a shared institutional identity.

Maria Simonsen is an associate professor of modern history at Aalborg University. Her research interests include the history of the book and publishing (from the nineteenth century onwards), the history of knowledge, and university history. She is currently part of the Wallenberg-funded research project "The Europeanisation of the Universities: Transforming Knowledge Institutions from Within, c. 1985–2010" led by Professor Johan Östling at Lund University. Her recent related publications include the article "Between Tradition and Experiment: The Idea of a New University" in the *Nordic Journal of Educational History* (2023) and *At bygge et universitet: Aalborg Universitet 1974–2024* (Nord Academic, 2024).

Bruno Hamnell
The Numinous, the Political, and the Epistemic: Analytical Categories for Exploring the Historical Intersections of Spirituality, Ideology, and Knowledge

Abstract: Historians of knowledge recognize that scientific knowledge is inseparable from ideology, which means that the intertwinement of *the epistemic* and *the political* constitutes a key topic of study. However, historians of knowledge have thus far not focused sufficiently on intersections with religiosity and spirituality. To address this gap, this article introduces *the numinous* as a complementary analytical category alongside the epistemic and the political with the aim of capturing these overlooked dimensions, which are essential to the *circulation* of knowledge. Through case studies regarding *holism* in the thought of Jan Smuts and Abraham Maslow, the article demonstrates how this expanded framework reveals the entanglement of scientific knowledge, ideology, and spirituality.

Keywords: analytical categories, boundary work, history of knowledge, science and religion, Jan Smuts, Abraham Maslow

Introduction

Ever since the postwar era, the history of science is no longer written as a Western story of progress separating science from culture. Instead, historians view science as a collective embodied material practice and a situated social construct tied to power. Even foundational epistemological concepts such as "truth" and "objectivity" have been denaturalized and relativized through historical scrutiny.[1] The breakthrough of this approach is often linked to works such as Thomas Kuhn's *The Structure of Scientific Revolutions* (1962) and Michel Foucault's *Les*

Note: This text has been improved thanks to the feedback of the anonymous reviewers and the journal's editors. It was supported by Åke Wibergs Stiftelse (Grant Number H22-0139).
1 See Lorraine Daston and Peter Galison, *Objectivity* (New York: Zone Books, 2007); and Steven Shapin, *A Social History of Truth: Civility and Science in Seventeenth-Century England* (Chicago, IL: University of Chicago Press, 1994).

Mots et les Choses (1966), even though important predecessors include Gaston Bachelard, Karl Mannheim, and Ludwik Fleck.

The history of knowledge has in the last decade emerged as a field extending and developing this approach by viewing knowledge as a social process in interplay with culture. Rather than solely focusing on the production and origins of the natural sciences, historians of knowledge examine the transformation, circulation, classification, and communication of various forms of knowledge in society.[2] However, there is an ongoing debate on whether the history of knowledge offers something novel compared to the history of science. Is it merely a more fitting label for what historians of science already do, or does it introduce new perspectives and methodologies?[3] I share the view of Martin Mulsow that the value of the history of knowledge lies in integrating "phenomena that have up till now been examined separately" by linking "scholarly and scientific knowledge [. . .] with other *forms of knowledge*" and political and social processes.[4] Perhaps its greatest contribution has consisted of sparking a theoretical and methodological debate that is worthwhile embracing regardless of whether we identify as historians of science or historians of knowledge.

However, there are examples of themes and approaches in the history of science that historians of knowledge have yet to sufficiently address. One is the relationship between science and religion.[5] In the last decades, historians of science have brought nuance to the picture of a "war" between science and religion stemming from the late nineteenth century. Rather than viewing their relationship as dichotomous, historians of science have increasingly studied interactions between science and religion, while stressing their local and temporal variations

---

[2] For introductions to the field, see Simone Lässig, "The History of Knowledge and the Expansion of the Historical Research Agenda," *Bulletin of the German Historical Institute* 59 (2016): 29–58; Johan Östling et al., eds., *Circulation of Knowledge: Explorations in the History of Knowledge* (Lund: Nordic Academic Press, 2018); and Peter Burke, *What is the History of Knowledge?* (Cambridge: Polity Press, 2016).

[3] For skeptical views regarding the novelty of the history of knowledge, see Lorraine Daston, "The History of Science and the History of Knowledge," *KNOW: A Journal on the Formation of Knowledge* 1, no. 1 (2017): 131–154; and Susanne Marchand, "How Much Knowledge is Worth Knowing? An American Intellectual Historian's Thoughts on the Geschichte des Wissens," *Berichte zur Wissenschaftsgeschichte* 42, no. 2–3 (2019): 126–149. For more optimistic views, see Philip Sarasin, "More Than Just Another Specialty: On the Prospects for the History of Knowledge," *Journal for the History of Knowledge* 1, no. 1 (2020): 1–5; and Johan Östling and David Larsson Heidenblad, "Fulfilling the Promise of the History of Knowledge: Key Approaches for the 2020s," *Journal for the History of Knowledge* 1, no. 1 (2020): 1–6.

[4] Martin Mulsow, "History of Knowledge," in *Debating New Approaches to History*, ed. Marek Tamm and Peter Burke (London: Bloomsbury, 2019), 160, 163. Emphasis in original.

[5] Which is not to say that it has been ignored. I return to examples below.

and aiming "to understand the scientific, theological, and cultural factors that determine the outcome in each situation."[6] Historians of knowledge would surely agree but have thus far not developed any distinct approaches for examining the subject of religion and spirituality. The present article aims to do exactly this and thus contribute to theoretical and conceptual developments in this field.

I propose an analytical framework for studying the historical intersections between knowledge, ideology, and spirituality by using the categories *the epistemic, the political,* and *the numinous*. The first two were the topic of a 2020 thematic issue of *KNOW: A Journal on the Formation of Knowledge*. These categories explain the social and ideological dimensions of knowledge production but do not account for the entanglement of religion, spirituality, and some metaphysical and existential matters with science. To bridge this gap, I adopt Rudolf Otto's notion of the numinous.[7] My aim, however, is not to do historical justice to Otto but to use his concept as theoretical inspiration, adapting it to form an analytical triad together with the categories of the political and the epistemic.

After outlining these analytical categories, I demonstrate how they are applied by using the example of *holism*—a contested term having circulated in various sciences since its coinage in 1926.[8] Holism has correctly been described as an epistemic notion with metaphysical and political connotations, which makes it well-suited for analyzing "the power effects of knowledge claims."[9] While the concept of holism predates the actual term, I focus on two figures who explicitly used it: Jan Smuts (1870–1950), who coined it, and psychologist Abraham Maslow (1908–1970). Analyzing their conceptions of holism by using the categories of the political, the epistemic, and the numinous illustrates how they challenged the boundaries of science by fusing it with ideological, spiritual, and existential matters. These intersections are crucial for understanding how holism came to leave the domains of science to circulate more broadly in culture around 1980. How-

---

6 For an overview of the modern relationship between science and religion as well as a list of key works, see Peter J. Bowler and Iwan Rhys Morus, "Chapter 16: Science and Religion," in *Making Modern Science: A Historical Survey*, 2nd ed. (Chicago, IL: University of Chicago Press, 2020), 377–404, quotation on p. 401.
7 Rudolf Otto, *The Idea of the Holy: An Inquiry into the Non-Rational Factor in the Idea of the Divine and Its Relation to the Rational*, 2nd ed., trans. John W. Harvey (London: Oxford University Press, 1950 [1923]).
8 *Oxford English Dictionary*, "Holism, n.," accessed June 19, 2024, https://doi.org/10.1093/OED/7388632619. On contested concepts (rather than terms), see W. B. Gallie, "Essentially Contested Concepts," *Proceedings of the Aristotelian Society* 56 (1955–1956): 167–198.
9 Andrew Jewett, "On the Politics of Knowledge: Science, Conflict, Power," in *American Labyrinth: Intellectual History for Complicated Times*, ed. Raymond J. Haberski and Andrew Hartman (Ithaca, NY: Cornell University Press, 2018), 299.

ever, my goal is not to present a comprehensive history of holism but rather to study two of its proponents in order to illustrate the importance of analyzing the entanglement of scientific knowledge, ideology, and spirituality.

"The Political" and "The Epistemic" as Analytical Categories

Analytical categories serve as tools for both formulating and addressing research problems. Just like searchlights, they illuminate specific aspects of the material being studied. Initially broad, these categories should then be fine-tuned to fit the specific context in which they are applied. In the best-known article on analytical categories in historical research, Joan Scott argues that due to the fact that "gender" cannot be neatly defined and that it has historically carried different meanings, it serves as a "useful category of historical analysis."[10] As a category, it is fundamentally unstable, which is why historians should resist offering a fixed definition, and instead uncover the shifting meanings attributed to gender in various contexts. Just like gender, categories related to knowledge, ideology, and spirituality are open and unstable and thus require historicization. I aim to develop an analytical model that examines the meanings attributed to (primarily scientific) knowledge, ideology, and spirituality in addition to the fluid, contested relationships between these. To this end, I propose using the analytical categories of the epistemic, the political, and the numinous.

In the introduction to a thematic issue published by *KNOW* on the first two categories, editors Kijan Espahangizi and Monika Wulz argue that in the early twentieth century, science became a "contested social practice" shaped by "social interactions, negotiations, controversies, critique, agreements, values, norms, ruptures, and even revolutions."[11] As traditional notions of objectivity were abandoned, knowledge production came to be seen as a social process guided by intersubjective agreements on what constitutes proof, evidence, and truth. Hence, science, knowledge, and epistemology must be considered "through the lens of the political."[12]

---

[10] Joan W. Scott, "Gender: A Useful Category of Historical Analysis," *The American Historical Review* 91, no. 5 (1986): 1053–1075.
[11] Kijan Espahangizi and Monika Wulz, "The Political and the Epistemic in the Twentieth Century: Historical Perspectives," *KNOW: A Journal on the Formation of Knowledge* 4, no. 2 (2020): 161–162.
[12] Ibid., 161.

The notion of the political, as contrasted to politics, comes from Carl Schmitt and Chantal Mouffe, who use this category to describe the social conflicts of interest in public life within which conventional politics occurs. The political is thus broader and encompasses politics, which mainly refers to phenomena typically studied in political science, such as the state, political parties, institutions, and elections.[13] While liberal politics focuses on deliberation, compromise, and consensus, Schmitt and Mouffe argue that it overlooks power and conflict, which are key to the political. They contend that political opinion is formed through positioning, difference, and contrast—that is, dividing people into "us" and "them."[14]

In order to capture the polemical nature of the political, Mouffe introduces the notion of *agonism* to describe situations in which different groups fundamentally disagree and see no path to consensus yet still recognize each other as legitimate.[15] She and Schmitt agree that all conflicts—moral, economic, ethnic, scientific, etc.—require positioning and difference, which thus makes them political.[16] As Schmitt points out, all political concepts are polemical, even the term political itself, which can be used to describe someone as being the opposite of objective or scientific.[17]

Mouffe and Schmitt do not discuss the relationship between science and the political all that extensively. However, conflicts encompassed by the political overlap with a politicized understanding of knowledge production. This link is highlighted by the category of the epistemic. Just like the political, the epistemic covers more than institutionalized and professional science, as it also incorporates the social and agonistic dimensions of science. It thus captures something broader and more fundamental than, for example, the politics of science or the role of scientists in policymaking.

Espahangizi and Wulz define the epistemic as "both nonfoundational and agonistic conditions in which knowledge emerges in an ever-changing multitude of forms and social contexts."[18] They view the epistemic and the political as fundamentally interconnected:

---

[13] Chantal Mouffe, *On the Political* (London: Routledge, 2005), 8; Carl Schmitt, *The Concept of the Political*, expanded ed., trans. George Schwab (Chicago, IL: University of Chicago Press, 2007 [1932]), 19–22.
[14] Mouffe, *On the Political*, 12–16; Schmitt, *The Concept of the Political*, 36–38.
[15] *Agonism* is juxtaposed to the *antagonism* between friend and enemy that is key for Schmitt's anti-democratic understanding of the political. In contrast to Schmitt, Mouffe argues that the task of democracy is to transform antagonism into agonism. See Mouffe, *On the Political*, 14–16, 19–21.
[16] Ibid., 10–14, 26–27, 69–72; Schmitt, *The Concept of the Political*, 25–37.
[17] Schmitt, *The Concept of the Political*, 31–32.
[18] Espahangizi and Wulz, "The Political and the Epistemic," 164.

> Inasmuch as *the political* is understood as a space of (dis)agreement, shifting not only in concert with the different actors that engage in it but also with the different epistemic practices, concepts, methods, and theories in which it is shaped, *the epistemic* cannot be separated from the political sphere since it is, in ways of both practice and theory, involved in creating the space of *the political,* and vice versa.[19]

The epistemic is thus not confined to scientific institutions but highlights the mutual impact of ideology and knowledge. Just as conflict is intrinsic to the political, it is also essential to the epistemic, which is not merely a matter of deliberation but "an arena of contesting and conflicting knowledge claims."[20] Epistemic conflicts also divide people into groups of "us" and "them." Knowledge actors have different interests, values, strategies, and norms but also varying views on the relationship between epistemology and ideology as well as between science and other forms of knowledge.[21] Of course, this all varies based on time, place, discipline, and among groups and individuals.

Analyzing the contested and ever-changing relationship between the political and the epistemic is related to what Thomas Gieryn refers to as "boundary work"; that is, how epistemic authority is established, legitimized, and enforced by separating scientific knowledge and practices from other knowledge-producing activities, politics, mysticism, and pseudoscience. While the ones who seek to demarcate science may present it as non-political, according to Gieryn, boundary work is ideological and always serves particular interests.[22] In contrast to Gieryn's focus on the demarcation of science, I will show that it is equally valuable to study those that seek to challenge or dissolve boundaries. This effort is also ideological and particularly relevant for historians of knowledge since the active attempt to blur distinctions between the epistemic, the political, and the numinous may be a crucial factor in terms of making knowledge *circulate*.[23]

While the political and the epistemic are useful categories, they are in some cases insufficient. As the example of holism will illustrate, knowledge sometimes

---

[19] Ibid., 165. Emphasis in original.

[20] Ibid.

[21] I borrow the notion of "knowledge actors" from Johan Östling, David Larsson Heidenblad, and Anna Nilsson Hammar, eds., *Knowledge Actors: Revisiting Agency in the History of Knowledge* (Lund: Nordic Academic Press, 2023).

[22] Thomas Gieryn, "Boundary-Work and the Demarcation of Science from Non-Science: Strains and Interests in Professional Ideologies of Scientists," *American Sociological Review* 48, no. 6 (1983): 781–795.

[23] The circulation of knowledge "beyond academia" is an important factor in what the editors of the present journal refer to as "intellectual culture." See Charlotte A. Lerg, Johan Östling, and Jana Weiß, "Introducing the Yearbook History of Intellectual Culture," *History of Intellectual Culture* 1 (2022): 5.

overlaps with religious and spiritual matters. To capture these intersections, I here introduce a third category: the numinous.

Bringing "the Numinous" into the History of Knowledge

Simone Lässig has suggested that historians of knowledge should analyze "the dialectical relationship and interconnections" between religion and knowledge while still viewing them as analytically distinct categories.[24] Similarly, Philip Sarasin suggests that science can never be entirely separated from non-science, and he uses Eastern esoterism as an example of a phenomenon that he does not believe merits being referred to as "knowledge," even though it may be analyzed using the tools of the history of knowledge.[25]

In contrast to Lässig and Sarasin, with whom I agree, other historians of knowledge view religion as (a form of) knowledge. While the boundaries between knowledge and belief are fluid and it is true that religions have incorporated non-religious knowledge in various ways, as well as having "structured the perception of the world and guided actions, in much the same way that scientific knowledge does,"[26] it does not follow that religion itself is knowledge. Anna Nilsson Hammar and Kajsa Brilkman argue that we should view it as such because "[r]eligions produce doctrine, theories, room for action, models for interaction and practice, for self-fashioning etc., all part of the interwoven production and circulation of knowledge in a given historical context."[27] Brilkman also promotes the narrower concept of "confessional knowledge" defined as "the systematic knowledge of creation and salvation that was developed in the framework of the early modern confessions."[28] I do not dispute that religions encompass various forms of knowledge or that, in Brilkman's example, "Lutheran dogmatics became

---

24 Lässig, "History of Knowledge," 39. See also Lässig, "Religious Knowledge and Social Adaptability," *History of Knowledge* (July 21, 2017), accessed January 26, 2025, doi: 10.58079/12pu7
25 Sarasin, "More Than Just Another Specialty," 2, 4.
26 Kajsa Brilkman and Anna Nilsson Hammar, "Religion as Knowledge," LUCK: Lund Centre for the History of Knowledge (April 24, 2019), accessed January 27, 2025, https://newhistoryofknowledge.com/2019/04/24/religion-as-knowledge/
27 Ibid.
28 Kajsa Brilkman, "Confessional Knowledge: How Might the History of Knowledge and the History of Confessional Europe Influence Each Other?" in *Forms of Knowledge: Developing the History of Knowledge*, ed. Johan Östling, David Larsson Heidenblad, and Anna Nilsson Hammar (Lund: Nordic Academic Press, 2020), 32.

social norms and an integral part of people's lifeworlds."[29] However, this approach risks blurring the distinctions between religion and knowledge too much. Moreover, by framing religion as knowledge, I believe that we miss something fundamental in religion—faith, belief, mystery, awe, wonder, and the experiential and phenomenal dimension.

In the following, I propose an alternative framework for analyzing religion that should resonate with historians of knowledge. However, I avoid using the term "religion" since my focus is not on religious institutions but rather on the personal and experiential aspects of belief.[30] I here draw on John Dewey, whose distinction between *religion* and *religious* parallels the distinction between science and the epistemic, as well as between politics and the political. Dewey describes religions as systems of authority, institutions, and beliefs. In contrast, the religious refers to an aspect of human experience that is essential to religiosity but not tied to any specific religion.[31] He suggests that religious experience emerges from viewing the self as "directed toward something beyond itself" and linked to "a larger whole," whether it be God, nature, or a community.[32] This experience is not necessarily transcendental but seeks to realize an ideal, offering both direction and values. Consequently, the religious—and, by extension, all specific religions—is not only "relative to the conditions of social culture" but also overlaps with "experience as aesthetic, scientific, moral, [and] political."[33]

Dewey's notion of the religious integrates well with the categories of the epistemic and the political. Even so, I find his terminology problematic. Despite Dewey's intentions, the term "religious" evokes institutionalized religions rather than something broader and more fundamental. Instead, I propose using Rudolf Otto's concept of the numinous, which aligns with Dewey's "religious" while avoiding these kinds of associations.

Like Dewey, Otto acknowledges the mystical or "non-rational" dimension of religiosity, which he describes as the "innermost core" of all religions.[34] Thus, the category of the numinous represents that which challenges our conceptual

---

[29] Ibid., 34.
[30] So, my approach is the opposite to that of Yves Gingras, who criticizes historians of science—especially John Hedley Brooke—for downplaying conflicts between the *institutions* of science and religion. Gingras, *Science and Religion: An Impossible Dialogue* (Cambridge: Polity Press, 2017), 5, 10–11. Brooke's *Science and Religion: Some Historical Perspectives* (Cambridge: Cambridge University Press, 1991) is a classic in the genre of science and religion.
[31] John Dewey, *A Common Faith* (1934), in *The Later Works 1925–1953*, Vol. 9 (Carbondale, IL: Southern Illinois University Press, 1986), 4, 8.
[32] Ibid., 14, 18.
[33] Ibid., 6, 9.
[34] Otto, *The Idea of the Holy*, 1–7.

thinking—while "it admits of being discussed, it cannot be strictly defined."[35] Otto describes it as a feeling of wonder and an experience arising when encountering aspects of reality that surpass our current rationality and comprehension.[36] Both he and Dewey recognize that the numinous overlaps with the aesthetic experience of the sublime, which also presents us with experiences that are both "daunting" and "attracting."[37] That said, Dewey adopts a broader notion of religiosity compared to that of Otto, arguing that the "religious"—or, as Otto would say, the "numinous"—encompasses moral and practical dimensions and is found in human relationships.[38] While Otto may not have agreed with Dewey's mission of integrating the natural and the supernatural, their combined perspectives provide a framework for analyzing how religious, spiritual, non-rational, and metaphysical elements intersect with the epistemic and the political in the creation and circulation of knowledge. Just like these categories, the numinous should be regarded as social, agonistic, and historically contingent.

Dewey and Otto address issues that resonate with contemporary debates on postsecularity, which challenge the "secularization thesis"—the notion that modernity inevitably leads to increased secularization and disenchantment. Instead, scholars speak of the "resurgence" or "return" of religion not only in public discourse but also in people's lives.[39] However, despite this talk of "return" and "*post*secularity," it would seem more accurate to argue that religion never disappeared. The concept of the postsecular has been criticized as "under-historicized"[40] and appears to be limited, as it primarily applies to certain (Western) societies assumed to be leading the way toward secularization since the nineteenth century. The category of the numinous offers an alternative perspective, even though paral-

---

35 Ibid., 7.
36 This point is summarized well by John W. Harvey, "Translator's Preface," in ibid., xvi–xvii.
37 Otto, *The Idea of the Holy*, 41–42. Dewey does not like the notion of the sublime, even though he does consider the aesthetic and the religious quality of experience to be intimately related, see *A Common Faith*, 17–18 and *Art as Experience* (1934), in *The Later Works 1925–1953*, Vol. 10 (Carbondale, IL: Southern Illinois University Press, 1987), 199, 275.
38 Dewey, *A Common Faith*, 15. In contrast, Otto describes the numinous as "'the holy' minus its moral factor." See *The Idea of the Holy*, 6. Emphasis in original. However, integrating Otto's numinous with ethics is done quite commonly. For an attempt that also seeks to fuse Otto with Dewey, see Henning Nörenberg, "The Numinous, the Ethical, and the Body: Rudolf Otto's 'The Idea of the Holy' Revisited," *Open Theology* 3, no. 1 (2017): 546–564.
39 See Jürgen Habermas, "Notes on a Post-Secular Society," *Sign and Sight* (June 18, 2008), accessed June 2, 2024, http://www.signandsight.com/features/1714.html; and Jayne Svenungsson, "The Return of Religion or the End of Religion? On the Need to Rethink Religion as a Category of Social and Political Life," *Philosophy & Social Criticism* 46, no. 7 (2020): 785–809.
40 Allan Megill, "History, Theoreticism, and the Limits of 'the Postsecular'," *History & Theory* 52, no. 1 (2013): 111.

lels do exist between these concepts. Like the numinous, the postsecular encourages studying the relationship between ideology, science, and religiosity. Furthermore, echoing Dewey's argument, proponents of the postsecular such as Dominick LaCapra have suggested that the secular and the sacred are not binary opposites. Instead, the postsecular should be regarded as an appeal to analyze this presumed dualism and the various ways in which it operates in society and people's lives, but also how this has changed historically. Like Otto and Dewey, LaCapra links the postsecular to aesthetics and the sublime while stressing its role in ideology.[41] Thus, the postsecular and the numinous share a number of similarities. However, the former remains more limited due to its association with a particular type of society.

While I find the numinous to be a more suitable term than spirituality, the postsecular, or Dewey's "religious," it is not perfect. It should be noted that in my use of the numinous, I do not adhere to Otto's original definition, which views it as strictly religious. Since I reject a rigid separation between the secular and the sacred, I extend the numinous to also include non-transcendental awe-inspiring experiences offering a sense of existential meaning. These may, for example, stem from nature, art, and science.

In the following, I demonstrate the application of these analytical categories in historical research by examining how Jan Smuts and Abraham Maslow use the term holism. As we will see, the term holism (or holistic), which originated in scientific discourse, gained broader cultural circulation around 1980. This expansion was enabled by figures such as Maslow and Smuts using this term in order to challenge the boundaries between (scientific) knowledge, spirituality, and ideology.

Jan Smuts' Holistic Worldview and Philosophy of Science

The term *holism* was officially coined in 1926 with the publication of the South African statesman and botanist Jan Smuts' *Holism and Evolution*. This book sought to replace the mechanistic-materialistic worldview with an organic one by

---

41 Dominick LaCapra, *History and its Limits: Human, Animal, Violence* (Ithaca, NY: Cornell University Press, 2009), 10, 57; and *Understanding Others: Peoples, Animals, Pasts* (Ithaca, NY: Cornell University Press, 2018), 170–173. For a critical discussion on LaCapra's notion of the postsecular, see Megill, "History, Theoreticism."

rethinking "our primary concepts of matter, life, mind and personality."[42] According to Smuts, mechanistic sciences only apply to simple lifeforms and fail to account for humans as spiritual beings with conscious minds and personalities. Moreover, they are unable to explain how higher forms of evolution occur in parallel with lower ones. Nevertheless, Smuts did not reject these sciences. In an antidualist manner, he argued that mechanism, materialism, reductionism, and realism must be integrated with their opposites: idealism, organicism, spiritualism, and vitalism.[43] Smuts thus sought to provide an epistemic framework for studying interconnectedness by describing holism as "the synthetic tendency in the universe" and the creative and progressive nature of evolution, "stretching from the inorganic beginnings to the highest level of spiritual creation."[44]

Smuts defined holism as the "fundamental factor operative towards the making or creation of wholes in the universe" and grounded this notion on recent scientific discoveries in evolutionary biology, colloid chemistry, and Einstein's new physics.[45] This idea, as Smuts himself notes, predates the term and can be traced to writings by Plato, Hippocrates, and the apostle Paul, with a semantic predecessor in the Greek term *holos*.[46] However, the German idealists—most notably Hegel—and Romantics at the beginning of the nineteenth century, as well as the French vitalist Henri Bergson represent more significant predecessors. Nevertheless, Smuts criticized these figures and insisted—unconvincingly according to his critics—that his concept of holism was distinct from theirs due to its basis in contemporary natural science.[47] Consequently, Smuts presented holism as an epistemic category. The fact that Smuts was elected president of the British Association for the Advancement of Science in 1931 in addition to the generally positive reception of *Holism and Evolution* show that it was recognized as such by the scientific community.[48]

The first four chapters of *Holism and Evolution* fall under the category of the epistemic, discussing how scientific discoveries reshape our understanding of matter, space, time, and life. The following four chapters introduce the concept of holism, while the final chapters expand into more speculative, spiritual, and exis-

---

[42] Jan C. Smuts, *Holism and Evolution* (Stirling, WA: Left of Brain Books, 2021[1926]), 1.
[43] Ibid., 9–11, 132.
[44] Ibid., 1.
[45] Ibid., 87.
[46] Ibid. See also, Linda Sargent Wood, *A More Perfect Union: Holistic Worldviews and the Transformation of American Culture after World War II* (Oxford: Oxford University Press, 2010), 13.
[47] Smuts, *Holism and Evolution*, 80, 84.
[48] After the initially positive reception, *Holism and Evolution* faced some severe criticism. See William Keith Hancock, *Smuts 2: The Fields of Force: 1919–1950* (Cambridge: Cambridge University Press, 1968), 188–192.

tential territory, addressing topics such as mind, values, and personality. Smuts concludes by outlining the *Weltanschauung* of the "holistic universe."[49] Thus, *Holism and Evolution* is not merely a work in the field of philosophy of science; it is also metaphysical, existential, and spiritual, seeking to give meaning, purpose, and direction to human life—matters belonging to the realm of the numinous.

The integration of religion and science was a common theme during the interwar period, as shown by Peter Bowler. He only mentions Smuts briefly, focusing more on similar books such as C. Lloyd Morgan's *Emergent Evolution* (1923) and Alfred N. Whitehead's *Process and Reality* (1929).[50] Something that these thinkers had in common was the impact of the new physics. Einstein's theory of relativity, quantum mechanics, Bohr's concept of complementarity, and Heisenberg's uncertainty principle contributed to a processual worldview that challenged reductionistic and mechanistic notions. As noted by John Hedley Brooke, these scientific developments led many scientists to adopt "a holistic philosophy" that was integrated with "religious critiques of reductionism."[51]

Smuts' holism was one of many interwar-era attempts to indirectly address Max Weber's notion of "disenchantment."[52] Like the Romantics, Smuts promoted an organic worldview that integrated natural science, philosophy, and religion, thereby seeking to reestablish a bond between humans and nature.[53] His biographer, William K. Hancock, writes that Smuts "was doing his best to keep God out of his book; but he could not keep God out of his mind. Ever since his student years, when the idea of the book first took shape, God had been its starting-point."[54] The topics of synthesis, wholes, and—inspired by Walt Whitman—personality, had

---

[49] Smuts, *Holism and Evolution*, 270.
[50] Peter J. Bowler, *Reconciling Science and Religion: The Debate in Early Twentieth-Century Britain* (Chicago, IL: University of Chicago Press, 2001).
[51] Brooke, *Science and Religion*, 330.
[52] Max Weber, "Science as a Vocation," in *Max Weber's 'Science as a Vocation'*, ed. Peter, Lassman, Irving Velody, and Hermínio Martins (London: Routledge, 2015). Cf. Anne Harrington, *Reenchanted Science: Holism in German Culture from Wilhelm II to Hitler* (Princeton, NJ: Princeton University Press, 1996), xv–xvii.
[53] See Andrew Cunningham and Nicholas Jardine, eds., *Romanticism and the Sciences* (Cambridge: Cambridge University Press, 1990), especially the editors' "Introduction: The Age of Reflexion," 1–9; and David Knight, "Romanticism and the Sciences," 13–24. Here, it is argued that Romanticism continued to influence the natural sciences throughout the nineteenth century. As Bowler shows, this went on well into the twentieth century. See his *Reconciling Science and Religion*, 2–4.
[54] Hancock, *Smuts 2*, 2, 194. However, the (largely implicit) religious nature of *Holism and Evolution* was noticed. Smuts' friend Frederick Kolbe sought to make it explicit in a book to which Smuts wrote the introduction. See Kolbe, *A Catholic View of Holism: A Criticism of the Theory put forward by General Smuts in his Book, 'Holism and Evolution'* (New York: MacMillan, 1928).

occupied Smuts since the 1890s.[55] Over half a century later, he wrote that: "Holism is [. . .] the approach towards the theistic concept from the side of nature, and it builds as it were a bridge between humanism and divinity."[56] Smuts lamented that science neglected spiritual issues related to the soul and values while arguing for a deeper engagement between science, philosophy, and the realm of the numinous—subjects traditionally left to theology, poetry, and the arts. He even envisioned a follow-up to *Holism and Evolution* addressing these themes, but such a work was never realized.[57]

Albeit not fully elaborated on in *Holism and Evolution*, Smuts' numinous visions are undeniable. For instance, he asserts that wholeness and holiness not only share a semantic origin but are also experientially similar.[58] His hierarchy of wholes further illustrates numinous aspects of holism. While all wholes are perfect and represent something more and different from their parts, wholes like atoms and molecules are classified as "poor empty, worthless stuff," while more complex organisms, such as plants and animals, are afforded a higher value.[59] At the pinnacle of Smuts' hierarchy are societies, artworks, spiritual values and ideals, and the human mind and personality. According to Smuts, the universe is inherently creative and progressive, achieving ever greater perfection and "ever widening degrees of freedom, until finally, at the human stage, freedom becomes self-conscious, creating the free ethical world of the Spirit."[60] Holism, therefore, is not merely a factor within the material universe but a metaphysical worldview, portraying the universe as opening "new paths and rendering possible new choices in the forward march, as creating freedom for the future and in a very fixed sense breaking the bondage of the past and its fixed determinations."[61] Yet, it remains unclear where this holistic process ultimately leads as its "bow," Smuts suggests, "is bent for the distant horizons, far beyond all human power of vision and understanding."[62] As these quotes illustrate, the leap from the epistemic to the numinous was never long for Smuts. A discussion on natural science could seamlessly transition into the mystical aspects of holism, infusing the cosmos, natural evolution, and human history with direction and meaning.

---

55 Smuts, *Holism and Evolution*, 2; William Keith Hancock, *Smuts 1: The Sanguine Years: 1870–1919* (Cambridge: Cambridge University Press, 1962), 47–51, 289–301.
56 Quoted in Hancock, *Smuts 2*, 523.
57 Ibid., 395, 399–401.
58 Smuts, *Holism and Evolution*, 293.
59 Ibid., 95.
60 Ibid., 87–88, 121.
61 Ibid., 80.
62 Ibid., 293.

Smuts' vision of the universe as holistic and progressive also extends to the political sphere. He described the universe as "friendly," "tolerant," and "co-operative" while applying the same language to organisms, which he characterized as "fundamentally a society in which innumerable members co-operate in mutual help in a spirit of the most effective disinterested service and loyalty to each other. Co-operation and mutual help are written large on the face of Nature."[63] As Peder Anker notes, this exemplifies how Smuts projected political ideals onto cells.[64] Just as cells cooperate to form a being greater than the sum of its parts, human individuals cooperate to build societies that transcend the sum of their members.

Smuts argued that humans, like organisms, cannot be isolated from their biological or social environments and that they only come into existence and develop inside communities. Consequently, he rejected "pure individualism."[65] Yet, he embraced the seemingly individualistic concept of self-realization, even advocating for a new science of personality to study the minds of great artists and intellectuals to uncover the "laws of personal evolution."[66] He described personality as "expressive of the universal order" and "the highest and completest of all wholes," thus turning it into an ideal that we should all strive toward—not only for personal benefit but also for the benefit of our society and the world.[67] However, he maintained that only a few individuals develop "strong" personalities characterized by greater freedom, harmony, and spirituality.[68]

Despite holism providing Smuts with a hierarchical view of the universe, the environment, humans, and societies, he was a progressive social liberal who held various ministerial posts for the Unionist Party of South Africa, including that of prime minister. He championed internationalism and human rights, describing the League of Nations as "the expression of the deeply-felt aspiration towards a more stable holistic human society."[69] Nevertheless, he also defended racial segregation and the oppression of black South Africans, and he argued that rights should be granted gradually since the holistic process of civilization must follow its internal rhythm.[70] As observed by Anker, this logic was consistent with Smuts'

---

[63] Ibid., 73, 187.
[64] Peder Anker, *Imperial Ecology: Environmental Order in the British Empire, 1895–1945* (Cambridge, MA: Harvard University Press, 2001), 71.
[65] Smuts, *Holism and Evolution*, 73, 209, 215.
[66] Ibid., 236, 240, 243, 253–254.
[67] Ibid., 225, 266.
[68] Ibid., 267.
[69] Ibid., 292–293.
[70] Anker, *Imperial Ecology*, 41, 48–51.

theory of stronger and weaker personalities, which led him "to draw a distinction between advanced and less advanced people, to develop a civilization ladder, and to think about human rights as 'a function of the personality' (distributing rights accordingly)."[71] Despite the obvious racist traits in Smuts' holistic politics, he insisted that it should not be equated with the similar *Ganzheit-Theorie* commonly found among proponents of national socialism in the Weimar Republic.[72] Although the politics advocated by Smuts was clearly not nazism, the theoretical differences between his own holism and *Ganzheit-Theorie* are far from obvious. While he dismissed *Ganzheit-Theorie* as "a ruthless scrapping of ideas" like "romanticism, racialism, ethics and religion,"[73] Smuts does not reflect on the fact that the same charge could be leveled at his own holism.

To summarize, Smuts' holism was epistemically grounded in recent scientific discoveries at the time, mainly Darwin's theory of evolution and the new physics. Based on these, he formulated a grand metaphysical theory infusing the universe with meaning, direction, spirituality, and ethical values. These numinous qualities of holism, in Smuts' mind, were intertwined with the political side of holism and led to a form of communitarian liberalism, according to which social changes should be slow and gradual.

Abraham Maslow's Utopian and Holistic-Humanistic Psychology

The terms holism and holistic started circulating in various scientific fields around 1930, most notably ecology, medicine, and psychology.[74] They took on a life of their own and were often used without reference to Smuts. Yet, the meaning of holism remained relatively stable. It went on serving as an agonistic term and positioned itself against what its proponents saw as the scientific mainstream characterized by materialism, mechanism, reductionism, atomism, specialization, and mind-body dualism. The intertwining of the epistemic, political, and numi-

---

71 Ibid., 45. Cf. Smuts, *Holism and Evolution*, 263–269.
72 Hancock, *Smuts 2*, 301. Cf. Peter Gay, *Weimar Culture: The Outsider as Insider* (Harmondsworth: Penguin Books, 1974); Fritz K. Ringer, *The Decline of the German Mandarins: The German Academic Community, 1890–1933* (Hanover, NH: University Press of New England, 1990); and Harrington, *Reenchanted Science*.
73 Quoted in Hancock, *Smuts 2*, 301.
74 This observation is based on a search for "holism OR holistic" on the Web of Science, accessed August 31, 2023, https://www.webofscience.com/wos/woscc/basic-search.

nous thus became a defining feature of holism, even for those unfamiliar with *Holism and Evolution*.

In psychology, holism became associated with Gestalt theory, which emerged in Germany around 1910 and was subsequently introduced to the United States by Kurt Koffka, Wolfgang Köhler, and Max Wertheimer. Like Smuts, the Gestalt theorists emphasized that wholes are more than, and different from, the sum of their parts and that the perception of a Gestalt—a form, pattern, or structure—precedes the perception of its components. A typical example is how we perceive a melody before identifying its notes.[75] While Koffka, Köhler, and Wertheimer did not use the term holism, the neurologist Kurt Goldstein, a German émigré loosely associated with Gestalt theory, did so.[76] As did Alfred Adler, perhaps the only psychologist who fully appreciated *Holism and Evolution*.[77] Even so, my next example does not involve the Gestalt theorists, Goldstein, or Adler, but rather someone influenced by them all: Abraham Maslow.

Like Smuts—whom he never directly referenced—Maslow viewed holism as both a starting point and a goal. He considered "the atomistic way of thinking [to be] a form of mild psychopathology" and criticized contemporary medicine and behaviorism—the dominant school of U.S. psychology in the early twentieth century and a primary target of Gestalt theory—for their narrow, mechanistic, and reductionist view of humans.[78] In contrast, he advocated for a humanistic and "holistic-dynamic" approach to psychology.[79] Maslow claimed that: "Holism is obviously true—after all, the cosmos is one and interrelated; any society is one and interrelated; any person is one and interrelated."[80] This statement reflects how holism provided Maslow with a worldview while also hinting at the interconnectedness of the epistemic, the political, and the numinous in his thought.

---

75 On the history of Gestalt theory, see D. Brett King and Michael Wertheimer, *Max Wertheimer and Gestalt Theory* (New Brunswick, NJ: Transaction Publisher, 2004); and Mitchell G. Ash, *Gestalt Psychology in German Culture, 1890–1967: Holism and the Quest for Objectivity* (Cambridge: Cambridge University Press, 1995).

76 *Holismus* does not appear in Kurt Goldstein's *Der Aufbau des Organismus* (1934), which instead uses the more common German concept of *Ganzheit*, which is translated as holism in the English edition, *The Organism: A Holistic Approach to Biology Derived from Pathological Data in Man* (Salt Lake City, UT: American Book Publishing, 1939).

77 Adler was the first who tried, but failed, to have *Holism and Evolution* translated into German. Still, it was thanks to him that the term *Holismus* appeared in German in 1932. See Anker, *Imperial Ecology*, 180–181.

78 Abraham H. Maslow, *Motivation and Personality*, 2nd ed. (New York: Harper & Row, 1970), xi.

79 Ibid., 299–302.

80 Ibid., xi.

Maslow did not reject the mechanistic sciences in which he was trained. Rather, he argued that they should be integrated into a broader holistic-humanistic framework looking upon humans as natural, social, and sacred beings who consist of mind, body, sense, intellect, emotion, and desire. This is a foundational epistemic presupposition in Maslow's psychology. For instance, it led him to argue that understanding an aggressive act requires a holistic view of the actor, including their values, relationships, and beliefs. To achieve this, Maslow developed a rigorous "holistic interviewing technique" to obtain "very full case-histories of whole lives and whole people."[81]

Maslow argued that psychology should not only become more attuned to the individual as a whole and their contexts but also, more crucially, that it had to shift away from its one-sided focus on psychopathology. Instead, psychology should evolve into a positive science of well-being and happiness, focusing on "the higher reaches of human nature."[82] These ideas took shape during World War II when Maslow began dreaming of "discovering a psychology for the peace table."[83] He set aside the research he was working on at the time to explore human nature and topics such as motivation, evil, religion, art, values, transcendence, self-actualization, and the good life. Maslow believed that understanding these issues was essential for achieving world peace—and that this task must be undertaken by psychologists. Convinced that only psychologists could save the world,[84] the war infused his scientific work with a social mission, thereby intertwining the epistemic and the political for the rest of his career. This profound sense of purpose arguably made him the most well-known American psychologist of his generation.

Maslow's 1954 bestseller *Motivation and Personality* introduced his theory of motivation, which proposes that human needs are hierarchically organized, with self-actualization at the top.[85] While he believed that all humans have the potential for self-actualization, he estimated that fewer than one percent achieve it. This, he argued, was unfortunate not only for individuals but also for society at large, as self-actualization involves striving for a cause greater than oneself. Self-

---

81 Abraham H. Maslow, *The Farther Reaches of Human Nature* (New York: The Viking Press, 1973), 75. See also *Motivation and Personality*, 19–33, 295–302.
82 Abraham H. Maslow, *The Psychology of Science: A Reconnaissance* (New York: Harper & Row, 1966), xv. See also *Motivation and Personality*, 281–293.
83 Mary Harrington Hall, "A Conversation with the President of the American Psychological Association Abraham H. Maslow," *Psychology Today* 2 (1968): 54.
84 Wood, *A More Perfect Union*, 165.
85 Maslow, *Motivation and Personality*, 46.

actualization is altruistic rather than individualistic and serves the common good.[86]

The political side of Maslow's holism is the most obvious in his vision of a peaceful and democratic society enabled by means of psychology. He called it "eupsychia"—a psychological utopia of "good souls." This would be a society with perfect synergy between individual and collective well-being: it would foster self-actualization and, in turn, be sustained by self-actualizers.[87] That is, healthy individuals driven by higher aspirations beyond fulfilling their basic needs. Self-actualizers cultivate their innate talents and possess positive qualities such as altruism and the ability to control their emotions. The act of self-realization is holistic because just as a painter paints or a musician composes, they lose their sense of time and place, and the dichotomy between the creator and the creation dissolves. Here, we encounter another one of Maslow's key concepts: the peak experience.[88] This notion is crucial for understanding the numinous aspects of his psychology.

Even though Maslow was a Jewish atheist and suspicious of religious institutions, he nevertheless drew inspiration from religion. For example, he advocated for a "Taoistic science" and compared the members of eupsychia to the bodhisattvas in Buddhism—enlightened individuals dedicated to the well-being and liberation of others.[89] His studies of self-actualizers revealed that many had undergone some kind of mystical experience that transformed their lives. These were not necessarily religious but could arise from "love and sex, from esthetic moments, from bursts of creativity, from moments of insight and discovery, from moments of fusion with nature."[90] While he drew inspiration from Otto's *The Idea of the Holy*, Maslow expanded the realm of the numinous to include transcendent moments of bliss, joy, and awe that need not involve supernatural beliefs. He regarded peak experiences as moments where the self is perceived as integrated with the universe. These experiences are necessary since a person may get "sick, violent, and nihilistic, or else hopeless and apathetic" without them.[91] We need transcendence in the sense of being part of something larger than ourselves,

---

[86] Abraham H. Maslow, *Toward a Psychology of Being*, 3rd ed. (New York: J. Wiley & Sons, 1999 [1962]), xliii, 224.
[87] Maslow, *Motivation and Personality*, 277–278; and *The Farther Reaches*, 142, 199–211, 237–238.
[88] Abraham H. Maslow, *Religions, Values, and Peak-Experiences* (Columbus, OH: Ohio State University Press, 1964), 59–68.
[89] Maslow, *The Psychology of Science*, 95–101; and *The Farther Reaches*, 346–347.
[90] Hall, "A Conversation with Abraham H. Maslow," 55.
[91] Maslow, *Toward a Psychology of Being*, xl.

which means that the experience of the numinous is an existential need deeply tied to meaning.

On the surface, it might seem contradictory that Maslow simultaneously called for both the "humanization" and the "resacralization" of science. Yet, like many holists, he rejected the dichotomy between the secular and the sacred, and between science and religion. He argued that science itself contains nonrational elements since it is a creative activity—and creativity stems from the nonrational.[92] "Science," he concluded in one of his books,

> is ultimately the organization of, the systematic pursuit of, and the enjoyment of wonder, awe, and mystery. [. . .] Science can be the religion of the nonreligious, the poetry of the nonpoet, the art of the man who cannot paint, the humor of the serious man, and the lovemaking of the inhibited shy man. Not only does science begin in wonder; it also ends in wonder.[93]

Maslow's vision of a future utopia where more individuals undergo transformative peak experiences and realize themselves as altruistic individuals working for the common good gave meaning and purpose to his scientific efforts. Like many proponents of holism, he envisioned a science that transcended and dissolved traditional boundaries.

The integration of political and numinous aspects into the epistemic made holism appealing to a broader audience. After having primarily been used in scientific contexts, the terms holism and holistic started circulating in broader culture around 1980.[94] By then, holistic ideas had been embraced by ecologists, advocates of alternative medicine, in the Californian counterculture, and the New Age movement, while being popularized in works such as Fritjof Capra's *The Tao of Physics* (1975).[95] Maslow played a key role in this shift through his involvement in the Esalen Institute in California, which served as an important hub for these movements.[96] By promoting a holistic worldview in which the boundaries be-

---

[92] Ibid., 228.
[93] Maslow, *The Psychology of Science*, 151.
[94] Google Books Ngram Viewer (Corpus: English 2019) shows that *holism* and *holistic* increased heavily in frequency during the late 1970s, https://books.google.com/ngrams. Searching for "holism OR holistic" on the Web of Science presents 40 records in 1975 and 246 in 1980. In the *New York Times*, a search for "Holism OR Holistic NOT Alcohol*" presents 22 records in 1975 and 117 in 1980. ProQuest Historical Newspapers: The New York Times with Index. All accessed August 31, 2023.
[95] For a discussion on Capra, see Brooke, *Science and Religion*, 334–336.
[96] Sargent Wood, "Chapter 6: The Esalen Institute: A Center for Holistic Pursuits," in *A More Perfect Union*. This is the most prominent study of holistic notions in the United States during the latter half of the twentieth century.

tween the epistemic, the political, and the numinous were constantly blurred, Maslow, just like Smuts before him, contributed to the circulation of holism in the broader culture.

Conclusion

This article has proposed complementing the analytical categories of the epistemic and the political with the numinous to better understand the historical intersections of knowledge, ideology, and spirituality. These categories are not only broader but also more fundamental than politics, science, and religion. They have not been given any exact definitions, as their meanings should be deliberated in relation to specific historical cases. Furthermore, I have argued that studies of scientific boundary work must include those who challenge established boundaries, as this is crucial for understanding the cultural circulation of knowledge—a key concern for historians of knowledge.

To illustrate the application of this framework, I examined holism in the thought of Jan Smuts and Abraham Maslow, respectively. For them—and for holistic thinkers generally—holism serves as an agonistic perspective infusing science with existential, spiritual, and sociopolitical meaning. Holists reject reductionism, materialism, atomism, individualism, mechanism, and specialization, along with dichotomies such as mind and body, fact and value, and the secular and the sacred. Instead, they advocate for a generalist approach to science, often interlinking it with philosophy and religion. Their views also carry political dimensions: by emphasizing that self-realization serves the common good, holists tend to support some form of social liberal communitarianism.

The case studies of Smuts and Maslow demonstrate how epistemic concepts may gain social and spiritual significance, which allows them to circulate beyond academic institutions. Recognizing the relationship between the numinous and the political with the epistemic while integrating these analytical categories into the history of knowledge enriches our understanding of how some ideas and concepts transcend epistemic boundaries and gain broader cultural significance.

Bruno Hamnell is a postdoctoral fellow in the history of ideas and sciences at Lund University, Sweden. His current project is called "All is One: Holistic Knowledge Ideals and Controversies from Fin de siècle to the Anthropocene." Hamnell's research interests include modern intellectual history, philosophy of history, and the history of knowledge. His thesis, *Two Quests for Unity: John Dewey, R. G. Collingwood, and the Persistence of Idealism*, was published in 2021.

Valentina Mann
Review Essay: The Return of Franz Boas?

Abstract: This essay examines the renewed attention lavished on anthropologist Franz Boas (1858–1914) in scholarly and popular publications over the past twenty years. Originating from many disciplinary and geographical quarters, this interest has resulted in a multiplication of Boases to fit various political and scholarly projects. This is a welcome development that offers openings for new approaches and counterbalances the (still present) traditional scholarly focus on the singular origin of Boas' ideas in Germany and a commitment to present Boas' politics in a positive light. New perspectives on intellectual change, transnational mobility, and the political implications of Boas' ideas on race and culture result in stimulating and often incompatible accounts. These, in turn, offer instructive snapshots of the rewards and challenges of recent efforts in intellectual history and the history of knowledge to include marginalised actors and address the transnational aspects of knowledge by focusing on mobility and circulation.

Keywords: anthropology, cultural relativism, race, Franz Boas, history of knowledge

Hans-Walter Schmul, ed., *Kulturrelativismus und Antirassismus: Der Anthropologe Franz Boas (1858–1942)* (Bielefeld: Transcript, 2009).
Michel Espagne and Isabelle Kalinowski, eds., *Franz Boas. Le travail du regard* (Paris: Armand Colin, 2013).
Regna Darnell et al., eds., *Franz Boas as Public Intellectual – Theory, Ethnography, Activism*, vol. 1 of *The Franz Boas Papers* (Lincoln, NE: University of Nebraska Press, 2015).
Ned Blackhawk and Isaiah Lorado Wilner, eds., *Indigenous Visions: Rediscovering the world of Franz Boas* (New Haven, CT: Yale University Press, 2018).
Charles King, *Gods of the Upper Air: How a Circle of Renegade Anthropologists Reinvented Race, Sex, and Gender in the Twentieth Century* (New York: Doubleday, 2019).
Rosemary Lévy-Zumwalt, *Franz Boas: The Emergence of the Anthropologist* (Lincoln, NE: University of Nebraska Press, 2019).
Rosemary Lévy-Zumwalt, *Franz Boas: Shaping Anthropology and Fostering Social Justice* (Lincoln, NE: University of Nebraska Press, 2022).

Introduction

Franz Boas was born in Minden, Westphalia in 1858 and lived in the German Empire until 1886, when he immigrated to the United States. Most frequently remembered as the founder or father of modern American anthropology, Boas is credited with watershed moments, both institutional and theoretical, in the history of the discipline. He helped turn anthropology into an academic discipline, established an independent department at Columbia University, and trained many of the anthropologists who went on to launch departments at other U.-S. universities. Starting in the twentieth century, he became a prominent public figure who argued against limiting European immigration based on race and condemned the unequal treatment of African Americans.[1] He also made two key conceptual moves in the development of the discipline. First, he rejected the nineteenth-century evolutionary paradigm and its understanding of culture as articulated in a series of discrete stages of mental and social development from 'primitive' to 'civilised'. Second, he separated culture and mental abilities from biological factors. Both of these developments were based on a new understanding of the term 'culture' as not being more or less advanced or 'modern' but simply multifaceted and shaped by migration, historical accident, and contact.[2]

The current political climate in the United States along with the confluence of two anniversaries – the 150th anniversary of Boas' birth in 2008 and the centenary of the original publication of his most famous work, *The Mind of Primitive Man* (1911), in 2011 – have yielded specialist and non-specialist publications that re-examine his legacy. This review essay examines seven publications on Boas from France, Germany, and the United States: a two-volume biography, a popular book on Boas and his students, and four edited volumes. Including the introductions, the contributions in the edited volumes amount to a total of sixty-five, featuring a mix of anthropologists, historians, philosophers, and political theorists. This precludes a detailed evaluation of each chapter; instead, I focus on how the editors frame the various volumes. When discussing the publications under review, I trace two recurring themes: (1) a renewed emphasis on Boas as a theorist and attempts to evaluate the originality and political implications of his views; and (2) expanding the origins of his theories.

These twin concerns are mainstays of scholarship on Boas in the United States and Europe. Before turning to the volumes under review, I provide an overview of the history of anthropology in the United States and highlight its emphasis on the origins of his ideas, the contradictions and tensions in his work, and the concept of 'culture'. Even though the publications under review do not

---

[1] Douglas Cole, *Franz Boas: The Early Years 1858–1906* (Toronto: Douglas & McIntyre, 1999); George W. Stocking Jr., ed., *A Franz Boas Reader: The Shaping of American Anthropology, 1883–1911* (Chicago: University of Chicago Press, 1989).
[2] Fredrik Barth et al., *The Halle Lectures: One Discipline, Four Ways: British, German, French, and American Anthropology* (Chicago: University of Chicago Press, 2005).

explicitly engage with the history of knowledge, the strongest and most thought-provoking pieces are the ones that critically analyse the circulation of knowledge and the constraints placed upon knowledge actors by public roles and colonial contexts. The final section compares and contrasts the monographs and articles in the edited volumes in order to assess the value of these publications and of the history of anthropology in general for historians of knowledge.

Boas and the History of Anthropology

In the decades after Boas passed away in 1942, many former students and colleagues published quasi-hagiographical celebrations of his life and work.[3] In the 1970s and 1980s, however, Boas fell out of favour with anthropologists for being un-theoretical; he was once described as 'someone who collected fish recipes [. . .] he meant well, but he didn't think much'.[4] Recently, some anthropologists have sought to recover Boas as a positive role model for both scholarly work and political activism.[5] Historians' engagement with Boas begins in earnest in postwar America with the work of George W. Stocking Jr. In his 1968 volume *Race, Culture, Evolution*, Stocking dispensed with presentist and internalist narratives of conversion by fieldwork to instead establish two lasting lenses through which to view the life and work of Boas: the importance of his German background and the presence of an unresolved tension in his thought.[6] These are also present in Stocking's presentation of some of Boas' publications and letters (1974) and in the edited volume *Volksgeist as Method and Ethic* (1996), whose many contributors adopt one or both of these lenses.[7] The emphasis on Boas' German background has at times turned a story of conceptual change into one of conceptual transfer from Germany to the United States. By tracing the origins of Boas' key theories

---

[3] Alfred Kroeber et al., *Franz Boas: 1858–1942* (Menasha, WI: American Anthropological Association, 1943); Robert H. Lowie, *Biographical Memoir of Franz Boas 1858–1942* (Washington, DC: National Academy of Sciences, 1944); Walter Goldschmidt, ed., *The Anthropology of Franz Boas: Essays on the Centennial of His Birth*, Memoir No. 89 of the American Anthropological Association (1959).
[4] Richard Handler, "An interview with Clifford Geertz", *Current Anthropology* 32, no. 5 (1991): 603–613 (609).
[5] AA.VV., *Proceedings of the American Philosophical Society* 154, no. 1 (2010).
[6] George W. Stocking Jr., *Race, Culture, Evolution: Essays in the History of Anthropology*, 2nd ed. (Chicago: University of Chicago Press, 1982 [1968]).
[7] Stocking, ed., *A Franz Boas reader*; George W. Stocking Jr., ed., *Volksgeist as Method and Ethic: Essays on Boasian Ethnography and the German Anthropological Tradition* (Madison, WI: University of Wisconsin Press, 1996).

and political commitments to his education and upbringing in Germany, Stocking highlighted the empirical 'liberal tradition' of German anthropology championed by ethnographer Adolf Bastian and physician Rudolf Virchow. Both were sceptical of or opposed to grand evolutionary schemes and had worked with Boas in Berlin after he received his PhD.[8] An alternative German source of Boas' ideas has been the research programme termed *Völkerpsychologie* developed in the 1850s and 1860s by Moritz Lazarus and Heymann Steinthal, whose central argument was that any study of the human mind had to consider the individual's community, particularly its beliefs and language.[9] Some have even claimed that 'the most eminent student of *Völkerpsychologie* in the United States was the German-born cultural anthropologist Franz Boas'.[10] This framing of Boas' key influences has enjoyed a long afterlife in the United States and France.[11]

The 'unresolved tension' in Boas' thought between law-seeking and historical-particularist impulses was often glossed by Stocking as a tension between the

---

8 Stocking, *Race, Culture, Evolution*, 133–160.
9 Ivan Kalmar, "The *Völkerpsychologie* of Lazarus and Steinthal and the modern concept of culture", *Journal of the History of Ideas* 48, no. 4 (1987): 671–690; Michel Espagne, "*Völkerpsychologie* et anthropogéographie: Le cas de Leipzig", in *Quand Berlin pensait les peuples. Anthropologie, ethnologie, psychologie 1850–1890*, ed. Céline Trautmann-Waller (Paris: CNRS, 2004), 185–196; Céline Trautmann-Waller, "La *Zeitschrift für Völkerpsychologie und Sprachwissenschaft* (1859–1890): entre *Volksgeist* et *Gesamtgeist*", in *Quand Berlin pensait les peuples. Anthropologie, ethnologie, psychologie 1850–1890*, ed. Céline Trautmann-Waller (Paris: CNRS, 2004), 105–119; Céline Trautmann-Waller, *Aux origines d'une science allemande de la culture: Linguistique et psychologie des peuples chez Heymann Steinthal* (Paris: CNRS, 2006); Uwe Wolfradt, *Ethnologie und Psychologie: Die Leipziger Schule der Völkerpsychologie* (Berlin: Reimer, 2011).
10 Egbert Klautke, *The Mind of the Nation: Völkerpsychologie in Germany, 1851–1955* (New York: Berghahn, 2013), 33.
11 Anne-Christine Taylor, "Américanisme tropicale, une frontière fossile de l'ethnologie", in *Histoires de l'anthropologie: XVIe-XIXe siècles (Colloque 'la pratique de l'anthropologie aujourd'hui', Sèvres, 19–21 Novembre 1981)*, ed. Britta Rupp-Eisenreich (Paris: Klincksieck, 1984), 213–234; H. Glenn Penny, "Bastian's museum: On the limits of Empiricism and the transformation of German ethnology", in *Worldly Provincialism: German Anthropology in the Age of Empire*, ed. Matti Bunzl and H. Glenn Penny (Ann Arbor, MI: University of Michigan Press, 2003), 86–126; Barth et al., *The Halle lectures*, 61–135, 257–348; Rainer Baehre, "Early anthropological discourse on the Inuit and the influence of Virchow on Boas", *Études/Inuit/Studies* 32, no. 2 (2008), 13–34; William Y. Adams, *The Boasians: Founding Fathers and Mothers of American Anthropology* (Lanham, MD: Hamilton Books, 2016); Adam Kuper, "Civilization, culture, and race: Anthropology in the nineteenth century", in *The Nineteenth Century*, ed. Warren Breckman and Peter E. Gordon, vol. 1 of *The Cambridge History of Modern European Thought*, ed. Warren Breckman and Peter E. Gordon (Cambridge: Cambridge University Press, 2019), 398–421.

natural sciences and the humanities.[12] Stocking tentatively linked this to the *Natur-/Geisteswissenschaft* debate – the attempt by late nineteenth-century historians and philosophers to provide the 'sciences of the mind' (in English sometimes termed 'human sciences' or even 'humanities') with distinctive methods and objects of study, thus making them independent from the sciences of nature. While Stocking cautiously avoided the wholesale transfer of this debate, he nevertheless helped to set up a central problem in the scholarship on Boas by juxtaposing 'physics', the search for laws, with 'history', the focus on particulars, and more broadly made the presence of a binary tension into a central aspect in the study of Boas' ideas.[13] While acknowledging a tension or contradiction has at times led to insightful analyses, it may also serve to minimise inconsistencies regarding, for example, the scientific study of race by reducing such inconsistencies to tensions between his nineteenth-century education and his more modern scholarly impulses, as highlighted below.

Moreover, studies on Boas seem to be incomplete if they do not reference the 'culture concept' with many different '-isms' being used in an attempt to pin down exactly what Boas meant by 'culture'. Even though the term 'cultural relativism' was coined by his students in the interwar years, 'cultural relativist' still represents the most common definition of Boas and stresses his rejection of evolutionary cultural hierarchy and his attention to understanding cultures as equal in value and as requiring the anthropologist to understand them on their own

---

[12] George W. Stocking Jr, "Boasian ethnography and the German anthropological tradition", in *Volksgeist as Method and Ethic: Essays on Boasian Ethnography and the German Anthropological Tradition*, ed. George W. Stocking Jr. (Madison, WI: University of Wisconsin Press, 1996), 3–8; Stocking, *Race, Culture, Evolution*, 155.

[13] Woodruff D. Smith, "The social and political origins of German diffusionist ethnology", *Journal of the History of the Behavioral Sciences* 14 (1978), 103–112; Douglas Cole, "'The value of a person lies in his *Herzensbildung*': Franz Boas' Baffin Island letter-diary, 1883–1884", in *Observers Observed: Essays on Ethnographic Fieldwork*, ed. George W. Stocking Jr. (Madison, WI: University of Wisconsin Press, 1983), 13–52; Matti Bunzl, "Franz Boas and the Humboldtian tradition: From *Volksgeist* and *Nationalcharakter* to an anthropological concept of culture", in *Volksgeist as Method and Ethic : Essays on Boasian Ethnography and the German Anthropological Tradition*, ed. George W. Stocking Jr. (Madison, WI: University of Wisconsin Press, 1996), 17–78; Julia E. Liss, "German culture and German science in the Bildung of Franz Boas", in *Volksgeist as Method and Ethic: Essays on Boasian Anthropology and the German Anthropological Tradition*, ed. George W. Stocking Jr. (Madison, WI: University of Wisconsin Press, 1996), 155–184 (155, 182); Regna Darnell, "Mind, body, and the Native point of view: Boasian theory at the centennial of *The mind of primitive man*", in *Franz Boas as Public Intellectual – Theory, Ethnography, Activism*, ed. Regna Darnell et al., vol. 1 of *The Franz Boas Papers*, ed. Regina Darnell et al. (Lincoln, NE: University of Nebraska Press, 2015), 3–17; Richard C. Powell, "The study of geography? Franz Boas and his canonical returns", *Journal of Historical Geography* 49 (2015), 21–30.

terms.[14] In 1999, Douglas Cole argued that 'cultural relativism' should primarily be understood as a method to guard against the type of *a priori* deduction that was common among evolutionists at the end of the nineteenth century.[15] Historians and anthropologists stressing the importance of migration and contact have favoured 'cultural diffusionism', while those emphasising the unique value and history of each culture have favoured 'cultural particularism' or 'historical particularism'.[16] This concern has continued into the second decade of the twenty-first century. In 2014, Tracy Teslow termed Boas a 'cultural essentialist', thus highlighting Boas' method of classifying myths, rites, and customs as originally 'foreign' or 'native' to the culture in question.[17] Conversely, Isaiah Wilner, one of the editors and authors being reviewed, has argued that Boas is best described as a 'cultural universalist' who recognised that all peoples had culture and that a culture was rarely the work of a single group.[18] As in earlier works, the efforts of these authors to define the term 'culture' often rely on reconstructions of the origins of Boas' thought and on identifying tensions and contradictions in his written work. With these key elements of Boas scholarship in mind, I now turn to examine the volumes under consideration.

Franz Boas in the 21st Century

This review section proceeds in chronological order. The first four volumes are edited collections resulting from academic conferences. The final two are monographs (where one consists of two volumes) – one addressed to a general audience and one to a specialist audience. In the case of the edited volumes, I focus on the editors' framing of the volume as a whole and on overall trends and arguments made by contributors. I examine some key chapters in greater depth in the

---

14 David Hollinger, "Cultural relativism", in *The Modern Social Sciences*, ed. Theodore M. Porter and Dorothy Ross, vol. 7 of *The Cambridge History of Science*, ed. David C. Lindberg and Ronald L. Numbers (Cambridge: Cambridge University Press, 2003), 708–720; Michel Espagne, "Introduction", in *Franz Boas: Le travail du regard*, ed. Michel Espagne and Isabelle Kalinowski (Paris: Armand Colin, 2013), 9–12; Adams, *The Boasians*.
15 Cole, *Franz Boas*, 275.
16 For cultural diffusionism, see Barth et al., *One Discipline, Four Ways*; Penny, "Bastian's Museum"; Bunzl, "Franz Boas and the Humboldtian tradition". For cultural particularism, see Petermann, *Geschichte der Ethnologie*.
17 Tracy Teslow, *Constructing Race: The science of Bodies and Cultures in American Anthropology* (Cambridge: Cambridge University Press, 2014), 4–5, 13.
18 Isaiah Lorado Wilner, "A global potlatch: Identifying the Indigenous influence on Western thought", *American Indian Culture and Research Journal* 37, no. 2 (2013), 87–114.

following section on 'the circulation of knowledge and knowledge actors'. The first two publications (from 2009 and 2013) originated from conferences held in Germany and France respectively. Before turning to these, I briefly examine how U.S. scholarship has influenced academic work on Boas in Europe.

Despite historians insisting on anthropological national traditions shaped by domestic and imperial politics, funding, and institutionalisation patterns, scholars often assume a shared set of theoretical turning points in the discipline derived from the history of anthropology in the U.S. One such development is the break with evolutionary schemes linking together physical and cultural traits and a turn towards relativistic stances that did away with evolutionary hierarchy, focused on cultures as distinct from physical traits, and sought to understand the former on their own terms.[19] In the late 1980s, Boas became central to the history of anthropology in Germany when Robert Proctor sought to refute the widespread *Sonderweg*-inspired narratives of German anthropology as an aberrant version of the discipline that inevitably resulted in German anthropologists endorsing and collaborating with National Socialism. Proctor argued that interwar German anthropology had not represented a particularly racist deviation from nineteenth-century German anthropology or nineteenth-century anthropology in Europe more broadly. To further undermine the *Sonderweg*-inflected narrative, Proctor identified the 'culturalist tradition' of Adolf Bastian and the thought of Franz Boas as proof of alternative nineteenth-century 'trends' in Germany.[20] Many historical accounts have since argued that the anti-racist, empirical, liberal German tradition of anthropology immigrated to the United States with Boas while Germany was left with competing strands of diffusionism and the increasingly ascendant *Rassenkunde*.[21] This narrative persists despite revisionist work by

---

[19] Barth et al., *One Discipline, Four Ways*; Henrika Kuklick, ed., *A New History of Anthropology* (Oxford: Blackwell, 2008).

[20] Robert N. Proctor, "From *Anthropologie* to *Rassenkunde* in the German anthropological tradition", in *Bones, Bodies, Behavior: Essays on Biological Anthropology*, ed. George W. Stocking Jr. (Madison, WI: University of Wisconsin Press, 1988), 130–179.

[21] Woodruff D. Smith, *Politics and the Sciences of Culture in Germany, 1840–1920* (Oxford: Oxford University Press, 1991), 104, 113; Bunzl, "Franz Boas and the Humboldtian tradition"; Matti Bunzl and H. Glenn Penny, "Introduction: Rethinking German anthropology, colonialism, and race", in *Worldly Provincialism: German Anthropology in the Age of Empire*, ed. Matti Bunzl and H. Glenn Penny (Ann Arbor, MI: University of Michigan Press, 2003), 1–30; Werner Petermann, *Die Geschichte der Ethnologie* (Wuppertal: Peter Hammer, 2004); Barth et al., *One Discipline, Four Ways*; Regna Darnell, "The North American traditions in anthropology: The historiographic baseline", in *A New History of Anthropology*, ed. Henrika Kuklick (Oxford: Blackwell, 2008), 35–51; H. Glenn Penny, "Traditions in the German language", in *A New History of Anthropology*, ed. Henrika Kuklick (Oxford: Blackwell, 2008), 79–95; Friedrich Pöhl, "Franz Boas: Feldforschung und Ethik", in

Andrew Zimmermann disputing the existence of a liberal and empirical tradition of anthropology in Berlin at the end of the nineteenth century.[22]

The edited volume *Kulturrelativismus und Antirassismus: Der Anthropologe Franz Boas (1858–1942)* [Cultural relativism and anti-racism: The anthropologist Franz Boas (1858–1942)], which is the result of a 2008 conference at the University of Bielefeld, adopts a sceptical approach to Boas' work. The editor Hans Walter-Schmul posits that Boas had clear 'theoretical presuppositions, which he just did not explicitly formulate'.[23] In uncovering these, the volume seeks to read Boas 'against the grain'; in other words, departing from heroic narratives about cultural relativism and antiracism. Reconstructing Boas' theoretical assumptions reveals many limits, both political and epistemological, and brings the ambivalences of his work into focus.[24]

Many contributors question the long-standing association of, on the one hand, evolutionism with bad politics and racism and, on the other hand, Boasian relativism with equality and freedom. Thus, Christian Geulen problematises the simplistic identification of 'race' with determinism and 'bad politics' and of 'culture' with free will and 'good politics'. He argues that Boas replaced biological determinism with cultural or environmental determinism; while the latter was more malleable, it also lent itself to social engineering. Ultimately, Boas was unable to escape the trap of determinism, which is why his ideas and the persistent

---

Franz Boas – Kultur, Sprache, Rasse: Wege einer antirassistischen Anthropologie, ed. Friedrich Pöhl and Bernhard Tilg (Münster: Lit, 2011), 55–76; Harry Liebersohn, "'Culture' crosses the Atlantic: The German sources of *The mind of primitive man*", in *Indigenous Visions: Rediscovering the World of Franz Boas*, ed. Ned Blackhawk and Isaiah Lorado Wilner (New Haven, CT: Yale University Press, 2018), 91–108.

22 Andrew Zimmermann, "Antisemitism as skill: Rudolf Virchow's *Schulstatistik* and the racial composition of Germany", *Central European History* 32 (1999), 409–429; Andrew Zimmermann, *Anthropology and Antihumanism in Imperial Germany* (Chicago: University of Chicago Press, 2001); Andrew Zimmermann, "Looking beyond history: The optics of German anthropology and the critique of Humanism", *Studies in the History and Philosophy of the Biological and Biomedical Sciences* 32, no. 3 (2001), 385–411; Andrew Zimmermann, "Ethnologie im Kaiserreich: Natur, Kultur und 'Rasse' in Deutschland und seine Kolonien", in *Das Kaiserreich Transnational: Deutschland in der Welt 1871–1914*, ed. Sebastian Conrad and Jürgen Osterhammel (Göttingen: Vandenhoeck & Ruprecht, 2004), 191–212.

23 Hans-Walter Schmul, "Einleitung", in *Kulturrelativismus und Antirassismus: Der Anthropologe Franz Boas (1858–1942)*, ed. Hans-Walter Schmul (Beileifeld: Transcript, 2009), 9–16 (13–15).

24 Schmul, "Einleitung", 13.

defence of these represent a cautionary tale rather than a positive example.²⁵ While often acknowledging Boas' intellectual background in Berlin anthropology, some contributors examine the limits of both his scientific arguments and his political activism in North American and interwar transatlantic contexts. For example, Doris Kauffmann examines Boas' work on indigenous art to argue that he was so focused on deconstructing evolutionism that he got stuck in a critical and hyper-empirical mode of writing that simply accumulated detailed descriptions upon detailed descriptions without providing any new frameworks or ideas.²⁶ While Kauffmann's arguments are openly presentist, assessing Boas in terms of much later developments in the anthropology of art, her charge that critique is not inherently constructive and generative is a welcome intervention in a field frequently focusing on this aspect of Boas' work.

Where *Kulturrelativismus und Antirassismus* departs from the anglophone focus on Boas' German background and problematises the narrative of a clean theoretical break, *Franz Boas: le travail du regard* (2013) [Franz Boas: The work of the gaze], which originated as a commemorative conference held in 2011 at the Musée de Quay Branly, is heavily indebted to this framework. Michel Espagne's introduction highlights the conceptual importance of Boas' break with evolutionary frameworks.²⁷ Gildas Salmon is even more forceful when stating that Boas represented an 'epistemological revolution' in anthropology.²⁸ Multiple contributors identify the transfer of a 'German tradition' to the United States as a key moment for anthropology: Boas is described as 'the ferryman [across the Atlantic] of the German tradition', and as 'arriv[ing] [in the United States] at the end of an intellectual education acquired entirely in the Wilhelmine Empire'.²⁹ In tracing

---

25 Christian Geulen, "Franz Boas und der Kulturdeterminismus", in *Kulturrelativismus und Antirassismus: Der Anthropologe Franz Boas (1858–1942)*, ed. Hans-Walter Schmul (Beilefeld: Transcript, 2009), 121–139.
26 Doris Kauffmann, "Die Entdeckung der 'Primitiven Kunst'. Zur Kulturdiskussion in der amerikanischen Anthropologie um Franz Boas, 1890–1940", in *Kulturrelativismus und Antirassismus: Der Anthropologe Franz Boas (1858–1942)*, ed. Hans-Walter Schmul (Beilefeld: Transcript, 2009), 211–230.
27 Michel Espagne, "Introduction", in *Franz Boas: Le travail du regard*, ed. Michel Espagne and Isabelle Kalinowski (Paris: Armand Colin, 2013), 9–10.
28 Gildas Salmon, "Forme et variante: Franz Boas dans l'histoire du comparatisme", in *Franz Boas: Le travail du regard*, ed. Michel Espagne and Isabelle Kalinowski (Paris: Armand Colin, 2013), 191–220 (202).
29 Emmanuel Desveaux, "L'anthropologie américaine avant et après Boas", in *Franz Boas: Le travail du regard*, ed. Michel Espagne and Isabelle Kalinowski (Paris: Armand Colin, 2013), 77–90 (88); Claude Imbert, "Boas, de Berlin à New York. Manières de vivres, manières de voir", in *Franz Boas: Le travail du regard*, ed. Michel Espagne and Isabelle Kalinowski (Paris: Armand Colin, 2013), 15–32.

the origins of this revolution to Germany, the editors and contributors follow the general lines of argument found in the secondary English-language scholarship, particularly Stocking's *Volksgeist as Method and Ethic*. This even extends to the structure of *Le travail du regard*, which concludes with a French translation of Boas' 1887 article 'The Study of Geography', the same essay that opens *Volksgeist as Method and Ethic*.[30] Another important influence is the scholarship on *transferts culturels*. This approach to cultural and intellectual history was formulated by Espagne, one of the editors of *Le travail du regard*, and focuses on the transfer of the human sciences and humanities across national borders, emphasising the movement of texts and ideas between France and Germany.[31] The 'German tradition' in *Le Travail du Regard* extends far beyond Berlin anthropology and Boas' direct engagement with scholars and scientists, as it ranges from early nineteenth-century experimental psychology and mathematics, to natural history, to von Humboldt's *Kosmos* (1845–1862), to the combination of comparison schemes drawn from philology and biology.[32]

A common thread in many of the chapters concerns explicit comparisons between Boas and Claude Lévi-Strauss (1908–2009), the French anthropological theoriser *par excellence*. Isabelle Kalinowski traces parallels and continuities between Lévi-Strauss and Boas; Aaron Glass notes that Boas 'anticipated' many aspects of Lévi-Strauss' work; Emmanuel Desveaux reconstructs Lévi-Strauss' explicit theoretical engagements with Boas and outlines improvements made by the former on the latter.[33] While Boas and Lévi-Strauss knew each other and corresponded, the contributors' emphasis on theoretical parallels and links rather than this archival material, most of which dates to the 1930s and concerns interwar politics, points to a distinctive trait of scholarship on the history of French anthropology: the trope of the 'late' development of anthropological theory in France. Accounts of late nineteenth-century French anthropology tend to focus on the *Société d'Anthropologie de Paris* and the debates between proponents of racial classification and supporters of evolutionism that persisted well into the twentieth

---

30 Franz Boas, "L'Étude de la géographie", trans. Camille Joseph, in *Franz Boas: Le travail du regard*, ed. Michel Espagne and Isabelle Kalinowski (Paris: Armand Colin, 2013), 271–280.
31 Michel Espagne, *Les transferts culturels Franco-Allemands* (Paris: PUF, 1999); Michel Espagne, *En deçà du Rhin. L'Allemagne des philosophes français au XIXe siècle* (Paris: CERF, 2004).
32 Respectively Imbert, "Boas, de Berlin à New York"; Carlo Severi, "Boas entre Biologie des images et Morphologie. Une généalogie intellectuelle", in *Franz Boas: Le travail du regard*, ed. Michel Espagne and Isabelle Kalinowski (Paris: Armand Colin, 2013), 33–51; Michel Espagne, "Franz Boas et la pensée géographique", in *Franz Boas: Le travail du regard*, ed. Michel Espagne and Isabelle Kalinowski (Paris: Armand Colin, 2013), 91–105.
33 Kalinowski, "Franz Boas et 'l'exubérance des formes'", 242–243; Glass, "Le Musée portatif", 116 ; Desveaux, "L'anthropologie américaine", 89.

century.[34] While some scholars have stressed the importance of the period 1890–1920 for the development of field research in France's African colonies, they concur with intellectual historians in terms of identifying the successful, albeit 'late', institutionalisation of an ethnographic, field-based, relativistic, and non-biological research programme in the interwar years with the founding the *Institut d'Ethnographie* in 1925.[35] Thus, linking Boas, credited with the discipline-defining theoretical break from the nineteenth century, to Lévi-Strauss offers a 'bridging' of sorts between national traditions and serves to reinsert French anthropology into a familiar narrative on the development of the field.

Compared to the sustained scepticism in *Kulturrelativismus und Antirassismus* and the general intellectual reverence in *Le travail du regard*, the first U.-S. publication under review presents an altogether more fragmented portrait of the discipline and the individual. *Franz Boas as Public Intellectual – Theory, Ethnography, Activism* is the first volume of "The Franz Boas Papers Documentary

---

[34] Claude Blackaert, "Histoires du terrain entre savoirs et savoir-faire", in *Le terrain de sciences humaines. Instructions et enquêtes (XVIIIᵉ – XXᵉ Siècle)*, ed. Claude Blanckaert (Paris: L'Harmattan, 1996), 9–55; Laurent Mucchielli, "Sociologie versus anthropologie raciale", *Gradhiva. Revue d'Histoire e d'Archives de l'Anthropologie* 21 (1997), 77–95; Laurent Mucchielli, *La découverte du social: Naissance de la sociologie en France (1870–1914)* (Paris: La Découverte, 1998), 21; Benoit Massin, "L'anthropologie raciale comme fondement de la science politique. Vacher de Lapouge et l'échec de l'"anthroposociologie' en France (1886–1936)", in *Les politiques de l'anthropologie. Discours et pratiques en France (1860–1940)*, ed. Claude Blanckaert (Paris: L'Harmattan, 2001), 269–336; Alice L. Conklin, *In the Museum of Man: Race, Anthropology, and Empire in France, 1850–1950* (Ithaca, NY: Cornell University Press, 2013).

[35] On the development of fieldwork in the Francophone context, see Emmanuelle Sibeud, "Ethnographie, ethnologie, et africanisme. La 'disciplinarisation' de l'ethnologie française dans le premier tiers du XXᵉ siècle", in *Qu'est-ce qu'une discipline?*, ed. Jean Boutier, Jean-Claude Passeron, and Jacques Revel (Paris: Éditions de l'École des Hautes Études en Sciences Sociales, 2006), 229–245; Emmanuelle Sibeud, "The metamorphosis of ethnology in France", in *A New History of Anthropology*, ed. Henrika Kuklick (Oxford: Blackwell, 2008), 96–110; Robert Parkin and Anne de Sales, "Introduction: Ethnographic practice and theory in France", in *Out of the Study and into the Field: Ethnographic Theory and Practice in French Anthropology*, ed. Robert Parkin and Anne de Sales (Oxford: Berghahn, 2010), 1–24. For the 'late' theoretical development in French anthropology, see Filippo Zerilli, *Il lato oscuro dell'etnologia. Il contributo dell'antropologia naturalista al processo di istituzionalizzazione degli studi etnologici in Francia* (Rome: Centro d'Informazione e Stampa Universitaria, 1998); Benoit de L'Estoile, "'Des races non pas inferieurs, mais différentes': De l'Exposition Coloniale au Musée de l'Homme", in *Les politiques de l'anthropologie. Discours et pratiques en France (1860–1940)*, ed. Claude Blanckaert (Paris: L'Harmattan, 2001), 391–476; Barth et al., *One Discipline, Four Ways*, 157–256; Claudine Gauthier, "Henri Gaidoz et l'institutionnalisation des études de folklore en France", in *De la Philologie allemande à l'anthropologie française: Les sciences humaines à l'EPHE (1868–1945)*, ed. Céline Trautmann-Waller (Paris: Honoré Champion, 2017), 349–366.

Edition Series", which aims to make his professional correspondence available to the public. A second volume, containing Boas' correspondence with his field collaborator James Teit, appeared in 2024, while the third volume, on Boas and Russian anthropology, is scheduled to be published in 2026.[36] *Franz Boas as Public Intellectual* serves as an introduction to Boas and his legacy. Made up of contributions from anthropologists and historians, this volume is a good example of the wide variety of scholarship on Boas being produced in the United States. Some of the contributions seek to crystallize Boas' thinking to better defend him from critics. One of the editors, anthropologist Regna Darnell, presents his 1911 publication *The Mind of Primitive Man* as a timeless distillation of his thought. She argues that Boas 'engaged in cultural relativism', without using this term, as he emphasised on the complexity, variability, and plasticity of humans and culture.[37] Herbert Lewis, also an anthropologist, gives himself the task of disproving the charge that Boas' conception of culture is essential and uniform, thereby rehabilitating it for contemporary use by practising anthropologists.[38] In both cases, the authors look for coherence in his writings and leave aside any analysis of change or tensions in his work. Many of the historians, however, focus on tracing changes in Boas' thought and conduct. These authors privilege the U.S., British Columbia, and the interwar years as key contexts for understanding Boas and highlight the formative importance of Boas' work with indigenous collaborators and students as well as his public role as a scientist.

The focus on indigenous collaborators takes centre stage in *Indigenous Visions: Rediscovering the World of Franz Boas*, which resulted from a 2011 conference at Yale University commemorating the centenary of three publications: *The Mind of Primitive Man*, *The Handbook of American Languages*, and the article 'Changes in bodily form of descendants of immigrants'. This is the most ambitious and most uneven of the volumes under review. Its editors, Ned Blackhawk and

---

36 Unfortunately, volume 2 appeared too late to be included in this review. See Andrea Laforet et al., ed., *Franz Boas, James Teit, and Early Twentieth-Century Salish Ethnography*, vol. 2 of *The Franz Boas Papers Documentary Edition*, ed. Regna Darnell et al. (Lincoln, NE: University of Nebraska Press, 2024). For the forthcoming volume 3, see https://www.nebraskapress.unl.edu/nebraska/9781496238825/the-franz-boas-papers-volume-3/.

37 Regna Darnell, "Mind, body, and the Native point of view: Boasian theory at the centennial of *The Mind of Primitive Man*", in *Franz Boas as Public Intellectual – Theory, Ethnography, Activism*, ed. Regna Darnell et al., vol. 1 of *The Franz Boas Papers Documentary Edition*, ed. Regna Darnell et al. (Lincoln, NE: University of Nebraska Press, 2015), 3–17.

38 Herbert S. Lewis, "The individual and individuality in Franz Boas's anthropology and philosophy", in *Franz Boas as Public Intellectual – Theory, Ethnography, Activism*, ed. Regna Darnell et al., vol. 1 of *The Franz Boas Papers*, ed. Regna Darnell et al. (Lincoln, NE: University of Nebraska Press, 2015), 19–41.

Isaiah Wilner, seek to pluralize the origins of Boas' ideas. One key source are the transformation narratives of the Kwakwaka'wakw in British Columbia amongst whom Boas carried out much of his research starting in the late 1880s. Wilner terms these narratives 'transcultural enlightenment', defined as 'an understanding of modernity as global interconnection and identity as multifaceted'.[39] Other sources are 'the German humanist tradition' that was 'activated' by Boas' encounter with U.S.-American multicultural society, late nineteenth-century 'expressive enlightenment' and its focus on speech as 'world making', and the 'the entire Goethe-Herder-Humboldt tradition'.[40] Boas' key contribution was institutional: he 'put in place, in the form of academic anthropology, a network that disseminated ideas across borders'.[41] What circulated were 'visions' of indigenous thinkers who articulated 'shared forms of belonging' and a more inclusive form of modernity.[42] These shaped Boas' thinking and emerge most clearly in *The Mind of Primitive Man*, which distilled a philosophy of equality and diversity completely opposed to evolutionary hierarchy.[43] Recovering this broad network thus reveals the non-European origin of modern ideas and values while also showing that the directionality of influence proceeded from indigenous collaborators to anthropologists. The structure of the volume reflects this argument – the first two sections, 'Origins and Erasures' and 'Worlds of Enlightenment', reconstruct these different influences, while the final two sections examine the circulation of 'Boasian' notions of 'race' and 'culture' through the network. While the volume offers many stimulating ideas, it exhibits two analytical drawbacks: it relies on the vagueness of the term 'enlightenment' to link everything from indigenous narratives to Herder, Kant, and early twentieth-century poetry, and it lacks a granular reconstruction of how the network of anthropology connected individuals and groups.

---

39 Isaiah Lorado Wilner, "Transformation masks: Recollecting the Indigenous origins of global consciousness", in *Indigenous Visions: Rediscovering the World of Franz Boas*, ed. Ned Blackhawk and Isaiah Lorado Wilner (New Haven, CT: Yale University Press, 2018), 3–41 (27).
40 Respectively Liebersohn, "'Culture' crosses the Atlantic"; Ryan Carr, "Expressive Enlightenment: Subjectivity and solidarity in Daniel Garrison Brinton, Franz Boas, and Carlos Montezuma", in *Indigenous Visions: Rediscovering the World of Franz Boas*, ed. Ned Blackhawk and Isaiah Lorado Wilner (New Haven, CT: Yale University Press, 2018), 61–90; James Tully, "Rediscovering the world of Franz Boas: Anthropology, equality/diversity, and world peace", in *Indigenous Visions: Rediscovering the World of Franz Boas*, ed. Ned Blackhawk and Isaiah Lorado Wilner (New Haven, CT: Yale University Press, 2018), 111–146 (127).
41 Ned Blackhawk and Isaiah Lorado Wilner, "Introduction", in *Indigenous Visions: Rediscovering the World of Franz Boas*, ed. Ned Blackhawk and Isaiah Lorado Wilner (New Haven, CT: Yale University Press, 2018), ix–xxii (xi).
42 Blackhawk and Wilner, "Introduction", xii–xiv.
43 Tully, "Rediscovering".

Finally, the monographs under review constitute much more straightforward defences of Boas' ideas and work and were clearly influenced by the polarised politics of the U.S. after 2016. Charles King's 2019 *Gods of the Upper Air: How a Circle of Renegade Anthropologists Reinvented Race, Sex, and Gender in the Twentieth Century*, covers the work of Franz Boas and some of his most well-known students: Ruth Benedict, Margaret Mead, Zora Neale Hurston, and Ella Cara Deloria. True to its subtitle, this book focuses on their ideas and the 'moral battle' to prove the oneness of humanity and to posit open-mindedness as a key scientific and human virtue.[44] Central to the worldview of these figures was 'cultural relativism', which King defines as an exhortation to understand others or 'the other' before judging them. The self-awareness that derives from this exercise in understanding yields further insights: it reveals the inability of science to rank humans and judge 'who is best' while also illustrating the fact that humans are cultural animals 'bound by the rules of our own making'.[45] The book is explicitly presentist, stressing that cultural relativism aims 'to enliven our moral sensibility' by highlighting the enduring prejudices of one's own culture and bemoaning the mid-century conservative backlash against it.[46]

An integral part of King's eloquent description and defence of 'cultural relativism' and the ideas of 'the Boas circle' is the emphasis on their 'homegrown' nature. The key context of this book is the U.S. in the early twentieth century, particularly the 1920s – a vibrant and multicultural 'laboratory' of humanity. This, rather than specific theories or experiences acquired in Germany, was what stimulated and directed Boas' work.[47] In his new country, scientists largely adhered to a rigid evolutionary framework that viewed history as having a single direction and being articulated in hierarchically ranked stages of development.[48] The belief that races were immutable and unequal was widespread and underpinned both discrimination against African Americans and opposition to immigration from Southern and Eastern Europe. This spurred Boas' work on the mutability and instability of physical traits and his insistence that scientists examine their own emotions and prejudices.[49] King's argument is further fleshed out when it comes to Boas' students, who used the opportunities for study he afforded them and the conceptual tools he imparted to them to make sense of their own experiences of

---

44 Charles King, *Gods of the Upper Air: How a Circle of Renegade Anthropologists Reinvented Race, Sex, and Gender in the Twentieth Century* (New York: Doubleday, 2019).
45 King, *Gods of the Upper Air*, Chapter 1: Away.
46 King, *Gods of the Upper Air*, Chapter 14: Home.
47 King, *Gods of the Upper Air*, Chapter 4: Science and Circuses.
48 King, *Gods of the Upper Air*, Chapter 3: Individuality.
49 King, *Gods of the Upper Air*, Chapter 5: Headhunters.

sexuality, gender roles, and racism. Margaret Mead's sense of non-belonging, compounded by her relationship with Ruth Benedict and her impatience with the expectation that she should become a doting wife and mother, shaped her interest in the internal lives of Samoan girls and women as well as her work on the cultural specificity of sexuality and gender roles.[50] Zora Neale Hurston worked on African-American folklore in the American South and presented it as a distinctive culture worthy of study and respect. Here, she set herself apart from prevailing views that contemporary black culture was 'degraded', a view held by Boas and many members of the Harlem Renaissance who sought to create new and 'high' cultural achievements for African Americans.[51]

2019 also saw the publication of *Franz Boas: The Emergence of the Anthropologist*, the first volume of a two-part biography on Franz Boas by folklorist Rosemary Lévy Zumwalt. The second volume, *Franz Boas: Shaping Anthropology and Fostering Social Justice*, was published in 2022. The only complete biography on Boas, this book is primarily addressed to the specialist and draws heavily on both his professional and personal correspondence.[52] Lévy Zumwalt focuses on the personal and emotional aspects of Boas' life.[53] While this allows her to paint a vivid picture of the protagonist, the wealth of archival details does not coalesce into clear narratives regarding Boas' ideas or the theoretical or institutional development of the discipline. Instead, the author relies heavily on ideas and themes from earlier scholarship.

The Emergence of the Anthropologist traces Boas' life from birth to 1906, the year when he resigned from the American Museum of Natural History and focused all his energies on the Department of Anthropology at Columbia University. The seeds of Boas' thinking are traced back to his childhood, when games and gardening marked both 'the beginning of a comparative approach' and a preoccupation with the relationship of details to 'generality'.[54] Later chapters cover his university years in Prussia, his early field experiences in Canada, and his search for employment in Europe and the U.S. Throughout, the author focuses on the more intimate aspects that drove Boas' decisions: his relationship with his

---

50 King, *Gods of the Upper Air*, Chapter 7: A Girl as Frail as Margaret and Chapter 8: Coming of Age.
51 King, *Gods of the Upper Air*, Chapter 9: Masses and Mountaintops.
52 Rosemary Lévy Zumwalt, *Franz Boas: The Emergence of the Anthropologist*, Critical Studies in the History of Anthropology Series (Lincoln, NE: University of Nebraska Press, 2019) and *Franz Boas: Shaping Anthropology and Fostering Social Justice*, Critical Studies in the History of Anthropology Series (Lincoln, NE: University of Nebraska Press, 2022).
53 Lévy Zumwalt, *Franz Boas: Shaping*, xviii.
54 Lévy Zumwalt, *Franz Boas: Emergence*, 49.

wife and family, his financial struggles, and his drive for scholarly recognition, which resulted in ever-changing patterns of alliance and animosity. *Shaping Anthropology and Fostering Social Justice* combines overviews of Boas' students with chapters on the funding of the anthropology department at Columbia University, the attempt to set up an international school of archaeology in Mexico City, Boas' experience of being censured by the public and the university during the First World War, and his efforts to find employment for displaced European scientists after 1933. The focus on social justice in the title serves as a common thread throughout the book and primarily centres on Boas' anti-racist scholarship and public activism. In a key chapter on 'Race and social justice', Lévy-Zumwalt not only seeks to describe Boas' activism but also to defend him against present-day criticism. This leads to an uncomfortable section that seems to equate far-right critics – who rely on antisemitic tropes to smear Boas, cultural relativism, and anti-racist science as a plot to weaken American civilization – with left-wing critiques that highlight the political and analytical limits of Boas' focus on individual racial prejudice.[55] While the author herself acknowledges shortcomings in Boas' work, she ultimately judges him to be a positive figure and explains his ambivalences as manifestations of a distinctive 'Boas paradox' rooted in the tension between nineteenth-century ways of thinking about race and Boas' own evolving cultural relativism.[56]

Knowledge Circulation and Knowledge Actors

Historically, work on Boas has implicitly or explicitly relied on narratives concerning intellectual transfer from one point to another rather than focusing on circulation as a longer and less linear process. *Indigenous Visions* represents a welcome departure from this trend, even though this project presents some clear weaknesses. In presenting the circulation of the concepts of 'race' and 'culture' as flowing from many points of origin through the network of academic anthropology to disparate fields and places, the editors upend schemes positing a central origin of knowledge, often in a European metropolis, which is then transmitted to

---

55 Lévy Zumwalt, *Franz Boas: Shaping*, 116ff. For the 'left' critique, see Marc Anderson, *From Boas to Black Power: Racism, Liberalism, and American Anthropology* (Stanford, CA: Stanford University Press, 2019).
56 Lévy Zumwalt, *Franz Boas: Shaping*, 97.

peripheries.[57] However, their framework maintains a focus on the origins of knowledge rather than on circulation or transit as key moments of knowledge production. Moreover, limited attention is paid to reconstructing the conditions and communities that made possible the 'anthropological network'. Instead, the network framework provided by the editors makes otherwise interesting chapters appear as weak links. A piece by Sean Hanretta placed in the section on the circulation of the concept of 'culture' examines the parallels of the 'liberatory culture concepts' of Liberian polymath Edward Wilmot Blyden and the 'German tradition', which here spans Hegel, Müller, Hölderlin, Waitz, Bastian, and Boas. While the theoretical arguments are stimulating, there is no acknowledgement that such a broad spectrum of 'culturalist' German thinkers contains vastly different positions. This might be explained by examining which interpretations or translations of these authors reached Blyden; however, there is no reconstruction of this process.[58]

Chapters focusing on the network of the modern university provide more detailed and at times surprising arguments regarding the circulation of 'race' and 'culture'. This confirms the emphasis among historians of knowledge on this institution.[59] Maria Lucia Pallares-Burke traces the transmission of Boas' ideas to Brazil via the anthropologist Rudiger Bilden, who was mentored by Boas while at Columbia University. Bilden, in turn, communicated Boasian ideas on cultural diversity, migration, and human variability to the young anthropologist Gilberto Freyre. These led Freyre to view miscegenation as something positive and to analyse social problems in terms of culture rather than race, thus enabling an appreciation of and pride in Brazil's diversity.[60] Eve Dunbar has a more sceptical view of the university. She examines the life and work of Zora Neale Hurston, who studied with Boas and authored important works in anthropology and in narrative non-fiction and fiction. Dunbar argues that Boas' theories and teaching cre-

---

57 Lissa Roberts, "Situating science in global history: Local exchanges and networks of circulation", *Itinerario* 33, no. 1 (2009), 9–30.
58 Sean Hanretta, "The river of salvation flows through Africa: Edward Wilmot Blyden, Rafael Armattoe, and the reception of the culture concept", in *Indigenous Visions: Rediscovering the World of Franz Boas*, ed. Ned Blackhawk and Isaiah Lorado Wilner (New Haven, CT: Yale University Press, 2018), 279–315.
59 Johan Östling et al., "The history of knowledge and the circulation of knowledge: An introduction", in *Circulation of Knowledge: Explorations in the History of Knowledge* (Lund: Nordic Academic Press, 2018), 9–33.
60 Maria Lucia Pallares-Burke, "A two-headed thinker: Rudiger Bilden, Gilberto Freyre, and the reinvention of Brazilian identity", in *Indigenous Visions: Rediscovering the World of Franz Boas*, ed. Ned Blackhawk and Isaiah Lorado Wilner (New Haven, CT: Yale University Press, 2018), 316–343.

ated space for an African American woman to train at Columbia and carry out research. However, racism, imperialism, and sexism limited her ability to thrive professionally both within and outside the university, thus consigning her valuable literary and scholarly contributions to oblivion for many decades.[61] In highlighting the limits of the modern university in relation to Hurston, Dunbar's chapter provides a stimulating counterpoint to the openness and connectivity of the university described by Pallares-Burke and its ability to alter rather than be constrained by society at large. Dunbar's arguments also resonate with King's observation that Hurston's emphasis on the value of black 'low' culture from rural areas was exceptional in both academic and literary circles at the time, putting her at odds with both the Boas Circle and the Harlem Renaissance.

While the above examples discuss the movements of ideas in the form of people or texts, one of the most insightful contributions in the edited volumes focuses on physical objects, another topic recently highlighted in the volume on the circulation of knowledge edited by Johan Östling et al.[62] In *Le Travail du Regard*, Rainer Hatoum presents a dynamic account of Boas' thinking by reconstructing the key role of indigenous masks from British Columbia as catalysts for Boas' thinking and interests. Hatoum reconstructs Boas' early encounter with these masks while working in Berlin in the mid-1880s and follows his sustained efforts to understand their purpose and meaning in the following decades. This, Hatoum argues, was a major motivating factor behind Boas' decision to travel to British Columbia and learn about the potlatch feasts and secret societies of the Kwakwaka'wakw, a topic that would stimulate and accompany him for the rest of his life.[63]

Analyses of Boas also provide fertile ground for thinking about knowledge actors. While there has been much focus in the history of knowledge on expanding the definition of a knowledge actor to marginalised figures while acknowledging the constraints placed upon them by their context, the invitation to consider constraints is also useful in the case of a public figure.[64] In the case of Boas, these might include learning to understand the public he was addressing, how to address it, and having to publicly express opinions or support he did not agree with in

---

[61] Eve Dunbar, "Woman on the verge of a cultural breakdown: Zora Neale Hurston in Haiti and the racial privilege of Boasian relativism", in *Indigenous Visions: Rediscovering the World of Franz Boas*, ed. Ned Blackhawk and Isaiah Lorado Wilner (New Haven, CT: Yale University Press, 2018), 231–257.
[62] Johan Östling et al., "The history of knowledge", 9–33.
[63] Rainer Hatoum, "La collection Boas au Musée d'Ethnologie du Berlin", in *Franz Boas: Le travail du regard*, 135–154.
[64] Johan Östling et al., "Introduction: Revisiting agency in the history of knowledge", in *Knowledge Actors: Revisiting Agency in the History of Knowledge*, ed. Johan Östling et al. (Lund: Nordic Academic Press, 2023), 9–23 (18–19).

private. An excellent piece by Julia Liss in *Franz Boas as Public Intellectual* historicises Boas' role as a public scholar and critic of political positions on both sides of the Atlantic. The First World War, she argues, 'mobilised' Boas' thinking and led him to use anthropological reflections on culture and language to dispute a link between German nationality and aggression. Despite Boas presenting his arguments as concerning the misapplication of scientific ideas to politics, possibly an honest mistake, his criticisms of U.S. scientists were not well-received. The frosty reception of Boas' critiques is best explained by the widespread anti-German sentiment at the time. Liss then traces a shift in the interwar period when Boas' public criticism increasingly targeted German antisemitism. Once his opponents were German scientists and a political regime that caused much concern and condemnation in the U.S., Boas was able to explicitly accuse scientists of acting in bad faith and putting ideology before science without alienating his readers.[65]

An even more granular analysis by Veronika Lipphardt in *Kulturrelativismus und Antirassismus* recovers Boas' interwar interactions with German Jewish scientists to draw out the ambivalences of Boas' public stance on science and race. In the 1930s Boas helped many Jewish scientists escape Germany and publicly supported their work on biological heredity. By this point, Boas was a well-known public figure who had written about the instability of human types as revealed by anthropometric measurements and had questioned the scientific standing of racial arguments. Boas himself viewed the social environment as being the more important determinant of human behaviour, but he recognised the risk of dismissing scientific work solely focused on biological heredity, especially since such studies were now based on a genetic foundation that Boas himself had no expertise in. Thus, while privately holding that biological heredity had little impact on human conduct, he publicly supported the work of Jewish scientists in the hope that they would disprove the findings of German racial science by using its very methods and focus.[66]

Turning to indigenous figures as key actors and interlocutors, scholarship on Boas presents contradictory and even incompatible arguments. In *Franz Boas as Public Intellectual*, Christopher Bracken, Isaiah Wilner, and Joshua Smith high-

---

[65] Julia E. Liss, "Franz Boas on war and empire: The making of a public intellectual", in *Franz Boas as Public Intellectual – Theory, Ethnography, Activism*, ed. Regna Darnell et al., vol. 1 of *The Franz Boas Papers*, ed. Regna Darnell et al. (Lincoln, NE: University of Nebraska Press, 2015), 293–328.

[66] Veronika Lipphardt, "'Investigation of biological changes'. Franz Boas in Kooperation mit deutsch-jüdischen Anthropologen, 1929–1940", in *Kulturrelativismus und Antirassismus: Der Anthropologe Franz Boas (1858–1942)*, ed. Hans-Walter Schmul (Beilefeld: Transcript, 2009), 163–186.

light the formative importance of Boas' work with indigenous collaborators and students. Smith argues that Boas was adamant regarding the need to involve indigenous populations in decision-making and that he and his former student Archie Phinney (Nez Perce) thought of indigenous issues in terms of treaty relations, sovereignty, and jurisdiction and pushed for a halt to assimilationist policies.[67] Bracken traces Boas' conceptual break with evolutionism to 1886, the year of his first fieldwork in British Columbia. Here, Boas witnessed the 'police dance', whose complex symbolic and political significance prompted him to focus on cultural dissemination and contact between peoples. According to Bracken, fieldwork did not serve as a conversion experience to modern anthropology but as a key site for changes in Boas' research focus and priorities.[68] An even stronger argument is made by Wilner, who reconstructs George Hunt's key role as Boas' teacher and guide. Hunt was a man of mixed Tlingit and European heritage who married into the Kawkwaka'wakw and collaborated with Boas for over twenty years collecting ethnographic material. Wilner argues that Hunt's insights and curiosities led Boas in new intellectual directions, and that getting to know someone else's mind represented a crucial influence on Boas.[69] As editor and contributor to *Indigenous Visions*, Wilner goes even further, claiming that the indigenous knowledge transmitted to Boas by Hunt constituted the core of Boas' anthropology. However, in *Kulturrelativismus und Antirassismus*, Jacqueline Holzer examines the contradictions between Boas' politics and his scientific practices in his interactions with indigenous communities. On the one hand, Boas opposed the potlatch ban in Canada and personally tried to intervene with Canadian authorities. On the other, he stole human remains from grave sites in British Columbia in the name of scientific research and convinced his indigenous collaborators,

---

67 Joshua Smith, "Cultural persistence in the age of 'hopelessness': Phinney, Boas, and U.S. Indian Policy", in *Franz Boas as Public Intellectual – Theory, Ethnography, Activism*, ed. Regna Darnell et al., vol. 1 of *The Franz Boas Papers*, ed. Regna Darnell et al. (Lincoln, NE: University of Nebraska Press, 2015), 263–276.

68 Christopher Bracken, "The police dance: Dissemination in Boas' field notes and diaries, 1886–1894", in *Franz Boas as Public Intellectual – Theory, Ethnography, Activism*, ed. Regna Darnell et al., vol. 1 of *The Franz Boas Papers*, ed. Regna Darnell et al. (Lincoln, NE: University of Nebraska Press, 2015), 43–64.

69 Isaiah Lorado Wilner, "Friends in this world: The relationship of Franz Boas and George Hunt", in *Franz Boas as Public Intellectual – Theory, Ethnography, Activism*, ed. Regna Darnell et al., vol. 1 of *The Franz Boas Papers*, ed. Regna Darnell et al. (Lincoln, NE: University of Nebraska Press, 2015), 163–190.

including George Hunt, to do the same.[70] These contrasting arguments illustrate the challenges of assigning agency to knowledge actors in colonial or imperial contexts without implying equal power in their relationships.[71]

Conclusion

Comparing and contrasting the publications under review underscores the rewards of moving away from or at least broadening the traditional historical foci on Boas. The strongest contributions in the edited volumes are attentive to the contexts of making and sharing knowledge, and they constitute valuable case studies for historians of knowledge. Pieces in *Le travail du regard* do this by drawing on visual and physical material, while the focus in *Kulturrelativismus und Antirassismus* on the many constraints placed on public intellectuals yields fascinating insights into Boas' thought and conduct. The more historically minded chapters in *Franz Boas as Public Intellectual* broaden the sites and actors of knowledge and contain excellent arguments regarding Boas' changing strategies of public criticism. While *Indigenous Visions* adopts an exciting conceptual approach that combines circulation, multipolarity, and the inclusion of non-Western actors, the collection as a whole does not bear out this scheme. Overall, these publications illustrate the many promises and challenges of recent trends in the history of anthropology and in the history of knowledge.

Valentina Mann is a historian of modern European intellectual history with a focus on the history of the social sciences. She is the co-editor of *Conceptions of Space in Intellectual History* (Routledge, 2021) and her article 'Mind and knowledge in the early thought of Franz Boas, 1887–1904', appeared in *History of the Human Sciences* in 2022. She is currently a Polonsky Academy Postdoctoral Fellow at the Van Leer Jerusalem Institute.

---

70 Jacqueline Holzer, "Franz Boas, die linguistische Anthropologie und die Sprachenpolitik der US-Regierung", in *Kulturrelativismus und Antirassismus: Der Anthropologe Franz Boas (1858–1942)*, ed. Hans-Walter Schmul (Beilefeld: Transcript, 2009), 49–68.
71 Kapil Raj, "Beyond postcolonialism . . . and postpositivism: Circulation and the global history of science", *Isis* 104, no. 2 (2013), 337–347.

Karl Haikola and Johan Östling

Review Essay: The Europeanisation of the Universities: An Emerging Topic of Historical Research

Abstract: In this review essay, the authors discuss new scholarly literature on the Europeanisation of the universities. This field has recently started to attract increasing interest among historians, partly as a new way of writing the history of the European integration and the so-called knowledge society. The authors review five books that approach these questions by means of different methods and perspectives. An important insight is that the Europeanisation of the universities is both a fairly recent phenomenon (with the 1980s serving as a kind of turning point) and a profound process altering the conditions for research and higher education in Europe. At the same time, the field is still young, and the authors call for more comparative studies and bottom-up approaches.

Keywords: Europeanisation, universities, knowledge society, higher education, contemporary history

Judith Marquand, *Democrats, Authoritarians and the Bologna Process: Universities in Germany, Russia, England and Wales* (Bingley: Emerald Publishing, 2018).
David John Frank and John W. Meyer, *The University and the Global Knowledge Society* (Princeton: Princeton University Press, 2020).
Veera Mitzner, *European Union Research Policy: Contested Origins* (Cham: Palgrave Macmillan, 2020).
Lars Lehmann, *"Das Europa der Universitäten": Die Europäische Rektorenkonferenz und die internationale Politik 1955–1975* (Berlin: De Gruyter Oldenbourg, 2021).
Marie-Gabrielle Verbergt, "The Price of History: Historical Research and Changing European Funding Regimes, 1970–Today" (PhD diss., Ghent University, 2024).

In October 2024, *Times Higher Education* published its annual, highly prestigious World University Ranking. While all top ten spots were occupied by universities in the United States and the United Kingdom, the ranking nevertheless revealed that these two countries were experiencing a significant drop in their average research and teaching reputation. Simon Marginson, professor of higher education at the University of Oxford, explained this as a matter of global competition rather than internal decline, as universities in countries such as China, France, and Germany were rapidly catching up in terms of resources, capabilities, and prestige. In the former case, this was largely due to massive government spending, while in the case of France and Germany, it was a result of European cooperation and integration: "On the whole", Marginson said, "Europeanisation – including Bologna-style cooperation and the framework research programmes, such as the current Horizon – have strengthened universities in continental Europe."[1]

The process discussed by Marginson may seem self-evident to a younger generation of European students and scholars. Today, European universities have been linked together through a series of large-scale supranational projects operated by the EU. Initiatives such as the Erasmus Programme, the Bologna Process, and the European Research Area have led to the creation of a common space for research and higher education. We should, however, remind ourselves that all of this would have been deemed unlikely only a few decades ago. For most of the postwar period, the rapid expansion of universities essentially occurred at the national level, and higher education and research were seen as peripheral matters in the context of the emerging Western European integration project. Up until the 1980s, the European academic landscape basically consisted of individual universities engaged in bilateral contacts and loose networks, not seldom based on personal contacts. With this in mind, we can better appreciate the truly groundbreaking nature of the current Europeanisation process. The changes initiated in the last couple of decades have indeed altered the conditions for universities in several ways, the increase in global competitiveness observed by Marginson being merely one such way. These changes must be seen as an important part of the history of European integration but also as a specific expression of a more general political and economic shift since the 1980s, commonly referred to as the emergence of the "knowledge society".[2]

While this process would seem to be of great interest to contemporary historians in various fields, there have so far been few efforts to analyse it from a historical perspective. To be sure, the history of the university as a field has experienced a process of strong revitalisation in the 2000s, but the *contemporary* history of European universities still essentially remains to be written.[3] A few valuable historical studies exist on changes in research policy in the 1980s and 1990s, although typically with a focus on particular countries and with the European dimension merely

---

1 "World University Rankings 2025: Results Announced", *Times Higher Education*, accessed 16 October 2024, https://www.timeshighereducation.com/news/world-university-rankings-2025-results-announced. The first Framework Programme for Research and Technological Development was launched by the European Commission in 1984. The current one, "Horizon" or "Horizon Europe", is the ninth programme and runs from 2021 to 2027.
2 There is a fairly rich literature on the "knowledge society", mainly from an economic, sociological, or other social science perspective. We discuss some of this scholarship later in this essay.
3 Johan Östling, "Contemporary Nordic Histories of the Universities: The Renewal of An Old Field", *Nordic Journal of Educational History* 10, no. 2 (2023).

looming in the background.⁴ Moreover, even though European integration history in a more general sense has as expanded as a field as of late, the integration of research and/or higher education has yet to take centre stage in this context.⁵ The recently published *The Cambridge History of the European Union* (2024), edited by Mathieu Segers and Steven Van Hecke, is a telling example. In this massive two-volume work, in total spanning 1,450 pages, there is but one short section on the Erasmus Programme, while European research policy is barely mentioned at all.⁶ In more general works on the contemporary history of Europe, these areas tend to be equally absent, seemingly overshadowed by the drama of the Cold War, the fall of the Berlin Wall, or transformative economic crises.

Fortunately, this situation seems to be changing. In recent years, we have seen a number of interesting works by historians or social scientists examining, for instance, the formation, institutionalisation, and consequences of a common European research policy, the background, implementations, and effects of the Bologna Process, or the various ideational and institutional antecedents of these processes. Several of these studies draw on some of the more promising methods and perspectives developed in recent European integration history. Furthermore, they are characterised by a richness in historical perspective, convincingly linking changes in the European university sector to larger contexts, be it the Cold War, the political radicalisation of the 1960s and 1970s, the austerity policies of the 1980s and 1990s, or the rise of the knowledge economy. While doing so, however, these studies also demonstrate that the contemporary history of European universities is important in its own right. We thus see an emerging tendency in

---

4 Jon Agar, *Science Policy under Thatcher* (London: UCL Press, 2019); Alexander Mayer, *Universitäten im Wettbewerb: Deutschland von den 1980er Jahre bis zur Exzellenzinitiative* (Stuttgart: Franz Steiner Verlag, 2019); Margit Szöllösi-Janze, "Archäologie des Wettbewerbs: Konkurrenz in und zwischen Universitäten in (West-)Deutschland seit den 1980er Jahren", *Vierteljahrshefte für Zeitgeschichte* 69, no. 2 (2021); Julian Lamberty, *Universitetet og konkurrencestaten: En studie af Syddansk Universitet 1990–2016* (Odense: Syddansk Universitetsforlag, 2022).
5 Barring a few mainly descriptive accounts focusing on the main actors and policy documents. See, for example, Luce Pépin, *The History of European Cooperation in Education and Training: Europe in the Making – An Example* (Luxemburg: Office for Official Publications of the European Communities, 2006). We return to the recent upsurge in European integration history in the concluding section.
6 Mathieu Segers and Steven Van Hecke, eds., *The Cambridge History of the European Union, Volume 1: European Integration Outside-In* (Cambridge: Cambridge University Press, 2024); Mathieu Segers and Steven Van Hecke, eds., *The Cambridge History of the European Union, Volume 2: European Integration Inside-Out* (Cambridge: Cambridge University Press, 2024).

the history of the university to focus on what we refer to as the *Europeanisation of the universities*.[7]

In this review essay, we discuss five recent key works in this new emerging field at some length, while pointing not only to their strengths but also their limitations. We wish to highlight both the insights and the new questions generated by previous studies yet to be answered. In that sense, the review essay is part of the larger project "The Europeanisation of the Universities: Transforming Knowledge Institutions from within, c. 1985–2010" that was recently launched at Lund University. Hopefully, our review essay will also be inspiring and useful for other scholars with similar interests.

The review essay is divided into five sections, all of which mainly focus on one particular work of research. To the extent that this has been possible, we have decided to review these studies in a somewhat chronological order with regard to the periods they focus on. In the first two sections, we discuss studies dealing with the postwar period. In the third section, we discuss a study stretching from the 1970s to the present, while in the fourth and fifth sections, we look at studies essentially focusing on the 2000s. We end our essay with a final section where we offer some concluding remarks on the studies reviewed, along with some thoughts on how to further investigate the Europeanisation of the universities.

Various and Competing Visions of Europeanisation

In her pioneering study *Universities and the Europe of Knowledge* (2005), British political scientist and education scholar Anne Corbett explains how higher education gradually emerged as a matter of European policy in the postwar era. At the time of her writing, the Bologna Process had recently been launched, and the focal point of Corbett's historical analysis was the EU and its forerunners in the

---

7 Another sign of the growing interest in the history of European research policy and higher education is the special issue of the *Journal of European Integration History* 30, no. 2 (2024) edited by David Irion and Darina Volf and titled "EUropeanisation in and through Science". Unfortunately, this issue was published after the present review essay had been finalised and could thus not be integrated into our text. The same goes for Raphaëlle Ruppen Coutaz and Simone Paoli, eds., *Building Europe Through Education, Building Education Through Europe: Actors, Spaces and Pedagogies in a Historical Perspective* (London: Routledge, 2025), which mainly focuses on education in a more general sense while also including some contributions specifically analysing postwar higher education institutions.

European Communities (EC).[8] Starting with the Messina Conference in 1955, where a common European University was proposed for the first time, and ending with the Bologna Declaration in 1999, Corbett points to an ideational continuity. Thus, calls for collaboration between, and the integration of, European universities were not as new as they may have seemed in the early 2000s.[9]

This was indeed an important observation. However, more recent studies show that there is an even greater story to be told about the early postwar period. While the European Coal and Steel Community (ECSC), formed in 1952 and later part of the EC, was primarily an economic arrangement, as opposed to educational or cultural, several other organisations took initiatives to promote European cooperation in the fields of research and higher education. One example is CERN, the European Council for Nuclear Research, launched outside of Geneva in 1954. Several centres of education and research had been formed a few years earlier with the purpose of promoting a common European culture and identity, such as the Collège de Europe in Bruges in 1949 and the Institut für Europäische Geschichte in Mainz in 1950. In a similar spirit, the Council of Europe, an intergovernmental organisation without any decision-making powers, issued recommendations to promote scientific and cultural exchanges between its member states. Finally, it is worth noting that newly created international organisations such as UNESCO, OEEC, and NATO all took different initiatives in the areas of research and education during this period.[10]

This diversity is stressed in Lars Lehmann's monograph *"Das Europa der Universitäten"* (2021), which is based on his dissertation from the Humboldt University of Berlin. This book analyses changes in European research and higher education from the 1950s to the 1970s and offers a thorough and multi-faceted narrative of conflicting and changing approaches to Europeanisation.[11] Lehmann

---

8 When speaking of forerunners, we refer to the European Coal and Steel Community (ECSC, created in 1952), the European Economic Community (EEC, created in 1957), and the European Atomic Energy Community (EAEC, or Euratom, created in 1957). With the Merger Treaty of 1967, the Commission and Council of the EEC assumed overarching responsibility for all three organisations while changing its name to the Commission of the European Communities. From that point on, they were collectively referred to as the European Communities (EC) until the European Union was established in 1993. Hence, the term EC is frequently used in this section and the next where the pre-EU period is in focus.
9 Anne Corbett, *Universities and the Europe of Knowledge: Ideas, Institutions and Policy Entrepreneurship in European Union Higher Education Policy, 1955–2005* (New York: Palgrave Macmillan, 2005).
10 Kiran Klaus Patel, *Projekt Europa: Eine kritische Geschichte* (Munich: C.H. Beck, 2018).
11 Lars Lehmann, *"Das Europa der Universitäten": Die Europäische Rektorenkonferenz und die internationale Politik 1955–1975* (Berlin: De Gruyter Oldenbourg, 2021).

explicitly draws on German historian Kiran Klaus Patel. In several more general works on the history of European integration, most notably *Projekt Europa* (2018) and *Europäische Integration* (2022), Patel points out that this history must be written without narrowly focusing on the EU. It is only in the last decades that the official European Union has become the main driving force behind Europeanisation. For a long time, other actors promoted their own brands thereof, sometimes successfully and often, as we shall see, in opposition to initiatives taken by the predecessors of the EU. Subsequently, Patel emphasises, we must not assume that the current dominance of the EU was the intended, natural, or unavoidable end goal of previous initiatives and processes.[12] This non-teleological perspective is aptly applied in *"Das Europa der Universitäten"* as well.

Lehmann specifically focuses on the Standing Conference of European Rectors (CRE), an organisation of European university rectors and vice-chancellors formed in the late 1950s. At this point in the Cold War, there was a widespread fear in Western Europe of a "technological gap"; that is, a notion of being far behind the United States and the Soviet Union in terms of technological and scientific competence, especially when it came to nuclear energy and other sectors vital to national security. As a result, Western collaboration in these areas seemed necessary. A proposal emerged from within NATO circles to create a European equivalent of the Massachusetts Institute of Technology (MIT). At the aforementioned Messina Conference, Walter Hallstein from West Germany launched an even bolder idea: a full-scale, supranational (Western) European university. When the European Atomic Energy Community (EAEC, or Euratom) was formed two years later, its treaty included similar ideas.

For heads of universities around Western Europe, carefully guarding their autonomy and influence, such ideas were seen as deeply threatening. This meant that resisting supranational interference was essentially the *raison d'être* of the CRE in its early years, often by using classical tropes such as "the autonomy of the university" and "academic freedom". The campaign was largely successful, as Lehmann concludes that the stern resistance of the CRE was an important reason why the idea of a pan-European university did not materialise, despite significant

---

[12] Patel, *Projekt Europa*; Kiran Klaus Patel, *Euroäische Integration: Geschichte und Gegenwart* (Munich: C.H. Beck, 2022). The significance of such an approach has been emphasised by other historians of European integration and Europeanisation as well. See, for example, Hartmut Kaelble, "Europäisierung", in *Dimensionen der Kultur- und Gesellschaftsgeschichte*, ed. Matthias Middell (Leipzig: Leipzig Universitätsverlag, 2007); Florian Greiner, Peter Pichler, and Jan Vermeiren, "Reconsidering Europeanization: An Introduction", in *Reconsidering Europeanization: Ideas and Practices of (Dis-)Integrating Europe since the Nineteenth Century* (Berlin: De Gruyter Oldenbourg, 2022).

political support. At the same time, he notes that the history of the early CRE is an example of what in German research has been called "Europäisierung wider Willen" ("involuntary Europeanisation") – opposition to Europeanisation in one form led to Europeanisation in another form; that is, to transnational cooperation and institution-building.[13]

The position of the CRE would eventually change. Around the mid-1960s, the growing number of students across the West represented an important factor behind the rise of the New Left, which, among many things, sought to create a more democratic and less hierarchical university system. Lehmann points out that this emerging climate of radicalisation created a new momentum for internationalisation and international collaboration. As for the CRE, many younger members in the 1970s came to embrace pan-European ideas, thereby rejecting the more traditional views of the older generation. This meant that an organisation originally being used to combat Europeanisation now turned into a vehicle for promoting it. In keeping with tradition, though, the new leaders of the CRE insisted on shaping university reforms themselves, rather than being given directives from political institutions. For instance, they launched a plan for a European University parliament where they themselves were to be the electors. Like many other transnational institutions proposed during this era, the university parliament was never put into practice. However, the sole fact that this idea originated from the CRE is indicative of a more widespread receptiveness to pan-European ideas in the university sector.[14]

The EC's Gradual Rise to Prominence

Such receptiveness was now manifest in the EC as well. It is important to link this observation to a more general reappraisal of the 1970s among historians of European integration. For a long time, this crisis-ridden decade was essentially seen as a minor dark age of *Eurosclerosis* and stagnation that was in sharp contrast to what would soon follow. In recent years, however, scholars have pointed out that the 1970s actually saw the EC expanding its sphere of interest and influence in new areas, thus paving the way for the more far-reaching integration efforts of the 1980s and 1990s.[15]

---

13 Lehmann, *"Das Europa der Universitäten"*, 119–147.
14 Lehmann, *"Das Europa der Universitäten"*, 149–180.
15 See, for example, Johnny Laursen, ed., *The Institutions and Dynamics of the European Community, 1973–83* (Baden-Baden: Nomos, 2014).

This reinterpretation seems highly accurate as far as research and higher education policy are concerned. In the years around 1970, the Commission of the European Communities launched several proposals regarding higher education, some of which aimed at establishing a framework of common standards among Western European universities. A dialogue was established in that context between politicians at the EC level and leading representatives of universities, which created the potential for a future common research and education policy. An important actor was German-British sociologist and politician Ralf Dahrendorf who, as a member of the Commission between 1970 and 1977, often came to play an intermediary role between the academic and political spheres. An institutional innovation during this period was the European University Institute established in Florence in 1976. That same year also saw the launch of the so-called Joint Study Programme – a direct forerunner to the more ambitious and more well-known Erasmus Programme from 1987.

In the context of our interest here, the 1970s thus hardly represented a period of stagnation but rather one in which things were set in motion. This interpretation is underlined in Finnish-American historian Veera Mitzner's *European Union Research Policy* (2020), which is based on a dissertation from the European University Institute. The institutionalisation of a common European research policy is often associated with the expansion period of the EC/EU in the 1980s and 1990s. However, in her carefully researched study, Mitzner demonstrates that the first steps were taken as far back as 1965, when the importance of research policy was discussed in a report published by PREST (Politique de la recherche scientifique et technique), a special working group formed within the EC. Early attempts like this one were decisively influenced by an instrumental outlook on research and science inherited from organisations such as the OEEC and the World Bank. According to this view, European cooperation in the fields of research and science constituted a means to assure technological progress, economic growth, and global competitiveness. This notion of *research for growth* would remain a guiding principle for the EC in the coming decades. Mitzner thus convincingly identifies threads of continuity and path dependence between the EC of the 1960s and the current EU in terms of both institutions and ideas.[16]

That being said, another merit of *European Union Research Policy* is its non-teleological approach, similar to that of Lehman and Patel: there was nothing inevitable in terms of the EC rising to prominence in the realm of research policy. On the contrary, Mitzner emphasises that the EC of the 1960s was a latecomer in

---

[16] Veera Mitzner, *European Union Research Policy: Contested Origins* (Cham: Palgrave Macmillan, 2020), 64–90.

this area, tentatively trying to carve out its own niche amongst competing, more established organisations. Furthermore, its attempts to enter this field tended to generate, or at least contribute to, competing initiatives from outside of the Community structure. In 1971, for instance, nineteen European countries formed the European Cooperation in Science and Technology (COST), a loosely composed intergovernmental forum for technological exchange. Three years later, the European Science Foundation (ESF) was established as an independent, non-governmental organisation.[17] While they play relatively marginal roles today, these organisations were at the time seen as serious challengers to the EC in the European research landscape.[18]

Nevertheless, the latter part of Mitzner's book narrates how the EC gradually became more dominant despite competition and setbacks along the way. Conversely, research policy within the Communities went from being a fringe phenomenon to becoming a strategic priority and a key competence to subsequently generate large-scale, costly programmes. How are we to account for this development? Mitzner points out that the instrumental conception of research and science adopted in the 1960s fitted well into the political climate of the 1980s. Indeed, the notion of academic knowledge as the most vital resource for economic growth was fundamental to the knowledge society discourse that was gaining ground at this time. Furthermore, the breakthrough of new information and communication technologies spawned fears of Western Europe lagging behind the United States and Japan in terms of scientific and technological know-how, much like the growing significance of nuclear energy in the early postwar period. "The return of the gap", as Mitzner calls it, resulted in a common research policy once again being seen as something urgent. Unlike in the 1950s, however, there was now an emerging institutional structure capable of putting such ideas into practice.[19] In an article published the year after Mitzner published her book, Kiran Klaus Patel adds that the economic logic of the EC was advantageous in yet another respect: presenting a European research policy as essentially an economic matter, as opposed to a political one, led to member states being far more willing to accept supranational intervention.[20]

---

17 See also Corinna R. Unger, "Making Science European: Towards a History of the European Science Foundation", *Contemporanea* 23, no. 3 (2020).
18 Mitzner, *European Union Research Policy*, 177–201.
19 Mitzner, *European Union Research Policy*, 215–224, quote on 215.
20 Kiran Klaus Patel, "Kooperation und Konkurrenz: Die Entstehung der europäischen Wissenschafts- und Forshungspolitik seit 1945", *Vierteljahrshefte für Zeitgeschichte* 69, no. 2 (2021).

Europeanisation through Research Funding

For the purposes of periodisation, one might thus argue that the 1980s marked the beginning of a new era characterised by the increasingly central role of the EC and later the EU, accompanied by the creation of new institutions for collaboration and integration. The EC launched its first Framework Programme for Research and Technological Development in 1984. Three years later, the importance of a common research policy was stated in the Single European Act. The turn of the century saw the launch of the European Research Area (ERA), a system connecting research programmes and resources within the union. ERA was closely tied to the Lisbon Strategy aimed at making the EU "the world's most competitive and dynamic knowledge-based economy" by 2010. This serves as yet another indication of the enormous importance ascribed to research and science in the union.

These later stages of Europeanisation through research policy formation have been explored in several works in recent years. Sociologists Tim Flink and Thomas König, from Germany and Austria respectively, have both studied the European Research Council (ERC) formed in 2007. In his dissertation *Die Entstehung des Europäischen Forschungsrates* (2016), Flink views the ERC as an offshoot of a more overarching geo-strategy.[21] König's *The European Research Council* (2017), on the other hand, is a detailed insider analysis. Between 2010 and 2013, König worked as a scientific advisor to Helga Nowotny, then president of the ERC and one of its founding figures. Rather than looking at the site of research policy in a geopolitical context, König emphasises the significance of individual academics in shaping the direction of the ERC.[22] The perspectives of Flink and König need not be seen as mutually exclusive – they simply differ from one another. Both studies are valuable reads alongside Mitzner's book as they illustrate the continuously growing significance of research policy after the 1980s. Yet, neither of them sheds much light on how this development has affected the European research community or the research produced in the EU.

Precisely this, however, is a main theme of a more recent study, the dissertation of Belgian historian Marie-Gabrielle Verbergt titled "The Price of History" (2024). Verbergt explores the history of European research funding and analyses its motives, methods, and effects. The dissertation is well-written and methodologically creative, while skilfully weaving different institutional levels together: the ideas and discourses related to research prevalent amongst European elites, the

---

21 Tim Flink, *Die Entstehung des Europäischen Forschungsrates: Marktimperative – Geostrategie – Frontier Research* (Weilerswist: Velbruck Wissenschaft, 2016).
22 Thomas König, *The European Research Council* (Cambridge & Malden: Polity Press, 2017).

different "funding regimes" shaped by such ideas and discourses, and the effects of these regimes on academia. As we may naturally assume, the latter have become all the more palpable and widely experienced with increased funding. While Verbergt, as the title indicates, mainly focuses on the discipline of history, she also offers a more general view of the European research landscape.

Verbergt identifies four different but partly overlapping funding regimes: a community-building regime (early 1980s to the late 1990s), a collaborative regime (early 1970s to the mid-2010s), a policy-oriented regime (from the mid-1990s and onwards), and a competitive regime (from the mid-2000s and onwards).[23] In the first one, historians were essentially employed by the European Commission as a modern version of the court chroniclers. In exchange for monetary support and access to archives, they were expected to write histories of European integration and identity that could offer meaning to the idea of a modern union. The ties between funders and funded were close, even though the latter group was small. In parallel with this funding regime, but independent of it, the European Science Foundation sponsored large-scale research programmes on comparative European history. Application processes were somewhat informal, and programmes with a pan-European orientation, such as the history of European state formation or the transformations of the Roman Empire, were favoured. International collaboration was treated as an end in itself. This meant that the ESF often took on an active role in both the formulation and execution of the programmes; for example, to make sure that scholars from as many European countries as possible participated.[24]

These funding regimes were called into question in the 1990s, in line with the austerity policies and neoliberal ideals of the time. For a younger generation of politicians and administrators in Brussels, as well as for many scholars and scientists, they seemed incompatible with transparency, efficiency, and accountability. A professionalisation process was set in motion with formalised procedures for evaluations and assessments. Peer review and streamlined application procedures became the norm. At the same time, European policymakers now in charge of funding prioritised policy-oriented research. So, while historians in the 1980s had been assigned to write edifying narratives on a common European past, they were now expected to produce "evidence-based" studies of practical use for decision-makers.[25]

---

23 Marie-Gabrielle Verbergt, "The Price of History: Historical Research and Changing European Funding Regimes, 1970–Today" (PhD diss., Ghent University, 2024), 12.
24 Verbergt, "Price of History", 29–66.
25 Verbergt, "Price of History", 75–104.

Around the turn of the century, at a time of general "europtimism", European research policy went into a higher gear.[26] The European Commission went from being a marginal to a central actor in this area, as its investments in research increased manifold. Drawing on political scientist Vivien A. Schmidt, Verbergt emphasises the importance of ideas, discourses, and visions in this context: suggestive concepts such as *knowledge economy* and a *Europe of knowledge* "worked together to sustain the idea that the EU needed to extend its activities in the domains of research and higher education and create, in these fields too, a Europe without borders."[27] Significantly, this idea was not only entertained by elites in the union but was also promoted and circulated by European academics themselves, often in prestigious outlets such as *Science*, *Nature*, and *Science and Public Policy*. These discussions ushered in the creation of the ERC in 2007, which, as Verbergt shows, has come to embody a fourth funding regime. This regime reinforced many of the virtues upheld since the 1990s, while also promoting a different kind of research than the policy-oriented regime. Opposed to the latter, the purpose of the ERC is to fund non-applied, basic research and direct utility for policy is not an explicit demand. However, a streamlined and highly competitive application process, focusing on concepts such as *excellence* and *frontier research*, is supposed to ensure that only the best and most ground-breaking projects are funded. Hence, while academics in the mid-2000s could argue that the ERC would create better evaluation standards and foster meritocracy, EU politicians could justify this as instrumental for enhancing European economic competitiveness.[28]

Verbergt notes that the competitive funding regime has come to dominate the European research landscape in a remarkably short period of time. Receiving a grant from the ERC is highly lucrative for individual scholars as well as their institutions. By the same token, such grants inevitably create material and symbolic differences between academic institutions. As for historians (a group which, by the way, does not seem to have played a very active role in the debates and campaigns preceding the ERC), Verbergt notes that the funding granted between 2007 and 2022 has clearly favoured large-scale research projects encompassing wide geographical areas and/or large time frames: big history, transnational history, and so forth. Moreover, projects aspiring to achieve conceptual or paradigmatical shifts have been prioritised, which is entirely in line with the notion of *frontier research*. Another interesting observation is that while immediate rele-

---

[26] This term has been used by political scientists and historians to refer to the enthusiasm spurred by the introduction of the euro in 1999 and the 2004 enlargement of the European Union. See Verbergt, "Price of History", 174.
[27] Verbergt, "Price of History", 178.
[28] Verbergt, "Price of History", 169–204.

vancy is not an explicit criterion for funding, the ERC does seem to prefer applications with a clearly stated link between the research topic and current issues.[29] In a critical concluding discussion, Verbergt highlights the risk of an emerging academic and epistemic monoculture in which only certain theories, perspectives, and research questions prevail. In connection to this, she points to the need for historians to critically examine Europeanisation and internationalism, just like they have deconstructed the nation-state and nationalism for the past 40 years.[30] "The Price of History" is an important contribution to such a project. However, further contributions are needed, especially as changes in research policy represent but one aspect of the Europeanisation of the universities.

Europeanisation through Higher Education

In tandem with the development in research policy described by Mitzner, Flink, König, and Verbergt, drastic changes have occurred towards integration and cooperation in higher education as well, the most obvious example being the Bologna Process. Gathered in the ancient North Italian university city in 1999, ministers of education from 29 different countries agreed to create a more unified European system for higher education. This was not an EU initiative, even though funding from the EU (for example, via the Erasmus Programme) has become increasingly important to Bologna, while non-EU countries are also welcome to join. In the following ten years, the Bologna Process was gradually implemented, eventually renamed the European Higher Education Area (EHEA). The most visible effect has been the introduction of a two-tier system with three-year first degrees (bachelor) followed by two-year master's degrees, as well as the introduction of a unified assessment system based on "learning outcomes and competences".

Historical research on these changes has been quite limited, barring Anne Corbett's *The University and the Europe of Knowledge*. Published as early as 2005, however, Corbett's book cannot serve as more than an essential backstory to the intensified integration processes set in motion since then. So far, then, research on the Bologna Process has for the most part been left to scholars in the field of education and pedagogy. Here, we may distinguish between critical discourse analyses of the central policies of Bologna, on the one hand, and studies of its effects on national education systems, on the other. Without disputing the value of

---

29 Verbergt, "Price of History", 262–303.
30 Verbergt, "Price of History", 309–317.

such approaches, there is undoubtedly a need for historical as well as comparative perspectives in this context.

One study that does apply the latter, as well as to some extent the former, is *Democrats, Authoritarians, and the Bologna Process* (2018) by British economist and education scholar Judith Marquand. Marquand looks at the motives for and implementations of Bologna in different national and local contexts. She analyses a number of universities in Germany, Russia, England, and Wales, mainly based on interviews with scholars, teachers, and administrators but also against the backdrop of contemporary history. As a result, the book presents a richer and more multi-faceted account than narratives focused either on the level of policy or on particular countries. Marquand argues that Bologna should not simply be seen as a homogenising package of entrepreneurial or neoliberal ideals enforced on member states from above. To be sure, homogenisation is, in a sense, precisely what it aims for, and Marquand's analysis demonstrates that individual universities may indeed perceive these reforms as being imposed on them without much of a dialogue. Furthermore, national political elites have sometimes used Bologna as a convenient excuse for unpopular reforms and budget cuts. Yet, Marquand emphasises the fundamentally non-binding character of the process: membership is voluntary and there is no legal framework or sanctions for enforcing reforms. Bologna operates mainly by means of peer pressure between states. This raises the question of why countries have chosen to join the process and how they have gone about implementing it.[31]

The comparison shows that the answers to both these questions may vary between countries. For example, Marquand points to interesting differences between England and Wales. Even though they are both part of the United Kingdom, Wales received its own assembly in 1999 with limited powers to formulate its own higher education policy. The United Kingdom was one of the original signatories of the Bologna Process, which at the time was found to be very much in line with educational reforms already implemented in the country in the previous decades. In spite of this, or perhaps as a result of this, enthusiasm for Bologna has been low or non-existent in the English university system. Furthermore, Marquand argues, the increasingly market-oriented higher education reforms imposed since then go beyond anything suggested in Bologna policies. Wales, by contrast, has adopted a much more positive and active approach to Bologna.[32]

---

31 Judith Marquand, *Democrats, Authoritarians and the Bologna Process: Universities in Germany, Russia, England and Wales* (Bingley: Emerald Publishing, 2018), 41–43, 51.
32 Marquand, *Democrats*, 127–175.

Germany was also one of the original signatories, although partly for different reasons. Whereas the English perceived themselves to be ahead of the process, German politicians saw Bologna as instrumental in solving various problems facing the German higher education system. One such problem was the persistent economic, institutional, and cultural differences between universities in the former Western and former Eastern parts of the country. However, the decentralisation of education policies in Germany's federal political system has rendered the implementation process cumbersome with notable differences between the various *Länder*. Meanwhile, Marquand also notes, German university staff have complained that their working situation has been taken over by the bureaucratic procedures necessitated by Bologna.[33] Indeed, the Bologna reforms were actually highly controversial among German university staff and students alike, provoking debates, critical writings, and street demonstrations.[34]

Russia is a different case, especially considering what has unfolded after *Democrats, Authoritarians, and the Bologna Process* was published. A signatory of the Bologna Declaration in 2003, Russia was excluded from the process after its invasion of Ukraine in early 2022. Marquand, who lived and worked in Russia for several years prior to her study, grapples with the question of why an increasingly authoritarian regime would be interested in a reform package that essentially applies liberal-democratic ideals to higher education. Her main conclusion is that Putin and his clique of oligarchs mistakenly saw Bologna as a shortcut to Western scientific and technological know-how. The reforms were communicated and imposed in a strictly hierarchical yet half-hearted manner: directives came down from Moscow to universities around the country lacking both clear guidelines and systematic follow-up mechanisms. At the same time, however, this allowed for a certain level of flexibility and heterogeneity. While changes in many places were superficial or merely rhetorical, certain Russian universities adhering to a Western or Humboldtian tradition, such as the Tomsk State University in Siberia, actively embraced Bologna.[35] This is particularly interesting in view of the inflamed debates raging in Germany around the same time, where the Humboldtian tradition was often invoked as an argument *against* the reform process.

The methodology of Marquand's book merits some discussion. To be fair, she admits that her study does not pretend to be particularly "rigorous" in that particular department, "but rather to provide a broad comparative picture of a relatively uncharted terrain" and reflect on "what lessons can be drawn" from the

---

33 Marquand, *Democrats*, 80–98.
34 Johan Östling, *Humboldt and the Modern German University: An Intellectual History* (Lund: Lund University Press, 2018), 207–220.
35 Marquand, *Democrats*, 103–125, 178.

individual case studies. Still, a somewhat more thorough methodological discussion would undoubtedly have been useful, not least regarding her selection of universities. As far as "lessons" to be drawn, the concluding chapter is surprisingly short and spans no more than five pages. Clearly, the many interesting observations contained in the preceding empirical chapters would have deserved a lengthier discussion. How does Bologna fit into a more general history of Europeanisation in the postwar period? And how does it fit into a larger context of globalisation, seeing as countries as diverse as China, Brazil, the United States, Morocco, and Australia have apparently shown an interest in the methods adopted by the EHEA?[36] Despite these objections, *Democrats, Authoritarians and the Bologna Process* is an interesting work illustrating how Europeanisation is always shaped and mediated by historical, cultural, and local factors. By doing so, it also points to the need for further comparative studies on this topic.

Universities in the Knowledge Society – A Global Bologna Process?

The final work to be reviewed here is *The University and the Global Knowledge Society* (2020) by American sociologists David John Frank and John W. Meyer, both of whom have previously written extensively on education, science, and universities, frequently from a transnational or global perspective. In the book discussed here, changes in research and higher education are also viewed as a global rather than regional phenomenon. Primarily drawing on global statistics rather than the archives of specific universities, Frank and Meyer aspire to form a general theory of the university. Consequently, their analytical scope encompasses the entire history of the university, even though their emphasis is clearly on the last few decades.[37] While these geographical and temporal scales obviously mean that *The University and the Global Knowledge Society* differs from the works reviewed above, it is important to discuss the book in this context for precisely that reason: future historians of the Europeanisation of the universities, we believe, need to engage with social scientists, who for decades have constructed theories and generalising narratives regarding the developments we wish to historicise.

---

36 Marquand, *Democrats*, 181.
37 David John Frank and John W. Meyer, *The University and the Global Knowledge Society* (Princeton: Princeton University Press, 2020).

The book is presented as a response to more pessimistic accounts of the state of Western universities that decry the marketisation or bureaucratisation of universities as well as the loss of academic freedom to external forces. Frank and Meyer object that such crisis narratives stem from a tunnel vision approach – a narrow focus on particular universities, disciplines, or regions. It is true, they admit, that universities in the last decades have come to be shaped and influenced by their social environments in ways previously unknown. However, pressures and influences go both ways, and the ways in which universities have come to shape and saturate societies and people's everyday lives are actually much more significant. The authors' chapter on this "academization of culture" is a captivating read, as the empirical evidence ranges from statistics on curricular expansion between 1895 and 2019 (indicating that the aspects of human existence under academic scrutiny have increased manifoldly) to close readings of how newspaper discourses have increasingly come to rely on scientific observations and scientific language.[38]

Moreover, and this is their main point, the truly remarkable trend from a global perspective is the enormous expansion of universities, not their decline. Here, they do not merely refer to the fact that there are now more universities in the world than ten, twenty, or thirty years ago but to a global embrace of academic knowledge as a concept. While not arguing that academic knowledge in any way is superior to other forms of knowledge, Frank and Meyer do stress that it differs by being characterised by its universalism and rationalism. Hence, we see a striking global convergence and isomorphism with regards to curricular structure and content, degrees and research. In one of several comparisons made to support this claim, Frank and Meyer look at the degrees offered at the University of Ibadan in Nigeria and the Universidad Nacional Autónoma de México, noting that they almost completely overlap:

> Even ostensibly local matters, such as Igbo and Latin American Studies, pack particularistic fillings into universalistic molds. They represent local instances of general phenomena: i.e., national languages and regional studies. [. . .] The similarity of curricular contents follows not from organizational standardization but from the nature of those contents, namely their aspiration to universalized explanation.[39]

As the quote implies, Frank and Meyer view the university as an idea more than anything else: a manifestation of the search for a particular kind of knowledge. By the same token, the knowledge society is to be understood as a cultural and political phenomenon rather than as an economic one, as universities abound in

---

[38] Frank and Meyer, *The University*, 73.
[39] Frank and Meyer, *The University*, 67–68.

all kinds of contemporary economies. Based on this perspective, the university is not an institution in crisis but one that is stronger than ever.

The University and the Global Knowledge Society obviously raises the question of whether a concept such as Europeanisation, at least in the context of the universities, is obsolete. After all, is not the entire world caught up in a Bologna Process of sorts, albeit not one we can smoothly trace back to specific political initiatives at specific dates in specific places? Yet, while acknowledging that Frank and Meyer's book is impressive in its analytical scope and offers plenty of food for thought, we should also point out that it comes with problems, many of which, as it happens, are due precisely to the authors' explicit lack of interest in the particularities of regions, countries, or individual universities. First of all, even though they draw extensively on global statistics, these statistics do not really support the strong claim that global similarities in degrees or curricula are indicative of a cultural and ideational convergence between different parts of the world, as opposed to just a more superficial isomorphism on an organisational level. The latter would obviously be important and interesting in its own right, but it would also be a different matter altogether. Furthermore, even if we do accept this claim, along with the much more credible claim of a general academisation of culture, this does not tell us all that much about the situation facing individual universities. Indeed, it is entirely possible to assume that *the university* as an abstract ideal flourishes and expands, while also assuming that *universities* as specific institutions in specific societal settings are being weakened. Hence, to the extent that Frank and Meyer wish to counter more pessimistic narratives concerning Western universities, they largely miss the target. We would argue that these flaws indicate the need for precisely that which the authors themselves find relatively unimportant, namely small-scale studies and comparisons that allow room for differences, not just similarities.

Concluding Remarks

Currently, discussions in and around the EU focus on topics such as the continued development of the European Higher Education Area or the design of the tenth Framework Programme for Research and Innovation for the period 2028–2034. While such discussions tend to focus on the future, the works reviewed in the preceding sections show that they can only be properly understood with a view to the past. On the one hand, this past may well be narrated as one of unforeseen shifts and changes. Indeed, Judith Marquand labels the Bologna Process "a quiet revolution", emphasising that it has fundamentally altered the higher education systems in its member states despite variations within and between countries.⁴⁰ Something similar could obviously be said on the role of the EU itself. As we have seen, the EC was a marginal player in terms of research and higher education well into the 1970s but eventually became the powerhouse behind large-scale and far-reaching initiatives such as the Erasmus Programme and the European Research Council. Indeed, the sole fact that present-day historians of the Europeanisation of the universities need to make a point of *not* focusing exclusively on the EU testifies to this dominance.

On the other hand, the narrative presented in the preceding sections also brings important continuities to light. Consider, for instance, how Europeanisation has been promoted and opposed throughout the decades. Reading Mitzner's book next to that of Verbergt, it becomes clear that the notion of "research for growth", developed in the context of research policy in the 1960s, is strikingly similar to the discourse underpinning the ERC's competitive funding regime in the early 2020s. Likewise, we also note that the arguments against Europeanisation used by European university rectors in the 1960s, analysed by Lehmann, were essentially repeated by German academics and students opposing the Bologna Process some fifty years later. This complex interplay between change and continuity is one reason why current discussions and initiatives must be seen against the backdrop of contemporary history.

Bearing that in mind, what else can we learn from the works reviewed here and what else needs to be done? To begin with the latter question, we believe that future historians of the Europeanisation of the universities have a lot to gain from drawing on perspectives recently developed in the more general field of European integration history. In the edited volume *Reconsidering Europeanization* (2022), Florian Greiner, Peter Pichler, and Jan Vermeiren note that the field is currently undergoing a process of diversification. Historians of Europeanisation have shifted their focus from the main political and economic institutions of the EU to a much wider array of actors and phenomena. Arguing for a continuation of this trend, they point to the importance of writing the history of Europeanisation "from the bottom-up", focusing, for instance, on the media, civil society, popular culture, or ordinary citizens as agents of Europeanisation.⁴¹ In the same vein, they also stress that historians must speak of Europeanisation processes in plural form, not as a single process. This concept must not be understood as simply referring to a supranational, unilinear, and irreversible process, but to a variety of processes, some of which are intended, others unintended, some of which

---

40 Marquand, *Democrats*, 35.
41 Greiner, Pichler, and Vermeiren, "Reconsidering Europeanization", 18.

integrative, others disintegrative.[42] It goes without saying that these perspectives are equally valid in the more specific context of the Europeanisation of the universities. Moreover, we would argue that they to some extent are present in several of the works discussed in the preceding sections.

Europeanisation processes – in the plural – are perhaps the most evident in the case of the early postwar decades. As we have seen, this period was characterised by a fairly wide range of pan-European ideas without there being an overarching plan for Europeanisation, let alone an institutional structure to execute such a plan. Initiatives towards international collaboration and integration tended to be met with opposition and counter-initiatives, thus manifesting and fostering other forms of international collaboration and integration. Indeed, both Lehmann and Mitzner show that such a reluctant or unintended Europeanisation represents a significant part of the story of the Europeanisation of the universities. However, the works of Verbergt and Marquand show that the growing dominance of the EC/EU in the following decades has not excluded a certain pluralism in this respect either. On the one hand, the different funding regimes identified by Verbergt with regard to the ERC over time may well be seen as different forms of Europeanisation, ranging from collaboration and common identity-building to competition and emulation. Marquand, on the other hand, shows that Europeanisation and "nationalisation" often went hand in hand in the sense that the former sometimes served as a tool for realising national or even nationalist projects, as in the case of the German and Welsh adaptions of the Bologna Process.

As for a bottom-up approach to Europeanisation, it must be said that the works discussed in this review essay offer a variety of perspectives. Whereas Mitzner, Flink, and König focus on international policy-making institutions – thereby adopting what Greiner, Pichler, and Vermeiren would refer to as a top-down approach – others highlight the varying effects of policy-making on other levels: the responses to Europeanisation by heads of universities (Lehmann), the effects of European research policies on a particular scholarly discipline (Verbergt), and the varying implementations and reinterpretations of European higher education policy in national and local contexts (Marquand). Thus, while undoubtedly focusing on "elites" in one sense or another, these studies nevertheless illustrate the value of analysing Europeanisation downstream from major institutions, indicating that these processes are never as uniform or homogenising as what may have been the intention.

Future historians of the Europeanisation of the universities would do well to stay on this course; that is, exploring the entanglements, overlaps, and conflicts

---

42 Greiner, Pichler, and Vermeiren, "Reconsidering Europeanization", 8–9.

between different forms of Europeanisation prevalent during specific periods. Looking at the very recent past, for instance, it is notable that the Europeanisation of higher education and research was essentially uninterrupted and in many ways flourished in the decade following the financial crises of 2007–2008 – a period generally associated with disintegration and major societal conflicts on a political level. Exploring this apparent paradox is one of many intriguing challenges awaiting historians. Furthermore, as indicated above, the bottom-up approach to Europeanisation can and should be applied to the history of universities in a multitude of new ways. A promising route would be to follow in the footsteps of Marquand's study by comparing the Europeanisation processes initiated at different European universities, albeit by adding a more elaborate historical perspective, on the one hand, and more methodological reflection, on the other.

Based on the works reviewed, we would like to conclude by identifying three key directions for research aimed at historicising the Europeanisation of the universities. First, the bottom-up approaches to Europeanisation, which we have advocated, must in no way prevent historians from engaging with social science theory. As indicated in our review of *The University and the Global Knowledge Society*, we find such a dialogue to be important. For one thing, historians need to reflect on the relationship between Europeanisation and globalisation. Is the Europeanisation of the universities simply part of a more general pattern of globalisation or can processes of Europeanisation rather be interpreted as reactions *against* globalisation? Indeed, as we may recall, Mitzner points out that attempts at Europeanising research policy in the 1960s and 1980s were largely driven by fears of the alleged technological superiority of other continents. It is likely that similar motives may prevail today. Moreover, Frank and Meyer's book is but one recent contribution to a longer theoretical discussion on the knowledge society (and similar concepts) that has been going on since the 1960s, with an increasing emphasis on the role of universities.[43] In other words, there is a host of theories from which historians may draw inspiration, while critically examining and expanding on these through empirical research. Alternatively, the influence of the knowledge society discourse on changes in higher education and research could itself constitute an object of historical study. Its influence has been assumed in several previous works, although without much of empirical studies.[44] Verbergt's

---

[43] See, for example, Anna-Katharina Hornidge, "'Knowledge Society' as Academic Concept and Stage of Development: A Conceptual and Historical Review", in *Beyond the Knowledge Trap: Developing Asia's Knowledge-Based Economies*, ed. Thomas Menkhoff et al. (Singapore: World Scientific Publishing, 2011).

[44] See, for example, Pépin, *History of European Cooperation*, 153–165; Florin D. Salajan, "The Rise of the Information Society amongst European Academics", *European Journal of Education* 43,

dissertation goes some way to confirm such claims, but a great deal of work remains to be done in that respect.

Second, as we have decided to present the works of different historians and social scientists in the form of a somewhat coherent narrative, we now see that there is indeed a bit of a chronological gap between the two groups. Historians (Lehmann and Mitzner) cover the postwar decades while social scientists (Flink, König, and Marquand) essentially zoom in on the 2000s without much of a historical perspective. Thus, there is still a need for fuller accounts of the Europeanisation of the universities linking current Europeanisation processes with those of the postwar period. Verbergt's dissertation exemplifies the advantages of such an approach, albeit only with a focus on research policy and its effects on one specific academic discipline.

Finally, when we speak of fuller accounts, we also refer to this in a thematic sense. For example, it is noteworthy that almost all works presented in this review essay view higher education policy and research policy as separate entities, focusing on one or the other but rarely on both. Taken together, however, these studies show that the two have often been closely aligned from the perspective of European institutions and that the Europeanisation of research and the Europeanisation of higher education have essentially been promoted using the same arguments. This alignment should be reflected in historical research as well.

Karl Haikola is a postdoctoral researcher in history at Lund University. His main research interests include Europeanisation, the history of the EU, the history of the university, and the history of knowledge. He is currently part of the research project "The Europeanisation of the Universities: Transforming Knowledge Institutions from within, c. 1985–2010", in which his empirical contribution focuses on Spain.

Johan Östling is a professor of history, director of the Lund Centre for the History of Knowledge (LUCK), and a Wallenberg Academy Fellow. His research mainly focuses on the history of knowledge and modern and contemporary European history. Recent publications include the trilogy *Circulation of Knowledge* (2018), *Forms of Knowledge* (2020), and *Knowledge Actors* (2023), as well as the introductory book *The History of Knowledge* (2023). Östling serves as PI of the research project "The Europeanisation of the Universities: Transforming Knowledge Institutions from within, c. 1985–2010".

---

no. 4 (2008); Jussi Välimaa and David Hoffman, "Knowledge Society Discourse and Higher Education", *Higher Education* 56, no. 3 (2008).

HIC Conversation with Mariama de Brito Henn, Friedrich Cain, Evangelia (Lina) Chordaki, Stella Andrada Kasdovasili, and Katerina Stavridi

To Play is to Know: Pushing the Boundaries of Doing Academia

Keywords: play, institution, boundaries, translation, in-betweenness, embodied epistemologies

... A crossing point is what this text is – a crossing point. To us, it is a snapshot capturing an ongoing conversation that we are not ready to forcefully end. This text is provisional, it is playful – and in its playfulness, it represents our formative experiences and re-appropriations within the world of academia, on the one hand, and as a group of people, on the other. This text is an attempt to make a linear representation of an irregular, polyphonic, and friendly exchange between two, five, at times three, or four individuals, who have thus far never convened in one physical space all at once but who met regularly for the better part of a year. Via Zoom, we span greater geographic and smaller intellectual distances and various levels of experience. We got to know each other, as people as well as colleagues in this academic world. Prior to this, we, the ones whose names are listed above in alphabetical order, had been linked together in highly different contexts that all feed into these pages.

What follows below started to be conceptualised at the invitation of the editors of *History of Intellectual Culture – International Yearbook of Knowledge and Society*, who approached one of us for a follow-up piece on a then recent workshop on knowledge institutions. While no capacities remained in relation to that matter, this context – our context – materialised when former bits of conversations were recalled, resumed, and re-connected until we declared our group "established". This link evolved around the notion of playing, which some of us had discussed in previous smaller exchanges and which we now sought to join into one, in *this* conversation.

Using *play* as the focal point of our discussions, we initiated an exploration of the dynamics that this term enfolds textually, theoretically, and emotionally while also experimenting with its limits in terms of both format and methods. The conceptualisation of play intentionally remains an ongoing project. As such, it can be understood as a process open to different ways of looking at play not only as a concept and methodology but also as a performative act of writing and producing knowledge.

During our first meetings, we gathered anecdotes from our own experiences in and around the twentysomething academic institutions around half the globe to which we, in one way or another, had been linked. Whether enrolled in or employed by them, we had made our ways into these institutions. We had co-created, stabilised, and sometimes challenged them. We had found ways to dwell within and beyond, to get lost (or not) in them, first as students and later as teachers, researchers, or fellows. As much as our experiences differed, we could all recall situations of searching, testing, and trying, which were frequently driven by insecurities and overwhelming structures. Even though we all approached this in our own ways, the notion of play was what helped us develop a vocabulary for critical but emphatic descriptions. Engaging with academia in a playful way and together with friends had offered and still offers hope. It helped build communities, and even if they only played out on sub-official levels, they were no less significant.

This text represents a crossing point and as such, it links this level to the surface of official academic practices, one of which is publishing. If we were to present an abstract of our conversation, we might suggest something like the following:

> *In this conversation, we discuss ways of moving within, beyond, as well as in and out of today's academic institutions and their ongoing neoliberal redesign. Based on our own experiences, we explore the intimacies, translations, emotions, practices, and movements occurring at all levels of academic life – from being a student to pursuing an academic career. Taking it a step further, we consider how to reclaim a notion of play that differs from learning in order to navigate institutional settings, to study, to get funding, to teach along preconceived outlines, and instead produce theory, research, and history through different ways of playing together with our friends. Here, the notion of play enfolds a crucial dynamic tension. It can help de-centre an academic game that is seemingly more grounded in competitiveness than cooperation. This notion may also be useful when critically examining epistemological orders. With its metaphorical connection to childhood activities, playing also helps open up new spaces for joyful, appreciative collaboration with emancipatory potentials and creative realms of academic practice.*

While this abstract captures what we talked about in several meetings, our practice of collecting experiences made us think about presentation, organisation, and the structure of arguments: How to write a conversation? How much of a playwright's craft do we need to stage this play? In order to transform our online meetings concerning universities and academia into a written text, we identified four major themes that have come up again and again in our discussions on *playing* with friends: *institutions, boundaries, translation,* and *in-betweenness*. As will be apparent in the following, these prompts, as we called them, are not distinct but overlap in more ways than we originally envisioned. On the one hand, we believe that what produces what we call the university is the conceptualisation of these prompts. On the other hand, this particular idea of the university as it comes out of these four prompts is the space in which we examine the notion of play.

Hence, we started ordering our gathered experiences in an attempt to ask a set of questions based on our first prompt.

> *How have academic* institutions *shaped our thinking, experience, and practice – both in terms of intellectual efforts and in terms of the challenges of navigating their structural constraints? What did it take to grasp the rules of the game and adapt to them, on the one hand, and how did it feel to not play along but with or beyond the rules, on the other? What or who helped in finding those spaces beyond?*

Stella A. Kasdovasili: Institutions have been a focal point of introspection throughout my academic life, shaping my lived experiences and my research. These complex structures and I are interlinked in a tight loop of constant transmutation and transformation that is constantly shifting whilst I grow and seek to construct linear narratives of progress. In each step of my academic career, the institution changes, it becomes something different or perhaps something additional in terms of its intricate modalities of operation, it becomes clearer.

The university as the locus of endless knowledge from my bachelor years became the neoliberal institution linking degrees to the job market during my master's degrees, and as the demand for philosophers – let alone female ones – is rather limited, I am left navigating structures that were not created to accommodate someone like me. Invisible boundaries and unspoken rules are at the heart of institutions, obscuring their inner workings to the untrained eye. However, as Foucault argues, "[t]he real political task in a society such as ours is to criticize the workings of institutions that appear to be both neutral and independent[. . .]".[1] Yet, that is not by any means an individual task but rather a collective one. Not all spaces (or institutions for that matter) are safe, but other people may help in making them feel safer, and I have been privileged to form bonds with others like me within the same institutions that often seem to abject us.

This liminal space of abjection, while vulnerable, is shared and as such, it can become a valuable and powerful tool for transformation. Echoing Laurent Berlant's work on intra-connectivity,[2] the complex affective interplay between us

---

[1] Noam Chomsky and Michel Foucault, *The Chomsky-Foucault Debate: On Human Nature* (New York: The New Press, 2006), 41.
[2] Lauren Berlant, *Cruel Optimism* (Durham, NC: Duke University Press, 2011).

and these structures brings an array of vulnerable positions to the surface, thereby facilitating the creation of social bonds that can help re-imagining said institutions and resisting oppressive structures. From my perspective, this non-institutionality of friendship[3] that Berlant's work brings forth is what has helped me make sense of the institutions having shaped me as a subject and transcend challenges and strict forms.

Evangelia (Lina) Chordaki: Reflecting on my engagement with various universities throughout my academic journey, spanning different geographical regions and educational systems – somewhere between the Mediterranean, Northern Europe, and the United States – I find myself contemplating these experiences as instances of navigating diverse environments, something that often feels like floating. This movement, this act of floating through different systems, has reshaped both me and the institutions I have encountered, as Stella argues above. These transformations emerged through the creation of space, our responses to the denial of space, or a combination of the two.

The institutions I engaged with were not uniform, which is why the nature of each encounter was distinct. I traversed the so-called central and peripheral European and American universities, from public, underfunded, and severely under-resourced institutions in Greece to a private, affluent Ivy League university in the United States. In doing so, I negotiated the spaces between my movement and these institutions. Despite the stark disparities in terms of human and material resources, one of the more nuanced and challenging aspects to articulate is the tension I felt in how I experienced the power of these institutions and their movements.

In the underfunded Greek universities, the institution felt like a ghost – undeniably present, yet invisible and intangible. I had to create my own space in order to exist within it. In contrast, at the well-resourced Ivy League university, the institution was an omnipresent force, close to the skin. Once I became a part of it, I felt as if though my body merged with the institution, embodying its institutionalisation. Floating and responding to the demands of continuous movement through such spaces involves varying levels of tangibility – a concept that I struggle to articulate. I am uncertain of the proper words to capture this sensation.

What intrigues me about this tension is not only how it is expressed and performed by institutions and their members (students, faculty, etc.) but also how the tangibility – or lack thereof – of these powerful structures shapes the ways in which I can interact with and play within them. How does my need to "play-to-exist" get mediated by these different levels of institutional tangibility? Which forms does this play take? How do I navigate or resist the power of a slippery,

---

3 Lauren Berlant, "Intimacy: A Special Issue", *Critical Inquiry* 24, no. 2 (1998): 281–288.

intangible institution? Conversely, how do I experience my body as a carrier of institutional power?

In grappling with such questions and in the challenge of describing the complex ways in which we float through institutions wielding varying degrees of control and power, I find resonance in Stella's reference to the work of Berlant. The intra-connectivity and non-institutionality of friendship open up the (im)possibilities of play as a mode of existence within Academia – with an uppercase "A" – or as a way of transforming it into a lighter, more accessible *academia* with a lowercase "a". Such extra-institutional socialities allow us to play and carve out new spaces within powerful structures, continuously pushing boundaries to expand the possibilities of interaction and existence.

I would suggest distinguishing between Academia with a majuscule "A" to refer to the institution as a historically situated, political, and seemingly stable entity, and academia with a minuscule "a", which signals a more fluid, vulnerable, and heterogeneous space composed of multiple, often contested, histories and forms. This differentiation echoes similar conceptual distinctions – such as between Theory and theory, where Theory points to an established, often canonical body of thought with institutional authority, while *theory* may refer to more localised, situated, or experimental forms of theorising; or between History and history, where the former denotes official, dominant narratives, and the latter encompasses alternative, marginalised, or plural historical accounts.

Katerina Stavridi: On the face of it, the task of reflecting on the ways in which my personal experiences of academic institutions have affected me seemed like a fairly straightforward one. However, as I delved into the project, a strange sense of unease began to emerge.

Initially, this feeling of unease arose from the tension related to the issue of time and temporality: How to untangle the threads of a long-term, intimate, and ongoing relationship – one in which I and the institutions themselves, as Stella aptly pointed out, are continuously and profoundly transforming each other? This tension then led to a deeper question at the heart of this sense of discomfort that reads like this: What is the position of the embodied, time-dependent, lived experience within the seemingly atemporal and rigidly disembodied notion of the institution? This deeper conflict – the clash in-between the dynamic nature of the lived experience and the rigidity of the institution – resonates with Lina's struggle to find the "correct" words to describe the (in)tangibility of institutionality.

To remain close to these tensions and their contradictory, yet productive nature, I am drawn to understanding the institution as a space, just as my studies at different levels and contexts have hard-coded me to do. Specifically, to carry out this project of self-reflection, I return to Doreen Massey's conceptualisation of space as an unfinished product, shaped by the relationships it forms simultaneously at multiple scales – from the global to the level of the body.[4] Massey's framework offers a way of situating my encounters with the institution within broader relational dynamics and of understanding the institution itself as produced through interactions and transformations.

With these conceptual tools in mind, I can only begin to understand my movement between academic institutions – from the margins of the European project to its centre and back – as deeply embedded within the contexts where these movements unfolded. From these first experiences as a student of architecture at the polytechnic school in a city and state in crisis to an urban studies master's programme in a Western European academic environment during the Covid-19 pandemic, my view of the university has oscillated between different and often contradictory states. On the one hand, it has appeared as a space with highly porous boundaries, open to the flows and movements of the city and the neighbourhood, yet intensely isolated within the broader uneven geographies of knowledge production. On the other hand, it has taken the form of a central point within expansive, albeit highly regulated global academic networks.

In both cases – the Greek university, with its "ghostliness" linked to its lack of resources and support, and the Western European university, with its limited interpersonal encounters amid intense flows and movements within uneven global geographies – a common characteristic emerges: The university as an institution has become one of the main sites for accelerating neoliberal processes in response to the unfolding of the multiple crises. Thus, the boundaries of the institution as a space of interactions were constantly and aggressively reconfigured.

Nevertheless, in the midst of these realignments, I am drawn to find solace in Lina and Stella's call to explore non-, extra-, and semi-institutional friendships. These relationships offer a way to reimagine and reclaim, even momentarily, the institution as a space of play and rupture. These moments, or fragments, of connection and play then become a site from which we might challenge the increasing rigidity of emerging material, disciplinary, regional, and epistemic boundaries.

Friedrich Cain: My first encounters with a university belong to my very early memories. My parents both hold doctoral degrees in the humanities, with my father at some point becoming a professor. Our family was structured according to what was a rather classical model at the time. Yet, although my mother stayed at home with three children, she took on different research projects and teaching appointments here and there to stay connected. That is how my sisters and I spent the greater part of our childhood in museums and institutes, meeting our

---

4 Doreen Massey, *For Space* (London: SAGE, 2005).

parents' colleagues at our family homes, soaking up terms, phrases, and anecdotes *en passant*. So, I literally grew into it and certainly had some kind of a head start when it came to an academic code of conduct. However, I did not realise that before I started studying myself.

Later, when I entered a university in my own right, it still took me a while to find my way around. Nevertheless, I experienced certain challenges quite differently than my friends from other backgrounds. While I now have Mauss' and Bourdieu's *habitus* conceptions at hand and could theorise on *rites de passage* and so on, I went through a lot of very personal situations in academic spaces before I learned to frame them accordingly. In hindsight, it is all about understanding understatements.

However, while I could make sense of certain ways of doing things – or dwelling – in Academia, I most certainly felt alienated, too. The role of the student was new and it came with quite some emotional chaos. I had no particular idea of the university and the campus I chose, let alone how to organise a whole life around it. In classes, I had to adapt to ways of reading and writing that I was not familiar with. When it comes to highly practical things, the stories I had overheard at home were not all that helpful: The disciplines were different, as were the times. So, apart from a certain feeling for the dos and don'ts, I still had to learn many intellectual and social rules. Finding friends, building solidarity, and all of that was not provided for at the centre of the academic structure, but rather at its margins or even beyond. Linking all the elements together was quite a personal challenge that I in the beginning experienced as a great deal of trial and error. Only later it became a matter of reflection over coffee and so on. Only after some time it became a matter of testing opportunities and pushing limits. Being somewhat familiar with the rules of the game is not the same as actually succeeding, and mastering the game is not necessarily the same as being creative. The notion of playing with friends evokes moving to or creating at the margins of institutional infrastructures in adaptive processes. It calls for emphatic practices in the first place. Rather than building an all-encompassing anthropology that reduces playing to a *homo ludens*,[5] a theory would have to be a praxiological reflection of emotion, of friendship, of care. I learned a lot about this from the Belarusian philosopher and activist Olga Shparaga, who writes about the care-based foundations of social change.[6]

---

[5] See Johan Huizinga, *Homo Ludens: A Study of the Play-Element in Culture* (London, Boston & Henley: Routledge & Kegan Paul, 1944 [1938]).

[6] See Olga Shparaga, *Die Revolution hat ein weibliches Gesicht. Der Fall Belarus* [The Face of the Revolution is Female: The Case of Belarus] (Berlin: Suhrkamp, 2021). See also Olga Shparaga on

Mariama de Brito Henn: Navigating institutions can be scary and alienating, or at least that was the case for me. This was due to the fact that I was one of the few who had to work alongside my university studies to even afford being a student, or because I too often was the only person of colour in a very white space, or because I always felt like being part of a play where I did not get the script. You quickly start to ask yourself if you truly belong and if it really should be this hard if you do belong. I tried to adapt, to play my expected role as best I could, filling in the missing lines with googled formalities and calculated responses. Hence, my existence in Academia became a performance. I dressed the part, talked the talk, and tucked away my more unpolished edges and uncomfortable experiences that I knew others would not be able to relate to. But when I entered museums and started working as a curator, I realised that what, how, and who I wanted to work with was heavily informed by the way I moved through the world, by all those untold experiences, all these at times rough edges. I was very lucky to find people in those spaces who demanded that I present myself in a way that is closer to who I am, to become someone who is no longer looking for a script written by someone else. I think that this is why creating spaces and finding a community, as mentioned above, really resonates with me. For me, community is what enables us to play our parts in academia without losing ourselves, what creates spaces where we can write new scripts or even dare to fail when improvising. When James Baldwin talked about love, he often talked about community, so when he wrote "love takes off the masks that we fear we cannot live without and know we cannot live within",[7] it rang true for the way I re-entered university for my PhD, unmasked.

> So, there is a great deal of in-betweenness in these first comments. Given the obstacles mentioned with regards to the institutionalised nature of the system, how can we describe what it feels like to be in-between and how does the notion of play help us exist and theorise around or against it?

Stella A. Kasdovasili: I would say that in a way, in-betweenness is constitutive of my academic career, a productive force that constructs me on a personal and professional level. I have felt lost, seemingly in-between worlds, as a first-generation university student trying to find my footing in a male-dominated field such as political philosophy. I have felt overwhelmed trying to write in-between Cixous'

Belarusian Academia in exile: "It is clear that something is happening in the field of education within and around Belarus", *Baltic Worlds* 18, no. 1 (2025): 86–92.

7 James Baldwin, *The Fire Next Time* (London: Penguin Books, 1992), 70.

écriture féminine[8] and citation politics.[9] I have experienced anguish trying to reconcile my class position with my academic aptitude, and I have felt excitement having found myself in-between theories and bodies of work that seem promising and invigorating. These are all emotions that I have encountered in this in-betweenness, this temporal and spatial space I consistently come across when my various identities overlap or conflict with ideas, institutions, people. Following Althusser, I have come to understand this in-betweenness as an encounter of various elements and structures.[10] This encounter is not in the least teleological and might also never last, might never produce a new structure, and the only way not to become all-consumed in attributing causality to the relationship between these elements is by engaging in play. It is in this in-betweenness where I reinvent myself or accrue new experiences allowing me to observe from multiple angles the constitutive elements of the multiple identities that grant me certain positions within structures. It is play that enables me to attempt to switch or reclaim certain positions and experience change, albeit at times followed by intense experiences on an emotional level. In that light, play is what allows me to transgress the limitations that my various identities and their interactions with structures such as Academia might set for me. Play also offers trust that in the event of something new emerging, everything will make sense retroactively, at least until the next lasting encounter.

Katerina Stavridi: Reflecting on my experiences in academic environments, in-betweenness emerges as a familiar, embodied positionality – one that encompasses a range of practices, encounters, relationships, and emotions that are often in conflict with one another. As someone having navigated the dual reality of working to afford being a student and a PhD candidate, existing in a space that is neither fully "inside" nor entirely "outside" academia can be exhausting and, at times, even disorienting.

At the same time, this experience of in-betweenness not only concerns institutional inclusion in general but also mundane, everyday, embodied, and linguistic negotiations within academia. Negotiating the distance between the positionality of a subject producing knowledge *in* and *from* Southern Europe and the expectation to perform the role of a "global" academic subject – one that moves fluidly within a globalised academic field – may generate a sense of frustration.

---

[8] Hélène Cixous, Keith Cohen, and Paula Cohen, "The Laugh of the Medusa", *Signs* 1, no. 4 (1976): 875–893.
[9] Sara Ahmed, *Living a Feminist Life* (Durham, NC: Duke University Press, 2017).
[10] Louis Althusser, *Philosophy of the Encounter: Later Writings, 1978–1987*, edited by François Matheron and Oliver Corpet, translated and with an introduction by G.M. Goshgarian (London & New York: Verso, 2006), 163–207.

This experience often becomes tangible through the very process of translation – a process linked to an uncanniness that echoes the sensation of Mariama's notion of lacking the script. This translation goes beyond words and permeates practices, gestures, nods, formal email greetings, tones of voice, and expressions. These are part of a maze-like set of codes and etiquette that are highly context-specific and signal the unspoken rules of the academic game – rules that seem intelligible only to the ones already "in the know".

Yet, hope and joy may also be found within this in-betweenness. It becomes a common (playing) ground, a space of playful encounters between subjects occupying similarly fuzzy positionalities – sharing this all-too-familiar sensation of not being taken seriously. This liminal space can become a point from which to redefine boundaries, precisely because of its marginality. The lack of funding and resources often results in not being fully integrated into the academic game – not fitting neatly into canonised relations related to academic competition. Yet, from this very position – under the radar of regulation and the increasing financialisation of knowledge production – a space of possibility emerges: the freedom to play with concepts, to blur disciplinary boundaries, and to engage with other subjects coded by this shared in-betweenness. In this context, *playing with* friends, peers, colleagues reflects the potential for disrupting the very definition of possibility in research and enabling new, often unpredictable, possibilities to emerge in spaces where boundaries are not fixed but continuously renegotiated and redrawn.

Friedrich Cain: Something I believe is very important with regard to being in-between is what I would describe as a perspective related to the moment. Of course, there is social background, institutions, and other contexts that, if we enter or leave them, are comfortable or uncomfortable. Yet, at the same time, experiencing these transitional moments can be important for our own identities or perhaps the processes of doing our own identities. Getting into or entering academia on a day-to-day basis – be it at a conference, entering a classroom to study or teach, going in and out of specific buildings, or as a passage into a new phase of life when taking up studies in the first place – is something that shapes us.

I think that *play* can help us look upon these things in many ways, starting at the linguistic level; for example, playing with the active and passive voice while thinking about forming and being formed, shaping and being shaped. This, I guess, is important when it comes to reflecting on position and potential. I think that we are fundamentally shaped in our thoughts and routines, and perhaps manners as well, by coming into contact with institutions, their subsections, and the people we meet there. I also believe that eternally fixed states do not exist – it is rather a question of narrative, of how we tell ourselves and our solidarities and how we change these accounts.

I was recently made aware of a podcast series on standpoint theory featuring Sandra Harding, Linda Alcoff, and Donna Haraway. As she has done elsewhere, Haraway warns of an essentialist misunderstanding of standpoint theory or her take on situated knowledges: These knowledges are ever-changing and never fixed. She talks about the situatedness of experience(s), which is not easy to describe. Rather, this is only possible through very difficult description practices that "are collectively invented, as well as inherited" and never work as a means for 1:1 representation.[11] Such practices develop along with the use of language. So, in addition to passive/active, there is also a problem of tropes. Once they are out, they cannot be controlled and need to be let go if there is a better one in the sense of being more fitting to a changing atmosphere.[12]

I like to think about this as playing, too. Rather than forging or welding words together in writing chambers, the constant exchange with friends about readings and impressions – experiences – as well as discussing my own work (that is, descriptions of historical situations) has never not benefited from being put out there for friendly comments. It is also about creating togetherness in kind interaction and thought; for example, also in activism for vulnerable groups at universities who experience racism, sexism, but also for non-professorial teaching staff. As Haraway says at the end of the interview: We need people "teaching you something you didn't know you needed to learn."[13]

Of course, such friendly togetherness also takes time that seems to be impossible to renumerate based on a neoliberal logic. In the interview I just mentioned, Haraway also points to the fact that being very busy all the time, feeling guilty about what is unfinished, and needing a new project is politically disempowering and does not help create a learning atmosphere for our students. I also wonder if there is a way to describe these academic processes along the lines of Anna Lowenhaupt Tsing's *Mushroom at the End of the World*,[14] in which the mycelium metaphor could do more than just illustrate.

> *Drawing on our exchange on in-betweenness, how does in-betweenness relate to boundaries and translation, and what may be the role of playing in connection with this?*

---

[11] "Standpoint theory was never supposed to be a theory about identity", interview with Donna Haraway by Alison Wylie, Emily Tilton, Karoline Paier, and Alex Bryant, accessed 28 March 2025, https://standpointtheory.com/podcast/, min. 27.
[12] "Standpoint theory was never supposed to be a theory about identity", min. 30, 37.
[13] "Standpoint theory was never supposed to be a theory about identity", min. 61.
[14] Anna Lowenhaupt Tsing, *The Mushroom at the End of the World: On the Possibility of Life in Capitalist Ruins* (Princeton, NJ: Princeton University Press, 2015).

Stella A. Kasdovasili: I find the struggle we faced when discussing in-betweenness, specifically in regard to its possible connection to boundaries and translation rather interesting, as if this in-betweenness is a quilting point, stitching together subjective positions and structures or, as Lacan puts it, a punctuation point that temporarily fixes signification, retroactively producing the notion of a "fixed" meaning.[15] We could then argue that, both boundaries and translation constitute different forms of stitches used to merge different discourses regarding the institutions that formulate us and the power dynamics that dictate the academic game. As far as I am concerned, translation and boundaries – or rather boundary setting – could easily be seen as two sides of the same coin, which is why I am inclined to argue that trying to approach them as two separate and distinct objectives might not be possible, as they are both needed and in a sense unavoidable when "playing" within Academia. We tend to face these invisible boundaries within the academic structure when we find ourselves in this in-betweenness, and these very boundaries are present in this liminal space of in-betweenness that pushes us to engage in the process of "translation" in our attempt to navigate them. This translation is what essentially allows us to continue existing within the structure, helps us contextualise boundaries and understand – or not – the dynamics and power relations producing them, and teaches us how we can overcome or transgress them. One could then argue that translation is the mechanism we develop in order to engage in academic play, thus attempting to influence these boundaries ourselves, and it is by means of translation that we get access to the possibility of setting our own boundaries.

Evangelia (Lina) Chordaki: When I started thinking about in-betweenness, I focused on how I feel, code, experience, and describe it. I then started thinking about what this "it" I was referring to actually consists of. Related to my experiences of doing Academia and operating in different institutional settings, I feel that in my view, in-betweenness first and foremost operates as a concept. It is probably a sweaty concept, using Sara Ahmed's theorisation.[16] While trying to articulate how it feels, it makes me feel that bodily sense of sweat – inscribing the difficulty of describing it. At the same time, in-betweenness is also a practice characterised by efforts to organise ourselves and our relationships to different knowledges and the multiple settings related to knowledge production. However, it may also operate as a condition – a condition that I often find myself in.

---

[15] Jacques Lacan, *The Psychoses: The Seminar of Jacques Lacan* (London: Routledge, 2013), https://doi.org/10.4324/9781315800189.

[16] Sara Ahmed, *Willful Subjects* (Durham, NC: Duke University Press, 2014); Athena Athanasiou, "Θεωρία φτιαγμένη από ιδρώτα", *Feministiqa* 3 (Autumn 2020), accessed 28 September 2023, https://feministiqa.net/theoria-ftiagmenh-apo-idrwta/.

The in-betweenness I am familiar with cannot be realised without the existence of boundaries. Such boundaries may be institutional, regional, disciplinary, geographical, etc. They produce orders and hierarchies in the name of protecting what is inside them. Such boundaries are in a constant relationship with us – a relationship (shifting between stability and crisis) mediated by gender, class, race, able-bodiedness, and, obviously, historicity. The study of how boundaries work on/against/with us has a long tradition in scholarly communities, especially the ones focusing on marginal social groups and identities. However, rather than focusing on how boundaries create exclusions and discipline our bodies, I am interested here in the relationship between boundaries and in-betweenness. Inevitably, I ask: Is the very existence of boundaries – their strong presence often accompanied by rigid movements or the denial of movements – what directly shapes in-betweenness? I argue that it is not. Instead, I believe that the practice of crossing boundaries is what creates in-betweenness. Crossing boundaries means that they expand and the parallel transformation of what is inside them. However, it also means creating a space shaped by the presence of the ones crossing the boundaries and the very movement of crossing. It is a space that touches the boundaries but is a separate entity allowing the freedom of movement while, at the same time, operating as an interface (a crossing point where things interact). The creation of in-betweenness requires a decision to move and a responsibility to cross, and in that sense, it is a political act. Now imagine someone working at the intersection of two disciplines, advocating for the importance of interdisciplinarity even though this is often a challenging task. (Our group could be the subject of this sentence!) In this case, what creates the in-betweenness that the scholar(s) may experience is not the interface of those two disciplines. Instead, what creates the in-betweenness is the political act of crossing both boundaries, allowing it to operate simultaneously as an interface, a space connected but being separated from the boundaries allowing the scholar to exist. Now situate the act of crossing such boundaries in the current political turmoil where the rise of the alt-right both in Europe and the United States, carried out through the multiple conceptualisations of "safety", is directly linked to an uncritical anti-expert ideology and anti-intellectualism, generalised attacks on science, education, and research (institutions, curricula, funding, and academic freedom) and obviously the rise and legitimisation of hate speech, including anti-gender narratives, sexism, transphobia, homophobia, racism, ableism, and classism. In this context, the act of crossing boundaries and creating in-betweenness is a work that requires much effort and has political weight for those who cross the boundaries at that moment but also for the effects that the space of in-betweenness will have on the future "invaders".[17]

Feeling in-betweenness means feeling uncomfortable, and feeling uncomfortable can be liberating. I recently started working on the concept of epistemic discomfort as an (im)possibility of becoming and a practice of resisting epistemic and thus social hierarchies. Here, however, I think it is important to focus more on the practices linked to in-betweenness and, more specifically, the practice of translation. When being in-between, one needs to constantly translate. Here, translation maintains its traditional meaning of converting a text from one language into another without changing the original meaning – this, of course, includes the disciplinary and/or institutional translations required in relation to terminologies and concepts. Nevertheless, it goes further than that. Translation also means creating bonds and shaping collective bodies. Thus, we can attribute a new characteristic in translation – that of stickiness.[18] Translation, as a practice arising in in-betweenness, works as a glue that helps subjects and objects stick together in order to further foster their existence.

Now, an alignment has been revealed. If (academic) institutions (as we know them) cannot exist without boundaries or be experienced outside the boundaries they create and are created by, what are the political possibilities of making them more democratic, especially in the current context? I believe that it is the practice of crossing boundaries and creating in-betweenness. Moreover, if in-betweenness is linked to the practices of translation operating as a survival act, what is the role of playing in Academia? For me, play is one of the primary feminist methodologies of doing Academia differently. This differs from the dominant view presenting/treating Academia as something that "requires that you have a strong stomach" and demands toughness and an ability to handle unpleasant situations. Play can be a fun, inclusive, constructive, and generative way of thinking, being, and practicing (in) Academia, treating it as an institutional and intellectual space of freedom, care, and critical thinking. Thus, play can become a radical epistemological entry point rather than a way to further discipline our epistemologies.

Mariama de Brito Henn: I really struggled with in-betweenness as, on the one hand, it is such an integral experience for me, even outside academia, and, on the other, when I think about in-betweenness in my research and work, I immediately link it to translation. Lina is right when saying that to be in-between, there must be boundaries – boundaries of belonging, of power, of class.

---

[17] Nirmal Puwar, *Space Invaders: Race, Gender and Bodies out of Place* (Oxford: Berg, 2004).
[18] For further theorisation regarding stickiness, see Sara Ahmed, *The Cultural Politics of Emotion* (Edinburgh: Edinburgh University Press, 2004).

While I understand and also relate to Lina's in-betweenness as something that exists between boundaries, I also think of it as this chasm that constantly moves with me, around me. Growing up as a person of colour in a predominantly white country like Germany, especially in the 1990s, it was made very clear who belonged and who did not. Be it the colour of your skin, your hair, or your family background, everything would warrant a "but you're not really from here". Hence, this chasm is formed. The gaps between you and the culture of your parents, the gap between you and how a "real" (insert any Western nation) has to look/talk/act, the gap between you and the world you move in. This rift becomes your companion, always changing and adapting, but never closing. So even when you cross boundaries, the chasm follows you, separates you, makes you in-between. Academia often further widens the gap. In such a historically white, upper-middle-class, male space, any and every intruder is made aware that perhaps they should not have crossed this boundary, or at least were not expected to do so. It is this othering, wilfully or unknowingly, that feeds such chasms, pushes people into these liminal spaces. While this liminal existence can and certainly is alienating, it is also a great tool. As the "Outsider Within",[19] as coined by Patricia Collins, you can see the chasms, not just around you but around others as well, and point them out, form links, and build connections. This is the freedom of moving in and out of spaces, of not belonging. You are not attached to the status quo, there is no tradition that you seek to uphold, as it was not yours to begin with. For a long time, translation was my tool for building bridges and creating networks. When I translate language or cultural concepts to my father, I build a connection between him and the country he chose to call his home. By building bridges, I might not be able to close the gaps, but I am able to cross them, connect with others, and understand the chasms that might make them in-between.

But the more I translate, the more I ask myself if I should. There are other ways of building bridges, of connecting. Translation always comes with some sort of hierarchy, such as the (often colonial) language into which we translate, for example, indigenous concepts and names without ever being able to do them justice. Or that our experiences of alienation and/or oppression only become valid if we can express them correctly, use the right words, the right tone. But why do I have to translate my culture, experiences, etc. into a language that is not my own, into a palpable and relatable anecdote, into a format that was not meant for me to begin with? So now I am at a point in my work where I am questioning for whom I translate and why? How can I play with my position as the outsider

---

[19] Patricia Hill Collins, "Learning from the Outsider Within: The Sociological Significance of Black Feminist Thought", *Social Problems* 33, no. 6 (1986): 14–32, https://doi.org/10.2307/800672

within, use my liminal existence to play with the concept of translation? How can I break away from these hierarchies? What do I translate and when do I expect others to engage with foreign concepts without translation? Is not the act of translation also an act of creation? So, how do I create something new? Not every gap has to be crossed by a bridge, sometimes a swing is sufficient.

Friedrich Cain: I wonder if I might not tell the story of getting to know the university as an institution in a different way and bring a historical perspective into it that also incorporates systemic changes. While there were things I might have learned "at home", I obviously struggled once taking my first steps into a university. In addition to all the intellectual struggle, there were all kinds of administrative challenges one can imagine.

For example, beyond a certain way of knowing what to do or perhaps a feeling of what is to be done, there is a certain area between institutions and educational systems that needs a great deal of translation, witful playing, and (ideally) friendly exchanges with those who know or come to understand the local specificities more quickly – or because they were there earlier.

I am thinking about moving from one university to another halfway through a study programme, beyond the constraints of a structured exchange scheme, more along the lines of medieval *peregrinatio academica*. Actually, the Europeanisation of higher education, with the introduction of the European Credit Transfer System (ECTS), certainly did not make it easier. I experienced this when moving from the University of Halle-Wittenberg to Bremen University after the first year during my BA and thus from one German university to another. During this process, the accreditation of courses in fairly similar programmes required roughly a year of administrative negotiating and back-to-back meetings with programme coordinators, who were luckily well-meaning and sufficiently imaginative to declare that the classes were comparable. Compared to that, it was much easier to get the classes acknowledged that I took during a semester abroad in Cracow one year later – at a university with a very different course structure and study experience. Still, other students in the programme, who went to other locations abroad, had very different experiences, as it turned out that the ECTS "currency" was not managed the same way in all institutions.

I guess in the end it is a matter of adapting creatively (and sometimes desperately) to Academia's game with all its social, intellectual, and economic rules, while at the same time making friends and creating new solidarities on and off campus that do not just follow the structure of the institution, but fill – or create – spaces in between.

In Lieu of a Conclusion

... A crossing point is what this text is – a crossing point. In this excerpt from our ongoing conversation, we explored the notion of *playing* and its potential to overcome the tensions between the neoliberal backlash in education and research and the takeover of new public management at universities, which fosters competitiveness rather than cooperation as the basis of the conceptual, institutional, and thus epistemological order. Our notion of *play* has a *responsive nature* and seeks to critically reclaim these ordered spaces. A second aspect of *play* is its proximity to the child – both as a not-fully-grown adult (a subject position typically reserved for women in canonical Western philosophy) and also as the symbol of hope when envisioning the future. Our critical reclaiming of *play* allows us to retrieve the enjoyment of collaborating with peers, moving beyond the manifested institutional resistance against creativity, focusing on the multileveled *emancipatory potentials* found in the historicity and embodiedness of *play* – our historicity and embodiedness – and allows us to rethink the university and academia as overarching systems, to rethink them as crossing points, at crossing points of different experiences, about which we need to hear and which we need to lay open in order to re-examine them in a way that helps us dwell in meaningful terms . . .

Mariama de Brito Henn has studied costume interpretation (BA) at the University of Arts in London, United Kingdom, and art history (MA) at the Ludwig-Maximilian-University in Munich, Germany. She is a textile and fashion historian who focuses on colonialism and textile/dress practices. She is currently working on her PhD project on the aesthetic practices of American afro-spiritual religions, such as Candomblé (Brazil) and Santería (Cuba). She also works as a curator. Recent exhibitions include: "Who Cares? – Exploring solidarity" (Augsburg, 2021) and "Coolness: Staging fashion in the 20th century" (Bocholt/Augsburg, 2022–23). Furthermore, she is also engaged in anti-racist work; for example, through workshops on coloniality in the German language.

Friedrich Cain is a postdoc assistant at the Faculty Center for Transdisciplinary Historical-Cultural Studies at the University of Vienna. He specializes in the history of science and the humanities with a special focus on political epistemologies in Central and Eastern Europe since the late 19th century. He has published a monograph on clandestine research carried out by Polish scholars under German occupation (1939–45), while he in his current project focuses on the history of science studies in East and West Germany between the 1960s and 1990s. He recently co-edited a special section on "Universities in Times of Crisis and Transformation" in *Baltic Worlds* (2025:1).

Evangelia (Lina) Chordaki is a specialist in science studies and gender studies, with a focus on the history and philosophy of science, anthropology of science and knowledge, and feminist epistemologies. She is currently a postdoctoral researcher at Princeton University. With a strong academic foundation and extensive interdisciplinary research experience, she has contributed significantly to the study of knowledge production and circulation, social and epistemological inequalities, and the entanglements of gender and technoscience since the late 20th century. She is the author of the book *Making Sense of Knowledge: Feminist Epistemologies in the Greek Birth Control Movement, 1974–1986* (Cambridge University Press, 2025).

Stella Andrada Kasdovasili holds a BA in political science and history and an MA in political philosophy and social theory, both from Panteion University of Social and Political Sciences in Athens, and an MA with distinction in gender studies from Central European University in Budapest. Her academic research focuses on emerging technologies, specifically artificial intelligence, and how they influence the formation of subjectivity. Currently an AI support engineer for a tech company in Amsterdam, she has worked as a social media analyst in the Friedrich-Ebert-Stiftung Foundation's research project "Migration Narratives in Europe 2017–2019," and co-organized the first "Feminism and Philosophy" workshop at Panteion University in 2019. Publications include "Where is the body of the other? Death and other affects," in: *Come Let Me Tell You: Feminist, Lesbian, and Queer Narratives of the Post-Dictatorship Period*, (ed. A. Karastathi and M. Polykarpou (Athens: FAC Press: 2021), 17–26 and "Emotive Humanoid," in: *Chimeras: Inventory of Synthetic Cognition*, ed. I. Manouach and A. Engelhardt (Athens: Onassis Publications, 2021), 335–337.

Katerina Stavridi is a PhD candidate at the School of Architecture, National Technical University of Athens (NTUA). Her current research explores the geopolitical dimensions of transnational dog rescue practices in Europe through urban ethnography, focusing on how notions of rescue are shaped through geographical imaginaries and multispecies encounters. She holds master's degrees in urban studies from the University of Amsterdam and in urban and spatial planning from NTUA. Recent publications include "Urban Hybrids: Relational Readings of the City through the Everyday Practices of Humans and Dogs," *Geographies* (2022) and "Posthuman Symbiosis Masterclass: [Un]learning with Donna Haraway and Rosi Braidotti," *Backchannels*, Society for Social Studies of Science (2024, co-author).

Contributors

Mariama de Brito Henn has studied costume interpretation (BA) at the University of Arts in London, United Kingdom, and art history (MA) at the Ludwig-Maximilian-University in Munich, Germany. She is a textile and fashion historian who focuses on textile/dress practices from colonial contexts. She is currently working on her PhD project on the aesthetic practices of American afro-spiritual religions, such as Candomblé (Brazil) and Santería (Cuba). She also works as a curator. Recent exhibitions include: "Who Cares? – Exploring solidarity" (Augsburg, 2021) and "Coolness: Staging fashion in the 20th century" (Bocholt/Augsburg, 2022–23). Furthermore, she is also engaged in anti-racist work; for example, through workshops on coloniality in the German language.

Friedrich Cain is a postdoc assistant at the Faculty Center for Transdisciplinary Historical-Cultural Studies at the University of Vienna. He specializes in the history of science and the humanities with a special focus on political epistemologies in Central and Eastern Europe since the late 19th century. He has published a monograph on clandestine research carried out by Polish scholars under German occupation (1939–45), while he in his current project focuses on the history of science studies in East and West Germany between the 1960s and 1990s. He recently co-edited a special section on "Universities in Times of Crisis and Transformation" in *Baltic Worlds* (2025:1).

Evangelia (Lina) Chordaki is a specialist in science studies and gender studies, with a focus on the history and philosophy of science, anthropology of science and knowledge, and feminist epistemologies. She is currently a postdoctoral researcher at Princeton University. With a strong academic foundation and extensive interdisciplinary research experience, she has contributed significantly to the study of knowledge production and circulation, social and epistemological inequalities, and the entanglements of gender and technoscience since the late 20th century. She is the author of the book *Making Sense of Knowledge: Feminist Epistemologies in the Greek Birth Control Movement, 1974–1986* (Cambridge University Press, 2025).

Karl Haikola is a postdoctoral researcher in history at Lund University. His main research interests include Europeanisation, the history of the EU, the history of the university, and the history of knowledge. He is currently part of the research project "The Europeanisation of the Universities: Transforming Knowledge Institutions from within, c. 1985–2010", in which his empirical contribution focuses on Spain.

Bruno Hamnell is a postdoctoral fellow in the history of ideas and sciences at Lund University, Sweden. His current project is called "All is One: Holistic Knowledge Ideals and Controversies from Fin de siècle to the Anthropocene." Hamnell's research interests include modern intellectual history, philosophy of history, and the history of knowledge. His thesis, *Two Quests for Unity: John Dewey, R. G. Collingwood, and the Persistence of Idealism*, was published in 2021.

David Larsson Heidenblad is an associate professor of history and deputy director of the Lund Centre for the History of Knowledge (LUCK). His research is centered on the history of investing in stock and the emergence of the knowledge society. Recent publications include "The Making of Everyman's Capitalism in Sweden" in *Enterprise & Society* (2023, with Orsi Husz) and *The History of Knowledge* (Cambridge, 2023, with Johan Östling).

Juliane Hornung is an associate professor at the History Department at the University of Cologne (*akadem. Rätin a.Z.*). She specializes in media history and the history of political violence in the nineteenth and twentieth centuries from a global perspective. Her current book project explores transnational kidnappings as political practices and how they were linked to political rule, international relations, and notions of trust, worth, and morality (ca. 1860–1980).

Stella Andrada Kasdovasili holds a BA in political science and history and an MA in political philosophy and social theory, both from Panteion University of Social and Political Sciences in Athens, and an MA with distinction in gender studies from Central European University in Budapest. Her academic research focuses on emerging technologies, specifically artificial intelligence, and how they influence the formation of subjectivity. Currently an AI support engineer for a tech company in Amsterdam, she has worked as a social media analyst in the Friedrich-Ebert-Stiftung Foundation's research project "Migration Narratives in Europe 2017–2019," and co-organized the first "Feminism and Philosophy" workshop at Panteion University in 2019. Publications include "Where is the body of the other? Death and other affects," in: *Come Let Me Tell You: Feminist, Lesbian, and Queer Narratives of the Post-Dictatorship Period*, (ed. A. Karastathi and M. Polykarpou (Athens: FAC Press: 2021), 17–26 and "Emotive Humanoid," in: *Chimeras: Inventory of Synthetic Cognition*, ed. I. Manouach and A. Engelhardt (Athens: Onassis Publications, 2021), 335–337.

Ewa Koźmińska-Frejlak is an associate professor at the Jewish Historical Institute (JHI) in Warsaw. Her research focuses on Jewish life during the Holocaust and its aftermath, Polish-Jewish relations during these periods, and the early Jewish historiography of the Holocaust. She is currently working on a book on the social history of the Central Jewish Historical Commission in Poland as well as on a book on the interviewers who collected testimonies from Holocaust survivors immediately after the war.

Fritz Kusch is a PhD candidate at the University of Bremen, Germany, and a research associate at the Collaborative Research Center 1342 "Global Dynamics of Social Policy." His research interests include the political and social history of tariffs and trade in the United States and German-American history. He is currently working on a PhD project on the history of protectionist advocacy groups in the United States and their impact on American trade policy in the late nineteenth and early twentieth centuries.

Charlotte A. Lerg is associate professor of North-American History at Ludwig-Maximilian University Munich and managing director of the Lasky Center for Transatlantic Studies. She has also taught at the Universities of Münster, Jena, and Bochum. Her research focuses on the cultural history of knowledge, visual media, and historical theory. Publications include *Universitätsdiplomatie: Prestige und Wissenschaft in den transatlantischen Beziehungen 1890–1920* (2019) and numerous articles on nineteenth and twentieth century transatlantic history. In her current project, funded by the German Research Foundation (DFG), she examines documentary drawing as part of the U.S. media landscape in the twentieth century.

Valentina Mann is a historian of modern European intellectual history with a focus on the history of the social sciences. She is the co-editor of *Conceptions of Space in Intellectual History* (Routledge, 2021) and her article 'Mind and knowledge in the early thought of Franz Boas, 1887–1904', appeared in *History of the Human Sciences* in 2022. She is currently a Polonsky Academy Postdoctoral Fellow at the Van Leer Jerusalem Institute.

Victoria Van Orden Martínez is a researcher at the Department of History at Lund University in Sweden. Her current research focuses on how survivors of Nazi persecution who became migrants and refugees after the war were involved in various sociohistorical processes, with a focus on gender and other differences. She is currently working on a project about women survivors of Nazi persecution who were medical professionals during and after the Second World War aiming to gain insight into how their wartime experiences impacted their lives and careers in medicine and science.

Johan Östling is a professor of history, director of the Lund Centre for the History of Knowledge (LUCK), and a Wallenberg Academy Fellow. His research mainly focuses on the history of knowledge and modern and contemporary European history. Recent publications include the trilogy *Circulation of Knowledge* (2018), *Forms of Knowledge* (2020), and *Knowledge Actors* (2023), as well as the introductory book *The History of Knowledge* (2023). Östling serves as PI of the research project "The Europeanisation of the Universities: Transforming Knowledge Institutions from within, c. 1985–2010".

Christine Schmidt is deputy director and head of research at The Wiener Holocaust Library. Her research has focused on the history of postwar tracing and documentation efforts, the concentration camp system in Nazi Germany, comparative studies of collaboration and resistance in France and Hungary, and women's roles in the collection of survivor accounts recorded by The Wiener Library in the 1950s and 1960s. Schmidt is co-editing (with Clara Dijkstra, Charlie Knight, and Sandra Lipner) *Holocaust Letters: Methodologies, Cases, Reflections* (Bloomsbury, 2026) and (with Elizabeth Anthony and Joanna Sliwa) *Older Jews and the Holocaust: Persecution, Displacement, and Survival* (Wayne State University Press in association with the US Holocaust Memorial Museum, 2026).

Maria Simonsen is an associate professor of modern history at Aalborg University. Her research interests include the history of the book and publishing (from the nineteenth century onwards), the history of knowledge, and university history. She is currently part of the Wallenberg-funded research project "The Europeanisation of the Universities: Transforming Knowledge Institutions from Within, c. 1985–2010" led by Professor Johan Östling at Lund University. Her recent related publications include the article "Between Tradition and Experiment: The Idea of a New University" in the *Nordic Journal of Educational History* (2023) and *At bygge et universitet: Aalborg Universitet 1974–2024* (Nord Academic, 2024).

Katerina Stavridi is a PhD candidate at the School of Architecture, National Technical University of Athens (NTUA). Her current research explores the geopolitical dimensions of transnational dog rescue practices in Europe through urban ethnography, focusing on how notions of rescue are shaped through geographical imaginaries and multispecies encounters. She holds master's degrees in urban studies from the University of Amsterdam and in urban and spatial planning from NTUA. Recent publications include "Urban Hybrids: Relational Readings of the City through the Everyday Practices of Humans and Dogs," *Geographies* (2022) and "Posthuman Symbiosis Masterclass: [Un]learning with Donna Haraway and Rosi Braidotti," *Backchannels*, Society for Social Studies of Science (2024, co-author).

Daniela Ozacky Stern is a scholar of Jewish resistance during the Holocaust and the Second World War. She is a lecturer in the Holocaust Studies Program at Western Galilee College, Israel. Ozacky Stern earned a PhD in Jewish History, specializing in Jewish partisans in Lithuania and Belarus during the Holocaust, and a master's degree focusing on Nazi propaganda under Joseph Goebbels.

She conducted post-doctoral research at Yad Vashem on Holocaust documentation and Jewish resistance movements. She was an Archive Fellow at the Fortunoff Video Archive for Holocaust Testimonies at Yale University, where she researched survivor testimonies and resistance narratives. Her publications deal with Jewish partisans in Eastern Europe, the Vilna Ghetto, and Holocaust documentation. She is the book review editor of the *Jewish Culture and History* journal.

Axel Vikström is a postdoctoral researcher at the Department of History, Lund University. His research is centered on the mediation of economic practices and the role of discourse and language in naturalising inequalities in terms of wealth and power. He recently published his thesis *The Mediated Representation of the Super-Rich: Secrecy, Wealth Taxation and the Tensions of Neoliberal Capitalism* (Örebro University).

Jana Weiß is DAAD Associate Professor at the University of Texas at Austin. With a focus on U.S. and transatlantic history, her research interests include nineteenth and twentieth century immigration, knowledge, and religious history as well as the history of racism. Recently, she has co-edited the special issue on the "International Knowledge Transfer and Circulation within the Brewing Industry" in the 2024 *Economic History Yearbook* (with Nancy Bodden) and launched a student-miniseries on "Texas Germans' Migration and Knowledge" on the *Migrant Knowledge* blog of the German Historical Institute in Washington, D.C.

www.ingramcontent.com/pod-product-compliance
Lightning Source LLC
Chambersburg PA
CBHW021938290426
44108CB00012B/881